05/07

UNIVERSITY OF
WOLVERHAMPTON

Centr

THE BODY

Critical Concepts in Sociology
Other titles in this series

THE BODY

Critical Concepts in Sociology

Edited by
THE ABERDEEN BODY GROUP
(Andrew Blaikie, Mike Hepworth,
Mary Holmes, Alexandra Howson,
David Inglis and Sheree Sartain)

Volume I

Knowing Bodies

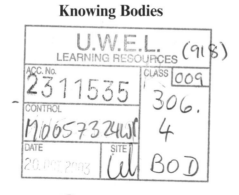
Routledge
Taylor & Francis Group

LONDON AND NEW YORK

First published 2004
by Routledge
11 New Fetter Lane, London EC4P 4EE

Simultaneously published in the USA and Canada
by Routledge
29 West 35th Street, New York NY 10001

Routledge is an imprint of the Taylor & Francis Group

Typeset in Times by RefineCatch Limited, Bungay, Suffolk
Printed and bound in Great Britain by MPG Books Ltd, Bodmin

British Library Cataloguing in Publication Data
A catalogue record for this book is available from the British Library

Library of Congress Cataloging in Publication Data
The body: critical concepts in sociology/edited by the Aberdeen
Body Group (Andrew Blaikie . . . [et al.])
p. cm. — (Critical concepts in sociology)
Includes bibliographical references and index.
Contents: v. 1. Knowing bodies — v. 2. Sociology, nature, and the
body — v. 3. Body history — v. 4. Living and dying bodies —
v. 5. Alternative bodies.
ISBN 0-415-26662-9 (set) – ISBN 0-415-26663-7 (v. 1) –
ISBN 0-415-26664-5 (v. 2) – ISBN 0-415-26665-3 (v. 3) –
ISBN 0-415-26666-1 (v. 4) – ISBN 0-415-32148-4 (v. 5)
1. Body, Human–Social aspects. 2. Body, Human–Philosophy.
3. Identity (Psychology) 4. Body, Human–Political aspects. 5. Body
image–Social aspects. I. Blaikie, Andrew. II. Aberdeen Body Group.
III. Series.
HM636.B59 2003
306.4–dc21   2003043200

ISBN 0–415–26662–9 (Set)
ISBN 0–415–26663–7 (Volume I)

Publisher's Note
References within each chapter are as they appear in the original
complete work.

CONTENTS

VOLUME I   KNOWING BODIES

CONTENTS

VOLUME II   SOCIOLOGY, NATURE AND THE BODY

vi

CONTENTS

VOLUME III   BODY HISTORY

PART 1
Thinking body history

CONTENTS

PART 2
Bodies in historical context

CONTENTS

CONTENTS

CONTENTS

VOLUME V 'ALTERNATIVE' BODIES

CONTENTS

ACKNOWLEDGEMENTS

The publishers would like to thank the following for permission to reprint their material:

MIT Press for permission to reprint S. Todes, 'The classic view of the way the human subject has his body, and Descartes's rejection of it', *Body and World*, Cambridge: MIT Press, 2001, pp. 10–22.

Descartes, R., 'Discourse 5' from *Discourses on Method*, Harmondsworth: Penguin, 1968, pp. 61–76. Copyright © F. E. Sutcliffe. Reproduced by permission of Penguin Books Ltd.

Cambridge University Press for permission to reprint E. Durkheim, 'Conceptual knowledge and sensory experience', in A. Giddens (ed.), *Emile Durkheim: Selected Writings*, Cambridge: Cambridge University Press, 1972, pp. 266–268.

S. Freud, 'Character and anal eroticism', *The Standard Edition of the Complete Psychological Works of Sigmund Freud*, London: Hogarth Press, 1962, pp. 168–175. Sigmund Freud © Copyrights, The Institute of Psycho-Analysis and The Hogarth Press for permission to quote from *The Standard Edition of the Complete Psychological Works of Sigmund Freud* translated and edited by James Strachey. Reprinted by permission of The Random House Group Ltd.

Taylor & Francis for permission to reprint Maurice Merleau-Ponty, 'The synthesis of one's own body', *The Phenomenology of Perception*, London: Routledge & Kegan Paul, 1966, pp. 148–153.

Simone de Beauvoir, 'Childhood', in H. M. Parshley (trans.) *The Second Sex*, Harmondsworth: Penguin, 1972 [1949], pp. 295–351. Extract from *The Second Sex* by Simone de Beauvoir, translated by H. M. Parshley published by Jonathan Cape. Used by permission of The Random House Group Ltd.

Michel Foucault, 'Technologies of the self', in H. Gutman and P. Hutton (eds), *Technologies of the Self: a seminar with Michel Foucault*, London:

Tavistock, 1988, pp. 16–49. Copyright © Random House 1988, Inc., New York. Originally published in French as La Volonte du Savoir copyright © Editions Gallimard 1976. Reprinted by permission of Georges Borchardt, Inc., for the Editions Gallimard.

L. Irigaray, 'This sex which is not one', reprinted from Luce Irigaray, *This Sex Which is Not One*, pp. 23–33, translated by Catherine Porter and Carolyn Burke. Translation copyright © 1985 Cornell University. Used by permission of the publisher, Cornell University Press.

Taylor & Francis for permission to reprint J. Butler, 'Bodies that matter', in *Bodies That Matter*, London and New York: Routledge, 1993, pp. 27–55.

Moira Gatens for permission to reprint M. Gatens, 'Towards a feminist philosophy of the body', B. Caine, E. A. Grosz and M. de Lepervanche (eds), *Crossing Boundaries: feminisms and the critique of knowledge*, Sydney: Allen & Unwin, 1988, pp. 59–70.

Taylor & Francis for permission to reprint E. Grosz, 'Notes towards a corporeal feminism', *Australian Feminist Studies* 5 (1987): 1–16.

Sage Publications Ltd for permission to reprint A. Hughes and A. Witz, 'Feminism and the matter of bodies: from de Beauvoir to Butler', *Body and Society* 3(1) (1997): 47–60.

Gale Group for permission to reprint S. Fisher, 'Body image', in D. Sills (ed.), *International Encyclopaedia of the Social Sciences*, New York: Macmillan & Glencoe: Freepress, 1968, pp. 113–116. Macmillan Library Reference © 1977 Macmillan Library Reference.

Sage Publications Ltd for permission to reprint N. Crossley, 'Body-subject/body-power: agency, inscription and control in Foucault and Merleau-Ponty', *Body and Society*, 2(2), (1996): 99–116.

Rutgers University Press for permission to reprint S. R. Bordo, 'The body and the reproduction of femininity: a feminist appropriation of Foucault', in Alison M. Jaggar and Susan R. Bordo (eds), *Gender/Body/Knowledge*,1989, pp. 13–31. Copyright © 1989 by Rutgers, The State University. Reprinted by permission of Rutgers University Press.

Macmillan Publishers Ltd for permission to reprint G. Ostrander, 'Foucault's disappearing body', A. Kroker and M. Kroker (eds), *Body Invaders, Sexuality and the Postmodern Condition*, London: Macmillan Educational, 1988, pp. 169–182.

International Philosophical Quarterly for permission to reprint R. T. Ames, 'The meaning of body in classical Chinese philosophy', *International Philosophical Quarterly* 24(1) (1984): 157–177.

State University of New York Press for permission to reprint J. M. Koller, 'Human embodiment: Indian perspectives', in T. P. Kasulis, R. T. Ames and Dissanayake, *Self as Body in Asian Theory and Practice*, New York: SUNY Press, 1993, pp. 45–58.

Disclaimer

The publishers have made every effort to contact authors/copyright holders of works reprinted in *The Body: Critical Concepts in Sociology*. This has not been possible in every case, however, and we would welcome correspondence from those individuals/companies who we have been unable to trace.

Chronological Table of Reprinted Articles and Chapters

Year	Author	Title	Reference		
1971	Mary Douglas	Do dogs laugh? A cross-cultural approach to body symbolism	*Journal of Psychosomatic Research* 15: 387–390.	III	33
1971	Erich Fromm	Psychoanalytic characterology and its relevance for social psychology	E. Fromm, *The Crisis of Psychoanalysis*, London: Cape, pp. 163–189.	III	35
1972	Simone de Beauvoir	Childhood	H. M. Parshley (trans.), *The Second Sex*, Harmondsworth: Penguin, pp. 295–351.	I	6
1972	Emile Durkheim	Conceptual knowledge and sensory experience	A. Giddens (ed.), *Emile Durkheim: Selected Writings*, Cambridge: Cambridge University Press, pp. 266–268.	I	3
1972	Susan Sontag	The double standard of aging	*Saturday Review* 55(39): 29–38.	IV	68
1973	Marcel Mauss	Techniques of the body	This article translated by Ben Brewster. *Economy and Society* 2(1): 70–88.	IV	53
1973	Richard L. Schoenwald	Training urban man: a hypothesis about the sanitary movement	H. J. Dyos and M. Wolff, *The Victorian City*, Vol. 2, London: Routledge & Kegan Paul, pp. 669–692.	III	47
1975	Kenneth Plummer	Interactionism and the forms of homosexuality	Kenneth Plummer. *Sexual Stigma: an interactionist account*, London: Routledge, pp. 93–101.	V	80
1976	Patricia R. Barchas	Physiological sociology: interface of sociological and biological processes	*Annual Review of Sociology* 2: 299–333.	II	28
1977	Paul Ekman	Biological and cultural contributions to body and facial movement	J. Blacking (ed.), *Anthropology of the Body*, New York: Academic Press, pp. 39–84.	IV	52
1978	Michel Foucault	The repressive hypothesis	M. Foucault, *The History of Sexuality: Volume One: Introduction*, London: Allen Lane, 1978, pp. 17–49.	III	36
1980	Sally Gadow	Body and self: a dialectic	*Journal of Medicine and Philosophy* 5(3): 172–185.	IV	54
1980	Iris Marion Young	Throwing like a girl: a phenomenology of feminine body comportment, motility and spatiality	*Human Studies* 3: 137–156.	IV	61

Chronological Table of Reprinted Articles and Chapters – continued

Date	Author(s)	Title	Source	Vol.	Ch.
1982	Mike Featherstone	The body in consumer culture	*Theory, Culture and Society* 1(2): 18–33.	III	44
1982	Orlando Patterson	Authority, alienation and social death	Orlando Patterson, *Slavery and social death: a comparative study*, Cambridge, MA: Harvard University Press, pp. 35–76.	V	87
1982	Bryan S. Turner	The government of the body: medical regimens and the rationalization of diet	*British Journal of Sociology* 33(2): 254–269.	V	73
1984	Roger T. Ames	The meaning of body in classical Chinese philosophy	*International Philosophical Quarterly* 24(1): 157–177.	I	18
1984	Robert Crawford	A cultural account of "health": control, release, and the social body	J. McKinlay (ed.), *Issues in the Political Economy of Health Care*, London: Tavistock, pp. 60–103.	IV	65
1984	Erving Goffman	Stigma and social identity	E. Goffman, *Stigma: notes on the management of spoiled identity*, Harmondsworth: Penguin, pp. 11–56.	IV	57
1984	Scott Lash	Genealogy and the body: Foucault, Deleuze, Nietzsche	*Theory, Culture and Society* 2(2): 1–18.	III	37
1984	Drew Leder	Medicine and paradigms of embodiment	*Journal of Medicine and Philosophy* 9(1): 29–43.	IV	55
1984	Emily Martin	Pregnancy, labor and body image in the United States	*Social Science and Medicine* 19(11): 1201–1206.	IV	64
1985	Norbert Elias	Ageing and dying: some sociological problems	N. Elias, *The Loneliness of the Dying*, Oxford: Basil Blackwell, pp. 68–91.	IV	70
1985	Pasi Falk	Corporeality and its fates in history	*Acta Sociologica* 28(2): 115–136.	III	41
1985	Donna Haraway	A manifesto for cyborgs: science, technology and socialist feminism in the 1980s	*Socialist Review* 80: 65–108.	V	74
1985	Elaine Scarry	The structure of torture: the conversion of real pain into the fiction of power	*The Body in Pain: the making and the unmaking of the world*, Oxford: Oxford University Press, pp. 27–59.	IV	66

Year	Author	Title	Reference		
1985	Jeffrey Weeks	Dangerous desires	J. Weeks, *Sexuality and its Discontents*, London: Routledge, pp. 157–181.	III	40
1986	J. M. Berthelot	Sociological discourse and the body	*Theory Culture and Society* 3(3): 155–164.	II	23
1986	Monique Canto	The politics of women's bodies: reflections on Plato	S. R. Suleiman (ed.), *The Female Body In Western Culture: contemporary perspectives*. Cambridge, Mass.: Harvard University Press, pp. 339–355.	III	31
1987	David Armstrong	Bodies of knowledge: Foucault and the problem of human anatomy	G. Scambler (ed.), *Sociological Theory and Medical Sociology*, London: Tavistock, pp. 59–76.	III	38
1987	Elizabeth Grosz	Notes towards a corporeal feminism	*Australian Feminist Studies* 5: 1–16.	I	11
1987	Dorothy E. Smith	A sociology of women	Dorothy E. Smith, *The Everyday World as Problematic: a feminist sociology*, Boston: Northeastern University Press, pp. 49–104.	II	20
1987	Bryan S. Turner	The rationalization of the body: reflections on modernity and discipline	S. Wimster and S. Lash (eds), *Max Weber, Rationality and Modernity*, Allen & Unwin, pp. 222–241.	III	48
1988	Michel Foucault	Technologies of the self	H. Gutman and P. Hutton (eds), *Technologies of the Self: a seminar with Michel Foucault*, London: Tavistock, pp. 16–49.	I	7
1988	Peter E. S. Freund	Bringing society into the body: understanding socialized human nature	*Theory and Society* 17: 839–864.	II	24
1988	Moira Gatens	Towards a feminist philosophy of the body	B. Caine, E. A. Grosz and M. de Lepervanche (eds), *Crossing Boundaries: feminism and the critique of knowledge*, Sydney: Allen & Unwin, pp. 59–70.	I	10
1988	Luce Irigaray	This sex which is not one	Irigaray, *This Sex Which is Not One*, Ithaca, NY: Cornell University Press, pp. 23–33.	I	8
1988	Greg Ostrander	Foucault's disappearing body	A. Kroker and M. Kroker (eds), *Body Invaders, Sexuality and the Postmodern Condition*, London: Macmillan Educational, pp. 169–182.	I	17

Chronological Table of Reprinted Articles and Chapters – continued

Date	Author(s)	Title	Source	Vol.	Ch.
1989	Susan R. Bordo	The body and the reproduction of femininity: a feminist appropriation of Foucault	A. M. Jaggar and S. R. Bordo (eds), *Gender/Body/Knowledge: feminist reconstructions of being and knowing*, New Brunswick: Rutgers University Press, pp. 13–31.	I	16
1989	Susan Sontag	AIDS and its Metaphors	S. Sontag, *AIDS and its Metaphors*, London: Allen Lane, pp. 80–95.	V	86
1990	Thomas J. Csordas	Embodiment as a paradigm for anthropology	*Ethos* 18(1): 5–47.	II	22
1991	Ted Benton	Biology and social science: why the return of the repressed should be given a (cautious) welcome	*Sociology* 25(1): 1–29.	II	29
1991	Mike Featherstone and Mike Hepworth	The mask of ageing and the postmodern life course	M. Featherstone, M. Hepworth and B. S. Turner (eds), *The Body: social process and cultural theory*, London: Sage, pp. 371–389.	IV	69
1991	Jocalyn Lawler	Embarrassment, social rules and the context of body care	J. Lawler, *Behind the Screens: nursing somology, and the problem of the body*, Edinburgh: Churchill Livingstone, pp. 135–154.	IV	71
1991	Irving Kenneth Zola	Bringing our bodies and ourselves back in: reflections on a past, present, and future "Medical Sociology"	*Journal of Health and Social Behaviour* 32(1): 1–16.	IV	59
1992	Dawn H. Currie and Valerie Raoul	Dissecting sexual difference in the body of knowledge	D. H. Currie and V. Raoul, *The Anatomy of Gender: women's struggle for the body*, Ottawa: Carlton University Press, pp. 1–34.	III	39
1993	Judith Butler	Bodies that matter	J. Butler, *Bodies That Matter: on the discursive limits of "sex"*, London and New York: Routledge, pp. 27–55.	I	9

Year	Author	Title	Reference		Page
1993	Thomas Kasulis	The body – Japanese style	T. P. Kasulis, R. T. Ames and W. Dissanayake, *Self as Body in Asian Theory and Practice*, New York: SUNY Press, pp. 299–319.	IV	56
1993	John M. Koller	Human embodiment: Indian perspectives	T. P. Kasulis, R. T. Ames and W. Dissanayake, *Self as Body in Asian Theory and Practice*, New York: SUNY Press, pp. 45–58.	I	19
1994	Norbert Elias	On blowing one's nose	N. Elias, *The Civilizing Process*, Oxford: Blackwell, pp. 117–125.	III	46
1994	M. L. Lyon and J. M. Barbalet	Society's body: emotion and the "somatization" of social theory	T. J. Csordas (ed.), *Embodiment and Experience: the existential ground of culture and self*, Cambridge: Cambridge University Press, pp. 48–66.	II	26
1994	Thorstein Veblen	Dress as an expression of the pecuniary culture	T. Veblen, *The Theory of the Leisure Class*, Mineola, NY: Dover, pp. 103–115.	III	43
1995	Anne Balsamo	Forms of technological embodiment: reading the body in contemporary culture	M. Featherstone and R. Burrows (eds), *Cyberspace/Cyberbodies/Cyberpunks*, London: Sage, pp. 213–237.	V	75
1995	Gillian Bendelow and Simon Williams	Pain and the mind–body dualism: a sociological approach	*Body and Society* 1(2): 83–103.	IV	67
1995	Robert W. Connell	Men's bodies	R. W. Connell, *Masculinities*, Cambridge: Polity, pp. 45–66.	IV	62
1995	Kathy Davis	From objectified body to embodied subject	Kathy Davis, *Reshaping the Female Body*, London and New York: Routledge, pp. 93–114.	V	78
1995	Mike Hepworth	Positive ageing: what is the message?	R. Buton, S. Nettleton and R. Burrows (eds), *The Sociology of Health Promotion: critical analyses of consumption, lifestyle and risk*. London: Routledge, pp. 176–190.	V	88
1995	Alan Radley	The elusory body and social constructionist theory	*Body and Society* 1(2): 3–23.	II	27

Chronological Table of Reprinted Articles and Chapters – continued

Date	Author(s)	Title	Source	Vol.	Ch.
1995	Robert J. C. Young	Sex and Inequality: the cultural construction of race	Robert J. C. Young, *Colonial Desire: hybridity in theory, culture and race.* London: Routledge, pp. 90–117.	III	42
1996	Nick Crossley	Body-subject/body-power: agency, inscription and control in Foucault and Merleau-Ponty	*Body and Society* 2(2): 99–116.	I	15
1996	Isabel Dyck	Body troubles: women, the workplace and negotiations of a disabled identity	R. Butler and H. Parr (eds), *Mind and Body Spaces: geographies of illness, impairment and disability,* London: Routledge, pp. 119–137.	IV	60
1996	Kristin G. Esterberg	"A certain swagger when I walk": performing lesbian identity	S. Seidman (ed.), *Queer Theory/Sociology,* Oxford: Blackwell, pp. 259–279.	V	81
1996	Sarah Pink	Breasts in the bullring: female physiology, female bullfighters and competing feminities	*Body and Society* 2(1): 45–64.	V	82
1997	Constance Classen	Engendering perception: gender ideologies and sensory hierarchies in Western history	*Body and Society* 3(2): 1–19.	III	45
1997	Alex Hughes and Anne Witz	Feminism and the matter of bodies: from de Beauvoir to Butler	*Body and Society* 3(1): 47–60.	I	12
1997	Bill Hughes and Kevin Paterson	The social model of disability and the disappearing body: towards a sociology of impairment	*Disability and Society* 12(3): 325–340.	IV	58
1997	Chris Shilling	The undersocialised conception of the embodied agent in modern sociology	*Sociology* 31(4): 737–755.	II	25
1997	Catherine Waldby	Revenants: the visible human project and the digital uncanny	*Body and Society* 3(1): 1–16.	V	89
1998	Julia Lawton	Contemporary hospice care: the sequestration of the unbounded body and "dirty dying"	*Sociology of Health and Illness* 20(2): 121–143.	IV	72

1998	Simon J. Williams	Emotions, cyberspace and the "virtual" body: a critical appraisal	G. Bendelow and S. J. Williams (eds), *Emotions in Social Life: theories and contemporary issues*, London: Routledge, pp. 120–134.	V	76
1998	Melissa Tyler and Pamela Abbott	Chocs away: weight watching in the contemporary airline industry	*Sociology* 32(3): 433–450.	V	83
1999	Roberta Sassatelli	Interaction, order and beyond: a field analysis of body culture within fitness gyms	*Body and Society* 5(2/3): 227–248.	V	85
1999	Paul Sweetman	Anchoring the (postmodern) self? Body modification, fashion and identity	*Body and Society* 5(2/3): 51–76.	V	84
2000	Pierre Bourdieu	Bodily knowledge	Pierre Bourdieu, *Pascalian Meditations*, Cambridge: Polity, pp. 128–163.	II	21
2000	David Inglis and Mary Holmes	Toiletry time: defecation, temporal strategies and the dilemmas of modernity	*Time and Society* 9(2/3): 223–245.	III	49
2000	Elspeth Probyn	Sporting bodies: dynamics of shame and pride	*Body and Society* 6(1): 13–28.	IV	63
2001	Rosi Braidotti	Meta(L)morphoses: the becoming-machine	R. Braidotti, *Metamorphoses: towards a materialist theory of becoming*, Cambridge: Polity, pp. 212–263.	V	77
2001	Alexandra Howson and David Inglis	The body in sociology: tensions inside and outside sociological thought	*Sociological Review* 49(3): 297–317.	II	30
2001	Samuel Todes	The classic view of the way the human subject has his body, and Descartes's rejection of it	Samuel Todes, *Body and World*, Cambridge: MIT Press, pp. 10–12.	I	1

GENERAL INTRODUCTION

The Sociology of the Body: genesis, development and futures

These volumes are intended to provide an overview of sociology's contribution towards understanding the human body in all its complexity and ambiguity. The sociology of the body has come in recent years to figure as a major arena for debate concerning the character of human being, stressing as it does the interconnections between social, cultural and biological factors in the constitution both of individual human bodies and of what it means to be human more generally. The main claim of sociological approaches to human corporeal life is that the body is always more than just 'nature'. It has an existence beyond the purely biological, being influenced by social and cultural forces which shape (or attempt to shape) it in their own image. As such forces vary in character from society to society, it follows that the sociology of the body stresses the diverse and heterogeneous nature of bodies, seeing each body's existence as socially mediated, and thus as profoundly enveloped by social mores and cultural forms. Sociological understandings of the body have as their main theme plurality, for they highlight the multiple ways in which, in variant social contexts, differing types of bodies are born, live and die.

The five volumes in this collection are intended to illustrate three key issues: firstly, the chronological development of the set of perspectives that makes up the sociology of the body; secondly, the range of these perspectives; thirdly, their thematic connectedness.

In terms of the first theme, although the term 'sociology of the body' is of relatively recent provenance, and although its modern manifestations have come to the fore explicitly within the discipline of sociology only in the past twenty or so years, it is nonetheless the case that ever since the beginning of their respective disciplines in the eighteenth and nineteenth centuries, both sociologists and anthropologists have been concerned with the social location of human bodies. After all, since human life is in one way or another dependent upon the activity of the bodies of the people who live in different societies, it is almost impossible not to deal with the body in some way while studying human life, even if the body is not explicitly problematised or is not understood as an object of investigation in itself.

1

As we will see below, social scientists of many different hues have for a long time been concerned in one way or another with the nature of human corporeal life. Yet it is only in the relatively recent past that the theme of 'the body' has come to figure as a dedicated analytic area of sociology in its own right. Bryan S. Turner's book, *Body and Society: explorations in social theory*, first published in 1984, is widely acknowledged as a landmark, since this work most firmly placed the body on the sociological agenda, as an object of sustained analysis, at least in the English-speaking world. However, Turner's work has antecedents in sociology and social thought more generally, including Marx, Feuerbach, Nietzsche and Parsons, and thus indicates that the sociological study of the body existed, although in fragmented and embryonic form, well before the 1980s. A key purpose of these volumes is to show the range of ideas that previous generations of analysts have provided for contemporary sociologists to draw upon for the study of human corporeality. These volumes contain selections that indicate sociological understandings of the body existed well before Turner's systematising and agenda-setting contribution.

By collecting pieces from a wide chronological period, we intend to illustrate a second key theme of the sociology of the body, namely its rich diversity. While there is now a field of study that can be called 'sociology of the body', it is inevitable that *within* that field, there is a vast array of perspectives, each with their own foci and analytic emphases. While all of these share a conviction that the human body is mediated, shaped, regulated and influenced by social and cultural forces, they differ in how such forces are to be conceptualised. This reflects the highly fragmented nature of contemporary sociology, which has been characterised by a bewildering proliferation of perspectives since the 1960s. We have tried to be as catholic as possible in our selection, endeavouring to represent as many viewpoints as possible. Some may lament a lack of consensus within sociology as to what the body 'means' and what it does. Conversely, our own attitude is that since diversity has provided so many stimulating ways of understanding human bodily life, the current nature of the sociology of the body – fragmented, polycentric, frequently fractious – has been hugely productive in the generation of new ways of seeing and thinking about the body. In one sense, therefore, these volumes are a celebration of the diversity of sociological perspectives on the body, which is highly appropriate given that most of these perspectives (despite their other disagreements) insist that the human body itself is a diverse and heterogeneous entity. Indeed, we should perhaps speak of different types of *bodies* in the plural rather than *body* in the singular.

The social roots of the sociology of the body

A sociological understanding of any phenomenon which did not explain its own interest in that particular subject matter would be a flawed one, for it would lack a reflexive consciousness both of its own historical genesis and of its tacit assumptions and dispositions. The sociology of the body (or rather, bodies) is no exception to this imperative. Its practitioners must be rigorously aware of what is involved in carrying out sociological studies of the body. Given this, we can identify several main reasons for the appearance in the past two decades of the sociology of the body as a dedicated area of study.

The first concerns what might be taken as mostly (but not exclusively) *intellectual* reasons for the genesis of the sociology of the body. Dissatisfaction among different groups of scholars as to how bodies were understood in Western thought in general, and *modern* Western thought in particular, is one root cause behind the appearance of the sociology of the body. Regarding the body as a mere physical appendage to 'higher' and more 'noble' mental faculties has arguably been part of the mainstream of Western modes of thought for a very long time. Although isolated thinkers in this tradition such as Friedrich Nietzsche attempted to place the body at the centre of philosophical debate (see Lash, Ch. 37, Vol. III), it remains the case that most Western thought, if not downright anti-corporeal, tends to gloss over or ignore the place bodies play in the constitution of the human being. Todes (Ch. 1, Vol. I) notes that despite important differences between their philosophical positions, both Plato and Aristotle regarded the human soul as rooted in the 'real' world by means of the body. The soul and the mind of the person were therefore regarded in an influential stream of Greek thought as being 'above' the body, in the twin sense of being morally superior to it, and of being lodged inside the body only unwillingly and temporarily. This Greek derogation of the body as a mere physical receptacle of the non-physical, mental capacities of the human being, in part shaped the Christian dislike of corporeal matter. As Bottomley (1979) shows, from the very beginning of Christianity, theologians were wont to heap abuse on the body as being a sinful mass of flesh, a reminder of the Fallen nature of Man, and a hindrance to the achievement of spiritual purity. As the medieval divine St Bernard put it, the body of the human being was 'nothing but fetid sperm, a bag of manure' (Camporesi 1995: 106).

It is therefore quite wrong to assert that a highly negative attitude towards the human body is a product only of Western *modernity*. Nonetheless, the early modern period pays witness to the development of a new, secular version of this form of Christian thinking. The French philosopher René Descartes (1596–1650) has come to play the role of *bete noire* in the work of certain authors working within the sociology of the body today. His conceptual revolution, one of the fundamental building blocks of modern Western epistemology, divides 'mind' from 'body' in a radical fashion, apparently leaving a chasm between the two. Whereas Christian thought had separated the two for theological reasons – the body's impurity was a sign of the mind's reaching after God – this new secular doctrine was a necessary move in the creation of a novel human-centred worldview, with the human mind seen to be at the centre of the Universe. The corollary of this shift in the nature of thought was that the body remained condemned as an inessential component of human life in comparison to the mental faculties. Yet this is far from being a 'natural' or inevitable viewpoint on the nature of human being. Outside the West, there are many other ways, both philosophical and more practical, of conceiving relations between 'mind' and 'body', and the nature of human being more generally (see the contributions by Ames on China and Koller on India, Chs 18 and 19, respectively, in Vol. I, and by Kasulis on Japan, Ch. 56, Vol. IV).

The viewpoint put forward by philosophers over a long course of Western history is thoroughly rooted in the perspective of intellectual groups, who stand to gain by the social valorisation of the mind; their main possession, tool and weapon. But the socially-generated dispositions of intellectuals who emphasise intellect over 'mere' physical life, is constitutive of an ideology, a partial perspective on the nature of life, rather than the basis for a more satisfactory and less myopic analysis of the nature of human life in general, and its bodily aspects in particular. Sociologists and others have come to cast a reflexive light on their own dispositions, as members of intellectual groups with an interest in downplaying the corporeal components of human existence. Consequently, they have sought to escape the shackles of what is not a 'natural' way of thinking but is instead the arbitrary product of a particular line of historical development, namely the creation and reproduction of a specifically 'intellectualist' mentality, generated and carried by different groups of Western intellectuals since the time of the ancient Greeks. The sociology of the body is both a rethinking of, and a rebellion against, the scholastic, anti-corporeal nature of much Western philosophical thought, which itself is understood to be rooted in the social conditions of existence of certain elite groups of intellectual producers (Mannheim 1985, Bourdieu 2000).

In one way, then, the sociology of the body is centrally comprised of a series of attempts to escape and transcend what is seen to be an overly restrictive (and if taken as 'natural', very misleading) conception of the relations between 'mind' and 'body'. However, this should not be taken to mean that the sociology of the body is a 'transcendent' viewpoint that has risen to a higher and more profound level of pure 'truth'. For one thing, the fractious nature of the field is such that different perspectives within the sociology of the body are sometimes perceived by their authors to have a monopoly on the truth, whereas rival perspectives are seen to be flawed and less compelling. There is no general agreement within the field (apart from the notion that the body is more than biology) as to how the social aspects of bodies are specifically to be understood.

In addition, the impulse behind many debates in the sociology of the body is not just intellectual; rather, many interventions are rooted in the political views of their authors. The exponents of particular political perspectives on human bodies may believe that their own perspective is truer than others, and that they are revealing the true nature – hitherto hidden or distorted – of the particular types of bodies they are concerned with. But since there are a number of different, sometimes competing, politicised viewpoints on the nature of bodies, which lie behind many of the interventions within the sociology of the body, it follows that this terrain is characterised more by a series of different claims to truth, rather than a consensus among all participants of what is 'the truth' of the body (and indeed, certain viewpoints associated with the post-modern version of semiotic thought deny that there is any pure 'truth' at all, both in general and in the specific terms of the body).

Given that political reasons often lie behind the scholarly contributions to the sociology of the body, a central theme is that of *power*. In particular, the focus has been on how certain types of bodies can be defined by powerful groups as 'normal', and how the bodies of less powerful groups are as a result labelled and denigrated as being 'abnormal', deficient or lacking in some crucial way. The field of sociology today is made up of a diversity of scholars from different backgrounds and with various political agendas. In particular, scholars operating with ideas forged inside feminism, disability studies, queer studies and post-colonial studies have conceptualised the body as a central site of power, domination, struggle and resistance. Authors from these sometimes overlapping perspectives have explored sexually-different, racially 'other', differently-abled, aged, altered and hybridised bodies in ways that seek fundamentally to challenge commonsense thinking about bodies, a commonsense seen to be saturated with ideas about 'normal' bodies that operate in the interests of powerful groups.

Many scholars have rejected the idea of the body as a self-evident and immediately 'knowable' object. For example, feminists have insisted on a focus on embodied experience in order to reinstate the body as part of the analysis of self and social identity. In no small part this insistence has developed through the women's health movement in the Anglophone world. Feminists associated with this movement have challenged the ways in which the body is defined within the sciences of health, and its constitution as an object of examination and intervention. A strong sense of body consciousness has been a product of feminist challenges to the power of contemporary Western medicine and is grounded in a sense of the body as a source of authentic meaning beyond the definitions given to women's bodies by the powerful professional groups controlling the apparatuses of health in Western countries. The production of alternative knowledges about the body, epitomised by texts such as the Boston Women's Health Book Collective (Philips and Rakusen 1971), *Our Bodies Ourselves*, has been one of the most powerful politicising forces behind the appearance of the sociology of the body in the past twenty years or so. Concerns about the nature of rapidly evolving new health technologies, and their ramifications for individual agency and empowerment, have been likewise influential.

Feminist sociologists and philosophers have particularly been concerned to overcome what they see as the patriarchal mentalities that underpin much of the Western philosophical tradition, especially the analytic separation of mind and body. It would be overly simplistic to suggest that pre-modern thought ignored women altogether, but they were often categorised as closer to 'nature', and thus more imprisoned in their bodies, than men. Classical Greek philosophy tended to associate women with irrational nature and man with cultured reason (Lloyd 1984). Women were thought to be less reasonable and more under the control of their bodily appetites than men were. Christianity even more closely associated women with 'flesh' (Riley 1988: 20–1). Meanwhile, Enlightenment thought, which saw itself as heralding the liberation of all humanity from the chains of such religious ideology, arguably was based around a 'masculinisation of thought', which further accentuated the association of men with reason and women with irrationality (Bordo 1987). In some versions of the Enlightened worldview of the eighteenth century, women were seen to be suffused with their sex, fated to be women rather than fully-rounded human beings, for women could not transcend their bodily existence in order to become wholly rational citizens of an Enlightened political order. It is this 'problem' of woman's immanence within, and apparent inability to escape from, the body that Simone de Beauvoir (Ch. 6, Vol. I) confronts in her now classic work, *The Second Sex* (1972). In the extract included here, she focuses on how girls learn to see their bodies as a problem. Whether the body is necessarily a 'problem' for women is an issue that has been confronted in the work of later feminist writers such as Gatens (Ch. 10, Vol. I) and Grosz (Ch. 11, Vol. I), who consider the potential of corporeal experience as a basis for reimagining subjectivity in a way more empowering for women.

Alternative knowledge of bodies has also been promoted by post-colonial and black writers challenging white Western corporeal hegemonies. For instance, bell hooks (1992) has questioned standards of bodily beauty based on whiteness. For writers on disability, it is also clear that in contemporary Western societies not all bodies are considered equal. Scholars here have attempted to challenge the narrowness of much understanding and measuring of bodies and bodily competence in terms of historically and culturally specific standards of 'normality'. The political message is that it might be the social and physical environment that is dis-abling rather than the person's impairment. A similar challenge to what counts as 'normal' has been mounted within queer studies, a project that seeks to bring to the forefront of thinking the claim that the homosexual body is neither naturally or inevitably 'deviant', and that its constitution as such, in both everyday practice and in some forms of academic analysis, is purely the result of heterosexist ideas prevalent in wider society. All of these attempts to challenge the nature of the 'normality' of bodies have been key factors in the genesis of a defined area of sociological study focused on human bodies.

The last factor to consider is the broader cultural configuration of Western (and other) societies that has been dominant since at least World War II. The sociology of the body can be seen to be a response to the changing circumstances of contemporary living, as issues surrounding the care, maintenance and grooming of the body become ever more important components both of what social life demands of individuals and what they come to expect of themselves. Clearly, we have to be careful not to overstate the novelty of such developments. All societies prescribe certain modes of bodily care and maintenance for their members. And the Western aristocracy and bourgeoisie in the nineteenth century were perhaps just as aware as people today of the importance of carefully composing one's bodily appearance, as one of the earliest analysts of such matters, Thorstein Veblen, points out (Ch. 43, Vol. III).

However, the Western world in the twentieth century may fairly be said to have taken concerns as to bodily appearance to new extremes. As Featherstone (Ch. 44, Vol. III) argues, the emergence of consumer culture throughout the twentieth century, but especially in the 1950s and after, leads to an increasing prioritisation (at least for some social groups) of how one's body looks to others, and growing preoccupations about its appearance, presentation, modification and control. For a large part of the population, a secure sense of self arguably now involves possessing the capacity to cultivate a lifestyle in which surface appearances are key expressions of individual worth. Sociological studies of the body have sought to interrogate this dominant cultural configuration, and its ramifications for the sense of self and identity by inquiring into the historical development of such important phenomena as dieting, beauty care and the cultivation of certain forms of physique. To this extent, the sociology of the body can be seen as an important way of describing, analysing and criticising the way we live now.

Critical resources

The specific ways in which present-day sociologists have sought to think about the social and cultural dimensions of the human body owe a great deal to the ideas put forward by earlier sociological thinkers. Nevertheless, as feminists and other critics of the sociological tradition have pointed out, these ideas cannot be unquestioningly absorbed, for they contain conceptual elements that may downgrade or ignore certain crucial features of social life.

Some earlier forms of sociology remain wedded to a generally Cartesian framework, the very mode of thought to which the sociology of the body is most hostile. This is the case with Emile Durkheim, who, in the extract we have selected (Ch. 3, Vol. I), regards the body of the human being as a purely physical, organic entity, while seeing the mind of the individual as being thoroughly a product of social forces, enculturated through the processes of primary socialisation. Yet, despite being based on what sociologists today would reject as an arbitrary division between 'social' mind and 'a-social' body, Durkheim's ideas on the social framing of the individual have been developed by those following in his footsteps in a manner that more satisfactorily deals with the social elements of bodily being. Both Marcel Mauss (Ch. 53, Vol. IV) and Mary Douglas (Ch. 33, Vol. III) take Durkheimian thought in more corporeal directions, the former through his analysis of how social mores shape different forms of physical comportment, and the latter in terms of how societies draw upon aspects of the body as powerful symbolic markers of group life and its boundaries.

One way in which contemporary sociology of the body can develop its intellectual heritage is to re-read previous sociological contributions in light of an explicit focus on the body. For example, the work of Georg Simmel (Chs 50 and 51, Vol. IV) remains an interesting resource for those wishing to consider the role of the human body, in this case the face, in the construction of socially-mediated emotional responses to particular interactional situations. His work also provides a stimulating way of thinking about the social shaping of sensory dispositions, a theme also dealt with by Karl Marx (Ch. 32, Vol. III). Marx places the human body, and its sufferings, under conditions of social power, at the centre of his analysis of human life. Both in his early writings on alienation, represented here in Volume III, and his later analyses of the capitalist system (Marx 1988), Marx emphasises that the 'sigh of the oppressed creature' comes from a body enmeshed within relations of domination that seek to crush its vital capacities. Power, partly as a result of Marx's intervention, is a key focus of analysis within sociology and, as we saw above, the forms of power within which bodies are entwined have constituted a crucial source of interest for contemporary sociologists of the body.

Although usually classed as a founder of modern psychology rather than sociology, Sigmund Freud may also be seen as a figure who makes a crucial contribution both to the understanding of social controls exerted over bodies, and the nature of power involved in forging those constraints. Freud was, like Marx, centrally concerned with bringing the social as well as the biological aspects of bodies to the fore through his analyses of sexually-based neuroses. Freud's thought encompasses the effects of social life on bodies both at the level of the individual and of the whole society. The former theme is dealt with in the extract from Freud's writings contained in Volume I. In terms of the latter, for Freud (1957) modern Western society was one marked by a particularly harsh repression of the sexual and coprophiliac desires of the human being in his or her 'natural', pre-socialised state. Freud sought to uncover the ways in which the body is repressed and regulated by the structures of modern society and culture. His work thus stands as one of the key (although often unacknowledged) sources of a central theme of contemporary sociology of the body, namely that social order requires the constraining of the body in certain ways. Later, and more 'sociological', developments of his ideas on the body are represented here by the pieces by Fromm and Schoenwald (Chs 35 and 47, respectively, Vol. III).

One especially influential application of a sociological understanding of power to the comprehension of bodily life is provided by Norbert Elias (Ch. 46, Vol. III). Although Elias rejects Freud's assumption that the constrictions of bodily behaviours have their roots in modern society's need to control unruly sexual dispositions, he nonetheless retains Freud's contention that Western modernity exercises particularly strict regulation over individuals and their bodies in comparison to pre-modern and non-Western societies. From Elias's perspective, power can be conceived of in terms of the pressures on individuals to manage their bodies in particular ways in defined social contexts. His masterwork, *The Civilizing Process* (1995), is an account of how, from the sixteenth century onwards, there developed in Western European countries increasingly circumscribed and regulatory patterns of social interaction, which in turn made more and more stringent demands on how the body was presented and managed in social settings. Much of Elias's understanding of the constraining circumstances in which bodies are located is encapsulated in his analysis of court society, especially that of the absolute monarchs of France in the seventeenth and eighteenth centuries. Elias detects in this aristocratic context the origins of all the subtle refinements of manners and etiquette that contribute to the negative emotions felt by modern people of all classes, of shame, embarrassment and guilt over bodily functions like excretion and sex. The example we represent here of the historical case studies that Elias used to support his theoretical analysis, shows the gradual shift to the use of the handkerchief in blowing one's nose. This indicates an increasing control over the 'natural' function of clearing the nasal passages and the emergence of the emotions of embarrassment, shame and guilt when a handkerchief is not used. Contemporary analyses of how bodies in modernity are publicly presented, groomed and supervised owe a great deal to Elias's ground-breaking analysis.

Another highly influential thinker in the development of the sociology of the body, Michel Foucault, like Elias owes much to Freud, but in a more sharply critical way. Foucault (Chs 7 and 36, Vols I and III respectively) rejects the Freudian idea that sexual dispositions are wholly repressed in modern society. Instead, modernity is productive of a whole series of 'sexualities', novel modes of understanding sexual dispositions and living them out. For Foucault, as for other thinkers of a semiotic and post-structuralist persuasion, there is no single body, no biologically determined entity, only a malleable phenomenon infinitely susceptible to the operations of power, which does not only repress bodies but also constructs new modes of bodily being. Foucault pursued this line of argument in a series of highly influential studies of how bodies are shaped and reshaped by what he called 'regimes of discourse'. These are sets of professional knowledges, such as medicine and psychiatry, which seek to label bodies in particular ways and render them into new configurations of corporeal existence. For Foucault, discourses of the body primarily involve systems of classification that establish 'expert' definitions of differences between bodies. As a result, certain bodies are pre-scribed as socially acceptable (for example, 'healthy' bodies; 'sane' minds) and those which should be excluded as deviant (for example, differences between 'healthy' and diseased bodies, and sexualities which are perceived as 'normal' and those which are 'abnormal'). Medical, psychiatric and other forms of discourse are, for Foucault, characterised by the creation of all the paraphernalia of contemporary human knowledge surrounding the expansion of categorisation: qualified personnel; professional academies and associations; ceremonies and rituals of status passage; libraries and archives; and a proliferation of learned publications.

It is out of this kind of analysis of 'normal' and 'abnormal' bodies that much of the work by scholars in queer, disability and post-colonial studies that we mentioned above has sprung. Indeed, Foucault's influence on the sociology of the body in general terms cannot be underestimated. Foucault's thinking on the enslavement *and* empowerment of bodies by regimes of discourse has been particularly influential within both studies of sexuality and feminist analyses of bodily matters (see below). Foucault's work has inspired a great deal of literature on how the body is discursively shaped in many different contexts. A good example of this way of understanding bodies is provided by Armstrong's Foucauldian analysis of human anatomy (Ch. 38, Vol. III). Armstrong discusses the strained relationship between the disciplines of biology and anatomy on the one hand and sociology on the other, each of which tries to establish disciplinary control over the ways in which the body is perceived. In this analysis of the struggles between these disciplines to define the ontology and epistemology of the body's make-up, Armstrong describes the discourse of human anatomy as a subfield of the 'biological vision' of the body (1985: 65). In addition to its role in alleviating bodily suffering, the power of medicine is also socially organised through claims of a professionally legitimated right to define our knowledge of the human body and its relationship to self and society.

Despite its huge influence on contemporary sociological studies of the body, Foucault's ideas are not without their critics (see e.g. Ostrander, Ch. 17, Vol. I). Seeing the body wholly as a discursive construction, with no biological or 'natural' bases at all, arguably is too strong a reaction against the Freudian idea that bodies have embedded within them certain sexual dispositions. If the body is purely a socially constructed fabrication of regimes of discourse, why is it that certain bodies seem to defy the standards and modes of behaviour expected by the particular discourse through which they have been constructed? The *unpredictability* and potentially anarchic nature of bodies is downplayed in this analysis, as is the possibility that there may be more to human bodily life than the elaboration of corporeality through discourse. Moreover, Foucauldian thought remains naïvely wedded to a semiotic, post-structuralist account of knowledge, whereby objects are seen never to have any inalienable properties in themselves but are always the products of modes of discursive labelling. While this approach may perhaps be suitable for objects that are purely cultural in character (artworks, for example), if the body has both socio-cultural and biological aspects, then Foucauldian and other forms of post-structuralist analysis are well equipped to deal with the former and very ill-equipped to deal with the latter. When a form of analysis denies the existence of things with which it cannot deal, one must be very wary as to the claims it makes, and not accept uncritically its myopic vision. Despite these admonitions, it remains the case that without the interventions of Foucault and his followers, sociology of the body would be much impoverished, both theoretically and empirically.

Bodies and lived experience

Like all macro-level forms of social thought, many of the ideas set out above, including those of Foucault, tend to bypass the actual experiences of embodied persons, in favour of analysing how social forces construct and constrain their bodies. The sociology of the body contains a strain within it that is more sensitive to how the body is lived, that is, how real people deal with and make sense of their bodily being. Perhaps the most influential theoretical influence on more phenomenological forms of analysing bodily life is that of the French philosopher Maurice Merleau-Ponty (1908–61) (Ch. 5, Vol. I; see also Crossley, Ch. 15, Vol. I). Merleau-Ponty's philosophy is an explicit attempt to think beyond the dualism of 'mind' and 'body' systematised by Descartes, by reorienting thought around an acceptance that these are not two separate entities but are instead fundamentally interwoven components of an indivisible human whole. The key idea here is of a 'body-subject' that is simultaneously both physical and mental. Merleau-Ponty sees the human body as the basis of human existence *per se*, in the sense that embodiment precedes and grounds reflective thought. A person's perception of the world is rooted in the position of their body within the world, rather than being the product of a free-floating intellect as Descartes alleges. As engagement with the world is carried out through modes of perception, especially, on Merleau-Ponty's account, the sense of sight, it follows that human being-in-the-world is thoroughly corporeal in nature. The ramification of this is that our bodies are not objects to us, because each of us *is* our body. Humans do not *possess* bodies, because that suggests the body 'belongs to the mind'. Instead, the body *is* the human subject, and likewise the human subject *is* his or her body.

An important implication of this position on the nature of bodily being is that although most of the time the human subject and his or her body are thoroughly intertwined, there are occasions when the subject is in a situation where he or she feels uncomfortable in their body and so confronts it as if it

11

were an external object (Leder, Ch. 55, Vol. IV). These conditions might arise through the experience of disease, frailty or pain, which may cause a person to become focused on bodily sensations and experiences. In such circumstances of phenomenological disruption we cease to take our bodies for granted and the lived body is experienced as an object, as something we are not fully at one with or in possession of.

The idea of the 'body-subject' is a philosophical trope rather than a sociological concept, but it has been taken in more sociological directions by thinkers such as Pierre Bourdieu (Ch. 21, Vol. II), who yokes its phenomenological concerns with the minutiae of individual corporeal experience to Durkheimian notions of social structure and Marxist ideas regarding the exercise of class power by and on bodies. The application of Merleau-Ponty's ideas to sociology is not without its problems, however, as Howson and Inglis show (Ch. 30, Vol. II). Combining phenomenological analysis of bodily particulars with more orthodox sociological accounts of macro-structures tends to result in a privileging of the latter over the former, and a loss of the context-specific details of particular modes of bodily activity.

Nonetheless, modified versions of Merleau-Ponty's phenomenological ideas can be, and have been, very useful for sociological studies of specific forms of lived experience. A particularly important explication and application of Merleau-Ponty's ideas in general, and the specific case of a subject confronting her body as a thing that she is not quite in full control of, is given by Iris Marion Young. In attempting to explain why gesture, comportment and styles of movement vary between men and women, Young (Ch. 61, Vol. IV) uses a Merleau-Pontian argument against those who hold that the different ways women and men use their bodies are explicable by recourse either to physiological attributes or some kind of gendered 'essence'. She avers that women do not make full use of their bodily potential since, unlike men, they do not engage their entire bodies in physical tasks. Women are more reactive and timid in activities such as sports, she argues, because they are hesitant to trust their bodies; and they are hesitant because they lack corporeal confidence. Young discerns a distancing from and objectification of the active female body as a thing apart. This is not a result of any 'natural' dispositions of the female body, but rather comes from the gender conditioning of patriarchal societies, where men are allowed to feel at ease with their bodies more than women, and where females are socialised into expecting to operate in corporeally demure and 'ladylike' ways.

How women's bodies are viewed and understood by men in a patriarchal society, and how women may come to understand their own corporeal being as a result, is the focus of Laura Mulvey's (1989) well-known psychoanalytic analysis of 'the male gaze'. Mulvey argues that women learn to look at themselves in the way that men look at them, thus objectifying their bodies as sources of a certain form of sexual pleasure. According to this argument, women can only enjoy their sexuality passively, through the pleasure their bodies offer men. The obvious problem with this analysis of women's lived experience is that it makes little or no reference to how real, living women perceive their bodies. This type of analysis remains content to operate wholly within the confines of theoretical argumentation, rather than empirical demonstration. Moreover, the theoretical framework itself is based on psychoanalytic principles that are certainly open to dispute. In addition, the implied lack of agency attributed to women in this account has been contested by other feminist writers (notably Gamman and Marshment 1988). Nonetheless, within the sociology of the body Mulvey's notion remains influential as a way of thinking about how patriarchal social relations are manifested at the level of perceptions, held by both men and women, as to how female bodies should look and ideals they should conform to what. Recent attempts to discern a 'female gaze' that seeks sexual pleasure from the objectification and fetishisation of certain types of male bodies illustrate the continuing utility of this sort of approach, if its psychoanalytic assumptions are tempered with more grounded sociological forms of evidence about the activities of actual social actors (Mort 1988).

Clearly, one crucial way of gaining insight into how particular people have experienced their bodies is by turning to historical evidence. Sociologists can learn from historians who, like Stephen Kern (1975), explore in their research the problem of corporeal nature. A key text in aiding understanding of the shifting nature of sensory experience over time is Alain Corbin's *The Foul and the Fragrant* (1986). This is a cultural history of odour and the sense of smell, which ingeniously and in vivid detail traces out affinities between variations in human sensitivity to body odour and the structure of the social imagination. Sociologists have conducted their own historical studies on bodily wastes (see Inglis and Holmes, Ch. 49, Vol. III) and other topics. In a similar vein, the social construction of ageing is considered in Hepworth and Featherstone's (1982) historically-informed analysis of the influence of consumer culture on changing conceptions of the ageing process from mid to later life (Featherstone, Ch. 44, Vol. III; Featherstone and Hepworth, Ch. 69, Vol. IV). Similarly, the historian Edward Shorter (1982) explored the influence of changing conceptions of the reproductive nature of the body of the woman as recorded in gynaecological texts, examining within the context of medical history conceptions of differences between men's and women's bodies and changing attitudes to sexual functions and sexual relations. As Laqueur (1990) has demonstrated, scientific thought did not always hold male and female sexes as 'opposite', with a 'one-sex' model dominant prior to the 1700s regarding women as supposedly 'imperfect' versions of men.

The implication of historical analyses which emphasise the mutable nature of ideas concerning, and practices involving, the human body, is that any simple form of biological essentialism is a misrepresentation of the complex and often ambiguous character of the history of bodies. While de Beauvoir (Ch. 6, Vol. I) notes that women appear to be victims of their reproductive anatomy her case is not an essentialist one, for she contends that menstru-ation, childbearing and menopause are only burdensome and delimiting within a particular set of social structures and cultural conditions. Women are not naturally or inevitably the 'second sex'. Like all forms of bodily being, how humans perceive their own bodies and those of others is a product of history, rather than a necessary and unalterable given.

The analysis of bodily experience necessarily also compels consideration of how ideas about the body held by social actors are made and remade through processes of mundane social interaction (Smith, Ch. 20, Vol. II). For example, the shaping of gendered bodies is attributable to how individuals reflect upon specific encounters in their everyday lives that resonate with sexual significance. Connell (Ch. 62, Vol. IV) focuses on 'body-reflexive prac-tices' in his discussion of masculinity. From this perspective, the agency of bodies is critical to understanding how social conduct and social processes are organised. This perspective suggests that an analytic model, which saw the social shaping of gender as a process that comes purely 'from above' the level of the individual, would be insufficient, in that it did not attend to the more active side of constructing modes of gender identity and practice engaged in by persons themselves.

Grounded analyses of human corporeal being suggest that the theorisa-tion of gender in terms of the essentialism-versus-constructionism couplet are insufficient. The dominance of particular bodily forms and the forms that dominance takes are closely linked to sexual desire, yet the very nature of desire itself is ambiguous. According to one viewpoint, neither a primeval, universal urge, nor a product of the individual will, its force can only be understood by reference to historically specific conditions of existence (Weeks, Ch. 40, Vol. III). Victorian sexologists presented male sexuality as a gushing torrent, incapable of being channelled, and like a volcano, prone to instinctive eruptions, thus excusing the supposedly untameable character of bodily urges that lead men to acts such as rape (Weeks, Ch. 40, Vol. III). This scientific construction was therefore an important force for the main-tenance of patriarchal power through violence. Clearly, then, the ideas and assertions of scientists as to the nature of bodies can be seen to be influenced by the social contexts in which they are compelled to operate. But a simple sociological 'demystification' of the claims of the natural sciences brings with it its own analytic problems. Here we come up against one of the most tricky issues sociologists of the body face. Clearly the nature of sexual desire is not a pure biological urge, in that it is culturally mediated in differ-ent ways in variant cultural contexts. But neither can desire be seen as purely a cultural construction, because every society has to deal with similar issues of restraining and channelling the human impulse to procreate. Quite how 'cultural' and 'biological' sexuality and other aspects of corporeal being are, continues to be a main source of dispute within the sociology of the body, and between it and other analytic perspectives.

The same issues appear when sociology turns towards the considerations of medicine and medicinal conceptions of the body. A key discourse that shapes widely held views of bodily being in the modern West is that of scientific medicine, which has defined the body as a relatively stable, predictable, objective entity (Gadow Ch. 54, Vol. IV), as being self-evident and unambiguous (Seymour 1998). The body is viewed as a complex biochemical machine that can be fixed by medical intervention (Freund and Maguire 1995). Pain is reduced to a system of signals in ways that can obscure its experiential aspects (Bendelow and Williams, Ch. 67, Vol. IV). In many medicalised settings, the classificatory regime imposed by treatment practices results in both fragmentation and a related objectification of the body and its workings. The damaged identities that result find parallels in the stigmatisation of those whose disabled bodies engender a status beyond which 'normals' cannot see (Goffman, Ch. 57, Vol. IV).

Emily Martin's (Ch. 64, Vol. IV) research into childbirth is one example of how bodies can be dealt with in medical contexts in ways that go beyond the neutrality alleged by the bio-medical model, reflecting aspects of the wider social configuration in which those medical contexts are embedded. Her study of women giving birth in a hospital setting indicates that labour in the sense of paid work is directly comparable to the travails of childbearing. Not only is the institutionalised birthing process comparable to the labour process in the roles adopted by the actors involved – obstetrician as manager, midwife as foreman, mother as labourer, and baby as product – but, because of how the process is controlled and managed by others, women respondents express a disturbing sense of distance from themselves, 'a marked sense of separation of self from the parts of the body'. Such a situation arises in part because in the present day, medical management has become increasingly institutionalised, hospitals and clinics effectively separating the treatment of the body from its everyday domestic settings (Aries 1974).

Issues surrounding the spatial location and management of bodies raise further important issues. Modern societies designate particular spaces and places for processes of death and dying. In particular, the hospice has become a space in which diseased and disintegrating bodies are set apart from mainstream society in order to maintain prevailing – and increasingly sanitised – views of the body and self (Lawton, Ch. 72, Vol. IV). But despite this veiling of corporeal practices from the wider public, within such locales much work has to be done, by both staff and patients, to ensure some sense of bodily 'normality' in conditions hardly conducive to such a desideratum. The aged and dying body can refuse to obey the demands placed on it, leaking effluvia at times and in places deemed unacceptable by more general social mores. In such a context, the potential for embarrassing situations to arise is almost boundless. For the professional carer, the job he or she has embarked on can often seem unpleasant and a threat to his or her own sense of bodily cleanliness. For patients, the body can become an object to oneself, no longer lived in a comfortable or familiar way, but as a recalcitrant alien entity over which control is increasingly unreliable and erratic (Lawler, Ch. 71, Vol. IV). Analysis which focuses on these kinds of situations provides an important critique of the notion that the human body is simply a product of discourses. If it were, then medical professionals, the very people who create and operate with these discourses, would not face so much difficulty in making certain bodies conform to particular expected modes of behaviour. Once again, the issue is raised as to what extent the body can *escape* social regulation and definition, disrupting strategies that attempt to confine it within certain normative boundaries.

The nature of ageing can be tackled sociologically in ways other than looking at the failings of the body in old age. The attempts made to keep the body looking youthful so that physical ageing is not admitted is a source of much discussion within the sociology of the body. In modern Western culture, there is a clear connection between women's bodies viewed as sex objects, youth being homologous with 'beauty', and systematic strategies that attempt to disguise the physical signs of ageing. Andrew Blaikie (1999), for example, discusses changing popular stereotypes of the ageing body. Today in the West the social importance of diet, exercise and cosmetics in maintaining the youthful body cannot be underestimated. There are also clear gender differences in this regard. Whereas older men can remain 'attractive' despite their evident ageing – baldness, grey hair, wrinkles – ageing is perceived as rendering women undesirable, hence the attribution of stereotypes such as 'hag' and 'crone' to the post-menopausal woman (Sontag, Ch. 68, Vol. IV).

For feminist theorists, the equation of female beauty with youthfulness is driven by a patriarchal fixation with control. Coward (1984) argues that mature women strive to achieve and maintain the visible body in its pre-pubescent stage by removing natural body hair and dieting to reduce full breasts and hips because men desire bodies over which they can sense power. Such modification is not done in response to explicit male invocation; rather, desires for the ideal body beautiful are implanted via visual culture, and particularly advertising. The ordinary woman, enjoined to feel guilty for failing to achieve this paragon, then fragments and objectifies her body in order to 'work on' the offending parts – the flabby thighs, the sagging breasts and so on. A particular feature of modern life in the West, which the sociology of the body has repeatedly pointed out, is that *dissatisfaction* with one's body is a seemingly ever more central component of the corporeal life of many social groups. It seems increasingly to be the case that many people are uncomfortable in their bodies, and that their physical frames confront them as objects and problems to be managed rather than as given and inevitable forms to live contentedly within.

Alternative bodies

The word 'alternative' might seem to reinforce a binary division between 'superior' normal and 'inadequate' other bodies. However, we deploy the term 'alternative' to describe fundamental challenges to thinking about bodies. A discussion of 'alternative' bodies (lesbian, disabled, intersex, and modified bodies, for instance) can trouble intellectual and actual body boundaries. The increasingly permeable boundaries of the body and the interplay between the 'natural' and the socio-cultural are especially evident in relation to the alteration of bodies. Techniques of body modification have proliferated due to dramatic changes in technology, prompting work on cyborgs and on the concept of the 'post-human body'. Often this work highlights how categories such as gender, race, sexuality, and disability intersect and interweave in the production of social hierarchies around bodies.

The queering or troubling of supposedly 'natural' hierarchies of bodies organised around sex/gender has been a particularly important area. Key theoretical pieces (e.g. Butler, Ch. 9, Vol. I) appear throughout these volumes – see, for example, the articles concerning difficulties women have in avoiding being objectified (e.g. Bordo, Ch. 16, Vol. I; Canto, Ch. 31, Vol. III; de Beauvoir, Ch. 6, Vol. I).

Arguments about gender to some extent apply to the difficulties of black embodiment, although there the issue is often one of invisibility rather than hypervisibility (Patterson, Ch. 87, Vol. V). The embodiment of non-Western peoples has been extensively rethought within post-colonial theoretical frameworks, largely following Edward Said. These have highlighted the influence of racist processes of colonisation and slavery in designating non-white bodies as ugly and uncivilised, and yet also as exotic and sexualised. Post-Colonial scholars have been influential in highlighting the bodily aspects of racialised notions of domination (see Young, Ch. 42, Vol. III).

Bodily hierarchies are also challenged by scholars associated with the disability movement, who have insisted on the necessity of 'bringing the body back in' to analysis of social life (Zola, Ch. 59, Vol. IV). The biophysical norms that are a fundamental part of the assumptions we make about the physical appearance of people were historically underpinned by assumptions about the physical requirements for economic productivity (Hughes and Paterson, Ch. 58, Vol. IV). While all societies develop somatic norms that are considered stigmatising (Freund and Maguire 1999), the norms that contribute to stigmatisation are themselves subject to social and historical change (Susman 1993). Nonetheless, it would seem that in the modern west, economically derived notions of the bio-physically normal body have particularly influenced social distinctions between physical ability, impairment and disability. While impairment refers to some loss of physiological or anatomical capacity, the term disability registers the repercussions of impairment and the difficulties a person may have engaging with the physical and built environment. Disability reflects not only the ways in which people with impairments are typically isolated and excluded from full social participation (Oliver 1996) but also that Western standards of disability are not universal. Whether or not impairment becomes a disability depends on the social and cultural contexts in which the impairment occurs or is acquired. Impairments can be found in all societies, but whether the status of disability is conferred upon impairment depends on the responses and social arrangements of the communities in which they occur. Nonetheless, categorising people on the basis of both physical appearance and physical function leads to social distinctions that may be stigmatising in their consequences (Zola 1982, 1993). These processes fuel considerable individual desires to alter 'imperfect' bodies.

Most bodies are subject to 'work' or management of some kind, as Featherstone's (Ch. 44, Vol. IV) widely read article outlines. This management can involve body modification practices ranging from diet (Turner, Ch. 73, Vol. V), to fitness regimes (Sassatelli, Ch. 85, Vol. V), to plastic surgery (Davis, Ch. 78, Vol. V). A focus on body modification helps in understanding bodies as in some sense achieved rather than naturally given. Such a perspective can challenge patterns of domination based on valuing some bodies and bodily expressions more highly than others. However, although individuals may have some agency in shaping their bodies, they may often do so not to display the importance of somatic diversity but in order to conform to dominant bodily standards. Symbolic interactionists have argued that bodies are in part achieved through working at appropriate forms of bodily display. Garfinkel's (Ch. 79, Vol. V) work on intersex individuals is a classic and early piece in this tradition. He argues that intersex people (those whose biological sex is unclear) highlight what is true for all: that sex is not a matter simply of anatomy but of managing the body in accordance with gendered expectations about how women's and men's bodies should look and act. These ideas have come to sociological attention partly via Judith Butler's (Ch. 9, Vol. I) philosophical writings on the performativity of gender in relation to sexed bodies. These and many other writings on 'alternative' bodies draw heavily on Foucault's (see Ch. 36, Vol. III) conceptualisation of corporeal disciplines within particular socio-historical discursive and institutional regimes.

Both the symbolic interactionist and Foucauldian traditions can be seen in sociological accounts of how material reshapings of bodies may be the outcome of internalising social norms about bodies. There are interesting similarities between these two perspectives but they are based on very different methodological approaches. Symbolic interactionists are concerned with everyday, observable bodily display and interaction. This influence is evident in Tyler and Abbott's (Ch. 83, Vol. V) observations of how thinness and other cultural expectations about femininity are enforced as part of the work practice of women flight attendants. Tyler and Abbott focus on women's day-to-day struggles to negotiate feminine bodily display in light of corporate attempts to direct that display. In contrast to symbolic interactionists' attention to watching people enact bodily norms, Foucault analyses the abstract historical processes, especially discursive processes, which have produced current forms of bodily governance. Although perhaps most obvious in the feminist work of Bordo (Ch. 16, Vol. I), Butler (Ch. 9, Vol. I), Haraway and Waldby (Chs 74 and 89, respectively, Vol. V), his influence may also be seen (although it is not specifically cited) within the piece by Davis (Ch. 78, Vol. V). She argues that women's stories about their plastic surgery highlight the paradox of women wishing to alter what are perceived as problematic aspects of their bodies in order to resist objectification.

The problems and possibilities of bodies might be thought of within a different framework, which could encourage attention to the *limitations* to social projects of body modification. Bodies themselves change over time in ways perhaps not desired; indeed modification may be aimed at circumventing such changes, and people must cope with the implications of disability, illness and/or age for bodily competence and body image. Technologies allow ever greater bodily manipulation, and this is frequently done in the service of maintaining youthful body appearance. However, as Mike Hepworth (Ch. 88, Vol. V) argues, ageing as a physical process cannot (yet?) be forever delayed – no matter how many technical or social forces are brought to bear.

Many feminist writers have stressed the importance of understanding the symbolic and material impact of new body technologies, which might go 'beyond the human'. The concept of the post-human body refers to the increasing difficulty of demarcating human bodies from the machinery sustaining and often incorporated within them. The advances of science and medicine, from drugs to transplants, have also broken down species boundaries. The diabetic survives on insulin made from pigs; baboons may become organ donors for humans. The figure of the cyborg describes the intermeshing of machine and flesh, and also becomes the metaphor for a new form of corporeal hybridity. Bodily hybridity increasingly emerges as a challenge to the nineteenth century legacy of pathologising and criminalising of bodies, as Braidotti (Ch. 77, Vol. V) argues. But whether post-human corporeality is a cause for concern or celebration is a matter of debate. That such corporeality is woven within rapid and complex changes affecting subjectivity/identity is largely agreed. Again, received wisdom draws upon Foucault's account of the discursive construction of the body for its interpretation. In a rather different vein, Haraway's (Ch. 74, Vol. V) analysis of the material, and not just discursive, aspects of what she calls 'the informatics of domination' has been influential. We reprint here an early statement of her position that makes clear the materialism underpinning her work. Similarly, Waldby (Ch. 89, Vol. V) argues that although new technologies have produced new ways of seeing bodies, these continue to produce hierarchies that devalue 'different' corporealities. What much sociology of the body reminds us is that we are not free to think whatever we like about our own or 'other' bodies, or to do with them wholly as we would wish.

Conclusion

As we noted above, the sociology of the body has as its central premise the notion that the human body is never just a purely biological entity but one which has social and cultural dimensions too. Within the field that is the sociology of the body, there are many different ways of understanding both the nature of those social and cultural aspects of the body, and the ways in which they relate to the body as a biological entity. These volumes are testament to the rich diversity of perspectives available today to anyone wishing to think about the human body as it exists in different social and culture contexts, each of which impacts upon it in one way or another.

Our sense of the current state of the sociology of the body is that much of the theoretical positions and analytic avenues that a study of the social and cultural aspects of the body require are now in place. The past two decades have seen the rapid development and consolidation of a whole host of inter-related (if sometimes antagonistic) theoretical resources for carrying out sociological analysis of human corporeality. It is doubtful whether now fundamentally novel theoretical positions will appear, unless radical changes in the nature of bodies themselves occur in the near future. Although much has been made in some quarters of cyborgs and new technologies that apparently diminish the divide between human and machine, and despite the often rather over stated controversies as to future developments in scientific modifications, it is likely that for most of us, for a long time to come, our everyday bodily lives will revolve around issues that are much more mundane, such as feeling embarrassed when an uncontrolled bodily emission escapes or when we have to interact with professional carers in hospitals or elsewhere. As the theoretical resources bequeathed by, among others, Elias, Foucault and Merleau-Ponty are now in place, we are inclined to advocate more empirical studies of particular forms of bodily life that draw upon – or challenge – these existing theoretical frameworks, in the excavation of specific contexts within which real people actually live their lives. This may seem to some like the advocation of a simplistic form of empiricism. But that is not what we mean. A situation where theorising is bereft of empirical data, and where theorists are constantly reinventing the wheel, is not a healthy one for any discipline or subdiscipline, and there is a danger that in the future the sociology of the body may fall into that trap. It is our belief that it is incumbent upon those who will take the sociology of the body forward in the future to deal with corporeal life as it is actually lived by different groups of people, rather than only as it is perceived in the seminar room and lecture hall.

The sociology of the body must also carefully consider its relationships with other disciplines, especially those of the natural sciences. It would be a reckless person indeed who claimed that the human body is *purely* a social and cultural product bearing within it no traces of biological life. Since the nineteenth century, there has been an increasing division of labour within academic life, splitting the arts and social sciences from the natural sciences. In the natural sciences, where human behaviour can be seen to be 'hard-wired' genetically (Dawkins 1989), the social and cultural aspects of human bodily life can seem so trivial and unimportant as to be hardly worth mentioning. Conversely, inside the universe inhabited by arts and social science scholars, biological factors might appear a complete irrelevance in understanding how human beings function.

Forms of disciplinary myopia characterise the more extreme contributions of those from each side of the social/natural science divide. While some contributions to the sociology of the body have been guilty of assuming that their own viewpoint on human existence is the only possible one, other scholars have sought to grapple explicitly with the thorny issue of the relations between biological and socio-cultural phenomena in the constitution of the human being. Authors such as Barchas, Benton, Freund and Radley (all represented in Vol. II) have each in their own distinctive ways sought to think through some of the difficulties involved in this debate. While putative solutions to such dilemmas are bound to remain controversial, these contributions focus attention on the need for the sociology of the body to reach beyond itself to other positions and viewpoints, and for it not to remain imprisoned by a churlish hostility to the natural sciences. The sociology of the body needs to encompass study not only of the bodies of humans but those of non-human animals as well. Only in this way can the similarities and differences between human corporeal life and the rest of nature truly be grasped. This demand suggests that the sociology of the body be part of a wider research programme, that of a systematic and open-minded sociology of nature, which would encompass attempts to comprehend both the 'natural' and 'cultural' dimensions of existence, human and extra-human, in all their complexity. The sociology of the body, as it has been constituted up to now, has already provided many crucial insights upon which such an ambitious endeavour could draw.

The sociology of the body has its roots in many different contributions from the history of sociology and other disciplines. But it has grown rapidly in recent years into a considerable field in its own right. The human body has now become an issue that sociology cannot shy away from. Endeavours in other areas of sociology (and indeed, the social sciences in general) can no longer legitimately disregard the fact that the people under study are embodied persons, an apparently simple fact but one which leads to enormous – and enormously stimulating – problems of analysis and investigation, not to mention of ethics and politics. The sociology of the body, in fact, should be seen as an indispensable component of all sociology, for without a focus on the corporeal, analysis of what human beings are, what they do and what they believe, would be impoverished indeed. Sociology of the body's crucial contribution to the understanding of the nature of life itself now cannot be ignored.

References

Aries, P. (1974) *Western Attitudes toward Death: from the Middle Ages to the present* Patricia M. Ranum (trans.), Baltimore and London: The Johns Hopkins University Press.

Armstrong, D. (1987) 'Bodies of knowledge: Foucault and the problem of human anatomy' in *Sociological Theory and Medical Sociology*, G. Scambler (ed.), London: Taristock.

Beauvoir, S. de (1972) *The Second Sex*, H.M. Parshley (trans.), Harmondsworth: Penguin.

Blaikie, A. (1999) *Ageing and Popular Culture*, Cambridge: Cambridge University Press.

Bottomley, F. (1979) *Attitudes to the Body in Western Christendom*, London: Lepus Books.

Bordo, S. (1987) 'The Cartesian masculinization of thought', in *Sex and Scientific Inquiry*, S. Hardins (ed.), Chicago: University of Chicago Press.

Bourdieu, P. (2000) *Pascalian Meditations*, Cambridge: Polity.

Camporesi, P. (1995) *The Juice of Life*, New York: Continuum.

Corbin, A. (1986) *The Foul and The Fragrant: odour and the French social imagination*, Leamington Spa: Berg Publishers.

Coward, R. (1984) 'The body beautiful', in R. Coward, *Female Desire: women's sexuality today*, London: Paladin, pp. 37–46.

Dawkins, R. (1989) *The Selfish Gene*, Oxford: Oxford University Press.

Elias, N. (1995) *The Civilizing Process: the history of manners*, Oxford: Blackwell.

Freud, S. (1957) *Civilization and its Discontents*, London: The Hogarth Press.

Freund, P. and Maguire, M. (1999) *Health, Illness and the Social Body*, New Jersey and London: Prentice Hall.

Gamman, L. and Marshment, M. (1988) *The Female Gaze: women as viewers of popular culture*, London: The Women's Press.

Hepworth, M. and Featherstone, M. (1982) *Surviving Middle Age*, Oxford: Basil Blackwell.

hooks, bell (1992) *Black Looks: race and representation*, Boston, Mass. Southend Press.

Kern, S. (1975) *Anatomy and Destiny: a cultural history of the body*, Indianapolis and New York: Bobbs-Merrill.

Laqueur, Thomas (1990) *Making Sex: body and gender from the Greeks to Freud*, Cambridge, Mass.: Harvard University Press.

Lloyd, Genevieve (1984) *The Man of Reason: 'male' and 'female' in Western philosophy*, London: Methuen.

Mannheim, K. (1985) *Ideology and Utopia: an introduction to the sociology of knowledge*, New York: Harcourt Brace.

Marx, K. (1988) *Capital*, Vol. I, Harmondsworth: Penguin.

Mort, F. (1988) 'Boy's own? Masculinity, style and popular culture', in R. Chapman and J. Rutherford (eds), *Male Order: unwrapping masculinity*, Lawrence & Wishart, pp. 193–224.

Mulvey, Laura (1989) 'Visual pleasure and narrative cinema', in *Visual and Other Pleasures*, London: MacMillan. First published in 1975 *Screen* 16(3): 6–18.

Oliver, M. (1996) *Understanding Disability*. London: Macmillan.

Phillips, A. and Rakusen, J., Boston Women's Health Collective (1971) *Our bodies ourselves: a health book by women for women*, Harmondsworth: Penguin.

Riley, D. (1988) *'Am I That Name?' Feminism and the Category of 'Women' in History*, Basingstoke: Macmillan.

Seymour, W. (1998) *Remaking the Body: rehabilitation and change*, London: Routledge.

Shorter, E. (1983) *A History of Women's Bodies*, London: Allen Lane.

Susman, J. (1993) 'Disability, stigma and deviance', *Social Science and Medicine* 38(1): 15–22.

Turner, B.S. (1984) *The Body and Society: explorations in social theory*, Oxford: Basil Blackwell.

Zola, I.K. (1982) *Missing Pieces: a chronicle of living with a disability*, Philadelphia: Temple University Press.

Zola, I.K. (1993) 'Self, identity and the naming question: reflections on the language of disability', *Social Science and Medicine* 36(2): 167–173.

1

THE CLASSIC VIEW OF THE WAY THE HUMAN SUBJECT HAS HIS BODY, AND DESCARTES'S REJECTION OF IT

S. Todes

Source: S. Todes, *Body and World*, Cambridge: MIT Press, 2001, pp. 10–22.

1.1 The classic view

According to Plato and Aristotle, the unity of the human subject ("soul") is complete only insofar as he comes to know (contemplate) the source of this world's order—for Plato, the realm of Ideas; and for Aristotle, pure thought thinking itself. They believed that one becomes, in respect to form, what one knows. Thus Plato and Aristotle held that the human subject is unified only insofar as he becomes identified with the ordering unity of the world. But they also believed that the human subject might not—and indeed, except for the rare exception of the true philosopher, does not—achieve very much of this unity. It is further questionable whether they even thought the true philosopher could achieve this unity perfectly, and it seems they thought that, while alive, he could not. For common men with distinctly lesser capacities, the difficulties were thought correspondingly greater. Nevertheless, they held that, despite the general failure of men to gain access to it, the perfectly unified source of the order of the world remains in being, is indeed "Being itself." Thus, for Plato and Aristotle, the unity of the world can be shared by the human subject insofar as he achieves perfection. But it rarely, if ever, is fully shared, so that, though access to the world's unity is the goal of the human subject, as it is of everything in the world, this unity is not *defined* in terms of the human subject, much less considered to derive its existence (or, more precisely, its being) from the human subject.

The actual living human subject is merely something (for Aristotle, a "substance") *in* the world, with the rare and seldom realized capacity to identify

25

himself somewhat imperfectly, through contemplation or *dianoia*, with the world's unity. And this identification, such as it is, is accomplished only by the human subject forsaking his bodily involvement as someone in the world. Thus, for my purposes, the view of Plato and Aristotle, the "classic view," is that the human subject begins, by virtue of his body, as something in the world, as one thing in the midst of others; and that, by virtue of his mind, he has the capacity to raise himself from this status to the status of being identified with the unity of the world itself. But insofar as a man achieves the higher status, he forsakes the lower.

For Plato especially, these two states are in opposition. It is one part, his body, that draws the human subject toward the lower state; and another part, his mind, that draws him (i.e., his soul) toward the upper state, requiring him in general to subdue rather than meet the claims of his body. Plato expounds this view at length, in its most simplified form, in the *Phaedo*; and more cursorily, in the same form, in the *Apology*. It is, in addition, implicit in the *Timaeus*. He gives the view more subtle form in the *Republic*, where he attempts to understand the transition of the human soul from one to the other of its two extreme states, depicted in the *Phaedo* as so sharply separated. A momentary exception to this general view occurs in the *Symposium*, where Diotima, speaking as the voice of inspired truth, tells Socrates that "love is not for the beautiful, as you think. . . . It is for begetting and birth in the beautiful," and yet, as she later says, "love is for immortality also." Insofar, thus, as Plato believes that the act of begetting the beautiful achieves immortality, he has a notion of how "mortality partakes of immortality, both *in body* [my italics] and in all other respects." But this line of thought is soon dropped in favor of Plato's dominant theme, which is expressed in Diotima's "higher revelation" of "the ladder of love," as it has come to be called in Platonic literature. This "higher revelation" teaches us that,

Whoever shall be guided so far towards the mysteries of love, by *contemplating* [my italics] beautiful things rightly in due order, approaches the last grade where he will suddenly behold a beauty marvelous in its nature, that very Beauty, for the sake of which all the earlier hardships had been borne . . . . This beauty will not show itself to him like a face or hands or any bodily thing *at all* [my italics] . . . but it is by itself with itself always in simplicity . . . . All the beautiful things elsewhere partake of this beauty in such manner, that when *they* are born and perish *it* [Plato's italics] becomes neither less nor more, and nothing at all happens to it.

In comparison to Plato, Aristotle believes there is less conflict between the demands raised by a man's mind and those raised by his body. Aristotle, unlike Plato, emphasizes a moderate norm of rational life, in which mind and body are mutually adjusted, neither being wholly subjected to the other. But Aristotle's greater acceptance of the importance, for a proper, rational human life, of meeting the claims of the body merely signals his greater acceptance than Plato of the imperfectibility of man, as contrasted, for example, with the perfection of the heavenly bodies. The latter, possessing a higher (more intelligible) grade of matter in their bodies than man, are, accordingly, conceived by Aristotle to have a more perfect norm of "life" or existence. Thus, for Aristotle as for Plato, insofar as the human body (human matter) plays a role in man's life, man is merely one substance among others in the world. Only insofar as some other element (the human intellect, human form) plays a role in his life does man have a measure of access to the ordering unity of the world. This access is in the form of identity. And the measure of identity with the unity of the world achieved by the nonbody element of the human subject is construed by both philosophers as a measure of release from being in the midst of things in the world, in favor of a state of pure thought beyond the world. For Aristotle, this identity with the unity of the world can be achieved only in a more partial and indirect way than for Plato. It is possible only through participation in the mediating active intellect;[1] and through "knowledge" of the merely analogical categories, and of what the Scholastics called "the Transcendentals," such as Being, Unity, Truth, Goodness, Thing, Other. Indirect and partial though it may be, the greatest happiness and the greatest good for man is nevertheless realized, according to Aristotle, in the contemplative life.[2] In this form of life, man is most nearly released from being in the midst of things, and most nearly identified with pure thought thinking itself *beyond* the *primum mobile*.

1.2 Descartes's rejection of the classic view

1.2.1 The discovery of human necessity, and its first consequences for the philosophy of the body

The first effective philosophic challenge to this classic view came with the work of Descartes. By the argument of the *cogito* the necessary (indubitable) existence of the human subject was demonstrated by showing that even the human attempt to dispense conceptually with this existence presupposes it. Descartes here introduced into philosophy, albeit merely on the conceptual level, a notion of *human necessity*—a notion colloquially familiar in reference to human life in all its aspects, as expressed by the phrase "the necessities of life." What is "necessary" in this sense is that which the human subject is unable to dispense with, try as he may, because he needs it even to undertake the act of dispensing with anything.

The primary consequence of this philosophic discovery of human necessity was that philosophy ceased to regard the human subject as a thing or substance *in* the world, and began instead to define the human subject in terms of the *world* in which things are. In the philosophy of Descartes himself, these consequences were only partially drawn; they were fully worked out only a century and a half later, by Kant. On the classic view, the human subject had been regarded as moored in the world by his body. As a direct consequence of the *cogito* argument in which he discovered the conceptual form of human necessity, Descartes cut this mooring. His reason, in effect, though he did not understand it this way, was that he had discovered no bodily form of it. Descartes's method had been to discover that about the human subject which is required by the very attempt to reject it, and is thus invulnerable to the subject's attempt to dispense with it intellectually. In short, Descartes sought to discover the human subject's indispensable beliefs.[3] Descartes discovered that what immediately resists a purely intellectual rejection is only the belief in the existence of one's own intellect—a point implicitly repeated in Leibniz's later criticism of Locke, "*Nihil est in intellectu . . . nisi ipse intellectus.*"[4] Descartes never thought of broadening his method in order to discover *all* that the human subject can not dispense with because he has to use it in order to dispense with anything. Instead, he concluded that whatever could be dispensed with in a purely intellectual way was not philosophically necessary to the human subject, that it was not "of the essence" of the human subject.[5] Thus, as the first result of his discovery of human necessity, he came to define the human subject solely as a "thinking substance."

I concluded that I was a substance whose whole essence or nature was only to think, and which, to exist, has no need of space nor of any material thing. Thus it follows that this ego, this soul, by which I am what I am, is entirely distinct from the body and easier to know than the latter, and that even if the body were not, the soul would not cease to be all that it now is.

True, Descartes elsewhere tries to modify the implausible extremism of this utter separation of mind and body, as in the *Meditations* (p. 64), where he writes, "I do not only reside in my body, as a pilot in his ship, but am intimately connected with it, and the mixture is so blended that something like a single whole is produced." But though Descartes sometimes insists, without satisfactory explication, that the human mind and body are "intimately" connected and "like" a single whole, he never gives up his fundamental position, which was the influential one in the history of philosophy: in "essence," mind and body are entirely distinct, so that one could exist without the other.

1.2.2 The ambiguity of Descartes's version of the human subject

Descartes's version of the human subject as a thinking substance leaves man hovering somewhat ambiguously between the world and things in the world. On the classic view, too, man hovers between these extremes, but in a different way. On the classic view, man hovers clearly between these extremes; he always has some definite position, and his "hovering" connotes merely that he can change his position, falling lower into association with material things in the world or ascending toward participation in the unity of the world itself ("Being as such"). But for Descartes, man's position as a thinking substance somewhere between things (elements of the one, infinite "extended substance") and the world's ordering unity (represented in Descartes's philosophy by God) is not so much variable as indeterminate.

The thinking subject, in existing outside of space and only in time, is conceived by Descartes to be outside the world; existing in time alone is not, for Descartes, existing in the world:

> I could imagine that I had no body, and that there was no world nor any place that I occupied, but I could not imagine for a moment that I did not exist.[6]

For the human subject to be in the world, the human body must be essential to him. But still, though Descartes raises the human subject from his classic status as placed (by his body) in the world, he does not quite raise him to the only definite alternate status of identification with the ordering unity of the world itself. Descartes seems confused about the relation between God and a thinking substance.

In some ways, Descartes treats the human subject in a manner that scholastic philosophy had reserved for God. In general, of course, Descartes replaces the Scholastics' central concern with God by a central concern with man. He concentrates on how *man* knows, on the proper "method" for human inquiry, whereas the Scholastics had concentrated on how *God* orders the world. But more specifically, Descartes's philosophy is built upon the argument of the *cogito*, which, in form, parallels the traditional ontological argument for the existence of God. In both cases, the necessary existence of the subject is held to be demonstrable from the mere conception of it; in both cases, the actuality of the subject is held to follow necessarily from its mere possibility, so that the *cogito* might well be called "the ontological argument for the existence of the human subject." As we will later see in discussing Kant, a new yet recognizable form of this argument is important in the work that at once consolidates the Cartesian venture and makes a fundamental point of refuting the ontological argument in its old form. This is additional evidence that the parallel is not fortuitous or merely verbal, but instead reflects the basic thinking of these philosophers.

In general, however, Descartes vacillates between identifying the human subject with the ordering unity of the world and giving him a lower status as what is perhaps best called "a fragment of the world," a status still above that of something merely in the world. This vacillation is rooted in Descartes's doctrine that the human subject does not experience things in the world but only (sensory) appearances or (conceptual) representations of these things. If things in the world are, however implicitly, *completely* represented (by appearances or representations) in the mind of the "thinking substance," then this substance (the human subject) is equivalent to the world in which things are. And if the representations in the mind follow from the very nature of the mental substance, as they do for Descartes insofar as he regards the representation as complete, then this mental substance is equivalent to the ordering unity of the world. On the other hand, if things in the world are *incompletely* represented in the thinking substance, then this substance is equivalent to a mere fragment of the world; it is neither the world nor something in it, but merely a fragmentary representation of it. On this view, we have fragmentary data from an original that we cannot directly experience, investigate, and know. However consistent a picture we make of our fragments, we can never be *sure* that the coherence is not simply a fortuitous condensation of representations of logically scattered fragments of things in the world; we can never be sure that this condensation is more than momentarily possible, and that it is not soon to be disrupted by new data from things in the world logically intermediate between the fragments already represented. As at a roulette table, if the winning numbers are successively, 1, 2, 3, . . . , 200, there is still no reason to believe the next number will be 201 (provided we know that the machine is not rigged), so, from the regularity of our impressions to date, we have no *reason*, if things in the world are incompletely represented in our mind, to believe that the next impression received will conform to the antecedently established pattern.

For Descartes, since all events in the world are rational effects of its first principles, and since man is always capable, if sufficiently careful, of indubitably correct inference from indubitably correct premises, it follows that, if man can have absolutely certain knowledge of the first principles of the world, there is in theory no upper limit short of completion to the possible extent of his knowledge of the world; there is no assignable limit of truths about the world beyond which he cannot in principle extend his knowledge. And conversely, since the "knowledge of causes from effects" can never be certain beyond doubt, it follows that, if these first principles are not accessible to man in his representations, there is in theory no lower limit above absolute ignorance to the possible extent of his knowledge of the world; there is no assignable minimum of truths about the world that he can be certain of possessing. Nor can we, using the term in Descartes's sense, hold that we "know" at least certain effects even though we do not know the causes from which they follow. For Descartes, "knowledge," being indubitable, must consist either of a self-evident principle or of a deductive inference from such a principle proceeding either directly to the given effects or indirectly, by an unbroken series of deductive inferences, to effects that can be understood as causes of the given effects. We could never prove to Descartes's satisfaction that simple data (representations merely of effects, but not of their causes) do not offer us illusory representations of the world of things.

Thus on Descartes's view, the extent to which the world of things is represented in the world of appearances, whether the world of appearances is an indefinitely complete or an indefinitely incomplete representation of the world of things, and accordingly, whether the human subject is equivalent to the ordering unity of the world or only to a fragment of the world, depends upon whether or not a perfect representation of the self-evident first principles about matters of fact in the world is possible for the finite thinking substance.

Descartes's answer to this crucial question is vacillating and confusing. In general, Descartes claims certainty but offers only uncertainty. He claims to be in possession of first principles from which all matters of fact about the world are in principle deducible—though the *de facto* capacity of man's finite mind to complete the deduction is in question. But there is a marked discrepancy between the philosophical ideal of certainly that he claims to have achieved and the scientific practice (scientific results) by which he claims to demonstrate that achievement. The scientific first principles that Descartes used in the treatises on optics, geometry, and meteors, to which the *Discourse* serves as an introduction, are explicitly given as only "hypotheses" justified by their explanation of observed "effects."[7] Descartes merely claims, but does not show, that these hypotheses are deducible from self-evident first principles, such as the *cogito*. Furthermore, Descartes's claims for the knowability of matters of fact on the basis of self-evident first principles rest upon the applicability of his four "rules of method" to our information about the world. He begins auspiciously with the statement that "I made a firm and unalterable *resolution* [my italics] not to violate them even in a single instance."[8] However, when he actually comes to "some questions of physics" and "the study of nature," he blandly admits that, descending to the consideration of particulars, he believes it "impossible for the human mind to distinguish the forms of species of objects found on earth from an *infinity* [my italics] of others which might have been there if God had so willed."[9] But, granted this "infinity," how can one possibly apply Descartes's fourth rule in accordance with his "unalterable resolution . . . to make enumerations so complete, and reviews so general, that I would be certain that nothing was omitted?"[10] Descartes's will (resolution) to judge seems here to outreach his capacity to understand, a condition that he elsewhere calls the source of error.

One might argue that these discrepancies between Descartes's claims and his demonstrations are only secondary. One might agree with Descartes's claim that he could have deduced his "hypotheses" from self-evident first principles, but merely chose not to do so in his published work; or that, however difficult to achieve, Descartes had at least outlined the correct *ideal* for knowledge. One might argue that the applicability of Descartes's method to general truths (e.g., about "skies, stars, an earth, and even, on the earth, water, air, fire, minerals"[11]) is sufficiently impressive, even though their applicability to "particulars" (objects on the earth) is questionable. Or one might attempt to save the applicability of the rule of complete enumeration to particulars, by weakening it so as to admit what Kant calls "limiting" predicates, such as "nonmortal." But this does not seem to be what Descartes intended.

The ambiguity of Descartes's version of the human subject, and the argument of the cogito

Descartes vacillates in a more crucial place between holding that the human subject is and is not in complete possession of a representation of the first principles from which, by God's will, the world of things is generated. Descartes vacillates not merely by exhibiting a discrepancy between the kind of investigation of matters of fact he claims is possible and the kind he actually reports. He also vacillates within his argument about the relation between the human subject and God, before he even broaches the question of man's knowledge of matters of fact, i.e., man's knowledge about things in the world, man's knowledge of extended substance. After having, to his satisfaction, demolished traditional belief, Descartes begins the reconstruction of philosophy by judging that he can "safely accept (the *cogito*) as the first principle"[12] of the philosophy he is seeking. From the *cogito* he derives the validity of the rule that clarity and distinctness are the criteria of truth, on the ground that he "sees" that the indubitability of the *cogito* is marked by these properties. From the *cogito* and these criteria, with the aid of the "evident" principle of "good sense" that nothing more perfect follows from something less perfect, he derives the existence of God.[13] Thus the initial thrust of Descartes's argument is to derive the existence of God from the existence of the human subject.

Descartes's attempt all along is to gain *knowledge*, in the strict sense, of matters of fact in the (extended) world. Granted Descartes's representational view of experience, he cannot derive any knowledge of the world of things merely from knowledge of the self and the contents of its consciousness. He first has to demonstrate the accuracy of experiential representation, by finding a bridge between its first principles and the first principles generating matters of fact in the world. These first principles must be self-evident principles of the purely rational intellect so that the finite thinking substance can share them, but they must also be endowed with the ability to create and order all things in the world. These self-evident principles, considered as endowed with the free capacity to create and order things down to the last detail, are what Descartes mainly means by "God"; God is for Descartes mainly the free rational architect of the world, the rational intellect that freely creates the world from one moment to the next. Thus, in deriving the existence of God from the existence of the human subject, Descartes proves that the ordering first principles of the world are accessible to man, so that man's representational world is indefinitely completable in correspondence to the world of things. It is in the spirit of this view that

Descartes is sometimes so optimistic as to suggest that he can actually bring his (purportedly) deductive investigations of the world to substantial completion. Thus he writes, "two or three further victories of equal importance would enable me to reach my goal."[14] Only on the basis of this view, furthermore, can Descartes even speak of the indefinite increase of our knowledge of the world.[15]

But Descartes here proves too much to keep man's world merely representational! By this proof, as we have seen, the human subject becomes equivalent to the creatively ordering unity of the world of things, because he becomes capable of generating a world of representations that corresponds to the world of things completely, or with indefinitely great completeness. But since knowledge of the unity of the world of things (God) has been *derived from* knowledge of the human subject, the human subject threatens to become not merely the originator of a corresponding world, but of the world of fact as well, so that the original is threatened with assimilation to its representation. This is so because of Descartes's "failure"[16] to distinguish between a reason and a cause. On Descartes's view, the logical and the causal sequence of things is the same, so that a proposition "p" implying a proposition "q" is, if true, about an event "e_p," which causes an event "e_q." Thus, if the existence of God is rationally implied by the existence of the human subject, it would seem to be also brought about or caused by the human subject, and, mediately, the world itself would be the product of the human subject.

Descartes cannot accept this, perhaps because he is convinced that "nothing more perfect can come from something less perfect," perhaps because of prudent regard for the power of the Church and a consequent unwillingness to publish his innermost thoughts,[17] or perhaps because his analysis of perceptual illusion and mistaken judgment has convinced him that experience is representational of a world that man might not know, and that he therefore cannot have originated. In any case, Descartes's representational view of human experience is incompatible with this originative view according to which the human subject would have occupied roughly the position of Spinoza's God.

Whatever his reasons, Descartes does not accept this originative view. Having derived knowledge of the existence of God from knowledge of the existence of the human subject and from the derivative criterion of truth, Descartes then writes that the criterion of truth is itself valid, and that all clearly and distinctly conceivable propositions, such as the *cogito*, are known to be true only because we know that they come to us from God.[18] This makes the knowledge, and therewith the existence, of the human subject derivative from that of God. It makes man a *passive* creature of God, receptive to His works in the world. In deriving the existence of man from the existence of God, Descartes, taken strictly, proves that the creative first principles of the world are inaccessible to man. For man is only one of their effects, and "knows" at best only himself. Yet from effects causes can never be judged with certainty. This position fits well with Descartes's views of perception as receptive, fragmentary, and fallible. It accounts well, moreover, for his emphasis on the usefulness of experiments, and for the position he sometimes takes that there are certain things that we cannot know except by experiment. For this position is that man is essentially passive, receiving his existence and all his representations from God, as an effect of God.[19]

This conclusion poses insuperable difficulties for Descartes's theory of knowledge. If man is not in possession of the very first principles of knowledge, then he cannot really know anything. The truth of man's beliefs is now radically in doubt, and man's representational fragment of a world may be indefinitely incomplete in its correspondence to the world of fact. And among all the propositions conceivable by man that are thus thrown in doubt is, of course, the very proposition Descartes has sought to sustain by this reversal, namely, "that all reality and truth within us come from a perfect and infinite Being," for this was proven only by regarding the *cogito* as independently certain. Hence, just as the derivation of the existence of God from that of man proved too much to keep man's world merely representational, the derivation of the existence of man from that of God proves too little to keep man's world faithfully representational. Since we cannot be certain of God's existence, being unable to argue validly from our representations as effects to Him as their cause, we cannot be certain that there is any material world at all of which the contents of the human mind are representations.

1.2.3 Summary of Descartes's view

By separating the human subject from his body, Descartes raises man from his classic status as being placed, by virtue of his body, *in* the world; but he does not quite raise man to the only definite alternate status envisaged by the classic tradition, viz., identification with the ordering unity of the world itself. Instead, Descartes is ambiguous and vacillating on this point. Sometimes he treats the human subject as equivalent to the ordering unity of the world, analyzing him primarily as an active deductive intellect capable of indubitable and unlimited knowledge of matters of fact. But sometimes he treats the human subject as merely a fragment of the world, analyzing him primarily as a passive perceiver capable of being deluded without limit about matters of fact. The uneasy balance, or better, imbalance, between these two sides of Descartes's thought is maintained by his view that the human subject does not experience things in the world but only representations corresponding variably to them. The inconsistency between these two sides of Descartes's thought comes to a head in the contradiction between Descartes's derivation of God's existence from that of the human subject, which assures the validity of our representations but threatens to make them legislative of the world; and his derivation of the existence of the human subject from that of God, which assures the representational character of our representations but threatens to deprive them of any validity as representing another world of fact. Insofar as our representations are shown to be valid, they do not seem to be merely representations, but rather to determine the nature of God. They seem, at least, to be the same as those of God, who is considered to create the world with a will of the same kind as our own;[20] it becomes in any case exceedingly difficult to distinguish the "object of the geometricians"[21] from extended substance itself. And on the other hand, insofar as our representations are shown to be merely representations, there does not seem to be any justification for holding them to be valid of the world of fact that they are supposed to represent; there does not seem to be any way of being sure from them that they are representations of anything else. In the former case, the implication of the world of fact by our experience is too strict to be representational; in the latter case, it is too loose to be so.

Notes

1 *On the Soul*, III, 5.

2 *Nicomachean Ethics*, X, 7.

3 ". . . I thought that I should . . . reject as absolutely false anything (primarily any of the opinions he had himself formerly held) of which I could have the least doubt, in order to see whether anything would be left after this procedure which could be called wholly certain" (*Discourse on Method*, p. 31). The pagination for citations from Descartes is as given in *Oeuvres de Descartes*, ed. Charles Adams and Paul Tannery (Paris: L. Cerf, 1897–1913). Quotations according to the Lafleur translations of the Library of Liberal Arts Press.

4 "Nothing is in the intellect except the intellect itself," *New Essays on the Understanding*, Bk. II, Ch. 1, Section 2.

5 ". . . other things of which (men) might think themselves more certain (than of the existence of God and of their souls), such as their having a body, or the existence of stars and of an earth, and other such things, are less certain. For even though we have a moral assurance of these things, such that it seems we cannot doubt them without extravagance, yet without being unreasonable we cannot deny that, as far as metaphysical certainty goes, there is sufficient room for doubt" (*Discourse*, pp. 37–38). Descartes never investigated whether this "moral assurance" might not be founded in a systematically undeniable necessity of some kind that was not purely intellectual; he assumed instead that it was founded in a merely *de facto* incredulity at the perfectly consistent "extravagance" of its denial.

6 *Discourse*, p. 33.

7 Ibid., p. 76.

8 Ibid., p. 18.

9 Ibid., p. 64.

10 *Meditations on First Philosophy*, p. 46.

11 Ibid., p. 64.

12 *Discourse*, p. 34.

13 Ibid., p. 32.

14 *Discourse*, p. 67.

15 E.g., *Meditations*, p. 37.

16 This "failure" is, however, so characteristic of Descartes's system of thought that it is not possible to determine what he would have thought without it. This is not so much a failure *in* his system, which Descartes could have "corrected," as a failure *of* his system as a whole. His system must be generally rejected or transformed insofar as the distinction between a real and a logical ground is upheld.

17 Such an interpretation suggests an explanation of Descartes's claimed fear that publication of his deduction of the first principles of his scientific investigations would encourage clever but hasty people in "building some extravagant phil-osophy on what they believe to be my principles." Was the extravagance Descartes feared the extravagance of an irrational instead of a rational subjectivity?

18 "If we did not know that all reality and truth within us came from a perfect and infinite Being, however clear and distinct our ideas might be, we would have no reason to be certain that they were endowed with the perfection of being true," (*Discourse*, p. 39.)

19 It is in this vein that Descartes, thinking of man as a fragment of the world, writes, "I am a mean between God and nothingness." Note he does not write, as a Greek theist might, "Between God and a thing in the world."

20 *Meditations*, p. 46.

21 *Discourse*, p. 36.

2

DISCOURSE 5

René Descartes

Source: R. Descartes, *Discourses on Method*, Harmondsworth: Penguin, 1968, pp. 61–76.

I should be very pleased to continue, and to show here the complete chain of the other truths that I deduced from these first ones; but as in order to do this it would now be necessary for me to speak of several questions about which the philosophers with whom I have no wish to embroil myself, are in dispute, I believe it will be better for me to abstain, and mention them only in general terms, in order to leave the more judicious to decide whether it would be useful that the public were informed of them in greater detail. I have always remained firm in the resolution I made not to suppose the existence of any other principle than that which I have just used to demonstrate the existence of God and of the soul, and not to accept anything as being true which did not seem to me more clear and certain than had previously the demonstrations of the geometers; and nevertheless, I dare to say that, not only have I found the means to satisfy myself in a short space of time, concerning all the principal difficulties which one usually treats of in philosophy, but also I have observed certain laws which God has so established in nature and of which he has impressed such notions in our souls, that having reflected on them sufficiently, we cannot be in any doubt that they are strictly observed in everything which exists or which happens in the world. Then, by considering the series of these laws, it appears to me that I have discovered many truths more useful and more important than anything I had learned before or even hoped to learn.

But, because I have tried to explain the most important of these in a treatise which a number of considerations prevent me from publishing, I could not make them better known than by saying here briefly what the treatise contains. It was my plan to include in it everything I thought I knew, before writing it down, concerning the nature of material things. But, in the same way that painters, being unable to represent equally well in a flat picture all the various faces of a solid body, choose one of the principal ones which they place alone in the light, and, putting the others in the shade, let them

37

appear only in so far as they can be seen while one is looking at the principal one, so, fearing that I would not be able to put into my discourse all that I had in my mind, I undertook only to expound fully what I understood about light; then, to take the opportunity to add to it something on the sun and the fixed stars, because light almost wholly stems from them; something about the firmament, because it transmits light; about the planets, comets and earth, because they reflect it; and in particular about all the bodies on earth, because they are either coloured, or transparent or luminous; and finally about man, because he sees all this. And in order to put all these new truths in a less crude light and to be able to say more freely what I think about them, without being obliged to accept or to refute what are accepted opinions among the philosophers and theologians, I resolved to leave all these people to their disputes, and to speak only of what would happen in a new world, if God were now to create, somewhere in imaginary space, enough matter to compose it, and if he were to agitate diversely and confusedly the different parts of this matter, so that he created a chaos as disordered as the poets could ever imagine, and afterwards did no more than to lend his usual preserving action to nature, and let her act according to his established laws. So, firstly, I described this substance, and tried to represent it such that, to my mind, there is nothing in the world clearer or more readily understandable, except what has already been said about God and the soul; for I even supposed expressly that there was in it none of those forms or qualities about which there is disagreement in the Schools, nor generally anything the knowledge of which was not so natural to our minds that one could not even pretend to be ignorant of it. Moreover, I showed what are the laws of nature and, without basing my reasonings on any other principle than on the infinite perfections of God, I tried to prove all those about which one might have had some doubt and to show that they are such that, if God had created many worlds, there could be none in which they failed to be observed. After this, I showed how most of the matter of this chaos must, in accordance with these laws, dispose and arrange itself in a certain way which would make it similar to our skies; how, in the meantime, some particles must compose an earth, others planets and comets, and still others a sun and fixed stars. And here, enlarging upon the subject of light, I explained at some length the nature of the light which is found in the sun and the stars, and how, from them, it crosses in an instant the immense expanses of the heavens, and how it is reflected from the planets and comets towards the earth. I added also many things about the substances, position, movements and all the different qualities of these heavens and stars; so that I thought I had said enough about them to show that there is nothing to be seen in those of this world which should not, or at least could not, appear just the same in those of the world I was describing. Next I came to speak of the earth in particular and to point out how it is that, although I had expressly supposed that God had put no weight in the matter of which it is composed, all its parts do nonetheless tend exactly towards its centre; how, there being water and air on its surface, the disposition of the heavens and the heavenly bodies, principally of the moon, must cause an ebb and flow in all respects similar to that which we see in our seas, and furthermore a certain current, as much of water as of air, from east to west, such as one notices between the tropics; how the mountains, seas, springs and rivers could form themselves naturally, and metals appear in the mines, and plants grow in the countryside, and in general, how all the bodies one calls mixed or composite could be engendered. And, among other things, because, apart from the stars, I knew nothing in the world except fire which produces light, I strove to make clearly understood everything belonging to its nature, how it is made, how it is fed, how sometimes there is only heat without light, and sometimes only light without heat; how it can introduce different colours into different bodies, and diverse other qualities; how it melts some things and hardens others; how it can consume almost everything or convert into ashes and smoke; and finally how from these ashes, by the mere power of its action, it forms glass; for as this transmutation of ashes into glass seems to me as wonderful as any other which happens in nature, I took particular pleasure in describing it.

However, I did not wish to infer from all these things that this world had been created in the way I described for it is very much more likely that, from the beginning, God made it as it was to be. But it is certain, and this is an opinion commonly held among the theologians, that the action by which he conserves it now is the same as that by which he created it; so that even though he did not at the beginning give it any other form than that of chaos, provided that he had established the laws of nature and lent it his preserving action to allow it to act as it does customarily, one can believe, without discrediting the miracle of creation, that in this way alone, all things which are purely material could in time have made themselves such as we see them today; and their nature is much easier to grasp when one sees them being fully made from the start.

From the description of inanimate objects and of plants I passed to that of animals, and particularly of man. But, because I had not yet enough knowledge to talk about it in the same way as the rest, that is to say, in proving effects by causes, and demonstrating from what elements and in what way nature must produce them, I contented myself with supposing that God made the body of man entirely similar to one of ours, as much in the outward shape of the members as in the internal conformation of the organs, without making it of a different matter from the one which I have described, and without putting in it at the beginning any rational soul, or any other thing to serve as a vegetative or sensitive soul, but merely kindling in his heart one of those fires without light that I had already explained and which I did not conceive as being of any other nature than that which heats hay when it has been stacked before it is dry, or which makes new wine ferment, when it is left to ferment on the lees. For, examining the functions which could, consequentially, be in this body, I found precisely all those which can be in us without our thinking of them, and therefore, without our soul, that is to say, that part distinct from the body about which it has been said above that its nature is only to think, contributing to them, and these are all the same functions in which one can say that the animals, devoid of reason, resemble us. But I was unable for all that to find any of those functions which, being dependent on thought, are the only ones which belong to us as men, whereas I found them all afterwards, once I had supposed that God created a rational soul, and joined it to this body in a particular way which I described.

But, so that one can see how I treated this matter there, I wish to give here the explanation of the movement of the heart and arteries, from which, being the first and most general that one observes in animals, one will be able to judge easily what one should think of all the others. And, so that one should have less difficulty in understanding what I shall say about it, I would like those who are not versed in anatomy to take the trouble, before reading this, to have cut open in front of them the heart of some large animal which has lungs, because it is, in all of them, similar enough to that of man, and to be shown its two ventricles or cavities. Firstly that in the right side, to which correspond two very large tubes: i.e. the *vena cava* (hollow vein), which is the main receptacle of the blood and is like the trunk of a tree of which all the other veins of the body are the branches; and the *vena arteriosa* (arterial vein) which is badly named thus because it is in fact an artery, which, originating in the heart, divides, having come out of the heart, into many branches which spread out throughout the lungs. Then the cavity in the left side, which similarly has two pipes which are in width equal to or larger than the preceding ones: i.e. the venous artery (*arteria venosa*), which also is badly named, being nothing other than a vein which comes from the lungs where it is divided into many branches, interlaced with those of the arterial vein and those of the tube called the windpipe, through which enters the air we breathe; and the great artery (*aorta*) which, coming out of the heart, sends its branches all through the body. I would also like them to be shown carefully the eleven little valvules which, like so many little doors, open and shut the four openings which are in these two cavities, i.e. three at the entrance of the hollow vein where they are so disposed that they can by no means prevent the blood it contains from flowing into the right-hand ventricle out of the heart, and at the same time prevent it completely from coming out of it; three at the entrance of the arterial vein, which, being placed the other way round, effectively permit the blood in this compartment to pass into the lungs, but not the blood which is in the lungs to return to it; and similarly two others at the entrance of the venous artery, which allow the blood from the lungs to flow into the left cavity of the heart, but which prevent its return; and three at the entrance of the great artery, which allow the blood to leave the heart but not to return. And there is no need to look for any other reason

40

for the number of these valvules, beyond the fact that the opening of the venous artery, being oval, on account of its position, can conveniently be closed with two, whereas the others, being round, can be more conveniently closed by three. In addition, I would like such persons to have pointed out to them that the grand artery and the arterial vein are of a much harder and firmer texture than the venous artery and the hollow vein; and that the two latter become larger before entering the heart and that they form there, as it were, two pouches, called the auricles of the heart, which are made of a substance similar to that of the heart itself; and that there is always more heat in the heart than anywhere else in the body; and finally that this heat is capable of causing any drop of blood which enters the heart's cavities immediately to expand and dilate, in the same way that all liquids do when they are allowed to fall drop by drop into some very hot vessel.

For, after that, I do not need to say anything else to explain the movement of the heart, except that when its cavities are not full of blood, blood necessarily flows from the hollow vein into the right and from the venous artery into the left; because these two vessels are always full of blood, and their openings which look towards the heart cannot then be blocked. But as soon as two drops of blood have thus entered the heart, one into each cavity, these drops, which cannot be other than very large because the openings by which they enter are very wide, and the vessels from which they come very full of blood, rarefy and dilate because of the heat they find there: by means of which, making the whole heart expand, they push against and close the five little doors which are at the entrances of the two vessels from which they flowed, thus preventing any more blood coming down into the heart, and, continuing to become more and more rarefied, they push open the six other little doors which are at the entrance to the two other vessels through which they leave the heart, in this way making all the branches of the arterial vein and the great artery swell, almost at the same moment as the heart, which straightaway afterwards contracts, as do these arteries also, because the blood which has entered them has cooled, and their six little doors shut again and the five of the hollow vein and the venous artery open again and let in two more drops of blood, which immediately make the heart and arteries expand, as before. And, because the blood which thus comes into the heart passes through these two pouches called auricles, so it comes about that their movement is contrary to that of the heart, and that they contract when the heart expands. Finally, so that those who do not know the force of mathematical demonstrations and who are not accustomed to distinguishing true reasons from mere verisimilitudes should not venture to deny this without examining it, I would like to warn them that this movement that I have just explained follows as necessarily from the mere disposition of the organs which may be observed in the heart by the eye alone, and from the heat which one can feel there with one's fingers, and from the nature of the blood which can be known by experience, as does that of a clock from the power, the position and the shape of its counterweights and its wheels.

But, if it be asked how it is that the blood in the veins is not exhausted, flowing in this way continually into the heart, and how it is that the arteries are not overfilled since all the blood which passes through the heart goes into them, I need only reply what an English doctor has already written about it, to whom must be given praise for having broken the ice on this topic, and for being the first who has taught that there are several little passages at the extremities of the arteries through which the blood which they receive from the heart enters the little branches of the veins, whence it returns immediately to the heart, so that its course is nothing other than a perpetual circulation. He proves this very well by the common experience of surgeons who, having bound the arm moderately tightly above the place at which they open the vein, cause more blood to come out than if they had not bound the arm, and the opposite result would occur if they bound the arm below, between the hand and the opening, or if they bound it above the opening very tightly. For it is obvious that a moderate binding, while being able to prevent the blood which is already in the arm from returning to the heart through the veins, cannot on that account prevent fresh blood from arriving from the arteries, because they are situated below the veins and because their texture, being harder than that of the veins, is less easy to compress, and also because the blood which comes from the heart tends to pass through the arteries to the hand with greater force than it does when returning from the hand to the heart by the veins. And since this blood comes out of the arm through the opening in one of the veins, there must necessarily be some passages below the ligature, that is to say, towards the extremities of the arm, through which it can come from the arteries. He also proves very well what he says about the circulation of the blood, by certain little pellicles which are so situated in various places along the veins that they do not allow the blood to pass from the centre of the body towards the extremities, but only to return from the extremities towards the heart; and moreover, from experience which shows that all the blood in the body can come out of it in a very short space of time through one artery if it is cut, even though it were tightly bound very near to the heart and cut between the heart and the ligature, so that one could not possibly have reason to imagine that the blood which flowed out came from anywhere other than the heart.

But there are many other things which bear witness that the true cause of this movement of the blood is as I have said: thus, firstly, the difference to be observed between the blood which comes out of the veins and that which issues from the arteries can only be due to the fact that, being rarefied and, as it were, distilled in passing through the heart, it is thinner, and more vigorous, and warmer straight after leaving the heart, that is to say, while it is in the arteries, than it is just before it goes into the heart, that is to say, in the veins; and, if one looks closely, one will find that this difference appears clearly only near the heart, and not so much so in the more remote parts of the body. In the next place, the hardness in texture of the arterial vein and the great artery shows sufficiently that the blood beats against them with more force than against the veins. And why should the left cavity of the heart and the great artery be larger and wider than the right-hand cavity and the arterial vein, if it were not that the blood from the venous artery, having been only in the lungs since it left the heart, is thinner and is rarefied to a greater degree, and more easily, than the blood which comes direct from the hollow vein? And what can the physicians discover from taking the pulse unless they know that, as the blood changes its nature, it can be rarefied by the heat of the heart more or less strongly and more or less quickly than before? And if one examines how this heat is communicated to the other organs of the body, must one not admit that it is by means of the blood, which, passing through the heart, is reheated and from there spreads throughout the body; from which it arises that if one removes the blood from some part, one removes the heat at the same time; and although the heart were as hot as a piece of glowing iron it would not suffice to warm the feet and hands as it does at present, unless it sent to these extremities a continuous supply of new blood. Then, also, one knows from this that the true use of respiration is to carry enough fresh air to the lungs, to enable the blood which enters the lungs from the right-hand cavity of the heart, where it has been rarefied and, as it were, changed into vapours, to thicken and convert once more into blood before falling into the left-hand cavity, without which it would not be fit to nourish the fire which is there. This is confirmed by the fact that we see that animals which do not have lungs, have only one cavity in the heart, and that children who cannot use their lungs while they are in their mothers' wombs, have an aperture through which blood flows from the hollow vein into the left-hand cavity of the heart, and a pipe through which it travels from the arterial vein into the great artery, without passing through the lung. Then how could digestion take place in the stomach if the heart did not send heat there by the arteries, and with it some of the more fluid parts of the blood, which help to dissolve the foods that have been put there? And is it not easy to understand the action which converts the juice of these foods into blood, if one considers that it is distilled in passing again and again through the heart, perhaps more than a hundred or two hundred times a day? And what else does one need to explain the feeding of the body with blood and the production of the various humours which are in the body other than to say that the force with which the blood, as it is rarefied, passes from the heart towards the extremities of the arteries, causes some of its parts to remain among those of the various members in which they find themselves, and taking the place there of others which they expel; and that according to the position, or the shape, or the smallness of the pores they encounter, some, rather than others, go to certain places, in the same way that, as everyone will have observed, different sieves which, having been pierced with different-sized holes, serve to separate different grains from each other? And, finally, what is most to be noticed in all this is the generation of the animal spirits, which are like a very subtle wind, or rather like a very pure and lively flame which, rising continually in great abundance from the heart to the brain, goes by means of the nerves into the muscles and gives movement to all the limbs, without its being necessary to suppose any other reason why it is that the parts of the blood which, being the most active and most penetrating, are the best suited to compose these spirits, direct themselves to the brain rather than elsewhere, than the fact that the arteries which carry them there are those which come from the heart in the straightest line of all, and that, according to the rules of mechanics, which are the same as the rules of nature, when many things tend together to move towards a same place where there is not enough space for them all, as in the case of the parts of the blood which leave the left-hand cavity of the heart and flow towards the brain, the weakest and least lively must be turned away from it by the strongest, which in this way alone arrive there.

I had explained all these things in some detail in the treatise which I earlier had it in mind to publish. And I had then shown there what must be the structure of the nerves and muscles of the human body, to enable the animal spirits, contained in the body, to have the power to move its limbs, as when one sees heads, shortly after having been cut off, still moving and biting the ground, even though they are no longer alive; what changes must take place in the brain to cause waking, sleep and dreams; how light, sounds, smells, tastes, heat and all the other qualities of external objects can imprint different ideas in the brain by means of the senses; how hunger, thirst and the other internal passions, can also transmit to it different ideas; what must be taken for the common sense in which these ideas are received, for memory which conserves them, and for the imagination, which can change them in different ways and make up new ones, and by the same means, distributing the animal spirits in the muscles, can make the limbs of this body move in as many different ways, and in a manner as suited to the objects which are presented to its senses, or to its internal passions, as our own bodies can move without the will conducting them. This will not appear in any way strange to those who, knowing how many different automata or moving machines the industry of man can devise, using only a very few pieces, by comparison with the great multitude of bones, muscles, nerves, arteries, veins and all the other parts which are in the body of every animal, will consider this body as a machine, which, having been made by the hands of God, is incomparably better ordered, and has in it more admirable movements than any of those which can be invented by men. And here I gave particular emphasis to showing that, if there were such machines which had the organs and appearance of a monkey or of some other irrational animal, we would have no means of recognizing that they were not of exactly the same nature as these animals: instead of which, if there were machines which had a

likeness to our bodies and imitated our actions, inasmuch as this were morally possible, we would still have two very certain means of recognizing that
they were not, for all that, real men. Of these the first is, that they could
never use words or other signs, composing them as we do to declare our
thoughts to others. For one can well conceive that a machine may be so made
as to emit words, and even that it may emit some in relation to bodily actions
which cause a change in its organs, as, for example, if one were to touch it in
a particular place, it may ask what one wishes to say to it; if it is touched in
another place, it may cry out that it is being hurt, and so on; but not that it
may arrange words in various ways to reply to the sense of everything that is
said in its presence, in the way that the most unintelligent of men can do.
And the second is that, although they might do many things as well as,
or perhaps better than, any of us, they would fail, without doubt, in
others, whereby one would discover that they did not act through knowledge,
but simply through the disposition of their organs: for, whereas reason is a
universal instrument which can serve on any kind of occasion, these organs
need a particular disposition for each particular action; whence it is that it is
morally impossible to have enough different organs in a machine to make it
act in all the occurrences of life in the same way as our reason makes us act.

Now by these two same means one can also tell the difference between
men and beasts. For it is particularly noteworthy that there are no men so
dull-witted and stupid, not even imbeciles, who are incapable of arranging
together different words, and of composing discourse by which to make their
thoughts understood; and that, on the contrary, there is no other animal,
however perfect and whatever excellent dispositions it has at birth, which can
do the same. Nor does this arise for lack of organs, for one sees that magpies
and parrots can utter words as we do, and yet cannot speak as we do, that is
to say, by showing that what they are saying is the expression of thought;
whereas men, born deaf and dumb, deprived as much as, or more than, the
animals of the organs which in others serve for speech, habitually invent for
themselves certain signs, by means of which they make themselves understood by those who, being fairly continuously in their company, have the
time to learn their language. And this shows not only that animals have less
reason than men, but that they have none at all; for we see that very little of it
is required in order to be able to speak; and since one notices inequality
among animals of the same species as well as among men, and that some are
easier to train than others, it is unbelievable that the most perfect monkey or
parrot of its species should not equal in this the most stupid child, or at least
a child with a disturbed brain, unless their souls were not of an altogether
different nature from our own. And one should not confuse words with the
natural movements which bear witness to the passions and can be imitated
by machines as well as by animals; neither should one think, as did certain of
the Ancients, that animals speak although we do not understand their language. For, if it were so, as they have many organs similar to our own, they

could make themselves understood by us as well as by their fellows. It is also particularly noteworthy that although there are many animals which show more skill than we do in certain of their actions, yet the same animals show none at all in many others; so that what they do better than we do does not prove that they have a mind, for it would follow that they would have more reason than any of us and would do better in everything; rather it proves that they do not have a mind, and that it is nature which acts in them according to the disposition of their organs, as one sees that a clock, which is made up of only wheels and springs, can count the hours and measure time more exactly than we can with all our art.

After this I had described the reasonable soul, and shown that it could not in any way be derived from the power of matter, as the other things of which I had spoken, but that it must be created expressly; and I had shown how it is not sufficient that it should be lodged in the human body, like a pilot in his ship, unless perhaps to move its limbs, but that it needs to be joined and united more closely with the body, in order to have, besides, sensations and appetites like our own, and in this way to constitute a true man. Finally, I treated at some length here the subject of the soul, because it is of the greatest importance: for, after the error of those who deny the existence of God, which error I think I have sufficiently refuted above, there is nothing which leads feeble minds more readily astray from the straight path of virtue than to imagine that the soul of animals is of the same nature as our own, and that, consequently, we have nothing to fear or to hope for after this life, any more than have flies or ants; instead, when one knows how much they differ, one can understand much better the reasons which prove that our soul is of a nature entirely independent of the body, and that, consequently, it is not subject to die with it; then, since one cannot see other causes for its destruction, one is naturally led to judge from this that it is immortal.

3

CONCEPTUAL KNOWLEDGE AND SENSORY EXPERIENCE

Emile Durkheim

Source: A. Giddens (ed.), *Emile Durkheim: Selected Writings*, Cambridge: Cambridge University Press, 1972, pp. 266–268.

(Man) has . . . everywhere conceived of himself as being formed of two radically heterogeneous beings: the body and the soul. Even when the soul is represented in a substantive form, it is not thought of as being of the same nature as that of the body. It is said that it is more ethereal, rarified and plastic, that it does not affect the senses as do the other objects to which they react, that it is not governed by the same laws as these objects, and so on. And not only are these two beings substantially different, they are to a large extent independent of each other, and are often even in conflict. For centuries it was believed that after this life the soul could escape from the body and lead an autonomous existence far from it. This independence was made manifest at the time of death when the body dissolved and disappeared, while the soul survived and continued to follow, under new conditions and for varying lengths of time, the path of its own destiny. It can even be said that, although the body and the soul are closely connected they do not belong to the same world. The body is an integral part of the material universe, since we come to know it through sensory experience; the dwelling-place of the soul is elsewhere, and it tends ceaselessly to return to it. This is the world of the sacred. Therefore, the soul is invested with a dignity that has always been denied to the body, which is considered essentially profane, and the soul inspires those feelings that are everywhere reserved for that which is divine. It is made of the same substance as are sacred beings: it differs from them only in degree.

A belief that is as universal and permanent as this cannot be purely illusory. There must be something in man that gives rise to this feeling that he possesses a dual nature, a feeling that man in all known civilisations has experienced. Psychological analysis has, in fact, confirmed the existence of this duality, showing it to be at the very heart of our inner life.

Our thought, like our actions, takes two very different forms: on the one hand, there are sensations and sensory tendencies; on the other, conceptual thought and moral activity. Each of these two parts of ourselves represents a separate pole of our existence, and these two poles are not only distinct from one-another but are opposed to one-another. Our sensory appetites are necessarily egoistic: they relate solely to our individuality. When we satisfy our hunger, our thirst, and so on, without involving any other tendency, it is ourselves, and ourselves alone, that we satisfy. The distinctive features of moral activity on the other hand are to be traced to the fact that the rules of conduct to which it conforms can be universalised. Thus by definition, they relate to impersonal ends. Morality begins with disinterest, with attachment to something other than ourselves. A sensation of colour or sound is closely dependent on my individual organism, and cannot be detached from the organism. In addition, it is impossible for me to make my awareness pass over into someone else. I can, of course, invite another person to face the same object and expose himself to its effect, but the perception that he will have of it will be his own, and specific to him, as mine is specific to me. Concepts, on the contrary, are always common to a plurality of men. They are formed by means of words, and neither the vocabulary nor the grammar of a language is the product of one particular person. They are rather the result of a collective elaboration, and they express the anonymous collectivity that employs them. The ideas of 'man' or 'animal' are not personal and restricted to me; I share them, to a large degree, with all the men who belong to the same social group. Because they are held in common, concepts are the supreme instrument of all intellectual exchange. Men communicate by means of them. No doubt, when an individual utilises the concepts that he receives from the community, he individualises them and marks them with his personal imprint; but there is nothing impersonal that is not open to this type of individualisation.

These two aspects of our psychic life are, therefore, as opposed to each other as the personal and the impersonal. There is in us a being that represents everything in relation to itself and from its own point of view; in everything that it does, this being has no other object but itself. There is another being in us, however, which knows things *sub specie aeternitatis*, as if it were sharing in some thought other than its own, and which tends through its actions to accomplish ends that surpass its own. The old formula *homo duplex* is therefore verified by the facts. Far from being simple, our inner life has something that is like a double centre of gravity. On the one hand there is our individuality and, more particularly, our body in which it is based; on the other there is everything in us that expresses something other than ourselves . . .

As we have said, the soul has everywhere been considered a sacred thing; it has been seen as a divine element which lives only a brief terrestrial life and tends, by itself, as it were to return to its place of origin. Thus the soul is opposed to the body, which is regarded as profane; and everything in our mental life that is related to the body – the sensations and the sensory appetites – has this same character. For this reason, we consider that sensations are inferior forms of activity, and we accord a higher respect to reason and moral activity, which are the faculties by which, so it is said, we communicate with god. Even the man who is freest from professed convictions makes this sort of differentiation, valuing our various psychic processes differently, and ranging them in a hierarchy, in which those that are most closely related to the body are placed at the bottom. Moreover, as we have shown, there is no morality that is not infused with religiosity. Even to the secular mind, duty, the moral imperative, is something dignified and sacred; and reason, the essential ally of moral activity, naturally inspires similar feelings. The duality of our nature is thus only a particular instance of that division of things into the sacred and the profane that is the foundation of all religions, and it must be explained on the basis of the same principles.

4

CHARACTER AND ANAL EROTICISM

Sigmund Freud

Source: S. Freud, *The Standard Edition of the Complete Psychological Works of Sigmund Freud*, London: Hogarth Press, 1962, pp. 168–175.

Among those whom we try to help by our psycho-analytic efforts we often come across a type of person who is marked by the possession of a certain set of character-traits, while at the same time our attention is drawn to the behaviour in his childhood of one of his bodily functions and the organ concerned in it. I cannot say at this date what particular occasions began to give me an impression that there was some organic connection between this type of character and this behaviour of an organ, but I can assure the reader that no theoretical expectation played any part in that impression.

Accumulated experience has so much strengthened my belief in the existence of such a connection that I am venturing to make it the subject of a communication.

The people I am about to describe are noteworthy for a regular combination of the three following characteristics. They are especially *orderly*, *parsimonious* and *obstinate*. Each of these words actually covers a small group or series of inter-related character-traits. 'Orderly'[1] covers the notion of bodily cleanliness, as well as of conscientiousness in carrying out small duties and trustworthiness. Its opposite would be 'untidy' and 'neglectful'. Parsimony may appear in the exaggerated form of avarice; and obstinacy can go over into defiance, to which rage and revengefulness are easily joined. The two latter qualities—parsimony and obstinacy—are linked with each other more closely than they are with the first—with orderliness. They are, also, the more constant element of the whole complex. Yet it seems to me incontestable that all three in some way belong together.

It is easy to gather from these people's early childhood history that they took a comparatively long time to overcome their infantile *incontinentia alvi* [faecal incontinence], and that even in later childhood they suffered from

50

isolated failures of this function. As infants, they seem to have belonged to the class who refuse to empty their bowels when they are put on the pot because they derive a subsidiary pleasure from defaecating;[2] for they tell us that even in somewhat later years they enjoyed holding back their stool, and they remember—though more readily about their brothers and sisters than about themselves—doing all sorts of unseemly things with the faeces that had been passed. From these indications we infer that such people are born with a sexual constitution in which the erotogenicity of the anal zone is exceptionally strong. But since none of these weaknesses and idiosyncracies are to be found in them once their childhood has been passed, we must conclude that the anal zone had lost its erotogenic significance in the course of development; and it is to be suspected that the regularity with which this triad of properties is present in their character may be brought into relation with the disappearance of their anal erotism.

I know that no one is prepared to believe in a state of things so long as it appears to be unintelligible and to offer no angle from which an explanation can be attempted. But we can at least bring the underlying factors nearer to our understanding by the help of the postulates I laid down in my *Three Essays on the Theory of Sexuality* in 1905.[3] I there attempted to show that the sexual instinct of man is highly complex and is put together from contributions made by numerous constituents and component instincts. Important contributions to 'sexual excitation' are furnished by the peripheral excitations of certain specially designated parts of the body (the genitals, mouth, anus, urethra), which therefore deserve to be described as 'erotogenic zones'. But the amounts of excitation coming in from these parts of the body do not all undergo the same vicissitudes, nor is the fate of all of them the same at every period of life. Generally speaking, only a part of them is made use of in sexual life; another part is deflected from sexual aims and directed towards others—a process which deserves the name of 'sublimation'. During the period of life which may be called the period of 'sexual latency'—i.e. from the completion of the fifth year[4] to the first manifestations of puberty (round about the eleventh year)—reaction-formations, or counter-forces, such as shame, disgust and morality, are created in the mind. They are actually formed at the expense of the excitations proceeding from the erotogenic zones, and they rise like dams to oppose the later activity of the sexual instincts. Now anal erotism is one of the components of the [sexual] instinct which, in the course of development and in accordance with the education demanded by our present civilization, have become unserviceable for sexual aims. It is therefore plausible to suppose that these character-traits of orderliness, parsimony and obstinacy, which are so often prominent in people who were formerly anal erotics, are to be regarded as the first and most constant results of the sublimation of anal erotism.[5]

The intrinsic necessity for this connection is not clear, of course, even to myself. But I can make some suggestions which may help towards an understanding of it. Cleanliness, orderliness and trustworthiness give exactly the impression of a reaction-formation against an interest in what is unclean and disturbing and should not be part of the body. ('Dirt is matter in the wrong place.')[6] To relate obstinacy to an interest in defaecation would seem no easy task; but it should be remembered that even babies can show self-will about parting with their stool, as we have seen above [p. 51], and that it is a general practice in children's upbringing to administer painful stimuli to the skin of the buttocks—which is linked up with the erotogenic anal zone—in order to break their obstinacy and make them submissive. An invitation to a caress of the anal zone is still used to-day, as it was in ancient times, to express defiance or defiant scorn, and thus in reality signifies an act of tenderness that has been overtaken by repression. An exposure of the buttocks represents a softening down of this spoken invitation into a gesture; in Goethe's *Götz von Berlichingen* both words and gesture are introduced at the most appropriate point as an expression of defiance.[7]

The connections between the complexes of interest in money and of defaecation, which seem so dissimilar, appear to be the most extensive of all. Every doctor who has practised psycho-analysis knows that the most refractory and long-standing cases of what is described as habitual constipation in neurotics can be cured by that form of treatment. This is less surprising if we remember that that function has shown itself similarly amenable to hypnotic suggestion. But in psycho-analysis one only achieves this result if one deals with the patients' money complex and induces them to bring it into consciousness with all its connections. It might be supposed that the neurosis is here only following an indication of common usage in speech, which calls a person who keeps too careful a hold on his money 'dirty' or 'filthy'.[8] But this explanation would be far too superficial. In reality, wherever archaic modes of thought have predominated or persist— in the ancient civilizations, in myths, fairy tales and superstitions, in unconscious thinking, in dreams and in neuroses—money is brought into the most intimate relationship with dirt. We know that the gold which the devil gives his paramours turns into excrement after his departure, and the devil is certainly nothing else than the personification of the repressed unconscious instinctual life.[9] We also know about the superstition which connects the finding of treasure with defaecation,[10] and everyone is familiar with the figure of the 'shitter of ducats [*Dukatenscheisser*]'.[11] Indeed, even according to ancient Babylonian doctrine gold is 'the faeces of Hell' (Mammon = *ilu manman*).[12] Thus in following the usage of language, neurosis, here as elsewhere, is taking words in their original, significant sense, and where it appears to be using a word figuratively it is usually simply restoring its old meaning.[13]

It is possible that the contrast between the most precious substance known to men and the most worthless, which they reject as waste matter ('refuse'),[14] has led to this specific identification of gold with faeces.

Yet another circumstance facilitates this equation in neurotic thought. The original erotic interest in defaecation is, as we know, destined to be extinguished in later years. In those years the interest in money makes its appearance as a new interest which had been absent in childhood. This makes it easier for the earlier impulsion, which is in process of losing its aim, to be carried over to the newly emerging aim.

If there is any basis in fact for the relation posited here between anal erotism and this triad of character-traits, one may expect to find no very marked degree of 'anal character' in people who have retained the anal zone's erotogenic character in adult life, as happens, for instance, with certain homosexuals. Unless I am much mistaken, the evidence of experience tallies quite well on the whole with this inference.

We ought in general to consider whether other character-complexes, too, do not exhibit a connection with the excitations of particular erotogenic zones. At present I only know of the intense 'burning' ambition of people who earlier suffered from enuresis.[15] We can at any rate lay down a formula for the way in which character in its final shape is formed out of the constituent instincts: the permanent character-traits are either unchanged prolongations of the original instincts, or sublimations of those instincts, or reaction-formations against them.[16]

Notes

1 ['*Ordentlich*' in German. The original meaning of the word is 'orderly'; but it has become greatly extended in use. It can be the equivalent of such English terms as 'correct', 'tidy', 'cleanly', 'trustworthy', as well as 'regular', 'decent' and 'proper', in the more colloquial senses of those words.]

2 Cf. Freud, *Three Essays on the Theory of Sexuality* (1905*d*), *Standard Ed.*, 7, 186.

3 [The material in the present paragraph is derived mainly from Section 5 of the first essay and Section 1 of the second (*Standard Ed.*, 7, 167 ff. and 176 ff.).]

4 [In the German editions before 1924 this read 'from the completion of the fourth year'.]

5 Since it is precisely the remarks in my *Three Essays on the Theory of Sexuality* about the anal erotism of infants that have particularly scandalized uncomprehending readers, I venture at this point to interpolate an observation for which I have to thank a very intelligent patient. 'A friend of mine', he told me, 'who has read your *Three Essays on the Theory of Sexuality*, was talking about the book. He entirely agreed with it, but there was one passage, which—though of course he accepted and understood its meaning like that of the rest—struck him as so grotesque and comic that he sat down and laughed over it for a quarter of an hour. This passage ran: "One of the clearest signs of subsequent eccentricity or nervousness is to be seen when a baby obstinately refuses to empty his bowels when he is put on the pot—that is, when his nurse wants him to—and holds back that function till he himself chooses to exercise it. He is naturally not concerned with dirtying the bed, he is only anxious not to miss the subsidiary pleasure attached to defaecating." [*Standard Ed.*, 7, 186.] The picture of this baby sitting on the pot and deliberating whether he would put up with a restriction of this kind upon his personal freedom of will, and feeling anxious, too, not to miss the pleasure

attached to defaecating,—this caused my friend the most intense amusement. About twenty minutes afterwards, as we were having some cocoa, he suddenly remarked without any preliminary: "I say, seeing the cocoa in front of me has suddenly made me think of an idea that I always had when I was a child. I used always to pretend to myself that I was the cocoa-manufacturer Van Houten" (he pronounced the name Van "Hauten" [i.e. with the first syllable rhyming with the English word 'cow']) "and that I possessed a great secret for the manufacture of this cocoa. Everybody was trying to get hold of this secret that was a boon to humanity but I kept it carefully to myself. I don't know why I should have hit specially upon Van Houten. Probably his advertisements impressed me more than any others." Laughing, and without thinking at the time that my words had any deep meaning, I said: "Wann haut'n die Mutter?" ['When does mother smack?' The first two words in the German phrase are pronounced exactly like 'Van Houten'.] It was only later that I realized that my pun in fact contained the key to the whole of my friend's sudden childhood recollection, and I then recognized it as a brilliant example of a screen-phantasy. My friend's phantasy, while keeping to the situation actually involved (the nutritional process) and making use of phonetic associations ("Kakao" ['cocoa'.—'Kaka' is the common German nursery word for 'faeces'—cf. a dream at the end of Section IX of Freud, 1923c] and "Wann haut'n"), pacified his sense of guilt by making a complete reversal in the content of his recollection: there was a displacement from the back of the body to the front, excreting food became taking food in, and something that was shameful and had to be concealed became a secret that was a boon to humanity. I was interested to see how, only a quarter of an hour after my friend had fended the phantasy off (though, it is true, in the comparatively mild form of raising an objection on formal grounds), he was, quite involuntarily, presented with the most convincing evidence by his own unconscious.'

6 [This sentence is in English in the original.]

7 [The scene occurs in Act III, when Götz is summoned by a Herald to surrender. In the later acting version of the play the words are toned down.]

8 [The English 'filthy' as well as the German '*filzig*' appears in the original. Freud had already commented on the usage mentioned here, in a letter to Fliess of December 22, 1897 (Freud, 1950a, Letter 79) and, later, in the first edition of *The Interpretation of Dreams* (1900a), *Standard Ed.*, **4**, 200.]

9 Compare hysterical possession and demoniac epidemics. [Freud discussed this at considerable length in Part III of his paper 'A Seventeenth Century Demonological Neurosis' (1923d). The legendary transformation of witches' gold into faeces and the comparison with the '*Dukatenscheisser*' below had already been mentioned by Freud in a letter to Fliess of January 24, 1897 (1950a, Letter 57).]

10 [Numerous examples of this derived from folklore are given in Freud and Oppenheim's paper on 'Dreams in Folklore' (1957a [1911]), *Standard Ed.*, **12**, 187 ff.]

11 [A term vulgarly used for a wealthy spendthrift.]

12 Cf. Jeremias (1904, 115n.). '"Mamon" ("Mammon") is "Manman" in Babylonian and is another name for Nergal, the God of the Underworld. According to Oriental mythology, which has passed over into popular legends and fairy tales, gold is the excrement of Hell.'

13 [For the occurrence of this in dreams, see a passage added in 1909 to *The Interpretation of Dreams, Standard Ed.*, **5**, 407.]

14 [In English in the original.]

15 [The connection between urethral erotism and ambition seems to find its first mention here. Freud occasionally returned to the point, e.g. in a sentence added in 1914 to *The Interpretation of Dreams, Standard Ed.*, **4**, 216 and in a footnote

added in 1920 to the *Three Essays* (1905*d*), ibid., **7**, 239. In a long footnote to Section III of *Civilization and its Discontents* (1930*a*) he brought the present finding into connection with his two other main lines of thought concerning enuresis— its symbolic association with fire and its importance as an infantile equivalent of masturbation. See also the still later paper on 'The Acquisition and Control of Fire' (1932*a*).]

16 [There are not many accounts by Freud of the nature of 'character' and the mechanism of its formation. Among them may be mentioned a passage near the end of the *Three Essays* (1905*d*), *Standard Ed.*, **7**, 238–9, some remarks in the paper on 'The Disposition to Obsessional Neurosis' (1913*i*), ibid., **12**, 323–4, and especially a discussion in the first half of Chapter III of *The Ego and the Id* (1923*b*), the gist of which is repeated in Lecture XXXII of the *New Introductory Lectures* (1933*a*).]

5

THE SYNTHESIS OF ONE'S OWN BODY

Maurice Merleau-Ponty

Source: M. Merleau-Ponty, *The Phenomenology of Perception*, London: Routledge & Kegan Paul, 1966, pp. 148–153.

The analysis of bodily space has led us to results which may be generalized. We notice for the first time, with regard to our own body, what is true of all perceived things: that the perception of space and the perception of the thing, the spatiality of the thing and its being as a thing are not two distinct problems. The Cartesian and Kantian tradition already teaches us this; it makes the object's spatial limits its essence; it shows in existence *partes extra partes*, and in spatial distribution, the only possible significance of existence in itself. But it elucidates the perception of the object through the perception of space, whereas the experience of our own body teaches us to embed space in existence. Intellectualism clearly sees that the 'motif of the thing' and the 'motif of space'[1] are interwoven, but reduces the former to the latter. Experience discloses beneath objective space, in which the body eventually finds its place, a primitive spatiality of which experience is merely the outer covering and which merges with the body's very being. To be a body, is to be tied to a certain world, as we have seen; our body is not primarily *in* space: it is of it. Anosognosics who describe their arm as 'like a snake', long and cold,[2] do not, strictly speaking, fail to recognize its objective outline and, even when the patient looks unsuccessfully for his arm or fastens it in order not to lose it,[3] he *knows* well enough where his arm is, since that is where he looks for it and fastens it. If, however, patients experience their arm's space as something alien, if generally speaking I can feel my body's space as vast or minute despite the evidence of my senses, this is because there exists an affective presence and enlargement for which objective spatiality is not a sufficient condition, as anosognosia shows, and indeed not even a necessary condition, as is shown by the phantom arm. Bodily spatiality is the deployment of one's bodily being, the way in which the body comes into being as a body. In trying to analyse it, we were therefore simply anticipating what we have to say about bodily synthesis in general.

We find in the unity of the body the same implicatory structure as we have already described in discussing space. The various parts of my body, its visual, tactile and motor aspects are not simply coordinated. If I am sitting at my table and I want to reach the telephone, the movement of my hand towards it, the straightening of the upper part of the body, the tautening of the leg muscles are enveloped in each other. I desire a certain result and the relevant tasks are spontaneously distributed amongst the appropriate segments, the possible combinations being presented in advance as equivalent: I can continue leaning back in my chair provided that I stretch my arm further, or lean forward, or even partly stand up. All these movements are available to us in virtue of their common meaning. That is why, in their first attempts at grasping, children look, not at their hand, but at the object: the various parts of the body are known to us through their functional value only, and their co-ordination is not learnt. Similarly, when I am sitting at my table, I can instantly visualize the parts of my body which are hidden from me. As I contract my foot in my shoe, I can see it. This power belongs to me even with respect to parts of the body which I have never seen. Thus certain patients have the hallucination of their own face *seen from inside*.[4] It has been possible to show that we do not recognize our own hand in a photograph, and that many subjects are even uncertain about identifying their own handwriting among others, and yet that everyone recognizes his own silhouette or his own walk when it is filmed. Thus we do not recognize the appearance of what we have often seen, and on the other hand we immediately recognize the visual representation of what is invisible to us in our own body.[5] In heautoscopy the double which the subject sees in front of him is not always recognized by certain visible details, yet he feels convinced that it is himself, and consequently declares that he sees his double.[6] Each of us sees himself as it were through an inner eye which from a few yards away is looking at us from the head to the knees.[7] Thus the connecting link between the parts of our body and that between our visual and tactile experience are not forged gradually and cumulatively. I do not translate the 'data of touch' 'into the language of seeing' or *vice versa*—I do not bring together one by one the parts of my body; this translation and this unification are performed once and for all within me: they are my body itself. Are we then to say that we perceive our body in virtue of its law of construction, as we know in advance all the possible facets of a cube in virtue of its geometrical structure? But—to say nothing at this stage about external objects—our own body acquaints us with a species of unity which is not a matter of subsumption under a law. In so far as it stands before me and presents its systematic variations to the observer, the external object lends itself to a cursory mental examination of its elements and it may, at least by way of preliminary approximation, be defined in terms of the law of their variation. But I am not in front of my body, I am in it, or rather I am it. Neither its variations nor their constant can, therefore, be expressly posited. We do not merely behold as spectators the relations between the parts of our body, and the correlations between the visual and tactile body: we are ourselves the unifier of these arms and legs, the person who both sees and touches them. The body is, to use Leibnitz's term, the 'effective law' of its changes. If we can still speak of interpretation in relation to the perception of one's own body, we shall have to say that it interprets itself. Here the 'visual data' make their appearance only through the sense of touch, tactile data through sight, each localized movement against a background of some inclusive position, each bodily event, whatever the 'analyser' which reveals it, against a background of significance in which its remotest repercussions are at least foreshadowed and the possibility of an intersensory parity immediately furnished. What unites 'tactile sensations' in the hand and links them to visual perceptions of the same hand, and to perceptions of other bodily areas, is a certain style informing my manual gestures and implying in turn a certain style of finger movements, and contributing, in the last resort, to a certain bodily bearing.[8] The body is to be compared, not to a physical object, but rather to a work of art. In a picture or a piece of music the idea is incommunicable by means other than the display of colours and sounds. Any analysis of Cézanne's work, if I have not seen his pictures, leaves me with a choice between several possible Cézannes, and it is the sight of the pictures which provides me with the only existing Cézanne, and therein the analyses find their full meaning. The same is true of a poem or a novel, although they are made up of words. It is well known that a poem, though it has a superficial meaning translatable into prose, leads, in the reader's mind, a further existence which makes it a poem. Just as the spoken word is significant not only through the medium of individual words, but also through that of accent, intonation, gesture and facial expression, and as these additional meanings no longer reveal the speaker's thoughts but the source of his thoughts and his fundamental manner of being, so poetry, which is perhaps accidentally narrative and in that way informative, is essentially a variety of existence. It is distinguishable from the cry, because the cry makes use of the body as nature gave it to us: poor in expressive means; whereas the poem uses language, and even a particular language, in such a way that the existential modulation, instead of being dissipated at the very instant of its expression, finds in poetic art a means of making itself eternal. But although it is independent of the gesture which is inseparable from living expression, the poem is not independent of every material aid, and it would be irrecoverably lost if its text were not preserved down to the last detail. Its meaning is not arbitrary and does not dwell in the firmament of ideas: it is locked in the words printed on some perishable page. In that sense, like every work of art, the poem exists as a thing and does not eternally survive as does a truth.

As for the novel, although its plot can be summarized and the 'thought' of the writer lends itself to abstract expression, this conceptual significance is extracted from a wider one, as the description of a person is extracted from the actual appearance of his face. The novelist's task is not to expound ideas or even analyse characters, but to depict an inter-human event, ripening and bursting it upon us with no ideological commentary, to such an extent that any change in the order of the narrative or in choice of viewpoint would alter the *literary* meaning of the event. A novel, poem, picture or musical work are individuals, that is, beings in which the expression is indistinguishable from the thing expressed, their meaning, accessible only through direct contact, being radiated with no change of their temporal and spatial situation. It is in this sense that our body is comparable to a work of art. It is a nexus of living meanings, not the law for a certain number of covariant terms. A certain tactile experience felt in the upper arm signifies a certain tactile experience in the forearm and shoulder, along with a certain visual aspect of the same arm, not because the various tactile perceptions among themselves, or the tactile and visual ones, are all involved in one intelligible arm, as the different facets of a cube are related to the idea of a cube, but because the arm seen and the arm touched, like the different segments of the arm, together *perform* one and the same action.

Just as we saw earlier that motor habit threw light on the particular nature of bodily space, so here habit in general enables us to understand the general synthesis of one's own body. And, just as the analysis of bodily spatiality foreshadowed that of the unity of one's own body, so we may extend to all habits what we have said about motor ones. In fact every habit is both motor and perceptual, because it lies, as we have said, between explicit perception and actual movement, in the basic function which sets boundaries to our field of vision and our field of action. Learning to find one's way among things with a stick, which we gave a little earlier as an example of motor habit, is equally an example of perceptual habit. Once the stick has become a familiar instrument, the world of feelable things recedes and now begins, not at the outer skin of the hand, but at the end of the stick. One is tempted to say that through the sensations produced by the pressure of the stick on the hand, the blind man builds up the stick along with its various positions, and that the latter then mediate a second order object, the external thing. It would appear in this case that perception is always a reading off from the same sensory data, but constantly accelerated, and operating with ever more attenuated signals. But habit does not *consist* in interpreting the pressures of the stick on the hand as indications of certain positions of the stick, and these as signs of an external object, since it *relieves us of the necessity* of doing so. The pressures on the hand and the stick are no longer given; the stick is no longer an object perceived by the blind man, but an instrument *with* which he perceives. It is a bodily auxiliary, an extension of the bodily synthesis. Correspondingly, the external object is not the geometrized projection or invariant of a set of perspectives, but something towards which the stick leads us and the perspectives of which, according to perceptual evidence are not signs, but aspects. Intellectualism cannot conceive any passage from the perspective to the thing itself, or from sign to significance otherwise than as an interpretation, an apperception, a cognitive intention. According to this view sensory data and perspectives are at each level contents grasped as (*aufgefasst als*) manifestations of one and the same intelligible core.[9] But this analysis distorts both the sign and the meaning: it separates out, by a process of objectification of both, the sense-content, which is already 'pregnant' with a meaning, and the invariant core, which is not a law but a thing; it conceals the organic relationship between subject and world, the active transcendence of consciousness, the momentum which carries it into a thing and into a world by means of its organs and instruments. The analysis of motor habit as an extension of existence leads on, then, to an analysis of perceptual habit as the coming into possession of a world. Conversely, every perceptual habit is still a motor habit and here equally the process of grasping a meaning is performed by the body. When a child grows accustomed to distinguishing blue from red, it is observed, that the habit cultivated in relation to these two colours helps with the rest.[10] Is it, then, the case that through the pair blue-red the child has perceived the meaning; 'colour'? Is the crucial moment of habit-formation in that coming to awareness that arrival at a 'point of view of colour', that intellectual analysis which subsumes the data under one category? But for the child to be able to perceive blue and red under the category of colour, the category must be rooted in the data, otherwise no subsumption could recognize it in them. It is necessary that, on the 'blue' and 'red' panels presented to him the particular kind of vibration and impression on the eye known as blue and red should be represented. In the gaze we have at our disposal a natural instrument analogous to the blind man's stick. The gaze gets more or less from things according to the way in which it questions them, ranges over or dwells on them. To learn to see colours it is to acquire a certain style of seeing, a new use of one's own body: it is to enrich and recast the body image. Whether a system of motor or perceptual powers, our body is not an object for an 'I think', it is a grouping of lived-through meanings which moves towards its equilibrium. Sometimes a new cluster of meanings is formed; our former movements are integrated into a fresh motor entity, the first visual data into a fresh sensory entity, our natural powers suddenly come together in a richer meaning, which hitherto has been merely foreshadowed in our perceptual or practical field, and which has made itself felt in our experience by no more than a certain lack, and which by its coming suddenly reshuffles the elements of our equilibrium and fulfils our blind expectation.

Notes

1 Cassirer, *Philosophie der symbolischen Formen*, III, Second Part, Chap. II.
2 Lhermitte, *L'Image de notre corps*, p. 130.
3 Van Bogaert, *Sur la Pathologie de l'Image de soi*, p. 541.
4 Lhermitte, *L'Image de notre corps*, p. 238.
5 Wolff, *Selbstbeurteilung und Fremdbeurteilung in wissentlichen und unwissentlichen Versuch*.
6 Menninger-Lerchental, *Das Truggebilde der eigenen Gestalt*, p. 4.
7 Lhermitte, *L'Image de notre corps*, p. 238.
8 The mechanics of the skeleton cannot, even at the scientific level, account for the distinctive positions and movements of my body. Cf. *La Structure du Comportment*, p. 196.
9 Husserl, for example, for a long time defined consciousness or the imposition of a significance in terms of the *Auffassung-Inhalt* framework, and as a *beseelende Auffassung*. He takes a decisive step forward in recognizing, from the time of his *Lectures on Time*, that this operation presupposes another deeper one whereby the content is itself made ready for this apprehension. 'Not every constitution is brought about through the *Auffassungsinhalt-Auffassung*.' *Vorlesungen zur Phänomenologie des inneren Zeitbewusstseins*, p. 5, note 1.
10 Koffka, *Growth of the Mind*, pp. 174 and ff.

6

CHILDHOOD

Simone de Beauvoir

Source: H. M. Parshley (trans.), *The Second Sex*, Harmondsworth: Penguin, 1972, pp. 295–351.

One is not born, but rather becomes, a woman. No biological, psychological, or economic fate determines the figure that the human female
presents in society; it is civilization as a whole that produces this creature,
intermediate between male and eunuch, which is described as feminine. Only
the intervention of someone else can establish an individual as an *Other*. In
so far as he exists in and for himself, the child would hardly be able to think
of himself as sexually differentiated. In girls as in boys the body is first of all
the radiation of a subjectivity, the instrument that makes possible the comprehension of the world: it is through the eyes, the hands, that children
apprehend the universe, and not through the sexual parts. The dramas of
birth and of weaning unfold after the same fashion for nurslings of both
sexes; these have the same interests and the same pleasures; sucking is at first
the source of their most agreeable sensations; then they go through an anal
phase in which they get their greatest satisfactions from the excretory functions, which they have in common. Their genital development is analogous;
they explore their bodies with the same curiosity and the same indifference;
from clitoris and penis they derive the same vague pleasure. As their sens-
ibility comes to require an object, it is turned towards the mother: the soft,
smooth, resilient feminine flesh is what arouses sexual desires, and these
desires are prehensile; the girl, like the boy, kisses, handles, and caresses her
mother in an aggressive way; they feel the same jealousy if a new child is
born, and they show it in similar behaviour patterns: rage, sulkiness, urinary
difficulties; and they resort to the same coquettish tricks to gain the love of
adults. Up to the age of twelve the little girl is as strong as her brothers, and
she shows the same mental powers; there is no field where she is debarred
from engaging in rivalry with them. If, well before puberty and sometimes
even from early infancy, she seems to us to be already sexually determined,
this is not because mysterious instincts directly doom her to passivity,
coquetry, maternity; it is because the influence of others upon the child is a

factor almost from the start, and thus she is indoctrinated with her vocation from her earliest years.

The world is at first represented in the newborn infant only by immanent sensations; he is still immersed in the bosom of the Whole as he was when he lived in a dark womb; when he is put to the breast or the nursing bottle he is still surrounded by the warmth of maternal flesh. Little by little he learns to perceive objects as distinct and separate from himself, and to distinguish himself from them. Meanwhile he is separated more or less brutally from the nourishing body. Sometimes the infant reacts to this separation by a violent crisis;[1] in any case, it is when the separation is accomplished, at about the age of six months, perhaps, that the child begins to show the desire to attract others through acts of mimicry that in time become real showing off. Certainly this attitude is not established through a considered choice; but it is not necessary to *conceive* a situation for it to *exist*. The nursling lives directly the basic drama of every existent: that of his relation to the Other. Man experiences with anguish his being turned loose, his forlornness. In flight from his freedom, his subjectivity, he would fain lose himself in the bosom of the Whole. Here, indeed, is the origin of his cosmic and pantheistic dreams, of his longing for oblivion, for sleep, for ecstasy, for death. He never succeeds in abolishing his separate ego, but at least he wants to attain the solidity of the in-himself, the *en-soi*, to be petrified into a thing. It is especially when he is fixed by the gaze of other persons that he appears to himself as being one.

It is in this perspective that the behaviour of the child must be interpreted: in carnal form he discovers finiteness, solitude, forlorn desertion in a strange world. He endeavours to compensate for this catastrophe by projecting his existence into an image, the reality and value of which others will establish. It appears that he may begin to affirm his identity at the time when he recognizes his reflection in a mirror – a time that coincides with that of weaning:[2] his ego becomes so fully identified with this reflected image that it is formed only in being projected. Whether or not the mirror actually plays a more or less considerable part, it is certain that the child commences towards the age of six months to mimic his parents, and under their gaze to regard himself as an object. He is already an autonomous subject, in transcendence towards the outer world; but he encounters himself only in a projected form.

When the child develops further, he fights in two ways against his original abandonment. He attempts to deny the separation: rushing into his mother's arms, he seeks her living warmth and demands her caresses. And he attempts to find self-justification through the approbation of others. Adults seem to him like gods, for they have the power to confer existence upon him. He feels the magic of the regard that makes of him now a delightful little angel, now a monster. His two modes of defence are not mutually exclusive: on the contrary, they complement each other and interpenetrate. When the attempt at enticement succeeds, the sense of justification finds physical confirmation in the kisses and caresses obtained: it all amounts to a single state of happy passivity that the child experiences in his mother's lap and under her benevo-lent gaze. There is no difference in the attitudes of girls and boys during the first three or four years; both try to perpetuate the happy condition that preceded weaning; in both sexes enticement and showing-off behaviour occur: boys are as desirous as their sisters of pleasing adults, causing smiles, seeking admiration.

It is more satisfying to deny the anguish than to rise above it, more radical to be lost in the bosom of the Whole than to be petrified by the conscious egos of others: carnal union creates a deeper alienation than any resignation under the gaze of others. Enticement and showing off represent a more complex, a less easy stage than simple abandon in the maternal arms. The magic of the adult gaze is capricious. The child pretends to be invisible; his parents enter into the game, trying blindly to find him and laughing; but all at once they say: 'You're getting tiresome, you are not invisible at all.' The child has amused them with a bright saying; he repeats it, and this time they shrug their shoulders. In this world, uncertain and unpredictable as the uni-verse of Kafka, one stumbles at every step.[3] That is why many children are afraid of growing up; they are in despair if their parents cease taking them on their knees or letting them get into the grown-ups' bed. Through the physical frustration they feel more and more cruelly the forlornness, the abandonment, which the human being can never be conscious of without anguish.

This is just where the little girls first appear as privileged beings. A second weaning, less brutal and more gradual than the first, withdraws the mother's body from the child's embraces; but the boys especially are little by little denied the kisses and caresses they have been used to. As for the little girl, she continues to be cajoled, she is allowed to cling to her mother's skirts, her father takes her on his knee and strokes her hair. She wears sweet little dresses, her tears and caprices are viewed indulgently, her hair is carefully done, older people are amused at her expressions and coquetries – bodily contacts and agreeable glances protect her against the anguish of solitude. The little boy, in contrast, will be denied even coquetry; his efforts at enticement, his play-acting, are irritating. He is told that 'a man doesn't ask to be kissed . . . A man doesn't look at himself in mirrors . . . A man doesn't cry'. He is urged to be 'a little man'; he will obtain adult approval by becoming independent of adults. He will please them by not appearing to seek to please them.

Many boys, frightened by the hard independence they are condemned to, wish they were girls; formerly, when boys were dressed in early years like girls, they often shed tears when they had to change from dresses to trousers and saw their curls cut. Certain of them held obstinately to the choice of femininity – one form of orientation towards homosexuality. Maurice Sachs (in *Le Sabbat*) says: 'I wished passionately to be a girl and I pushed my unawareness of the grandeur of being male to the point of pretending to urinate in a sitting position.'

But if the boy seems at first to be less favoured than his sisters, it is because great things are in store for him. The demands made upon him at once imply a high evaluation. Maurras relates in his memoirs that he was jealous of a younger brother whom his mother and grandmother were cajoling. His father took his hand and drew him from the room, saying to him: 'We are men, let us leave those women.' The child is persuaded that more is demanded of boys because they are superior; to give him courage for the difficult path he must follow, pride in his manhood is instilled into him; this abstract notion takes on for him a concrete aspect: it is incarnated in his penis. He does not spontaneously experience a sense of pride in his sex, but rather through the attitude of the group around him. Mothers and nurses keep alive the tradition that identifies the phallus and the male idea; whether they recognize its prestige in amorous gratitude or in submission, or whether they get a sense of revenge in coming upon it in the nursling in a very humble form, they treat the infantile penis with remarkable complacency. Rabelais tells us about the tricks and comments of Gargantua's nurses, and history has preserved those of the nurses of Louis XIII. More modest women still give a nickname to the little boy's sex, speaking to him of it as of a small person who is at once himself and other than himself: they make of it, according to the expression already cited, an 'alter ego usually more sly, more intelligent, and more clever than the individual'.[4]

Anatomically the penis is well suited for this role; projecting free of the body, it seems like a natural little plaything, a kind of puppet. Elders will lend value to the child, then, in conferring it upon his double. A father told me about one of his sons who at the age of three still sat down to urinate; surrounded with sisters and girl cousins, he was a timid and sad child. One day his father took him to the lavatory, saying: 'I am going to show you how men do it.' Thereafter the child, proud of urinating while standing, scorned girls 'who urinate through a hole'; his disdain originally arose not because they lacked an organ but because they had not been singled out and initiated by the father, as he had. Thus, far from the penis representing a direct advantage from which the boy could draw a feeling of superiority, its high valuation appears on the contrary as a compensation – invented by adults and ardently accepted by the child – for the hardships of the second weaning. Thus he is protected against regret for his lost status as nursling and for his not being a girl. Later on he will incarnate his transcendence and his proud sovereignty in his sex.[5]

The lot of the little girl is very different. Mothers and nurses feel no reverence or tenderness towards her genitals; they do not direct her attention towards that secret organ, invisible except for its covering, and not to be grasped in the hand; in a sense she has no sex organ. She does not experience this absence as a lack; evidently her body is, for her, quite complete; but she finds herself situated in the world differently from the boy; and a constellation of factors can transform this difference, in her eyes, into an inferiority.

There are few questions more extensively discussed by psychoanalysts than the celebrated feminine 'castration complex'. Most would admit today that penis envy is manifested in very diverse ways in different cases.[6] To begin with, there are many little girls who remain ignorant of the male anatomy for some years. Such a child finds it quite natural that there should be men and women, just as there is a sun and a moon: she believes in essences contained in words and her curiosity is not analytic at first. For many others this tiny bit of flesh hanging between boys' legs is insignificant or even laughable; it is a peculiarity that merges with that of clothes or haircut. Often it is first seen on a small newborn brother and, as Helene Deutsch puts it, 'when the little girl is very young she is not impressed by the penis of her little brother'. She cites the case of a girl of eighteen months who remained quite indifferent to the discovery of the penis and attached no importance to it until much later, in accordance with her personal interests. It may even happen that the penis is considered to be an anomaly: an outgrowth, something vague that hangs, like wens, breasts, or warts; it can inspire disgust. Finally, the fact is that there are numerous cases where the little girl does take an interest in the penis of a brother or playmate; but that does not mean that she experiences jealousy of it in a really sexual way, still less that she feels deeply affected by the absence of that organ; she wants to get it for herself as she wants to get any and every object, but this desire can remain superficial.

There is no doubt that the excretory functions, and in particular the urinary functions, are of passionate interest to children; indeed, to wet the bed is often a form of protest against a marked preference of the parents for another child. There are countries where the men urinate while seated, and there are cases of women who urinate standing, as is customary with many peasants, among others; but in contemporary Western society, custom generally demands that women sit or crouch, while the erect position is reserved for males. This difference constitutes for the little girl the most striking sexual differentiation. To urinate, she is required to crouch, uncover herself, and therefore hide: a shameful and inconvenient procedure. The shame is intensified in the frequent cases in which the girl suffers from involuntary discharge of urine, as for instance when laughing immoderately; in general her control is not so good as that of the boys.

To boys the urinary function seems like a game, with the charm of all games that offer liberty of action; the penis can be manipulated, it gives opportunity for action, which is one of the deep interests of the child. A little girl on seeing a boy urinating exclaimed admiringly: 'How convenient!'[7] The stream can be directed at will and to a considerable distance, which gives the boy a feeling of omnipotence. Freud spoke of 'the burning ambition of early diuretics'; Stekel has discussed this formula sensibly, but it is true, as Karen Horney says,[8] that the 'fantasies of omnipotence, especially those of sadistic character, are frequently associated with the male urinary stream'; these fantasies, which are lasting in certain men,[9] are important in the child. Abraham speaks of the 'great pleasure women derive from watering the garden with a hose'; I believe, in agreement with the theories of Sartre and of Bachelard,[10] that identifying the hose with the penis is not necessarily the source of this pleasure – though it is clearly so in certain cases. Every stream of water in the air seems like a miracle, a defiance of gravity: to direct, to govern it, is to win a small victory over the laws of nature; and in any case the small boy finds here a daily amusement that is denied his sisters. It permits the establishment through the urinary stream of many relations with things such as water, earth, moss, snow, and the like. There are little girls who in their wish to share these experiences lie on their backs and try to make the urine spurt upwards or practise urinating while standing. According to Karen Horney, they envy also the possibility of exhibiting which the boy has. She reports that 'a patient, upon seeing a man urinating in the street, suddenly exclaimed: "If I could ask one gift from Providence, it would be to have for once in my life the power of urinating like a man."' To many little girls it seems that the boy, having the right to touch his penis, can make use of it as a plaything, whereas their organs are taboo.

That all the factors combine to make possession of a male sex organ seem desirable to many girls is a fact attested by numerous inquiries made and confidences received by psychiatrists. Havelock Ellis[11] cites these remarks made by a patient of Dr S. E. Jelliffe, called Zenia: 'The gushing of water in a jet or spray, especially from a long garden hose, has always been highly suggestive to me, recalling the act of urination as witnessed in childhood in my brothers or even in other boys.' A correspondent, Mrs R. S., told Ellis that as a child she greatly desired to handle a boy's penis and imagined scenes involving such behaviour with urination; one day she was allowed to hold a garden hose. 'It seemed delightfully like holding a penis.' She asserted that the penis had no sexual significance for her; she knew about the urinary function only. A most interesting case, that of Florrie, is reported by Havelock Ellis[12] (and later analysed by Stekel); I give here a detailed summary:

The woman concerned is very intelligent, artistic, active, biologically normal, and not homosexual. She says that the urinary function played a great role in her childhood; she played urinary games with her brothers, and they wet their hands without feeling disgust. 'My earliest ideas of the superiority of the male were connected with urination. I felt aggrieved with nature because I lacked so useful and ornamental an organ. No teapot without a spout felt so forlorn. It required no one to instil into me the theory of male predominance and superiority. Constant proof was before me.'

She took great pleasure in urinating in the country. 'Nothing could come up to the entrancing sound as the stream descended on crackling leaves in the depth of a wood and she watched its absorption. Most of all she was fascinated by the idea of doing it into water' [as are many little boys]. Florrie complains that the style of her knickers prevented her from trying various desired experiments, but often during country walks she would hold back as long as she could and then suddenly relieve herself standing. 'I can distinctly remember the strange and delicious sensation of this forbidden delight, and also my puzzled feeling that it came standing.' In her opinion, the style of children's clothing has great importance for feminine psychology in general. 'It was not only a source of annoyance to me that I had to unfasten my drawers and then squat down for fear of wetting them in front, but the flap at the back, which must be removed to uncover the posterior parts during the act, accounts for my early impression that in girls this function is connected with those parts. The first distinction in sex that impressed me – the one great difference in sex – was that boys urinated standing and that girls had to sit down ... The fact that my earliest feelings of shyness were more associated with the back than the front may have thus originated.' All these impressions were of great importance in Florrie's case because her father often whipped her until the blood came and a governess had once spanked her to make her urinate; she was obsessed by masochistic dreams and fancies in which she saw herself whipped by a school mistress under the eyes of all and having to urinate against her will, 'an idea that gives one a curious sense of gratification'. At the age of fifteen it happened that under urgent need she urinated standing in a deserted street. 'In trying to analyse my sensations I think the most prominent lay in the shame that came from standing, and consequently greater distance the stream had to descend. It seemed to make the affair important and conspicuous, even though clothing hid it. In the ordinary attitude there is a kind of privacy. As a small child, too, the stream had not far to go, but at the age of fifteen I was tall and it seemed to give one a glow of shame to think of this stream falling unchecked such a distance. (I am sure that the ladies who fled in horror from the urinette at Portsmouth[13] thought it most indecent for a woman to stride across an earthenware boat on the ground, a leg on each side, and standing there to pull up her clothes and do a stream which descended unabashed all that way.)' She renewed this experience at twenty and frequently thereafter. She felt a mixture of shame and pleasure at the idea that she might be surprised and that she would be incapable of stopping. 'The stream seemed to be drawn from me without my consent, and *yet with even more pleasure than if I were doing it freely*. [The italics are Florrie's.] This curious feeling – that it is being drawn away by some unseen power which is determined that one shall do it – is an entirely feminine pleasure and a subtle charm ... There is a fierce charm in the torrent that binds one to its will by a mighty force.' Later Florrie developed a flagellatory eroticism always combined with urinary obsessions.

This case is of great interest because it throws light on several elements in the child's experience. But there are evidently special circumstances that confer enormous importance upon them. For normally reared little girls, the urinary privilege of the boy is something too definitely secondary to call forth directly a feeling of inferiority. The psychoanalysts who, following

Freud, suppose that the mere discovery of the penis by a little girl would be enough to cause a trauma profoundly misunderstand the mentality of the child; this mentality is much less rational than they seem to suppose, for it does not envisage clear-cut categories and it is not disturbed by contradiction. When the small girl sees the penis and declares: 'I had one, too,' or 'I will have one, too,' or even 'I have one, too,' it is not an insincere self-justification; presence and absence are not mutually exclusive; as his drawings show, the child believes much less in what he *sees* with his eyes than in significant *types* that he has set up once for all. He often draws without looking, and in any case his perceptions are strongly coloured by what he puts into them. In emphasizing just this point, Saussure[14] cites this important observation of Luquet: 'Once a sketch is seen to be erroneous, it is as if non-existent; the child *literally no longer sees it*, being in a way hypnotized by the new sketch that replaces it, just as he pays no attention to accidental lines on his paper.' The male anatomy constitutes a powerful formation that often impresses itself upon the little girl's attention; and she *literally no longer sees* her own body. Saussure mentions the case of a little girl of four who, while trying to urinate like a boy between the bars of a gate, said that she wished she had 'a long little thing that streams'. She was affirming at once that she had and did not have a penis, which is in harmony with the thinking by 'participation' described in children by Piaget. The little girl readily believes that all children are born with a penis but that later the parents cut off some of them to make girls; this idea satisfies the artificialism of the child, who, deifying her parents, 'conceives of them as the source of everything she has', as Piaget puts it; the child does not at first see castration as a punishment.

In order for her state to assume the character of a frustration, it is necessary for the little girl to be already, for some reason, dissatisfied with her situation; as Helene Deutsch justly remarks, an exterior event like the sight of a penis could not in itself bring about an internal development: 'The sight of the male organ can have a traumatic effect,' she says, 'but only provided that a long chain of earlier experiences calculated to produce this effect has preceded it.' If the little girl finds herself unable to satisfy her desire by masturbation or exhibition, if her parents repress her auto-eroticism, if she feels she is less loved, less admired than her brothers, then she will project her dissatisfaction upon the male organ. 'The discovery made by the little girl of her anatomical difference from the boy serves to confirm a need previously felt; it is her rationalization of it, so to speak.'[15] And Adler has insisted precisely on the fact that it is the valuation established by the parents and associates that lends to the boy the prestige of which the penis becomes the explanation and symbol in the eyes of the little girl. People consider her brother superior; he is himself swollen with pride in his manhood; so she envies him and feels frustrated. Sometimes she holds it against her mother, more rarely against her father; or she may blame herself for the mutilation, or she may console herself in thinking that the penis is hidden in the body and will come out some day.

But even if the young girl has no serious penis envy, the absence of the organ will certainly play an important role in her destiny. The major benefit obtained from it by the boy is that, having an organ that can be seen and grasped, he can at least partially identify himself with it. He projects the mystery of his body, its threats, outside of himself, which enables him to keep them at a distance. True enough, he does scent danger in connection with his penis, he fears its being cut off; but this is a fright easier to overcome than the diffuse apprehension felt by the little girl in regard to her 'insides', an apprehension that will often be retained for life. She is extremely concerned about everything that happens inside her, she is from the start much more opaque to her own eyes, more profoundly immersed in the obscure mystery of life, than is the male. Because he has an *alter ego* in whom he sees himself, the little boy can boldly assume an attitude of subjectivity; the very object into which he projects himself becomes a symbol of autonomy, of transcendence, of power; he measures the length of his penis; he compares his urinary stream with that of his companions; later on, erection and ejaculation will become grounds for satisfaction and challenge. But the little girl cannot incarnate herself in any part of herself. To compensate for this and to serve her as *alter ego*, she is given a foreign object: a doll. It should be noted that in French the word *poupée* (doll) is also applied to the bandage around a wounded finger; a dressed-up finger, distinguished from the others, is regarded with amusement and a kind of pride, the child shows signs of the process of identification by his talk to it. But it is a statuette with a human face – or, that lacking, an ear of corn, even a piece of wood – which will most satisfyingly serve the girl as substitute for that double, that natural plaything: the penis.

The main difference is that, on the one hand, the doll represents the whole body, and, on the other, it is a passive object. On this account the little girl will be led to identify her whole person and to regard this as an inert given object. While the boy seeks himself in the penis as an autonomous subject, the little girl cuddles her doll and dresses her up as she dreams of being cuddled and dressed up herself; inversely, she thinks of herself as a marvellous doll. By means of compliments and scoldings, through images and words, she learns the meaning of the terms *pretty* and *plain*; she soon learns that in order to be pleasing she must be 'pretty as a picture'; she tries to make herself look like a picture, she puts on fancy clothes, she studies herself in a mirror, she compares herself with princesses and fairies. Marie Bashkirtsev gives us a striking example of this childish coquetry. It is not by chance that, being weaned late – at three and a half – she felt strongly, at the age of four to five, the need to make herself admired, to live for others. The shock of weaning must have been violent in a child so old, and she must have tried the more passionately to compensate for the separation inflicted upon her; in her journal she writes: 'At five I dressed in my mother's laces, with flowers in my hair, and went to dance in the drawing-room. I was the great dancer Petipa, and the whole family were there to *look at me*.'

This narcissism appears so precociously in the little girl, it will play so fundamental a part in her life as a woman, that it is easy to regard it as arising from a mysterious feminine instinct. But we have seen above that in reality it is not an anatomical fate that dictates her attitude. The difference that distinguishes boys is a fact that she can take in a number of ways. To have a penis is no doubt a privilege, but it is one whose value naturally decreases when the child loses interest in its excretory functions. If its value is retained in the child's view beyond the age of eight or nine, it is because the penis has become the symbol of manhood, which is socially valued. The fact is that in this matter the effect of education and surroundings is immense. All children try to compensate for the separation inflicted through weaning by enticing and show-off behaviour; the boy is compelled to go beyond this state; he is rid of narcissism by having his attention directed to his penis; while the little girl is confirmed in the tendency to draw attention to herself, which all young children have in common. The doll is a help, but it no longer has a determining role; the boy, too, can cherish a teddy bear, or a puppet into which he projects himself; it is within the totality of their lives that each factor – penis or doll – takes on its importance.

Thus the passivity that is the essential characteristic of the 'feminine' woman is a trait that develops in her from the earliest years. But it is wrong to assert that a biological datum is concerned; it is in fact a destiny imposed upon her by her teachers and by society. The great advantage enjoyed by the boy is that his mode of existence in relation to others leads him to assert his subjective freedom. His apprenticeship for life consists in free movement towards the outside world; he contends in hardihood and independence with other boys, he scorns girls. Climbing trees, fighting with his companions, facing them in rough games, he is aware of his body as a means for dominating nature and as a weapon for fighting; he takes pride in his muscles as in his sex; in games, sports, fights, challenges, trials of strength, he finds a balanced exercise of his powers; at the same time he absorbs the severe lessons of violence; he learns from an early age to take blows, to scorn pain, to keep back the tears. He undertakes, he invents, he dares. Certainly he tests himself also as if he were another; he challenges his own manhood, and many problems result in relation to adults and to other children. But what is very important is that there is no fundamental opposition between his concern for that objective figure which is his, and his will to self-realization in concrete projects. It is by *doing* that he creates his existence, both in one and the same action.

In woman, on the contrary, there is from the beginning a conflict between her autonomous existence and her objective self, her 'being-the-other'; she is taught that to please she must try to please, she must make herself object; she should therefore renounce her autonomy. She is treated like a live doll and is refused liberty. Thus a vicious circle is formed; for the less she exercises her freedom to understand, to grasp and discover the world about her, the less resources will she find within herself, the less will she dare to affirm herself as subject. If she were encouraged in it, she could display the same lively exuberance, the same curiosity, the same initiative, the same hardihood, as a boy. This does happen occasionally, when the girl is given a boyish bringing up; in this case she is spared many problems.[16] It is noteworthy that this is the kind of education a father prefers to give his daughter; and women brought up under male guidance very largely escape the defects of femininity. But custom is opposed to treating girls like boys. I have known of little village girls of three or four being compelled by their fathers to wear trousers. All the other children teased them: 'Are they girls or boys?' – and they proposed to settle the matter by examination. The victims begged to wear dresses. Unless the little girl leads an unusually solitary existence, a boyish way of life, though approved by her parents, will shock her entourage, her friends, her teachers. There will always be aunts, grandmothers, cousins around to counteract the father's influence. Normally he is given a secondary role with respect to his daughters' training. One of the disadvantages that weigh heavily upon women – as Michelet has justly pointed out – is to be left in women's hands during childhood. The boy, too, is brought up at first by his mother, but she respects his maleness and he escapes very soon;[17] whereas she fully intends to fit her daughter into the feminine world.

We shall see later how complex the relations of mother to daughter are: the daughter is for the mother at once her double and another person, the mother is at once overweeningly affectionate and hostile towards her daughter; she saddles her child with her own destiny: a way of proudly laying claim to her own femininity and also a way of revenging herself for it. The same process is to be found in pederasts, gamblers, drug addicts, in all who at once take pride in belonging to a certain confraternity and feel humiliated by the association: they endeavour with eager proselytism to gain new adherents. So, when a child comes under their care, women apply themselves to changing her into a woman like themselves, manifesting a zeal in which arrogance and resentment are mingled; and even a generous mother, who sincerely seeks her child's welfare, will as a rule think that it is wiser to make a 'true woman' of her, since society will more readily accept her if this is done. She is therefore given little girls for playmates, she is entrusted to female teachers, she lives among the older women as in the days of the Greek gynaeceum, books and games are chosen for her which initiate her into her destined sphere, the treasures of feminine wisdom are poured into her ears, feminine virtues are urged upon her, she is taught cooking, sewing, housekeeping, along with care of her person, charm, and modesty; she is dressed in inconvenient and frilly clothes of which she has to be careful, her hair is done up in fancy style, she is given rules of deportment: 'Stand up straight, don't walk like a duck'; to develop grace she must repress her spontaneous movements; she is told not to act like a would-be boy, she is forbidden violent exercises, she is not allowed to fight. In brief, she is pressed to become, like her elders, a servant and an idol. Today, thanks to the conquests of feminism, it is becoming more and more normal to encourage the young girl to get an education, to devote herself to sports; but lack of success in these fields is more readily pardoned in her than in a boy; and success is made harder by the demands made upon her for another kind of accomplishment: at any rate she must be *also* a woman, she must not *lose* her femininity.

When very young the girl child resigns herself to all this without too much trouble. The child moves on the play and dream level, playing at being, playing at doing; to do and to be are not clearly distinguished when one is concerned only with imaginary accomplishments. The little girl can compensate for the present superiority of the boys by the promises that are inherent in her womanly destiny and that she already fulfils in play. Because she knows as yet only her childhood universe, her mother at first seems to her to be endowed with more authority than her father; she imagines the world to be a kind of matriarchate; she imitates her mother and identifies herself with her; frequently she even reverses their respective roles: 'When I am big, and you are little . . .' she likes to say to her mother. The doll is not only her double; it is also her child. These two functions do not exclude each other, inasmuch as the real child is also an *alter ego* for the mother. When she scolds, punishes, and then consoles her doll, she is at once vindicating herself as against her mother and assuming, herself, the dignity of a mother: she combines in herself the two elements of the mother-daughter pair. She confides in her doll, she brings it up, exercises upon it her sovereign authority, sometimes even tears off its arms, beats it, tortures it. Which is to say she experiences subjective affirmation and identification through the doll. Frequently the mother is associated in this imaginary life: The child plays with her mother at being father and mother of the doll, making a couple that excludes the man. Here again there is no 'maternal instinct', innate and mysterious. The little girl ascertains that the care of children falls upon the mother, she is so taught; stories heard, books read, all her little experiences confirm the idea. She is encouraged to feel the enchantment of these future riches, she is given dolls so that these values may henceforth have a tangible aspect. Her 'vocation' is powerfully impressed upon her.

Because the little girl feels that children will be her lot, and also because she is more interested in her 'insides' than is the boy, she is especially curious about the mystery of procreation. She soon ceases to believe that babies are born in cabbages, carried in the doctor's bag, or brought by storks; she soon learns, especially if brothers and sisters arrive, that babies develop in the mother's body. Besides, modern parents make less of a mystery about it than was formerly the custom. The little girl is generally more amazed than frightened, because the phenomenon seems magical to her; she does not as yet grasp all the physiological implications. At first she is unaware of the father's part and supposes that a woman becomes pregnant from eating certain foods. This is a legendary theme (in stories queens give birth to a little girl or a fine boy after having eaten a certain fruit, or a special kind of fish), and one that later leads certain women to associate the idea of gestation with that of the digestive system. These problems and discoveries together engage much of the interest of the young girl and help to nourish her imagination. I will bring forward as typical one of Jung's cases,[18] which has remarkable similarities with that of little Hans, analysed by Freud at about the same time:

Towards three, Anna began to ask where babies came from, and for a time believed they were little angels. At four she had a new brother, without having appeared to notice her mother's pregnancy. On returning from a short visit to her grandmother's she showed jealousy of the new baby, misbehaving in various ways and frequently accusing her mother of not telling the truth, because she suspected her of having lied about the birth. She asked whether she would become a woman like her mother. She called to her parents at night, saying she was frightened by what she had heard about an earthquake and asking questions about it. One day she asked point-blank where her brother was before he was born, why he did not come sooner, and the like. She seemed pleased to be told that he grew like a plant inside the mother; but she asked how he got out, since he couldn't walk, and if there was a hole in the chest, and so on. Then she declared she knew storks brought babies; but she ceased to worry about earthquakes. A little later, seeing her father in bed, she asked if he too had a plant growing inside him. She dreamed that the little animals fell out of her Noah's ark through a hole in the bottom. She put her doll under her skirt and then had it 'come out'. She was wondering about the father's role, and one day lay on his bed face-down and, kicking with her legs, asked if that wasn't what Papa did. Later she asked if eyes and hair are planted in the head, after she had planted some seeds in the garden. Her father explained that they were present as germs in the child before developing, and she asked how her little brother got inside Mamma, who had planted him there, how he got out. Her father asked what she thought, and she indicated her sex organ; he said that was right. But she still wanted to know how he got in, and so her father explained that it is the father who furnishes the seed. This seemed to satisfy her, and being almost informed by the time she was five, she had no further trouble with the subject.

This history is characteristic, though often the little girls asks less precisely about the role of the father, or the parents are evasive on this point. Many a little girl puts a pillow under her apron to play at being pregnant, or walks with a doll in the folds of her skirt and drops it in the cradle; she may give it the breast. Boys, like girls, wonder at the mystery of motherhood; all children have an imagination 'of depth' which makes them conceive the idea of secret riches in the interior of things; they all feel the miracle of encasements, of dolls that contain other similar dolls, of boxes containing other boxes, of pictures that contain replicas of decreasing size; all are delighted to see a bud taken apart, to observe the chick in its shell, to watch as 'Japanese flowers' expand when floated in a dish of water. It was a small boy who cried with delight: 'Oh, it's a mother!' when he opened an Easter egg filled with small sugar eggs. To make a baby emerge from one's body: that is as fine as any feat of legerdemain. The mother seems to be endowed with marvellous fairy powers. Many boys regret the lack of such a privilege; if, later on, they steal birds' eggs and trample down young plants, if they destroy life about them in a kind of frenzy, it is in revenge for their inability to bring forth life; while the little girl takes pleasures in the thought that she will create life one day.

In addition to this hope which playing with dolls makes concrete, family life provides the little girl with other opportunities for self-expression. A good deal of the housework is within the capability of a very young child; the boy is commonly excused, but his sister is allowed, even asked, to sweep, dust, peel potatoes, wash the baby, keep an eye on the cooking. In particular, the eldest sister is often concerned in this way with motherly tasks; whether for convenience or because of hostility and sadism, the mother thus rids herself of many of her functions; the girl is in this manner made to fit precociously into the universe of serious affairs; her sense of importance will help her in assuming her femininity. But she is deprived of happy freedom, the carefree aspect of childhood; having become precociously a woman, she learns all too soon the limitations this estate imposes upon a human being; she reaches adolescence as an adult, which gives her history a special character. A child overburdened with work may well become prematurely a slave, doomed to a joyless existence. But if no more than an effort suited to her powers is asked of her, she is proud to feel herself as capable as a grown-up, and she enjoys sharing responsibility with adults. This equal sharing is possible because it is not a far cry from child to housekeeper. A man expert in his trade is separated from the stage of childhood by his years of apprenticeship. Thus the little boy finds his father's activities quite mysterious, and the man he is to become is hardly sketched out in him at all. On the contrary, the mother's activities are quite accessible to the girl; 'she is already a little woman,' as her parents say; and it is sometimes held that she is more precocious than the boy. In truth, if she is nearer to the adult stage it is because this stage in most women remains traditionally more or less infantile. The fact is that the girl is conscious of her precocity, that she takes pride in playing the little mother towards the younger children; she is glad to become important, she talks sensibly, she gives orders, she assumes airs of superiority over her baby brothers, she converses on a footing of equality with her mother.

In spite of all these compensations, she does not accept without regret the fate assigned to her; as she grows, she envies the boys their vigour.

Parents and grandparents may barely conceal the fact that they would have preferred male offspring to female; or they may show more affection for the brother than the sister. Investigations make it clear that the majority of parents would rather have sons than daughters. Boys are spoken to with greater seriousness and esteem, they are granted more rights; they themselves treat girls scornfully; they play by themselves, not admitting girls to their group, they offer insults: for one thing, calling girls 'prissy' or the like and thus recalling the little girl's secret humiliation. In France, in mixed schools, the boys' caste deliberately oppresses and persecutes the girls' caste.

If the girls want to struggle with the boys and fight for their rights, they are reprimanded. They are doubly envious of the activities peculiar to the boys: first, because they have a spontaneous desire to display their power over the world, and, second, because they are in protest against the inferior status to which they are condemned. For one thing, they suffer under the rule forbidding them to climb trees and ladders or go on roofs. Adler remarks that the notions of high and low have great importance, the idea of elevation in space implying a spiritual superiority, as may be seen in various heroic myths; to attain a summit, a peak, is to stand out beyond the common world of fact as sovereign subject (ego); among boys, climbing is frequently a basis for challenge. The little girl, to whom such exploits are forbidden and who, seated at the foot of a tree or cliff, sees the triumphant boys high above her, must feel that she is, body and soul, their inferior. And it is the same if she is left *behind* in a race or jumping match, if she is thrown *down* in a scuffle or simply kept on the side lines.

As she becomes more mature, her universe enlarges, and masculine superiority is perceived still more clearly. Very often identification with the mother no longer seems to be a satisfying solution; if the little girl at first accepts her feminine vocation, it is not because she intends to abdicate; it is, on the contrary, in order to rule; she wants to be a matron because the matrons' group seems privileged; but when her company, her studies, her games, her reading, take her out of the maternal circle, she sees that it is not the women but the men who control the world. It is this revelation – much more than the discovery of the penis – that irresistibly alters her conception of herself.

The relative rank, the hierarchy, of the sexes is first brought to her attention in family life; little by little she realizes that if the father's authority is not that which is most often felt in daily affairs, it is actually supreme; it only takes on more dignity from not being degraded to daily use; and even if it is in fact the mother who rules as mistress of the household, she is commonly clever enough to see to it that the father's wishes come first; in important matters the mother demands, rewards, and punishes in his name and through his authority. The life of the father has a mysterious prestige: the hours he spends at home, the room where he works, the objects he has around him, his pursuits, his hobbies, have a sacred character. He supports the family, and he is the responsible head of the family. As a rule his work takes him outside, and so it is through him that the family communicates with the rest of the world: he incarnates that immense, difficult, and marvellous world of adventure; he personifies transcendence, he is God.[19] This is what the child feels physically in the powerful arms that lift her up, in the strength of his frame against which she nestles. Through him the mother is dethroned as once was Isis by Ra, and the Earth by the Sun.

But here the child's situation is profoundly altered: she was to become one day a woman like her all-powerful mother – she will never be the sovereign father; the bond attaching her to her mother was an active emulation – from her father she can but passively await an expression of approval. The boy thinks of his father's superiority with a feeling of rivalry; but the girl has to accept it with impotent admiration. I have already pointed out that what Freud calls the Electra complex is not, as he supposes, a sexual desire; it is a full abdication of the subject, consenting to become object in submission and adoration. If her father shows affection for his daughter, she feels that her existence is magnificently justified; she is endowed with all the merits that others have to acquire with difficulty; she is fulfilled and deified. All her life she may longingly seek that lost state of plenitude and peace. If the father's love is withheld, she may ever after feel herself guilty and condemned; or she may look elsewhere for appreciation of herself and become indifferent to her father or even hostile. Moreover, it is not alone the father who holds the keys to the world: men in general share normally in the prestige of manhood; there is no occasion for regarding them as 'father substitutes'. It is directly, as men, that grandfathers, older brothers, uncles, playmates, fathers, family friends, teachers, priests, doctors, fascinate the little girl. The emotional concern shown by adult women towards Man would of itself suffice to perch him on a pedestal.[20]

Everything helps to confirm this hierarchy in the eyes of the little girl. The historical and literary culture to which she belongs, the songs and legends with which she is lulled to sleep, are one long exaltation of man. It was men who built up Greece, the Roman Empire, France, and all other nations, who have explored the world and invented the tools for its exploitation, who have governed it, who have filled it with sculptures, paintings, works of literature. Children's books, mythology, stories, tales, all reflect the myths born of the pride and the desires of men; thus it is that through the eyes of men the little girl discovers the world and reads therein her destiny.

The superiority of the male is, indeed, overwhelming: Perseus, Hercules, David, Achilles, Lancelot, the old French warriors Du Guesclin and Bayard, Napoleon – so many men for one Joan of Arc; and behind her one descries the great male figure of the archangel Michael! Nothing could be more tiresome than the biographies of famous women: they are but pallid figures compared with great men; and most of them bask in the glory of some masculine hero. Eve was not created for her own sake but as a companion for Adam, and she was made from his rib. There are few women in the Bible of really high renown: Ruth did no more than find herself a husband. Esther obtained favour for the Jews by kneeling before Ahasuerus, but she was only a docile tool in the hands of Mordecai; Judith was more audacious, but she was subservient to the priests, and her exploits, of dubious aftertaste, is by no means to be compared with the clean, brilliant triumph of young David. The goddesses of pagan mythology are frivolous or capricious, and they all tremble before Jupiter. While Prometheus magnificently steals fire from the sun, Pandora opens her box of evils upon the world.

There are in legend and story, to be sure, witches and hags who wield fearful powers. Among others, the figure of the Mother of the Winds in Andersen's *Garden of Paradise* recalls the primitive Great Goddess; her four gigantic sons obey her in fear and trembling, she beats them and shuts them up in sacks when they misbehave. But these are not attractive personages. More pleasing are the fairies, sirens, and undines, and these are outside male domination; but their existence is dubious, hardly individualized; they intervene in human affairs but have no destiny of their own: from the day when Andersen's little siren becomes a woman, she knows the yoke of love, and suffering becomes her lot.

In modern tales as in ancient legends man is the privileged hero. Mme de Ségur's books are a curious exception: they describe a matriarchal society where the husband, when he is not absent, plays a ridiculous part; but commonly the figure of the father, as in the real world, is haloed with glory. The feminine dramas of *Little Women* unfold under the aegis of a father deified by absence. In novels of adventure it is the boys who take a trip around the world, who travel as sailors on ships, who live in the jungle on breadfruit. All important events take place through the agency of men. Reality confirms what these novels and legends say. If the young girl reads the papers, if she listens to the conversation of grown-ups, she learns that today, as always, men run the world. The political leaders, generals, explorers, musicians, and painters whom she admires are men; certainly it is men who arouse enthusiasm in her heart.

This prestige is reflected in the supernatural world. As a rule, in consequence of the large part played by religion in the life of women, the little girl, dominated by her mother more than is her brother, is also more subject to religious influences. Now, in Western religions God the Father is a man, an old gentleman having a specifically virile attribute: a luxuriant white beard.[21] For Christians, Christ is still more definitely a man of flesh and blood, with a fair beard. Angels have no sex, according to the theologians; but they have masculine names and appear as good-looking young men. God's representatives on earth: the Pope, the bishop (whose ring one kisses), the priest who says Mass, he who preaches, he before whom one kneels in the secrecy of the confessional – all these are men. For a pious little girl, her relations with the everlasting Father are analogous to those she has with the earthly father; as the former develop on the plane of imagination, she knows an even more nearly total resignation. The Catholic religion among others exerts a most confused influence upon the young girl.[22] The Virgin hears the words of the angel on her knees and replies: 'Behold the *handmaid* of the Lord.' Mary Magdalene lies at Christ's feet, washing them with her tears and drying them with the hairs of her head, her woman's long hair. The saints kneel and declare their love for the shining Christ. On her knees, breathing the odour of incense, the young girl abandons herself to the gaze of God and the angels: a masculine gaze. There has been frequent insistence on the similarities between erotic language and the mystical language spoken by women; for instance, St Theresa writes of Jesus: 'Oh, my Well-Beloved, through Thy love I am reconciled not to feel, here below, the inexpressible kiss of Thy mouth . . . but I pray Thee to fire me with Thy love . . . Ah, let me in my burning frenzy hide within Thy heart . . . I would become the prey of Thy love . . .' and so on.

But it is not to be concluded that these effusions are always sexual; the fact is rather that when feminine sexuality develops, it is pervaded with the religious sentiment that women ordinarily direct towards man from early childhood. True it is that the little girl experiences in the presence of her confessor, and even when alone at the foot of the altar, a thrill very similar to what she will feel later in her lover's embrace: this means that feminine love is one of the forms of experience in which a conscious ego makes of itself an object for a being who transcends it; and these passive delights, too, are the enjoyment of the young feminine devotee lingering in the shadowy church.

Head bowed, face buried in her hands, she knows the miracle of renunciation: on her knees she mounts towards heaven; her surrender to the arms of God assures her an Assumption fleecy with clouds and angels. It is from this marvellous experience that she copies her earthly future. The child can find it also through many other roads: everything invites her to abandon herself in daydreams to men's arms in order to be transported into a heaven of glory. She learns that to be happy she must be loved; to be loved she must await love's coming. Woman is the Sleeping Beauty, Cinderella, Snow White, she who receives and submits. In song and story the young man is seen departing adventurously in search of woman; he slays the dragon, he battles giants; she is locked in a tower, a palace, a garden, a cave, she is chained to a rock, a captive, sound asleep: she waits.

Un jour mon prince viendra . . . Some day he'll come along, the man I love – the words of popular songs fill her with dreams of patience and of hope.

Thus the supreme necessity for woman is to charm a masculine heart; intrepid and adventurous though they may be, it is the recompense to which all heroines aspire; and most often no quality is asked of them other than their beauty. It is understandable that the care of her physical appearance should become for the young girl a real obsession; be they princesses or shepherdesses, they must always be pretty in order to obtain love and happiness; homeliness is cruelly associated with wickedness, and one is in doubt, when misfortunes shower on the ugly, whether their crimes or their ill-favoured looks are being punished. Frequently the beautiful young creatures, with a glorious future in store, are seen at first as victims; the stories of Genevieve of Brabant, of Griselda, are not so simple as they seem; love and suffering are disquietingly mingled in them; woman assures her most delicious triumphs by first falling into depths of abjection; whether God or a man is concerned, the little girl learns that she will become all-powerful through deepest resignation: she takes delight in a masochism that promises supreme conquests. St Blandine, her white body blood-streaked under the lion's claws, Snow White laid out as if dead in a glass coffin, the Beauty asleep, the fainting Atala, a whole flock of delicate heroines bruised, passive, wounded, kneeling, humiliated, demonstrate to their young sister the fascinating prestige of martyred, deserted, resigned beauty. It need not astonish us that while her brother plays the hero, the young girl quite willingly plays the martyr: pagans throw her to the lions, Bluebeard drags her by the hair, her husband, the King, exiles her to forest depths; she submits, she suffers, she dies, and her head wears the halo of glory. 'While still a little girl,' writes Mme de Noailles, 'I wanted to attract the affection of men, to disquiet them, to be rescued by them, to die in their arms.' We find a remarkable example of these masochistic day-dreamings in Marie Le Hardouin's *Voile noire*:

At seven, from I know not what rib, I created my first man. He was tall, slender, very young, dressed in black satin with long sleeves trailing to the ground. He had blond hair in long, heavy curls . . . I called him Edmond . . . Then I gave him two brothers, Charles and Cedric, and the three, alike in dress and appearance, made me feel strange delights . . . Their tiny feet and fine hands gave me all kinds of inner movements . . . I became their sister Marguerite . . . and loved to feel myself wholly at their mercy, Edmond having the right of life and death over me . . . He had me whipped on the slightest pretext . . . When he spoke to me I was overcome with fear and could only stammer: 'Yes, my lord,' feeling the strange pleasure of being idiotic . . . When my sufferings became too great, I begged for mercy and kissed his hand, while, my heart finally breaking, I reached that state in which one wants to die from excess of pleasure.

More or less precociously the little girl dreams that she is old enough for love; at nine or ten she amuses herself by making up her face, she pads her bodice, disguises herself as a grown-up lady. But she does not seek any actual erotic experience with little boys: if she happens to hide with them and play at 'showing things to each other', it is only a matter of sexual curiosity. But the partner in her amorous reveries is an adult, either purely imaginary or based upon real individuals; in the latter case, the child is satisfied to love at a distance. A very good example of these childish daydreams will be found in the memoirs of Colette Audry, *Aux yeux du souvenir*; she relates that she discovered love at the age of five:

That, of course, had nothing to do with the little sexual pleasures of childhood, the satisfaction I felt, for example, when I sat astride on a certain chair or caressed myself before going to sleep . . . All they had in common was that I carefully hid both from those about me . . . My love for this young man consisted in thinking of him before going to sleep and imagining wonderful stories . . . I was in love successively with all my father's head clerks . . . I was deeply grieved when they left, for they were hardly more than a pretext for my dreams . . . When I went to bed I took my revenge for being too young and timid. I made careful preparations; I found no trouble in making him seem present, but I had to transform myself so that I could see myself ceasing to be 'I' and becoming 'she'. First of all, I was eighteen and beautiful . . . I had a lovely box of sweets . . . I had brown hair in short curls and was dressed in a long muslin gown. An absence of ten years had separated us. He returned looking scarcely older, and the sight of this marvellous creature overwhelmed him. She seemed hardly to remember him, she was full of ease, indifference, and wit. I composed truly brilliant dialogue for this first meeting. There followed misunderstandings, a whole difficult conquest, cruel hours of discouragement and jealousy for him. At last, driven to extremes, he avowed his love. She listened in silence and just when he thought all was lost, she said she had never ceased loving him, and they embraced a little . . . I saw the two near together, on a bench in a park usually, heard their murmurs, and at the same time I felt the warm contact of their bodies. But from that point everything came apart. I never got as far as marriage[23] . . . The next morning I thought about it a little, while washing. I admired my soapy face (though at other times I did not consider myself beautiful) and felt that somehow it hopefully beckoned me towards the distant future. But I had to hurry; once my face was wiped, all was over, and in the glass I saw more my commonplace childish head, which no longer interested me.

Games and daydreams orient the little girl towards passivity; but she is a human being before becoming a woman, and she knows already that to accept herself as a woman is to become resigned and to mutilate herself; if the resignation is tempting, the mutilation is hateful. Man, Love, are still far in the mists of the future; at present the little girl seeks activity and independence, like her brothers. The burden of liberty is not heavy upon children, because it does not imply responsibility; they know they are safe under adult protection: they are not tempted to run away. Her spontaneous surge towards life, her enjoyment of playing, laughing, adventure, lead the little girl to view the maternal sphere as narrow and stifling. She would like to escape from her mother's authority, an authority that is exercised in a much more intimate and everyday manner than is anything the boys have to accept. Rare indeed are the instances when the mother's authority is as comprehending and discreet as in the case of that 'Sido' whom Colette has lovingly depicted. Apart from the quasi-pathological cases – and they are common[24] – where the mother is a kind of brute, satisfying on the child her will to domination and her sadism, her daughter is the privileged object before whom she claims to stand as sovereign subject; this claim leads the child to rise in revolt. Colette Audry has described this revolt of a normal child against a normal mother:

> I could not have replied with the truth, however innocent it might have been, for I never felt innocent before Mamma. She was the great essential person, and I had such a grudge against her that I have not got over it yet. There was deep within me a kind of savage open sore that I was sure to find always inflamed . . . Without regarding her as too severe or beyond her rights, I just thought: 'No, no, no,' with all my might. I did not reproach her for her arbitrary power, her orders and prohibitions, but for her *desire to humble me*, sometimes plainly stated, sometimes read in her eyes or voice. When she told lady visitors that children are much more amenable after a punishment, her words stuck in my gorge, unforgettable: I could not vomit them up, nor could I swallow them. This anger represented my guilt before her and also my shame before myself (for after all she scared me, and by way of reprisal I had to my credit only a few violent words and insolent attitudes), but it was also my glory, in spite of everything: as long as the sore was there, and while there lived the mute rage that seized me at the mere repetition of the words *to humble, amenable, punishment, humiliation* – for so long I would not be humbled.

The rebellion is the more violent when, as often happens, the mother has lost her prestige. She is the one who waits, submits, complains, weeps, makes scenes: an ungrateful role that in daily life leads to no apotheosis; as a victim she is looked down on; as a shrew, detested; her fate seems the prototype of rapid *recurrence*: life only repeats itself in her, without going anywhere; firmly set in her role as housekeeper, she puts a stop to the expansion of existence, she becomes obstacle and negation. Her daughter wishes *not* to be like her, worshipping women who have escaped from feminine servitude: actresses, writers, teachers; she engages avidly in sports and in study, she climbs trees, tears her clothes, tries to rival the boys.

Usually she has a best friend in whom she confides; it is an exclusive friendship like an amorous passion, which ordinarily involves the sharing of sexual secrets, the little girls exchanging and discussing such information as they have been able to obtain. Often enough a triangle is formed, one of the girls liking her friend's brother. So in *War and Peace* Sonia is Natasha's best friend and loves her brother Nicolas. In any case such friendship is shrouded in mystery, and it may be said in general that at this stage children love to have secrets; the girl makes a secret of the most insignificant things, in reaction against the mystery-making that is often the response to her curiosity. Having secrets is also one way of giving herself importance, something she seeks in every way to acquire: trying to interfere with grown-ups, inventing stories for their benefit in which she only half believes and in which she plays an important part, and the like. Among her companions she pretends to scorn the boys as much as they do her; she and her friends form a separate group, giggling and making fun of the boys.

But in fact she is pleased when they treat her on a footing of equality, and she tries to gain their approval. She would like to belong to the privileged caste. The same movement that in the primitive horde woman directed against male dominance is manifested in each new initiate through refusal of her lot: in her, transcendence condemns the absurdity of immanence. She does not like being intimidated by the rules of decency, bothered by her clothes, enslaved to household cares, stopped short in all her flights. Numerous inquiries have been made on this point, almost all[25] giving the same result: practically all the boys – like Plato in his time – declared that they would be horrified to be girls; almost all the girls regretted not being boys. According to Havelock Ellis's statistics, one boy in a hundred would like to be a girl; more than 75 per cent of the girls would prefer to change sex. According to Karl Pipal's research (quoted by Baudouin in *L'Âme enfantine*, out of 20 boys of twelve to fourteen, 18 said they would prefer anything in the world to being girls. Out of 22 girls, 19 wanted to be boys, giving the following reasons: 'Boys are better off, they do not have to suffer as women do ... My mother would love me more ... A boy does more interesting work ... A boy has more aptitude for studies ... I would have fun scaring girls ... I would no longer be afraid of boys ... They are freer ... Boys' games are more fun ... They are not bothered by their clothes'. This last point often recurs: most girls complain that their dresses bother them, that they do not have liberty of movement, that they are obliged to be careful not to spot their light-coloured skirts and dresses.

At ten or twelve years of age most little girls are truly *garçons manqués* – that is to say, children who lack something of being boys. Not only do they feel it as a deprivation and an injustice, but they find that the régime to which they are condemned is unwholesome. In girls the exuberance of life is restrained, their idle vigour turns into nervousness; their too sedate occupations do not use up their superabundant energy; they become bored, and, through boredom and to compensate for their position of inferiority, they give themselves up to gloomy and romantic day-dreams; they get a taste for these easy escape mechanisms and lose their sense of reality; they yield to their emotions with uncontrolled excitement; instead of acting, they talk, often commingling serious phrases and senseless words in hodge-podge fashion. Neglected, 'misunderstood', they seek consolation in narcissistic fancies: they view themselves as romantic heroines of fiction, with self-admiration and self-pity. Quite naturally they become coquettish and stagy, these defects becoming more conspicuous at puberty. Their malaise shows itself in impatience, tantrums, tears; they enjoy crying – a taste that many women retain in later years – largely because they like to play the part of victims: at once a protest against their hard lot and a way to make themselves appealing. Little girls sometimes watch themselves cry in a mirror, to double the pleasure.

Most young girls' dramas concern their family relationships; they seek to break their ties with mother: now they show hostility towards her, now they retain a keen need for her protection; they would like to monopolize father's love; they are jealous, sensitive, demanding. They often make up stories, imagining that their parents are not really their parents, that they are adopted children. They attribute to their parents a secret life; they muse on their relationships; they often imagine that father is misunderstood, unhappy, that he does not find in his wife an ideal companion such as his daughter could be for him; or, on the contrary, that mother regards him rightly as coarse and brutal, that she is horrified at all physical relations with him. Fantasies, histrionics, childish tragedies, false enthusiasms, odd behaviour – the reason for all these must be sought not in a mysterious feminine soul but in the child's environment, her situation.

It is a strange experience for an individual who feels himself to be an autonomous and transcendent subject, an absolute, to discover inferiority in himself as a fixed and preordained essence: it is a strange experience for whoever regards himself as the One to be revealed to himself as otherness, alterity. This is what happens to the little girl when, doing her apprenticeship for life in the world, she grasps what it means to be a woman therein. The sphere to which she belongs is everywhere enclosed, limited, dominated, by the male universe: high as she may raise herself, far as she may venture, there will always be a ceiling over her head, walls that will block her way. The gods of man are in a sky so distant that in truth, for him, there are no gods: the little girl lives among gods in human guise.

The situation is not unique. The American Negroes know it, being partially integrated in a civilization that nevertheless regards them as constituting an inferior caste; what Bigger Thomas, in Richard Wright's *Native Son*, feels with bitterness at the dawn of his life is this definitive inferiority, this accursed alterity, which is written in the colour of his skin: he sees aeroplanes flying by and he knows that because he is black the sky is forbidden to him. Because she is a woman, the little girl knows that she is forbidden the sea and the polar regions, a thousand adventures, a thousand joys: she was born on the wrong side of the line. There is this great difference: the Negroes submit with a feeling of revolt, no privileges compensating for their hard lot, whereas woman is offered inducements to complicity. I have previously[26] called to mind the fact that along with the authentic demand of the subject who wants sovereign freedom, there is in the existent an inauthentic longing for resignation and escape; the delights of passivity are made to seem desirable to the young girl by parents and teachers, books and myths, women and men; she is taught to enjoy them from earliest childhood; the temptation becomes more and more insidious; and she is the more fatally bound to yield to those delights as the flight of her transcendence is dashed against harsher obstacles.

But in thus accepting her passive role, the girl also agrees to submit unresistingly to a destiny that is going to be imposed upon her from without, and this calamity frightens her. The young boy, be he ambitious, thoughtless, or timid, looks towards an open future; he will be a seaman or an engineer, he will stay on the farm or go away to the city, he will see the world, he will get rich; he feels free, confronting a future in which the unexpected awaits him. The young girl will be wife, mother, grandmother; she will keep house just as her mother did, she will give her children the same care she herself received when young – she is twelve years old and already her story is written in the heavens. She will discover it day after day without ever making it; she is curious but frightened when she contemplates this life, every stage of which is foreseen and towards which each day moves irresistibly.

This explains why the little girl, more than her brothers, is preoccupied with the mysteries of sexuality. Boys are also passionately interested in these matters; but they are not most concerned about their role as husband and father, in their futures. Whereas for the girl marriage and motherhood involve her entire destiny; and from the time when she begins to glimpse their secrets, her body seems to her to be odiously threatened. The magic of maternity has been dissipated: by more or less adequate means the girl has been informed, and whether early or late she knows that the baby does not arrive by chance in the maternal body and that it is not caused to emerge by the wave of a wand; she questions herself anxiously. Often it no longer seems marvellous but rather horrible that a parasitic body should proliferate within her body; the very idea of this monstrous swelling frightens her.

And how will the baby get out? Even if no one has told her about the screams and the pains of childbirth, she has overheard remarks or read the words of the Bible: 'In sorrow thou shalt bring forth children'; she has a presentiment of tortures that she cannot even imagine in detail; she devises strange operations in the umbilical region. If she supposes that the foetus will be expelled through the anus, she gets no reassurance from that idea: little girls have been known to undergo attacks of psychosomatic constipation when they thought they had discovered the birth process. Precise explanations will not prove to be of great assistance: pictures of swelling, tearing, haemorrhage, will haunt her. The young girl will suffer the more from these visions the more imaginative she is; but none can face them without a shudder. Colette relates how her mother found her in a faint after reading in a novel by Zola the description of a birth, in crude and shocking terms and in minute detail.

The reassurances given by grown-ups leave the child uneasy; as she gets older, she learns not to take the word of adults any more, and it is often in just these matters concerning reproduction that she catches them lying. She knows also that they regard the most frightful things as normal; if she has experienced some violent physical shock – a tonsillectomy, a tooth pulled, a felon lanced – she will project the pain she remembers upon a future childbirth.

The physical nature of pregnancy and birth at once suggests that 'something physical' takes place between husband and wife. The word *blood* frequently occurring in such expressions as 'child of the same blood', 'pure blood', 'mixed blood', sometimes gives direction to the childish imagination; it may be supposed, for instance, that marriage involves some solemn rite of transfusion. But more often the 'something physical' is connected with the urinary and excremental apparatus; in particular, children are inclined to believe that the man urinates into the woman. The sexual operation is thought of as *dirty*. This is extremely upsetting to the child for whom 'dirty' things have been severely tabooed: how then can adults accept such things as an integral part of life? The child is kept from being scandalized at first by the absurdity of what he discovers: he sees no sense in what he hears, or reads, or writes: it all seems unreal to him. In Carson McCullers's novel *The Member of the Wedding*, the young heroine comes upon two lodgers naked in bed, and the very anomaly of the situation prevents her from feeling it to be important.

When children are warned against strangers or when a sexual incident is explained to them, it is likely that reference will be made to the diseased, to maniacs, to the insane; it is a convenient explanation. A child touched by her neighbour at the cinema, or one who has seen a passer-by expose himself, believes that she has had to do with a madman. To be sure, it is unpleasant to encounter insanity: an epileptic attack, a hysterical outburst, or a violent quarrel, upsets the order of the adult world, and the child who sees it feels endangered; but after all, just as there are in a harmonious society a certain number of beggars, of the lame, and of the infirm with hideous sores, so there may be found in it also certain abnormals, without disturbance of its foundations. It is when parents, friends, teachers, are suspected of celebrating black Masses in secret that the child becomes really frightened. An incident in point is cited from Dr Liepmann's *Jeunesse et sexualité*.

When I was first told about the sexual relations between man and woman, I denied that such things were possible since my parents would have had to do likewise, and I thought too highly of them to believe it. I said that it was much too disgusting for me ever to do it. Unfortunately I was to be undeceived shortly after, when I heard what my parents were doing ... that was a fearful moment; I hid my face under the bedclothes and stopped my ears, and wished I were a thousand miles from there.

How make the transition from the thought of clothed and dignified people who enjoin decency, reserve, the life of reason, to that of two naked animals confronting each other? Here, indeed, is a self-defamation of adults which shakes their pedestal, which darkens the sky. Frequently the child obstinately refuses to accept the revelation: 'My parents don't do that,' she insists. Or she tries to construct for herself a decent picture of coition: as one little girl put it, 'When a child is wanted, the parents go to the doctor's surgery; they undress, they blindfold themselves because they mustn't look; then the doctor attaches them together and sees to it that all goes well'; she had transformed the act of love into a surgical operation, unpleasant, no doubt, but as correct as a session with the dentist. Yet in spite of denial and flight from reality, uneasiness and doubt creep into the childish heart, and an effect is produced as painful as that of weaning: it is no longer a matter of separating the girl from the mother's flesh, but of the crumbling around her of the protective universe; she finds herself without a roof over her head, abandoned, absolutely alone before a dark future.

And what increases the little girl's distress is that she fails to discern clearly the shape of the equivocal curse that weighs upon her. Her information is incoherent, the books are contradictory; even technical explanations fail to dissipate the thick darkness; a hundred questions arise: Is the sexual act painful? Or delightful? How long does it last – five minutes or all night? One reads here that a woman has become a mother after a single embrace, there that she remains sterile after hours of sexual pleasure. Do people 'do it' every day? Or only occasionally? The child seeks to inform herself by reading the Bible, by consulting dictionaries, by asking her friends about it, and so she gropes in obscurity and disgust. Dr Liepmann's research produced an interesting document on this matter. Here are some of the replies given him by young girls concerning their first knowledge of sexuality:

I continued to go astray among my odd and nebulous ideas. No one broached the subject, neither my mother nor my schoolteachers; no book treated the subject fully. A kind of perilous and ugly mystery was woven about the act, which at first had seemed to me so natural. The big girls of twelve made use of crude jokes to bridge the chasm between themselves and my classmates. All that was still vague and disgusting; we argued as to where the baby was formed; if perhaps the thing took place only once in man, since marriage was the occasion for so much fuss. My menstruation at fifteen was a new surprise . . .

Sexual initiation! Not to be mentioned in our house! . . . I hunted in books, but wore myself out without finding the road . . . For my school-teacher the question did not seem to exist . . . A book finally showed me the truth, and my over-excitement disappeared; but I was most unhappy, and it took me a long time to understand that eroticism and sexuality alone constitute real love.

Stages of my initiation: (I) First questions and unsatisfactory notions, age three and a half to eleven . . . No answers . . . My pet rabbit had young when I was seven, and my mother told me that in animals and people the young grew inside the mother and emerged through the flank, which seemed to me unreasonable . . . a nursemaid told me about pregnancy, birth and menstruation . . . At length, to my last question on his function, my father replied with vague stories about pistil and pollen. (II) There were some attempts at personal initiation, age eleven to thirteen. I consulted an encyclopaedia and a medical book . . . Only theoretical information in strange, big words. (III) Some command of acquired knowledge, age thirteen to twenty: (*a*) through daily life; (*b*) through scientific books.

At eight I played with a boy of the same age. I repeated to him what my mother had told me: A woman has many eggs inside her . . . a child is born from one of these eggs whenever the mother strongly desires it . . . He called me stupid and said that when the butcher and his wife wanted a baby, they went to bed and acted indecently. I was shocked . . . When I was twelve and a half we had a maid who told me scandalous tales of all kinds . . . From shame I said nothing of this to Mamma; but when I asked her if sitting on a gentleman's knees could give one a baby, she explained everything to me as well as she could.

I learned at school where babies come from, and I felt it was something frightful. But how did they come into the world? Two of us formed a monstrous idea of it all; especially after meeting a man one dark winter morning, who showed his sexual parts and asked us if that were not something good to devour. We felt the deepest repugnance and were literally nauseated. Until I was twenty-one I thought babies were born through the navel.

A little girl asked me if I knew where babies come from. Finally she called me a goose and said they come from inside women and to make them it was necessary for women to do something quite disgusting with men. Then she went into details, but I was unable to believe that such things could be possible. Sleeping in my parents' room, I later heard take place what I had thought was impossible, and I was ashamed of my parents. All this made of me another being. I felt frightful moral suffering, regarding myself as a depraved creature because I was now aware of things.

It should be said that even clear instruction would not solve the problem; with the best will in the world on the part of parents and teachers, it is impossible to put the erotic experience into words and concepts; it is to be comprehended only in living it; any analysis, however serious, is bound to have a comic side and it will fail to express the truth. When, beginning with the poetic amours of the flowers and the nuptials of fishes, and proceeding by way of the chick, the kitten, and the kid, one has attained the level of the human species, one can very well elucidate in theory the mystery of generation – but the mystery of sexual pleasure and love remains complete.

How is one to explain the pleasure of a kiss or a caress to the passionless child? Family kisses are given and received, sometimes even on the lips; why should that contact of mucous membranes have, in certain cases, vertiginous effects? It is like describing colours to the blind. As long as there is no intuition of the excitement and the desire that give its meaning and its unity to the erotic function, the various elements that compose it will seem shocking and monstrous. In particular, the little girl is revolted when she realizes that she is virginal and closed, and that, to change her into a woman, it will be necessary for a man's sexual organ to penetrate her. Because exhibitionism is a widespread perversion, many young girls have seen the penis in a state of erection; in any case, they have seen the sex organs of male animals, and unfortunately that of the horse has often drawn their gaze; this may well be frightening. Fear of childbirth, fear of the male sex organ, fear of the 'crises' that threaten married people, disgust for indecent behaviour, mockery for actions that are without any significance – all this often leads the little girl to declare: 'I will never get married.'[27] That would be the surest defence against the pain, the foolishness, the obscenity. In vain the attempt to explain to her that one day neither defloration nor childbirth would seem so terrible to her, that millions of women have gone through with it all and have been none the worse for the experience. When a child has fear of some external occurrence, we rid her of it; but if we predict that later she will accept it quite naturally, then she feels dread of encountering herself – changed, astray – in the distant future. The metamorphosis of the caterpillar into chrysalis and then into butterfly makes the child uneasy: Is it still the same caterpillar after its long sleep? Will it recognize itself in this bright winged thing? I have known little girls whom the sight of a chrysalis plunged into a frightened reverie.

And yet the metamorphosis does take place. The little girl does not grasp its meaning, but she notices that something is changing subtly in her relations with the world and with her own body: she is aware of contacts, tastes, odours, that were formerly indifferent to her; strange pictures pass through her mind; she hardly recognizes herself in mirrors; she feels 'funny', things seem 'funny'. Such is little Emily, whom Richard Hughes describes in *A High Wind in Jamaica*:

It was her own tenth birthday . . . Emily, for coolness sat up to her chin in water, and hundreds of infant fish were tickling with their inquisitive mouths every inch of her body, a sort of expressionless light kissing.

Anyhow she had lately come to hate being touched – but this was abominable. At last, when she could stand it no longer, she clambered out and dressed.

Even the tranquil Tessa in Margaret Kennedy's *The Constant Nymph* felt this strange distraction:

Suddenly she had become intensely miserable. She stared down into the darkness of the hall, cut in two by the moonlight which streamed in through the open door. She could not bear it. She jumped up with a little cry of exasperation. 'Oh!' she exclaimed. 'How I hate it all!' . . . She ran out to hide herself in the mountains, frightened and furious, pursued by a desolate foreboding which seemed to fill the quiet house. As she stumbled up towards the pass she kept murmuring to herself: 'I wish I could die! I wish I was dead!'

She knew that she did not mean this; she was not in the least anxious to die. But the violence of such a statement seemed to satisfy her . . .

This disturbing moment is described at length in Carson McCullers's book *The Member of the Wedding*.

What is happening in this time of unrest is that the child's body is becoming the body of a woman and is being made flesh. Except in cases of glandular insufficiency, where the subject remains fixed at an infantile stage, the crisis of puberty supervenes at about the age of twelve or thirteen.[28] This crisis begins much earlier in the girl than in the boy, and it brings much more important changes. The young girl meets it with uneasiness, with displeasure. When the breasts and the body hair are developing, a sentiment is born which sometimes becomes pride but which is originally shame; all of a sudden the child becomes modest, she will not expose herself naked even to her sisters or her mother, she inspects herself with mingled astonishment and horror, and she views with anguish the enlargement of this firm and slightly painful core, appearing under each nipple, hitherto as inoffensive as the navel. She is disturbed to feel that she has a vulnerable spot; this sore spot is surely a slight matter in comparison with the pain of a burn or a toothache; but whether from injuries or sicknesses, pains were always something abnormal; whereas the young breast is normally the seat of one knows not what dull disaffection. Something is taking place – not an illness – which is implied in the very laws of existence, but still is of the nature of a struggle, a laceration. From infancy to puberty the girl has grown, of course, but she has never been conscious of her growth: day after day her body was always a present fact, definite, complete; but now she is 'developing'. The very word seems horrifying; vital phenomena are reassuring only when they have reached a state of equilibrium and have taken on the fully formed aspect of a fresh flower, a glossy animal; but in the development of her breasts the girl senses the ambiguity of the word *living*. She is neither gold nor diamond, but a strange form of matter, ever changing, indefinite, deep within which unclean alchemies are in course of elaboration. She is accustomed to a head of hair quietly rippling like a silken skein; but this new growth in her armpits and at her middle transforms her into a kind of animal or alga. Whether or not she is well forewarned, she feels in these changes the presentiment of a finality which sweeps her away from selfhood: she sees herself thrown into a vital cycle that overflows the course of her private existence, she divines a dependence that dooms her to man, to children, and to death. In themselves her breasts would seem to be a useless and obtrusive proliferation. Arms, legs, skin, muscles, even the rounded bottom on which she sits – up to now all these have had their obvious usefulness; only her sex, clearly a urinary organ, has seemed to be somewhat dubious, but secret and invisible to others. Under her sweater or blouse her breasts make their display, and this body which the girl has identified with herself she now apprehends as flesh. It becomes an object that others see and pay attention to. 'For two years,' a woman told me, 'I wore a cape to hide my chest, I was so ashamed of it.' And another: 'I still recall the strange confusion I felt when a friend of the same age, but more developed than I was, bent down to pick up a ball and I saw through the opening of her bodice two breasts that were already full. I blushed on my own account at the sight of this body so near mine in age, on which mine would be modelled.' Still another woman told me this: 'At thirteen I was taking a walk, wearing a short dress and with my legs bare. A man, chuckling, made some comment on my large calves. Next day my mother had me wear stockings and lengthen my skirts, but I shall never forget the sudden shock I felt at being seen *naked*.' The young girl feels that her body is getting away from her, it is no longer the straightforward expression of her individuality; it becomes foreign to her; and at the same time she becomes for others a thing: on the street men follow her with their eyes and comment on her anatomy. She would like to be invisible; it frightens her to become flesh and to show her flesh.

This distaste is expressed by many young girls through the wish to be thin; they no longer want to eat, and if they are forced to, they have vomiting spells; they constantly watch their weight. Others become pathologically timid; for them it is torture to enter a drawing-room or even to go out in the street. From such beginnings psychoses may now and then develop. A typical case of this kind is described by Janet in *Les Obsessions et la psychasthénie*, under the name Nadia:

Nadia, a young girl of wealthy and intelligent family, was stylish, artistic, and an excellent musician; but from infancy she was obstinate and irritable. 'She demanded excessive affection from family and servants, but she was so exigent and dominating that she soon alienated people; when mockery was used as a means of reforming her, she acquired a sense of shame with reference to her body.' Then, too, her need for affection made her wish to remain a spoiled child, made her fear growing up . . . A precocious puberty added to her troubles: 'since men like plump women, she would remain thin'. Pubic hair and growing breasts added to her fears. From the age of eleven it seemed to her that everybody eyed her legs and feet. The appearance of menstruation drove her half mad, and believing that she was the only one in the world having the monstrosity of pubic hair, she laboured up to the age of twenty to rid herself of this 'savage decoration' by depilation . . . She was so afraid of becoming plump – when she 'would be ashamed to show herself' – that she tried all kinds of prayers and conjurations to prevent normal growth, for 'no one would love her if she became fat'. Finally she decided not to eat, so as 'to remain a little girl'; and when she yielded to her mother's pleas to take some food, she knelt for hours, writing out vows and tearing them up. Her mother died when she was eighteen, and then she imposed on herself so severe a régime that she gnawed on her handkerchief and rolled on the floor from excess of hunger. She was pretty, but believed that her face was puffy and covered with pimples, asserting that her doctor, who could not see them, lacked understanding of her condition. She left her family and hid in a small apartment, never going out; there she lived most of the time in the dark, thinking that her appearance was so horrible that to be seen was intolerable.

Very often the parental attitude serves to inculcate in the girl a sense of shame regarding her appearance. One woman reported to Stekel[29] as follows:

I suffered from a very keen sense of physical inferiority, which was accentuated by continual nagging at home ... Mother, in her excessive pride, wanted me to appear at my best, and she always found many faults which required 'covering up' to point out to the dressmaker; for instance, drooping shoulders! Outstanding hips! Too flat in the back! Bust too prominent! And so on. I was particularly worried on account of the appearance of my limbs ... and I was nagged on account of my gait ... There was some truth in every criticism ... but sometimes I was so embarrassed, particularly during my 'flapper' stage, that at times I was at a loss to know how to move about. If I met someone my first thought was: 'If I could only hide my feet!'

This feeling of shame leads the girl to act awkwardly and to blush incessantly; this blushing increases her timidity and itself involves a phobia.

Sometimes the girl does not as yet feel ashamed of her body, in what may be called the stage of pre-puberty, before the appearance of the menses; she is proud of becoming a woman and watches the maturing of her bosom with satisfaction, padding her dress with handkerchiefs and taking pride in it before her elders; she does not yet grasp the significance of what is taking place in her. Her first menstruation reveals this meaning, and her feelings of shame appear. If they were already present, they are strengthened and exaggerated from this time on. All the evidence agrees in showing that whether the child has been forewarned or not, the event always seems to her repugnant and humiliating. Frequently her mother has neglected to inform her; it has been noted[30] that mothers more readily explain to their daughters the mysteries of pregnancy, childbirth, and even sexual relations than the fact of menstruation. They themselves seem to abhor this feminine burden, with a horror that reflects the ancient mystical fears of males and that the mothers pass on to their offspring. When the girl finds the suspicious spots on her clothing, she believes she is a victim of a diarrhoea or a fatal haemorrhage or some shameful disease. According to a study reported in 1896 by Havelock Ellis, among 125 pupils in an American high school, 36 knew absolutely nothing on the subject at the time of their first menses, 39 had some vague knowledge; more than half, that is, were in ignorance of the matter. According to Helene Deutsch, things were much the same in 1946. Instances of attempted suicide are not unknown, and indeed it is natural enough for the young girl to be frightened as her life blood seems to be flowing away, perhaps from some injury to the internal organs. Even if wise instruction spares her too vivid anxiety, the girl feels ashamed, soiled; and she hastens to the bathroom, she tries to cleanse or conceal her dirty linen. In *Aux yeux du souvenir*, Colette Audry describes at length a typical experience, here given in abbreviated form.

One night, when undressing, I thought I must be ill, but said nothing in the hope that it would be gone in the morning ... Four weeks later it happened again, more excessively, and I put my underwear in the basket for soiled clothes. My mother came to my room to explain things. I cannot recall the effect her words had on me, but when my sister Kiki looked in curiously, I was upset and cried to her to go away. I wanted my mother to punish her for coming in without knocking. My mother's air of calm satisfaction maddened me, and when she went out I was plunged into a brutal night.

Two memories came back to me all of a sudden: An old physician meeting us on the street remarked: 'Your daughter is growing up, madame,' and all at once I detested him without knowing why. A little later Kiki saw my mother putting a package of small napkins in a drawer and in reply to Kiki's question she said, with the lofty air of grown-ups who reveal a quarter of the truth while withholding three quarters: 'They are for Colette, before long.' Speechless, incapable of framing a single question, I detested my mother.

All through that night I turned and twisted in bed. It couldn't be possible. I would wake up, Mamma was wrong, it would pass and not return ... Next day, secretly changed and soiled, I must confront the others. I hated my sister, suddenly though unknowingly given such superiority over me. Then I began to hate men, who would never experience that, who knew about it. And I detested women, who took it so easily and who, if they knew about me, would gleefully think: 'Now it is your turn.' ... I walked uneasily and dared not run ... It was over, and I began again to hope foolishly that it would not happen again. A month later I had to yield to the evidence ... Thenceforth there was in my memory a 'before'. The rest of my life would be no more than an 'after'.

Things happen in analogous fashion for most young girls. Many of them are horrified at the thought of revealing their secret to family and associates. A friend of mine, who had no mother and lived with her father and governess, told me she passed three months in fear and shame, hiding her spotted underwear, before her condition was discovered. Even peasant women, who supposedly would be hardened by their acquaintance with the cruder aspects of animal life, regard this curse with horror because menstruation still carries a taboo in the country. I knew a young farmer's wife who during a whole winter washed her linen secretly in an icy brook and even put on her chemise still wet in order to conceal her unspeakable secret. I could mention a hundred similar facts. Even avowal of this surprising misfortune does not mean deliverance. No doubt the mother who brutally slapped her daughter, saying: 'Idiot, you are too young,' is exceptional. But more than one will show bad humour; most fail to give the child adequate information, and the latter remains filled with anxiety concerning the new status that the first menstruation inaugurates. She wonders whether the future may not have further painful surprises in store for her; or she fancies that henceforth she can become pregnant through the mere presence or touch of a man and thus feels real terror in regard to males. Even if she is spared these pangs through intelligent explanations, she is not so easily given peace of mind. Previously the little girl, with a bit of self-deception, could consider herself as still a sexless being, or she could think of herself not at all; she might even dream of awakening changed into a man; but now, mothers and aunts whisper flatteringly: 'She's a big girl now'; the matron's group has won: she belongs to it. And so she is placed without recourse on the woman's side. It may be that she is proud of it; she thinks that she has become a grown-up and that this will revolutionize her existence. For instance, Thyde Monnier says in *Moi*:

> Several of us had become 'big girls' during vacation; others reached that estate while at school, and then one after another we went 'to see the blood' in the courtyard water-closets where they sat enthroned like queens receiving their subjects.

But the little girl is soon undeceived, for she sees that she has gained no new privileges at all, life following its usual course. The only novelty is the untidy event that is repeated each month; there are children who weep for hours when they realize that they are condemned to this fate. And what strengthens their revolt still further is the knowledge that this shameful blemish is known also to men; they would prefer at least that their humiliating feminine condition might remain shrouded in mystery for males. But no; father, brothers, cousins, all the men know, and even joke about it sometimes. Here disgust at her too fleshly body arises or is exacerbated in the girl. And though the first surprise is over, the monthly annoyance is not similarly effaced; at each recurrence the girl feels again the same disgust at this flat and stagnant odour emanating from her – an odour of the swamp, of wilted violets – disgust at this blood, less red, more dubious, than that which flowed from her childish abrasions. Day and night she must think of making her changes, must keep watch of her underwear, her sheets, must solve a thousand little practical and repugnant problems. In economical families the sanitary napkins are washed each month and put back with the clean handkerchiefs; she must put these excreta from herself in the hands of whoever does the washing – laundress, maid, mother, or older sister. The pads sold by chemists are thrown away after use; but on trips, visits or excursions it is not so easy to get rid of them, especially when disposal in the lavatory is expressly forbidden. The young girl, when at her period, may feel horrified at the sanitary napkin and refuse to undress except in the dark, even before her sister. This annoying and cumbersome object may be displaced during violent exercise, and it is a worse humiliation than losing her knickers in the street. Such a dreadful prospect sometimes gives rise to psycho-pathological states. By a kind of natural malice, certain illnesses and pains often begin only after the flow, which may at first pass unnoticed; young girls are often not yet regulated: they run the risk of being surprised while out for a walk, in the street, visiting friends; they run the risk – like Mme de Chevreuse[31] – of spotting their clothes or whatever they are seated on; some girls are kept in constant apprehension by such a possibility. The more repellent this feminine blemish seems to the young girl, the more watchful she must be against exposing herself to the dread humiliation of an accident or a sharing of her secret.

Dr W. Liepmann, in *Jeunesse et sexualité*, obtained, among others, the following statements on this matter during the course of his research on juvenile sexuality:

At sixteen, when I was indisposed for the first time, I was very much frightened when I discovered it one morning. Truth to tell, I knew it had to happen; but I was so ashamed of it that I stayed in bed all the morning and to all questions I replied that I could not get up.

I was astounded when at twelve I menstruated for the first time. I was scared, and as my mother simply remarked that it would happen every month, I considered it a great indecency and refused to admit that it did not happen also to men.

My mother had told me about menstruation, and I was much disappointed when, being indisposed, I joyfully ran to wake my mother saying: 'Mamma, I have it!' and she only said: 'And you wake me up for that!' Nevertheless I considered the event a real revolution in my life.

I was greatly frightened when, at my first menstruation, I saw that the flow did not stop after a few minutes. Yet I said nothing to anybody. I was just fifteen; moreover, I suffered very little pain from it. Only once I had such pains that I fainted and lay on the floor in my room for three hours. Still I said nothing about it.

It happened first when I was almost thirteen. I had talked it over with girls at school and felt quite proud of becoming a grown-up. I explained importantly to my gymnastics teacher that today it was impossible for me to join the class because I was indisposed.

95

My mother did not warn me. In her case it began at nineteen, and in fear of being scolded for dirtying her underwear, she went out and buried the clothes in a field.

At eighteen I had my period for the first time, without foreknowledge. That night I suffered from a great flow and severe cramps. In the morning I went sobbing to my mother for advice. She only reprimanded me severely for soiling the bed, without further explanation. I wondered in anguish what crime I had committed.

I already knew about it. I awaited the event impatiently, because I hoped that then my mother would tell me how babies were made. The great day arrived: but my mother said nothing. None the less I thought joyfully: 'Now you too can make children: you are a woman.'

This crisis occurs at a still tender age; the boy reaches adolescence only at fifteen or sixteen; the girl changes to a woman at thirteen or fourteen. But it is not from this difference in ages that the essential difference in their experience comes; no more does it reside in the physiological phenomena that give the girl's experience its shocking force: puberty takes on a radically different significance in the two sexes because it does not portend the same future to both of them.

It is true enough that at the moment of puberty boys also feel their bodies as an embarrassment, but being proud of their manhood from an early age, they proudly project towards manhood the moment of their development; with pride they show one another the hair growing on their legs, a manly attribute; their sex organ is more than ever an object of comparison and challenge. Becoming adult is an intimidating metamorphosis: many adolescent boys are worried at the thought of the exigent liberty to come; but they joyfully assume the dignity of being male.

The little girl, on the contrary, in order to change into a grown-up person, must be confined within the limits imposed upon her by her femininity. The boy sees with wonder in his growing hairiness vague promises of things to come; the girl stands abashed before the 'brutal and prescribed drama' that decides her destiny. Just as the penis derives its privileged evaluation from the social context, so it is the social context that makes menstruation a curse. The one symbolizes manhood, the other femininity; and it is because femininity signifies alterity and inferiority that its manifestation is met with shame. The girl's life has always seemed to her to be determined by that vague essence to which the lack of a penis has not been enough to give a positive shape: but she becomes aware of herself in the red flow from between her thighs. If she has already accepted her condition, she greets the event with joy – 'Now you are a woman.' If she has always refused to accept her condition, the bloody verdict stuns her; most often she falters: the monthly uncleanness makes her inclined to feel disgust and fear. 'So that is what is meant by the words "to be a woman"!' The set fate that up to now weighed upon her indistinctly and from without is crouching in her belly; there is no escape; she feels she is caught.

In a sexually equalitarian society, woman would regard menstruation simply as her special way of reaching adult life; the human body in both men and women has other and more disagreeable needs to be taken care of, but they are easily adjusted to because, being common to all, they do not represent blemishes for anyone; the menses inspire horror in the adolescent girl because they throw her into an inferior and defective category. This sense of being declassed will weigh heavily upon her. She would retain her pride in her bleeding body if she did not lose her pride in being human. And if she succeeds in keeping this last, she will feel much less keenly the humiliation of her flesh; the young girl who opens up for herself the avenues of transcendence in athletic, social, intellectual, and mystical activities will not regard her sexual specialization as a mutilation, and she will easily rise above it. If the young girl at about this stage frequently develops a neurotic condition, it is because she feels defenceless before a dull fatality that condemns her to unimaginable trials; her femininity means in her eyes sickness and suffering and death, and she is obsessed with this fate.

An example that strikingly illustrates these anxieties is one of a patient described by Helene Deutsch[32] under the name of Molly. An abbreviated synopsis follows:

Molly was fourteen when she began to suffer from psychic disorders; she was the fourth child in a family of five siblings. Her father is described as extremely strict and narrow-minded. He criticized the appearance and behaviour of his children at every meal. The mother was worried and unhappy; and every so often the parents were not on speaking terms; one brother ran away from home. The patient was a gifted youngster, a good tap dancer; but she was timid, took the family troubles seriously, and was afraid of boys. She took the greatest interest in her older sister's pregnancy, knew the details, and heard that women often die in childbirth. She took care of the baby for two months; when the sister left the house, there was a terrible scene and the mother fainted. Molly's thoughts were much concerned with separation, fainting, and death.

The mother reported that the patient had begun to menstruate several months previously. She was rather embarrassed about it and told her mother: 'The thing is here.' She went with her sister to buy some menstrual pads; on meeting a man in the street, she hung her head. In general she acted 'disgusted with herself'. She never had pain during her periods, but tried to hide them from her mother, even when the latter saw stains on the sheets. She told her sister: 'Anything might happen to me now. I might have a baby.' When told: 'You have to live with a man for that to happen,' she replied: 'Well, I am living with two men – my father and your husband.'

The father did not permit his daughters to go out after dark on account of soldiers being in the town and because one heard stories of rape. These fears helped to give

Molly the idea of men being redoubtable creatures. From her first menstruation her anxiety about becoming pregnant and dying in childbirth became so severe that after a time she refused to leave her room, and now she sometimes stays in bed all day; if she goes out to play, the thought of leaving the immediate vicinity gives her an attack of 'shaking'. She lies awake listening to hoises, and fears that someone is trying to enter the house; she has fits of weeping, she daydreams, and she writes poetry. She has eating spells, to keep her from fainting; she fears to go in cars, cannot go to school or otherwise lead a normal life.

An analogous case history is that of Nancy, which is not concerned with the onset of menstruation but with the anxiety of the little girl in regard to her insides.[33]

Towards the age of thirteen the little girl was on intimate terms with her older sister, and she had been proud to be in her confidence when the sister was secretly engaged and then married: to share the secret of a grown-up was to be accepted among the adults. She lived for a time with her sister; but when the latter told her that she was going 'to buy' a baby, Nancy got jealous of her brother-in-law and of the coming child: to be treated again as a child to whom one made little mysteries of things was unbearable. She began to experience internal troubles and wanted to be operated on for appendicitis. The operation was a success, but during her stay at the hospital Nancy lived in a state of severe agitation; she made violent scenes with a nurse she disliked; she tried to seduce the doctor, said she 'knew everything', and tried to get him to spend the night with her – probably sure he would not agree, but wishing he would accept her as a grown-up. She accused herself of being to blame for the death of a little brother some years before. And in particular she felt sure that they had not removed her appendix or had left a part of it inside her; her claim that she had swallowed a penny was probably intended to make sure an X-ray would be taken.

This desire for an operation – especially the removal of the appendix – is often met with at that age; young girls express in this way their fantasies of rape, pregnancy, and childbirth. They feel vague threats inside them, and they hope that the surgeon will save them from this unknown danger that lies in wait for them.

And it is not the appearance of her menses alone that announces her womanly destiny to the girl. Other dubious phenomena are appearing in her. So far her erotic feeling has been clitorid. It is difficult to find out whether masturbation is less common in the girl than in the boy; she engages in the practice during her first two years, perhaps even from the first months of her life; it would seem that she gives it up at about two, to take it up again later. The anatomical conformation of that stalk planted in the male flesh makes it more tempting to touch than is a hidden mucous area; but chance contacts – the child climbing ropes or trees, or riding a bicycle – the friction of clothes, touching in games, or even initiation by playmates, older children, or adults, may often make the girl aware of sensations which she endeavours to revive manually.

In any case the pleasure, when it is obtained, is an independent sensation: it has the light and innocent character of all childish diversions.[34] The girl hardly connects these private enjoyments with her womanly destiny; her sexual relations with boys, if any existed, were based essentially on curiosity. And now she feels herself shot through with confused emotions in which she does not recognize herself. The sensitivity of the erogenous zones is developing, and these are so numerous in woman that her whole body may be regarded as erogenous. This fact is revealed to her by family caresses, innocent kisses, the indifferent touch of a dressmaker, a doctor, or a hairdresser, by a friendly hand upon her hair or the nape of her neck; she comes to know, and often deliberately to seek, a deeper thrill in play relations, in wrestling with boys or girls. So it was with Gilbertine grappling with Proust in the Champs-Elysées; she felt strange languors while in the arms of her partners as she danced under the unsuspicious eye of her mother. Then, too, even a well-protected maidenhood is exposed to more specific experiences; in 'well-bred' circles silence is maintained with one accord concerning these regrettable incidents. But very often some of the caresses of family friends, uncles and cousins, not to mention grandfathers and fathers, are much less inoffensive than the mother imagines; a teacher or a priest or a doctor may have been bold, indiscreet. Accounts of such experiences will be found in Violette Leduc's *Asphyxie*, in S. de Tervagnes's *Haine maternelle*, in Yassu Gauclère's *Orange bleue*, and in Casanova's *Memoirs*. Stekel regards grandfathers, among others, as often very dangerous.

I was fifteen. The day before the funeral my grandfather came to stay at our house. Next morning, after my mother had got up, he came and wanted to get in bed to play with me; I rose at once without answering him ... I began then to be afraid of men.

Another young girl remembered having had a severe shock at eight or ten when her grandfather, an old man of seventy, tampered with her genitals, inserting his finger. The child felt severe pain but was afraid to speak of the incident. From that time she had great fear of everything sexual.[35]

Such incidents are usually unmentioned by the little girl because of shame. Besides, if she tells her parents, their reaction is often to scold her: 'Don't say such things.' 'You are naughty.' She keeps silent also regarding certain peculiar actions of strangers. A girl related the following to Dr Liepmann:[36]

We had rented a basement room from a cobbler. When our landlord was alone, he often came to find me, took me in his arms, and held me in a long embrace, moving backward and forward. Moreover, his kiss was not superficial, as he put his tongue in my mouth. I detested him on account of this way of acting. But I never said a word about it, being very much scared.

In addition to enterprising playmates and perverse friends, there is that knee pressed against the little girl's in the cinema, that hand which at night in the train glides along her leg, those young fellows who titter as she goes by, those men who follow her in the street, those embraces, those furtive touches. She has little idea of the meaning of these adventures. There is often a strange jumble in the head of the fifteen-year-old, because her theoretical knowledge and these actual experiences do not blend. She has already felt all the heat of roused senses and desire, but she fancies – like Francis Jammes's Clara d'Ellébeuse – that a man's kiss would be enough to make her a mother. Clara had exact information concerning genital anatomy, but when her dancing partner embraced her, she blamed a migraine for the emotion she felt.

No doubt young girls are better informed now than formerly, but some psychiatrists hold that not a few adolescent girls are still unaware that the genitals have other than a urinary function.[37] At any rate, they see little relation between their sexual emotions and the existence of their genital organs, because there is no sign as clear as the masculine erection to indicate this correlation. Between their romantic daydreams of men – that is, love – and the crudity of certain facts known to them, there exists such a hiatus that they arrive at no synthesis of the two. Thyde Monnier[38] relates that she and some friends swore to ascertain how a man is constructed and report on it to the others:

Having entered my father's room purposely without knocking, I reported as follows: 'It looks like a leg-of-mutton sleeve; that is, it is like a roller and then comes something round.' It was difficult to explain. I made a drawing, three in fact, and each took one away, hidden down her neck, and from time to time looked at it and burst out laughing, and then became dreamy ... How could innocent girls like us make any connection between this object and the sentimental songs, the pretty little romantic stories in which love, wholly composed of respect, timidity, sighs, and hand-kissings, is sublimated to the point of castration?

Nevertheless, through reading, conversation, sights seen and words over-heard, the young girl attaches meaning to the disturbances of her flesh; she becomes all appeal, desire. In and through her excitements, thrills, moistenings, vague discomforts, her body takes on a new and disquieting dimension. The young man openly welcomes his erotic tendencies because he joyfully assumes his virile estate; with him sexual desire is aggressive and grasping in nature; in it he sees affirmation of his subjectivity, his transcendence; he boasts of it among his fellows; his sex organ continues to serve as a double in which he takes pride; the urge that drives him towards the female is of the same kind as that which throws him against the world, and he recognizes himself in both. The sexual life of the little girl, on the contrary, has always been secret; when her eroticism changes and invades all her flesh, its mystery becomes agonizing: she suffers from the disturbance as from a shameful illness; it is not active: it is a state from which, even in imagination, she cannot find relief by any decision of her own. She does not dream of taking, shaping, violating: her part is to await, to want; she feels dependent; she scents danger in her alienated flesh.

For her diffuse hopefulness, her dream of happy passivity, reveals her body to her clearly as an object destined for another; she would fain realize the sexual experience only in its immanence; it is the *contact* of the hand, of the mouth, of another flesh that she wants and not the hand, mouth, and flesh of the other. She leaves in shadow the image of her partner, or she loses it in ideal mists. Yet, she cannot prevent his presence from haunting her. Her juvenile terrors and revulsions in regard to man have taken on a more equivocal character than formerly, and at the same time one more agonizing. Those feelings arose before from a profound divorce between her childish organism and her adult future; now they have their source in the very complexity the young girl senses in her flesh. She realizes that she is destined for possession, since she wants it; and she revolts against her desires. She simultaneously longs for and dreads the shameful passivity of the willing prey. The thought of appearing nude before a man overwhelms her with excitement; but she feels also that she will then be helpless under his gaze. The hand that lays hold on her, that touches her, has a yet more imperious urgency than have the eyes: her fright is still greater. But the most obvious and the most detestable symbol of physical possession is penetration by the sex organ of the male. The young girl hates to think that someone can perforate this body which she identifies with herself as one perforates leather, or can tear it as one tears cloth. But what the young girl objects to more than the injury and its accompanying pain is that the injury and the pain should be *inflicted*. A young girl once said to me: 'It is horrible to think of being *impaled* by a man.' It is not fear of the virile member that gives rise to horror of the male, but the fear is the corroboration and symbol of the horror; the idea of penetration acquires its obscene and humiliating sense within a more general frame, of which it is, in turn, an essential element.

The young girl's anxiety is expressed in tormenting nightmares and haunting phantoms: the very time she feels within herself an insidious willingness is just when the idea of rape in many cases becomes obsessing. This idea is manifested in dreams and in behaviour through numerous more or less definite symbols. Before going to sleep the girl looks under the bed in fear of finding some robber with dubious intentions; she thinks she hears burglars in the house; an attacker comes in through the window, armed with a knife, to stab her. Men frighten her more or less. She begins to feel a certain disgust for her father; the smell of his tobacco becomes unbearable, she hates to go to the bathroom after him; even if she is still affectionate, this physical repulsion is often felt; she assumes an exasperated air, as if the child were already hostile to her father, as often happens with younger sisters. Psychiatrists say they often meet with a certain dream in their young patients: they fancy they have been violated by a man in the presence of an older woman who permits the act. Clearly they are in symbolical fashion asking their mother's permission to yield to their desires.

For one of the constraints that bear upon them most odiously is that of hypocrisy. The young girl is dedicated to 'purity' and 'innocence' just when she is discovering in herself and all around her the mysterious stirrings of life and sex. She is supposed to be white as snow, transparent as crystal, she is dressed in filmy organdie, her room is papered in dainty colours, voices are lowered at her approach, she is forbidden salacious books. Now, there is not a 'good little girl' who does not indulge in 'abominable' thoughts and desires. She strives to conceal them even from her closest friend, even from herself; she wants to live and to think only according to rules; her distrust of herself gives her a sly, unhappy, sickly air; and later on, nothing will be more difficult for her than to overcome these inhibitions. And despite all her repressions, she feels crushed under the weight of unspeakable transgressions. She undergoes her metamorphosis into a woman not only in shame but in remorse.

It is understandable that the awkward age should be for the girl a period of painful disturbance. She does not want to remain a child. But the adult world seems frightening or boring. As Colette Audry says:

> So I wanted to grow up, but I never thought seriously of leading a life such as I saw adults leading . . . and thus the wish to grow up without ever assuming adult status was still kept alive within me, never would I make one with parents, housekeepers, home-makers, and heads of families.

The young girl would rid herself of her mother's yoke, but she feels also a keen need of her protection. What makes this refuge necessary is the series of transgressions that weighs on her conscience, such as solitary practices, dubious friendships, and improper reading. The following letter written by a girl of fifteen and cited by Helene Deutsch[39] is characteristic:

> Mother wants me to wear a long dress at the big dance party at the Ws' – my first long dress. She is surprised that I don't want to. I begged her to let me wear my short pink dress for the last time. I am so afraid. The long dress makes me feel as if Mummy were going on a long journey and I did not know when she would return. Isn't that silly? And sometimes she looks at me as though I were still a little girl. Ah, if she knew! She would tie my hands to the bed, and despise me.

In Stekel's *Frigidity in Woman* will be found a remarkable account of a feminine childhood. In it a Viennese girl (*Backfisch*) presents a detailed confession at the age of twenty-one. It constitutes a concrete synthesis of all the phenomena we have studied separately. A condensed version follows:

'At the age of five I chose for my playmate Richard, a boy of six or seven . . . For a long time I had wanted to know how one can tell whether a child is a girl or a boy. I was told: by the earrings . . . or by the nose. This seemed to satisfy me, though I had a feeling that they were keeping something from me. Suddenly Richard expressed a desire to urinate . . . Then the thought came to me of lending him my chamber-pot . . . When I saw his organ, which was something entirely new to me, I went into highest raptures: "What have you there? My, isn't that nice! I'd like to have something like that, too." Whereupon I took hold of the membrum and held it enthusiastically . . . My great-aunt's cough distracted us . . . and from that day on our doings and games were carefully watched.'

At nine she played 'marriage' and 'doctor' with two other boys of eight and ten; they touched her parts and one day one of the boys touched her with his organ, saying that her parents had done just the same thing when they got married. 'This aroused my indignation: "Oh no! They never did such a nasty thing!" ' She kept up these games for a long time in a strong sexual friendship with the two boys. One day her aunt caught her and there was a frightful scene with threats to put her in the reformatory. She was prevented from seeing Arthur, whom she preferred, and she suffered a good deal from it; her school work went badly, her writing was deformed, and she became cross-eyed. She started another intimacy with Walter and Franz. 'Walter became the goal of all thoughts and feeling. I permitted him very submissively to reach under my dress while I sat or stood in front of him at the table, pretending to be busy with a writing exercise; whenever my mother . . . opened the door, he withdrew his hand instantly; I, of course, was busy writing . . . In the course of time we also behaved as husband and wife; but I never allowed him to stay long; whenever he thought he was inside me, I tore myself away saying that somebody was coming . . . I did not reflect that this was "sinful" . . .

'My childhood boy friendships were now over. All I had left were girl friends. I attached myself to Emmy, a highly refined, well-educated girl. One Christmas we exchanged gilded heart-shaped lockets with our initials engraved on them – we were, I believe, about twelve years of age at the time – and we looked upon this as a token of "engagement"; we swore eternal faithfulness "until death do us part". I owe to Emmy a good part of my training. She taught me also a few things regarding sexual matters. As far back as during my fifth grade at school I began seriously to doubt the stork story. I thought that children developed within the body and that the abdomen must be cut open before a child can be brought out. She filled me with particular horror of self-abuse. In school the Gospels contributed a share towards opening our eyes with regard to certain sexual matters. For instance, when Mary came to Elizabeth, the child is said to have "leaped in her womb"; and we read other similarly remarkable Bible passages. We underscored these words; and when this was discovered the whole class barely escaped a "black mark" in deportment. My girl friend told me also about the "ninth month reminder" to which there is a reference in Schiller's *Die Räuber* . . . Emmy's father moved from our locality and I was again alone. We corresponded, using for the purpose a cryptic alphabet which we had devised between ourselves; but I was lonely and finally attached myself to Hedl, a Jewish girl. Once Emmy caught me leaving school in Hedl's company; she created a scene on account of her jealousy . . . I kept up my friendship with Hedl until I entered the commercial school. We became close friends. We both dreamed of becoming sisters-in-law sometime, because I was fond of one of her brothers. He was a student. Whenever he spoke to me I became so confused that I gave him an irrelevant answer. At dusk we sat in the music room, huddled together on the little divan, and often tears rolled down my cheek for no particular reason as he played the piano.

'Before I befriended Hedl, I went to school for a number of weeks with a certain girl, Ella, the daughter of poor people. Once she caught her parents in a "tête-à-tête". The creaking of the bed had awakened her . . . She came and told me that her father had crawled on top of her mother, and that the mother had cried out terribly; and then the father said to her mother: "Go quickly and wash so that nothing will happen!" After this I was angry at her father and avoided him in the street, while for her mother I felt the greatest sympathy. (He must have hurt her terribly if she cried out so!)

'Again with another girl I discussed the possible length of the male membrum; I had heard that it was 12 to 15 cm. long. During the fancy-work period (at school) we took the tape-measure and indicated the stated length on our stomachs, naturally reaching to the navel. This horrified us; if we should ever marry we would be literally impaled.'

She saw a male dog excited by the proximity of a female, and felt strange stirrings inside herself. 'If I saw a horse urinate in the street, my eyes were always glued to the wet spot in the road; I believe the length of time (urinating) is what always impressed me.' She watched flies in copulation and in the country domesticated animals doing the same.

'At twelve I suffered a severe attack of tonsillitis. A friendly physician was called in. He seated himself on my bed and presently he stuck his hand under the bedclothes, almost touching me on the genitalia. I exclaimed: "Don't be so rude!" My mother hurried in; the doctor was much embarrassed. He declared I was a horrid little monkey, saying he merely wanted to pinch me on the calf. I was compelled to ask his forgiveness . . . When I finally began to menstruate and my father came across the blood-stained cloths on one occasion, there was a terrible scene. How did it happen that he, so clean a man, had to live among such dirty females? . . . I felt the injustice of being put in the wrong on account of my menstruation.'

At fifteen she communicated with another girl in shorthand 'so that no one else could decipher our missives. There was much to report about conquests. She copied for me a vast number of verses from the walls of lavatories; I took particular notice of one. It seemed to me that love, which ranged so high in my fantasy, was being dragged in the mud by it. The verse read: "What is love's highest aim? Four buttocks on a stem." I decided I would never get into that situation; a man who loves a young girl would be unable to ask such a thing of her.

'At fifteen and a half I had a new brother. I was tremendously jealous, for I had always been the only child in the family. My friend reminded me to observe "how the baby boy was constructed", but with the best intentions I was unable to give her the desired information ... I could not bear to look. At about this time another girl described to me a bridal night scene ... I think that then I made up my mind to marry after all, for I was very curious; only the "panting like a horse", as mentioned in the description, offended my aesthetic sense ... Which one of us girls would not have gladly married then, to undress before the beloved husband and be carried to bed in his arms? It seemed so thrilling!'

It may be objected – although the case is normal and not pathological – that this child was exceptionally 'perverse'; but in truth she was only watched less closely than others. If the curiosities and the desires of 'well-bred' girls are not expressed in acts, they none the less exist in the form of fantasies and games. I once knew a young girl who was very pious and disconcertingly innocent – since become a thorough woman, steeped in maternity and devotion – who, quivering with excitement, said one night to an older sister: 'How marvellous it must be to undress before a man! Make believe you are my husband'; and she undressed herself, trembling with emotion. No education can prevent the little girl from becoming conscious of her body and from musing on her destiny; at most, strict repression can be imposed, which will later weigh heavily upon her sexual life. What is desirable is that she should be taught, on the contrary, to accept herself without being self-satisfied and without shame.

We are now acquainted with the dramatic conflict that harrows the adolescent girl at puberty: she cannot become 'grown-up' without accepting her femininity; and she knows already that her sex condemns her to a mutilated and fixed existence, which she faces at this time under the form of an impure sickness and a vague sense of guilt. Her inferiority was sensed at first merely as a deprivation; but the lack of a penis has now become defilement and transgression. So she goes onward towards the future, wounded, shameful, culpable.

Notes

1 Judith Gautier relates in her memoirs that she wept and pined so pitifully when taken from her nurse that they had to bring her back, and she was not weaned until much later.

2 This theory was proposed by Dr Lacan in *Les Complexes familiaux dans la formation de l'individu*. This observation, one of primary importance, would explain how it is that in the course of its development 'the ego retains the ambiguous aspect of a spectacle'.

3 In her *Orange bleue*, Yassu Gauclère relates anecdotes of childhood illustrating the inconsistent behaviour of both her father and her mother; her childish conclusion was that 'the conduct of grown-ups is decidedly incomprehensible'.

4 A. BALINT, *La Vie intime de l'enfant.* cf. Book One, p. 79.

5 See Book One, pp. 79–80.

6 In addition to the works of Freud and Adler, an abundant literature on the subject is in existence. Karl Abraham was first to voice the idea that the little girl might consider her sex as a wound resulting from a mutilation. Karen Horney, Jones, Jeanne Lampt de Groot, Helene Deutsch, and A. Balint have studied the question from the psychoanalytic point of view. Saussure essays to reconcile psychoanalysis with the ideas of Piaget and Luquet. See also POLLACK, *Les Idées des enfants sur la différence des sexes.*

7 Cited by A. Balint.

8 'The Genesis of the Castration Complex in Woman', *International Journal of Psychoanalysis*, 1923–4.

9 cf. MONTHERLANT, Book One, p. 239.

10 See Book One, p. 77.

11 *Studies in the Psychology of Sex*, 'Undinism'.

12 H. ELLIS, op. cit., vol. III, p. 121.

13 In allusion to an episode previously related: at Portsmouth a modern retiring room for ladies was opened which called for the standing position; all the ladies were seen to depart hastily as soon as they entered.

14 'Psychogenèse et psychanalyse', *Revue française de psychanalyse*, 1933.

15 See HELENE DEUTSCH, *The Psychology of Women* (Grune & Stratton, 1944), vol. I, pp. 319ff. She cites also the authority of K. Abraham and J. H. W. van Ophuijsen.

16 At least during early childhood. Under present social conditions, the conflicts of adolescence, on the contrary, may well be exaggerated.

17 There are of course many exceptions; but we cannot undertake here to study the part played by the mother in the boy's development.

18 From *Les Conflits de l'âme enfantine.*

19 'His generous presence inspired great love and extreme fear in me,' says Mme de Noailles in speaking of her father. 'At first he astounded me. The first man astounds a little girl. I felt strongly that everything depended upon him.'

20 It is noteworthy that the worship of the father is to be met with especially in the eldest of the children, and indeed a man is more interested in his first paternity than in later ones: he often consoles his daughter, as he consoles his son, when their mother is monopolized by newcomers, and she is likely to become ardently attached to him. On the contrary, a younger sister never can have her father all to herself, without sharing him; she is commonly jealous at once of him and of her elder sister: she attaches herself to that same elder sister whom the father's favour invests with high prestige, or she turns to her mother, or she revolts against the family and looks for help outside. In many families the youngest daughter gains a privileged position in some other way. Many things, of course, can motivate special preferences in the father. But almost all the cases I know of confirm this observation on the different attitudes of the older and younger sisters.

21 'I no longer suffered from my inability to *see* God, for I recently succeeded in imagining him in the image of my late grandfather, an image that to tell the truth was rather human; but I had soon made it more Godlike by separating my grandfather's head from the torso and mentally placing it against a background of blue sky where white clouds formed a collar for it,' confides Yassu Gauclère in her *Orange bleue.*

22 Beyond question the women are infinitely more passive, more subservient to man, servile, and abased in the Catholic countries, such as Italy, Spain, or France, than in such Protestant regions as the Scandinavian and Anglo-Saxon countries. And that flows in large part from the women's own attitude: the cult of the Virgin, confession, and the rest lead them towards masochism.

23 Counter to the masochistic imaginings of Marie Le Hardouin, those of Colette Audry are of a sadistic type. She wants the beloved to be wounded, in danger, and she saves him heroically, not without having humiliated him. This is a personal note, characteristic of a woman who will never accept passivity and will seek to win her independence as a human being.

24 cf. V. LEDUC, *L'Asphyxie*; S. DE TERVAGNES, *La Haine maternelle*; H. BAZIN, *Vipère au poing*.

25 An exception is a school in Switzerland where boys and girls, getting the same education under favourable conditions of comfort and freedom, all said they were satisfied; but such circumstances are exceptional. Assuredly girls *could* be quite as happy as boys; but in existing society the fact is that they commonly are not.

26 Introduction, p. 20.

27 A passage from YASSU GAUCLÈRE'S *Orange bleue* expresses this feeling: 'Filled with repugnance, I prayed God to vouchsafe me a religious vocation in which I would escape the laws of maternity. And after having thought long upon the repugnant mysteries that in spite of myself I possessed within me, and fortified by such repulsion as by a sign from heaven, I decided that chastity was certainly my vocation.' For one thing, the idea of perforation horrified her. 'So that is what makes the wedding night terrible! This discovery overwhelmed me, adding to my earlier disgust the physical fear of this operation, which I fancied extremely painful. My terror would have been still greater if I had supposed that birth took place through the same channel, but having long known that children were born from the mother's belly. I believed that they separated off from it by a process of segmentation.'

28 The physiological processes concerned have been described in Book One, chap. 1.

29 In *Frigidity in Woman*.

30 cf. the works of Daly and Chadwick, cited by HELENE DEUTSCH in *The Psychology of Women*, p. 152.

31 Mme de Chevreuse was disguised as a man during the period of civil wars called the *Fronde*, and was unmasked, after a long ride on horseback, by the spots of blood that were noticed on her saddle.

32 *The Psychology of Women*, vol. I, pp. 175–8.

33 ibid., pp. 59–71. Much abbreviated here.

34 Except, of course, in the many cases where the direct or indirect intervention of parents, or religious scruples, make it a sin.

35 STEKEL, *Frigidity of Women*.

36 *Jeunesse et sexualité*.

37 HELENE DEUTSCH, *The Psychology of Women*, vol. I, p. 175.

38 In *Moi*.

39 *The Psychology of Women*, vol. I, p. 121.

7

TECHNOLOGIES OF THE SELF

Michel Foucault

Source: H. Gutman and P. Hutton (eds), *Technologies of the Self: a seminar with Michel Foucault*, London: Tavistock, 1988, pp. 16–49.

I
Technologies of the self

When I began to study the rules, duties, and prohibitions of sexuality, the interdictions and restrictions associated with it, I was concerned not simply with the acts that were permitted and forbidden but with the feelings represented, the thoughts, the desires one might experience, the drives to seek within the self any hidden feeling, any movement of the soul, any desire disguised under illusory forms. There is a very significant difference between interdictions about sexuality and other forms of interdiction. Unlike other interdictions, sexual interdictions are constantly connected with the obligation to tell the truth about oneself.

Two facts may be objected: first, that confession played an important part in penal and religious institutions for all offenses, not only in sex. But the task of analyzing one's sexual desire is always more important than analyzing any other kind of sin.

I am also aware of the second objection: that sexual behavior more than any other was submitted to very strict rules of secrecy, decency, and modesty so that sexuality is related in a strange and complex way both to verbal prohibition and to the obligation to tell the truth, of hiding what one does, and of deciphering who one is.

The association of prohibition and strong incitations to speak is a constant feature of our culture. The theme of the renunciation of the flesh was linked to the confession of the monk to the abbot, to telling the abbot everything that he had in mind.

I conceived of a rather odd project: not the evolution of sexual behavior but the projection of a history of the link between the obligation to tell the truth and the prohibitions against sexuality. I asked: How had the subject been compelled to decipher himself in regard to what was forbidden? It is a question of the relation between asceticism and truth.

Max Weber posed the question: If one wants to behave rationally and regulate one's action according to true principles, what part of one's self should one renounce? What is the ascetic price of reason? To what kind of asceticism should one submit? I posed the opposite question: How have certain kinds of interdictions required the price of certain kinds of knowledge about oneself? What must one know about oneself in order to be willing to renounce anything?

Thus I arrived at the hermeneutics of technologies of the self in pagan and early Christian practice. I encountered certain difficulties in this study because these practices are not well known. First, Christianity has always been more interested in the history of its beliefs than in the history of real practices. Second, such a hermeneutics was never organized into a body of doctrine like textual hermeneutics. Third, the hermeneutics of the self has been confused with theologies of the soul—concupiscence, sin, and the fall from grace. Fourth, a hermeneutics of the self has been diffused across Western culture through numerous channels and integrated with various types of attitudes and experience so that it is difficult to isolate and separate it from our own spontaneous experiences.

Context of study

My objective for more than twenty-five years has been to sketch out a history of the different ways in our culture that humans develop knowledge about themselves: economics, biology, psychiatry, medicine, and penology. The main point is not to accept this knowledge at face value but to analyze these so-called sciences as very specific "truth games" related to specific techniques that human beings use to understand themselves.

As a context, we must understand that there are four major types of these "technologies," each a matrix of practical reason: (1) technologies of production, which permit us to produce, transform, or manipulate things; (2) technologies of sign systems, which permit us to use signs, meanings, symbols, or signification; (3) technologies of power, which determine the conduct of individuals and submit them to certain ends or domination, an objectivizing of the subject; (4) technologies of the self, which permit individuals to effect by their own means or with the help of others a certain number of operations on their own bodies and souls, thoughts, conduct, and way of being, so as to transform themselves in order to attain a certain state of happiness, purity, wisdom, perfection, or immortality.

These four types of technologies hardly ever function separately, although each one of them is associated with a certain type of domination. Each implies certain modes of training and modification of individuals, not only in the obvious sense of acquiring certain skills but also in the sense of acquiring certain attitudes. I wanted to show both their specific nature and their constant interaction. For instance, one sees the relation between manipulating things and domination in Karl Marx's *Capital*, where every technique of production requires modification of individual conduct—not only skills but also attitudes.

Usually the first two technologies are used in the study of the sciences and linguistics. It is the last two, the technologies of domination and self, which have most kept my attention. I have attempted a history of the organization of knowledge with respect to both domination and the self. For example, I studied madness not in terms of the criteria of formal sciences but to show how a type of management of individuals inside and outside of asylums was made possible by this strange discourse. This contact between the technologies of domination of others and those of the self I call governmentality.

Perhaps I've insisted too much on the technology of domination and power. I am more and more interested in the interaction between oneself and others and in the technologies of individual domination, the history of how an individual acts upon himself, in the technology of self.

The development of technologies of the self

I wish to sketch out the development of the hermeneutics of the self in two different contexts which are historically contiguous: (1) Greco-Roman philosophy in the first two centuries A.D. of the early Roman Empire and (2) Christian spirituality and the monastic principles developed in the fourth and fifth centuries of the late Roman Empire.

Moreover, I wish to discuss the subject not only in theory but in relation to a set of practices in late antiquity. These practices were constituted in Greek as *epimelēsthai sautou*, "to take care of yourself," "the concern with self," "to be concerned, to take care of yourself."

The precept "to be concerned with oneself" was, for the Greeks, one of the main principles of cities, one of the main rules for social and personal conduct and for the art of life. For us now this notion is rather obscure and faded. When one is asked "What is the most important moral principle in ancient philosophy?" the immediate answer is not "Take care of oneself" but the Delphic principle, *gnothi sauton* ("Know yourself").

Perhaps our philosophical tradition has overemphasized the latter and forgotten the former. The Delphic principle was not an abstract one concerning life; it was technical advice, a rule to be observed for the consultation of the oracle. "Know yourself" meant "Do not suppose yourself to be a god." Other commentators suggest that it meant "Be aware of what you really ask when you come to consult the oracle."

In Greek and Roman texts, the injunction of having to know yourself was always associated with the other principle of having to take care of yourself, and it was that need to care for oneself that brought the Delphic maxim into operation. It is implicit in all Greek and Roman culture and has been explicit since Plato's *Alcibiades I*. In the Socratic dialogues, in Xenophon, Hippocrates, and in the Neoplatonist tradition from Albinus on, one had to be concerned with oneself. One had to occupy oneself with oneself before the Delphic principle was brought into action. There was a subordination of the second principle to the former. I have three or four examples of this.

In Plato's *Apology*, 29^e, Socrates presents himself before his judges as a master of *epimeleia heautou*. You are "not ashamed to care for the acquisition of wealth and for reputation and honor," he tells them, but you do not concern yourselves with yourselves, that is, with "wisdom, truth and the perfection of the soul." He, on the other hand, watches over the citizens to make sure they occupy themselves with themselves.

Socrates says three important things with regard to his invitation to others to occupy themselves with themselves: (1) His mission was conferred on him by the gods, and he won't abandon it except with his last breath. (2) For this task he demands no reward; he is disinterested; he performs it out of benevolence. (3) His mission is useful for the city—more useful than the Athenians' military victory at Olympia—because in teaching people to occupy themselves with themselves, he teaches them to occupy themselves with the city.

Eight centuries later, one finds the same notion and the same phrase in Gregory of Nyssa's treatise, *On Virginity*, but with an entirely different meaning. Gregory did not mean the movement by which one takes care of oneself and the city; he meant the movement by which one renounces the world and marriage and detaches oneself from the flesh and, with virginity of heart and body, recovers the immortality of which one has been deprived. In commenting on the parable of the drachma (Luke 15:8–10), Gregory exhorts one to light the lamp and turn the house over and search, until gleaming in the shadow one sees the drachma within. In order to recover the efficacy which God has printed on one's soul and which the body has tarnished, one must take care of oneself and search every corner of the soul (*De Virg.* 12).

We can see that Christian asceticism, like ancient philosophy, places itself under the same sign of concern with oneself. The obligation to know oneself is one of the elements of its central preoccupation. Between these two extremes—Socrates and Gregory of Nyssa—taking care of oneself constituted not only a principle but also a constant practice.

I have two more examples. The first Epicurean text to serve as a manual of morals was the *Letter to Menoeceus* (Diogenes Laërtius 10.122–38). Epicurus writes that it is never too early, never too late, to occupy oneself with one's soul. One should philosophize when one is young and also when one is old. It was a task to be carried on throughout life. Teachings about everyday life were organized around taking care of oneself in order to help every member of the group with the mutual work of salvation.

Another example comes from an Alexandrian text, *On the Contemplative Life*, by Philo of Alexandria. He describes an obscure, enigmatic group on the periphery of Hellenistic and Hebraic culture called the Therapeutae, marked by its religiosity. It was an austere community, devoted to reading, to healing meditation, to individual and collective prayer, and to meeting for a spiritual banquet (*agapē*, "feast"). These practices stemmed from the principal task, concern for oneself (*De Vita Cont.* 36).

This is the point of departure for some possible analysis for the care of the self in ancient culture. I would like to analyze the relation between care and self-knowledge, the relation found in Greco-Roman and Christian traditions between the care of oneself and the too-well-known principle "Know yourself." As there are different forms of care, there are different forms of self.

Summary

There are several reasons why "Know yourself" has obscured "Take care of yourself." First, there has been a profound transformation in the moral principles of Western society. We find it difficult to base rigorous morality and austere principles on the precept that we should give ourselves more care than anything else in the world. We are more inclined to see taking care of ourselves as an immorality, as a means of escape from all possible rules. We inherit the tradition of Christian morality which makes self-renunciation the condition for salvation. To know oneself was paradoxically the way to self-renunciation.

We also inherit a secular tradition which respects external law as the basis for morality. How then can respect for the self be the basis for morality? We are the inheritors of a social morality which seeks the rules for acceptable behavior in relations with others. Since the sixteenth century, criticism of established morality has been undertaken in the name of the importance of recognizing and knowing the self. Therefore, it is difficult to see concern with oneself as compatible with morality. "Know thyself" has obscured "Take care of yourself" because our morality, a morality of asceticism, insists that the self is that which one can reject.

The second reason is that, in theoretical philosophy from Descartes to Husserl, knowledge of the self (the thinking subject) takes on an ever-increasing importance as the first step in the theory of knowledge.

To summarize: There has been an inversion between the hierarchy of the two principles of antiquity, "Take care of yourself" and "Know thyself." In Greco-Roman culture knowledge of oneself appeared as the consequence of taking care of yourself. In the modern world, knowledge of oneself constitutes the fundamental principle.

II

The first philosophical elaboration of the concern with taking care of oneself that I wish to consider is found in Plato's *Alcibiades I*. The date of its writing is uncertain, and it may be a spurious Platonic dialogue. It is not my intention to study dates but to point out the principal features of the care of self which is the center of the dialogue.

The Neoplatonists in the third or fourth century A.D. show the significance given to this dialogue and the importance it assumed in the classical tradition. They wanted to organize Plato's dialogues as pedagogy and as the matrix for encyclopedic knowledge. They considered *Alcibiades* to be the first dialogue of Plato, the first to be read, the first to be studied. It was *arche*. In the second century Albinus said that every gifted young man who wanted to stand apart from politics and practice virtue should study the *Alcibiades*. It provided the point of departure and a program for all Platonic philosophy. "Taking care of oneself" was its first principle. I would like to analyze the care of self in the *Alcibiades I* in terms of three aspects.

1. How is this question introduced into the dialogue? What are the reasons Alcibiades and Socrates are brought to the notion of taking care of one's self?

Alcibiades is about to begin his public and political life. He wishes to speak before the people and be all-powerful in the city. He is not satisfied with his traditional status, with the privileges of his birth and heritage. He wishes to gain personal power over all others both inside and outside the city. At this point of intersection and transformation, Socrates intervenes and declares his love for Alcibiades. Alcibiades can no longer be the beloved; he must become a lover. He must become active in the political and the love game. Thus, there is a dialectic between political and erotic discourse. Alcibiades makes his transition in specific ways in both politics and love.

An ambivalence is evident in Alcibiades' political and erotic vocabulary. During his adolescence Alcibiades was desirable and had many admirers, but now that his beard is growing, his lovers disappear. Earlier, he had rejected them all in the bloom of his beauty because he wanted to be dominant, not dominated. He did not wish to be dominated in youth, but now he wants to dominate others. This is the moment Socrates appears, and he succeeds where the others have failed: He will make Alcibiades submit, but in a different sense. They make a pact—Alcibiades will submit to his lover, Socrates, not in a physical but in a spiritual sense. The intersection of political ambition and philosophical love is "taking care of oneself."

2. In that relationship, why should Alcibiades be concerned with himself, and why is Socrates concerned with that concern of Alcibiades? Socrates asks Alcibiades about his personal capacity and the nature of his ambition. Does he know the meaning of the rule of law, of justice or concord? Alcibiades clearly knows nothing. Socrates calls upon him to compare his education with that of the Persian and Spartan kings, his rivals.

113

Spartan and Persian princes have teachers in Wisdom, Justice, Temperance, and Courage. By comparison, Alcibiades' education is like that of an old, ignorant slave. He doesn't know these things so he can't apply himself to knowledge. But, says Socrates, it's not too late. To help him gain the upper hand—to acquire *technē*—Alcibiades must apply himself, he must take care of himself. But Alcibiades doesn't know to what he must apply himself. What is this knowledge he seeks? He is embarrassed and confused. Socrates calls upon him to take heart.

In 127^d of the *Alcibiades* we find the first appearance of the phrase, *epimelēsthai sautou*. Concern for self always refers to an active political and erotic state. *Epimelēsthai* expresses something much more serious than the simple fact of paying attention. It involves various things: taking pains with one's holdings and one's health. It is always a real activity and not just an attitude. It is used in reference to the activity of a farmer tending his fields, his cattle, and his house, or to the job of the king in taking care of his city and citizens, or to the worship of ancestors or gods, or as a medical term to signify the fact of caring. It is highly significant that the concern for self in *Alcibiades I* is directly related to a defective pedagogy, one which concerns political ambition and a specific moment of life.

3. The rest of the text is devoted to an analysis of this notion of *epimelēsthai*, "taking pains with oneself." It is divided into two questions: What is this self of which one has to take care, and of what does that care consist?

First, what is the self (129^b)? Self is a reflexive pronoun, and it has two meanings. *Auto* means "the same," but it also conveys the notion of identity. The latter meaning shifts the question from "What is this self?" to "What is the plateau on which I shall find my identity?"

Alcibiades tries to find the self in a dialectical movement. When you take care of the body, you don't take care of the self. The self is not clothing, tools, or possessions. It is to be found in the principle which uses these tools, a principle not of the body but of the soul. You have to worry about your soul—that is the principal activity of caring for yourself. The care of the self is the care of the activity and not the care of the soul-as-substance.

The second question is: How must we take care of this principle of activity, the soul? Of what does this care consist? One must know of what the soul consists. The soul cannot know itself except by looking at itself in a similar element, a mirror. Thus, it must contemplate the divine element. In this divine contemplation, the soul will be able to discover rules to serve as a basis of just behavior and political action. The effort of the soul to know itself is the principle on which just political action can be founded, and Alcibiades will be a good politician insofar as he contemplates his soul in the divine element.

Often the discussion gravitates around and is phrased in terms of the Delphic principle, "Know yourself." To take care of oneself consists of knowing oneself. Knowing oneself becomes the object of the quest of concern for self. Being occupied with oneself and political activities are linked. The dialogue ends when Alcibiades knows he must take care of himself by examining his soul.

This early text illuminates the historical background of the precept "taking care of oneself" and sets out four main problems that endure throughout antiquity, although the solutions offered often differ from those in Plato's *Alcibiades*.

First, there is the problem of the relation between being occupied with oneself and political activity. In the later Hellenistic and imperial periods, the question is presented in an alternative way: When is it better to turn away from political activity to concern oneself with oneself?

Second, there is the problem of the relationship between being occupied with oneself and pedagogy. For Socrates, occupying oneself with oneself is the duty of a young man, but later in the Hellenistic period it is seen as the permanent duty of one's whole life.

Third, there is the problem of the relationship between concern for oneself and the knowledge of oneself. Plato gave priority to the Delphic maxim, "Know yourself." The privileged position of "Know yourself" is characteristic of all Platonists. Later, in the Hellenistic and Greco-Roman periods, this is reversed. The accent was not on the knowledge of self but on the concern with oneself. The latter was given an autonomy and even a preeminence as a philosophical issue.

Fourth, there is the problem of the relationship between the care of self and philosophical love, or the relation to a master.

In the Hellenistic and imperial periods, the Socratic notion of "taking care of oneself" became a common, universal philosophical theme. "Care of the self" was accepted by Epicurus and his followers, by the Cynics, and by such Stoics as Seneca, Rufus, and Galen. The Pythagoreans gave attention to the notion of an ordered life in common. This theme of taking care of oneself was not abstract advice but a widespread activity, a network of obligations and services to the soul. Following Epicurus himself, the Epicureans believed that it's never too late to occupy oneself with oneself. The Stoics say you must attend to the self, "retire into the self and stay there." Lucian parodied the notion. It was an extremely widespread activity, and it brought about competition between the rhetoricians and those who turned toward themselves, particularly over the question of the role of the master.

There were charlatans, of course. But certain individuals took it seriously. It was generally acknowledged that it was good to be reflective, at least briefly. Pliny advises a friend to set aside a few moments a day, or several weeks or months, for a retreat into himself. This was an active leisure—to study, to read, to prepare for misfortune or death. It was a meditation and a preparation.

Writing was also important in the culture of taking care of oneself. One of the main features of taking care involved taking notes on oneself to be reread, writing treatises and letters to friends to help them, and keeping notebooks in order to reactivate for oneself the truths one needed. Socrates' letters are an example of this self-exercise.

In traditional political life, oral culture was largely dominant, and therefore rhetoric was important. But the development of the administrative structures and the bureaucracy of the imperial period increased the amount and role of writing in the political sphere. In Plato's writings, dialogue gave way to the literary pseudodialogue. But by the Hellenistic age, writing prevailed, and real dialectic passed to correspondence. Taking care of oneself became linked to constant writing activity. The self is something to write about, a theme or object (subject) of writing activity. That is not a modern trait born of the Reformation or of romanticism; it is one of the most ancient Western traditions. It was well established and deeply rooted when Augustine started his *Confessions*.

The new concern with self involved a new experience of self. The new form of the experience of the self is to be seen in the first and second century when introspection becomes more and more detailed. A relation developed between writing and vigilance. Attention was paid to nuances of life, mood, and reading, and the experience of oneself was intensified and widened by virtue of this act of writing. A whole field of experience opened which earlier was absent.

One can compare Cicero to the later Seneca or Marcus Aurelius. We see, for example, Seneca's and Marcus's meticulous concern with the details of daily life, with the movements of the spirit, with self-analysis. Everything in the imperial period is present in Marcus Aurelius's letter of 144-45 A.D. to Fronto:

Hail, my sweetest of masters.

We are well. I slept somewhat late owing to my slight cold, which seems now to have subsided. So from five A.M. till 9, I spent the time partly in reading some of Cato's *Agriculture*, partly in writing not quite such wretched stuff, by heavens, as yesterday. Then, after paying my respects to my father, I relieved my throat, I will not say by gargling—though the word *gargarisso* is, I believe, found in Novius and elsewhere—but by swallowing honey water as far as the gullet and ejecting it again. After easing my throat I went off to my father and attended him at a sacrifice. Then we went to luncheon. What do you think I ate? A wee bit of bread, though I saw others devouring beans, onions, and herrings full of roe. We then worked hard at grape-gathering, and had a good sweat, and were merry and, as the poet says, "still left some clusters hanging high as gleanings of the vintage." After six o'clock we came home.

I did but little work and that to no purpose. Then I had a long chat with my little mother as she sat on the bed. My talk was this:

"What do you think my Fronto is now doing?" Then she: "And what do you think my Gratia is doing?" Then I: "And what do you think our little sparrow, the wee Gratia, is doing?" Whilst we were chattering in this way and disputing which of us two loved the one or other of you two the better, the gong sounded, an intimation that my father had gone to his bath. So we had supper after we had bathed in the oil-press room; I do not mean bathed in the oil-press room, but when we had bathed, had supper there, and we enjoyed hearing the yokels chaffing one another. After coming back, before I turn over and snore, I get my task done and give my dearest of masters an account of the day's doings, and if I could miss him more, I would not grudge wasting away a little more. Farewell, my Fronto, wherever you are, most honey-sweet, my love, my delight. How is it between you and me? I love you and you are away.

This letter presents a description of everyday life. All the details of taking care of oneself are here, all the unimportant things he has done. Cicero tells only important things, but in Aurelius's letter these details are important because they are you—what you thought, what you felt.

The relation between the body and the soul is interesting too. For the Stoics, the body was not so important, but Marcus Aurelius speaks of himself, his health, what he has eaten, his sore throat. That is quite characteristic of the ambiguity about the body in this cultivation of the self. Theoretically, the culture is soul-oriented, but all the concerns of the body take on a huge importance. In Pliny and Seneca there is great hypochondria. They retreat to a house in the countryside. They have intellectual activities but rural activities as well. They eat and engage in the activity of peasants. The importance of the rural retreat in this letter is that nature helps put one in contact with oneself.

There is also a love relationship with Aurelius and Fronto, one between a twenty-four-year-old and a forty-year-old man. *Ars erotica* is a theme of discussion. Homosexual love was important in this period and carried over into Christian monasticism.

Finally, in the last lines, there is an allusion to the examination of conscience at the end of the day. Aurelius goes to bed and looks in the notebook to see what he was going to do and how it corresponds to what he did. The letter is the transcription of that examination of conscience. It stresses what you did, not what you thought. That is the difference between practice in the Hellenistic and imperial periods and later monastic practice. In Seneca too there are only deeds, not thoughts. But it does prefigure Christian confession.

This genre of epistles shows a side apart from the philosophy of the era. The examination of conscience begins with this letter writing. Diary writing comes later. It dates from the Christian Era and focuses on the notion of the struggle of the soul.

III

In my discussion of Plato's *Alcibiades*, I have isolated three major themes: first, the relation between care for oneself and care for the political life; second, the relation between taking care of the self and defective education; and third, the relation between taking care of oneself and knowing oneself. Whereas we saw in the *Alcibiades* the close relation between "Take care of yourself" and "Know yourself," taking care of yourself eventually became absorbed in knowing yourself.

We can see these three themes in Plato, also in the Hellenistic period, and four to five centuries later in Seneca, Plutarch, Epictetus, and the like. If the problems are the same, the solutions and themes are quite different and, in some cases, the opposite of the Platonic meanings.

First, to be concerned with self in the Hellenistic and Roman periods is not exclusively a preparation for political life. Care of the self has become a universal principle. One must leave politics to take better care of the self.

Second, the concern with oneself is not just obligatory for young people concerned with their education; it is a way of living for everybody throughout their lives.

Third, even if self-knowledge plays an important role in taking care of oneself, it involves other relationships as well.

I want to discuss briefly the first two points: the universality of the care of the self independent of political life, and the care of the self throughout one's life.

1. A medical model was substituted for Plato's pedagogical model. The care of the self isn't another kind of pedagogy; it has to become permanent medical care. Permanent medical care is one of the central features of the care of the self. One must become the doctor of oneself.

2. Since we have to take care throughout life, the objective is no longer to get prepared for adult life, or for another life, but to get prepared for a certain complete achievement of life. This achievement is complete at the moment just prior to death. This notion of a happy proximity to death—of old age as completion—is an inversion of the traditional Greek values on youth.

3. Lastly, we have the various practices to which cultivation of self has given rise and the relation of self-knowledge to these.

In *Alcibiades I*, the soul had a mirror relation to itself, which relates to the concept of memory and justifies dialogue as a method of discovering truth in the soul. But, from the time of Plato to the Hellenistic age, the relationship between care of the self and knowledge of the self changed. We may note two perspectives.

In the philosophical movements of Stoicism in the imperial period there is a different conception of truth and memory, and another method of examining the self. First, we see the disappearance of dialogue and the increasing

118

importance of a new pedagogical relationship—a new pedagogical game where the master/teacher speaks and doesn't ask questions and the disciple doesn't answer but must listen and keep silent. A culture of silence becomes more and more important. In Pythagorean culture, disciples kept silent for five years as a pedagogical rule. They didn't ask questions or speak up during the lesson, but they developed the art of listening. This is the positive condition for acquiring truth. The tradition is picked up during the imperial period, where we see the beginning of the culture of silence and the art of listening rather than the cultivation of dialogue as in Plato.

To learn the art of listening, we have to read Plutarch's treatise on the art of listening to lectures (*Peri tou akouein*). At the beginning of this treatise, Plutarch says that, following schooling, we have to learn to listen to *logos* throughout our adult life. The art of listening is crucial so you can tell what is true and what is dissimulation, what is rhetorical truth and what is falsehood in the discourse of the rhetoricians. Listening is linked to the fact that you're not under the control of the masters but you must listen to *logos*. You keep silent at the lecture. You think about it afterward. This is the art of listening to the voice of the master and the voice of reason in yourself.

The advice may seem banal, but I think it's important. In his treatise *On the Contemplative Life*, Philo of Alexandria describes banquets of silence, not debauched banquets with wine, boys, revelry, and dialogue. There is instead a teacher who gives a monologue on the interpretation of the Bible and a very precise indication of the way people must listen (*De Vita Cont.* 77). For example, they must always assume the same posture when listening. The morphology of this notion is an interesting theme in monasticism and pedagogy henceforth.

In Plato the themes of contemplation of self and care of self are related dialectically through dialogue. Now in the imperial period we have the themes of, on one side, the obligation of listening to truth and, on the other side, of looking and listening to the self for the truth within. The difference between the one era and the other is one of the great signs of the disappearance of the dialectical structure.

What was an examination of conscience in this culture, and how does one look at oneself? For the Pythagoreans, the examination of conscience had to do with purification. Since sleep was related to death as a kind of encounter with the gods, you had to purify yourself before going to sleep. Remembering the dead was an exercise for the memory. But in the Hellenistic and the early imperial periods, you see this practice acquiring new values and signification. There are several relevant texts: Seneca's *De Ira*, and *De Tranquilitate* and the beginning of Marcus Aurelius's fourth book of *Meditations*.

Seneca's *De Ira* (book 3) contains some traces of the old tradition. He describes an examination of conscience. The same thing was recommended by the Epicureans, and the practice was rooted in the Pythagorean tradition. The goal was the purification of the conscience using a mnemonic device. Do good things, have a good examination of the self, and a good sleep follows together with good dreams, which is contact with the gods.

Seneca seems to use juridical language, and it seems that the self is both the judge and the accused. Seneca is the judge and prosecutes the self so that the examination is a kind of trial. But if you look closer, it's rather different from a court. Seneca uses terms related not to juridical but to administrative practices, as when a comptroller looks at the books or when a building inspector examines a building. Self-examination is taking stock. Faults are simply good intentions left undone. The rule is a means of doing something correctly, not judging what has happened in the past. Later, Christian confession will look for bad intentions.

It is this administrative view of his own life much more than the juridical model that is important. Seneca isn't a judge who has to punish but a stock-taking administrator. He is a permanent administrator of himself, not a judge of his past. He sees that everything has been done correctly following the rule but not the law. It is not real faults for which he reproaches himself but rather his lack of success. His errors are of strategy, not of moral character. He wants to make adjustments between what he wanted to do and what he had done and reactivate the rules of conduct, not excavate his guilt. In Christian confession, the penitent is obliged to memorize laws but does so in order to discover his sins.

For Seneca it isn't a question of discovering truth in the subject but of remembering truth, recovering a truth which has been forgotten. Second, the subject doesn't forget himself, his nature, origin, or his supernatural affinity, but the rules of conduct, what he ought to have done. Third, the recollection of errors committed in the day measures the distinction between what has been done and what should have been done. Fourth, the subject is not the operating ground for the process of deciphering but is the point where rules of conduct come together in memory. The subject constitutes the intersection between acts which have to be regulated and rules for what ought to be done. This is quite different from the Platonic conception and from the Christian conception of conscience.

The Stoics spiritualized the notion of *anachoresis*, the retreat of an army, the hiding of an escaped slave from his master, or the retreat into the country away from the towns, as in Marcus Aurelius's country retreat. A retreat into the country becomes a spiritual retreat into oneself. It is a general attitude and also a precise act every day; you retire into the self to discover—but not to discover faults and deep feelings, only to remember rules of action, the main laws of behavior. It is a mnemotechnical formula.

IV

I have spoken of three Stoic techniques of self: letters to friends and disclosure of self; examination of self and conscience, including a review of what was done, of what should have been done, and comparison of the two. Now I want to consider the third Stoic technique, *askēsis*, not a disclosure of the secret self but a remembering.

For Plato, one must discover the truth that is within one. For the Stoics, truth is not in oneself but in the *logoi*, the teaching of the teachers. One memorizes what one has heard, converting the statements one hears into rules of conduct. The subjectivization of truth is the aim of these techniques. During the imperial period, one couldn't assimilate ethical principles without a theoretical framework such as science, as for example in Lucretius's *De Rerum Naturae*. There are structural questions underlying the practice of the examination of the self every night. I want to underscore the fact that in Stoicism it's not the deciphering of the self, not the means to disclose secrecy, which is important; it's the memory of what you've done and what you've had to do.

In Christianity asceticism always refers to a certain renunciation of the self and of reality because most of the time your self is a part of that reality you have to renounce in order to get access to another level of reality. This move to attain the renunciation of the self distinguishes Christian asceticism.

In the philosophical tradition dominated by Stoicism, *askēsis* means not renunciation but the progressive consideration of self, or mastery over oneself, obtained not through the renunciation of reality but through the acquisition and assimilation of truth. It has as its final aim not preparation for another reality but access to the reality of this world. The Greek word for this is *paraskeuazō* ("to get prepared"). It is a set of practices by which one can acquire, assimilate, and transform truth into a permanent principle of action. *Aletheia* becomes *ethos*. It is a process of becoming more subjective.

What are the principle features of *askēsis*? They include exercises in which the subject puts himself in a situation in which he can verify whether he can confront events and use the discourses with which he is armed. It is a question of testing the preparation. Is this truth assimilated enough to become ethics so that we can behave as we must when an event presents itself?

The Greeks characterized the two poles of those exercises by the terms *meletē* and *gymnasia*. *Meletē* means "meditation," according to the Latin translation, *meditatio*. It has the same root as *epimelēsthai*. It is a rather vague term, a technical term borrowed from rhetoric. *Meletē* is the work one undertook in order to prepare a discourse or an improvisation by thinking over useful terms and arguments. You had to anticipate the real situation through dialogue in your thoughts. The philosophical meditation is this kind of meditation: It is composed of memorizing responses and reactivating those memories by placing oneself in a situation where one can imagine how one would react. One judges the reasoning one should use in an imaginary exercise ("Let us suppose . . .") in order to test an action or event (for example, "How would I react?"). Imagining the articulation of possible events to test how you would react—that's meditation.

The most famous exercise of meditation is the *premeditatio mallorum* as practiced by the Stoics. It is an ethical, imaginary experience. In appearance it's a rather dark and pessimistic vision of the future. You can compare it to what Husserl says about eidetic reduction.

The Stoics developed three eidetic reductions of future misfortune. First, it is not a question of imagining the future as it is likely to turn out but to imagine the worst which can happen, even if there's little chance that it will turn out that way—the worst as certainty, as actualizing what could happen, not as calculation of probability. Second, one shouldn't envisage things as possibly taking place in the distant future but as already actual and in the process of taking place. For example, imagining not that one might be exiled but rather that one is already exiled, subjected to torture, and dying. Third, one does this not in order to experience inarticulate sufferings but in order to convince oneself that they are not real ills. The reduction of all that is possible, of all the duration and of all the misfortunes, reveals not something bad but what we have to accept. It consists of having at the same time the future and the present event. The Epicureans were hostile to it because they thought it was useless. They thought it was better to recollect and memorize past pleasures in order to derive pleasure from present events.

At the opposite pole is *gymnasia* ("to train oneself"). While *meditatio* is an imaginary experience that trains thought, *gymnasia* is training in a real situation, even if it's been artificially induced. There is a long tradition behind this: sexual abstinence, physical privation, and other rituals of purification.

Those practices of abstinence have other meanings than purification or witnessing demonic force, as in Pythagoras and Socrates. In the culture of the Stoics, their function is to establish and test the independence of the individual with regard to the external world. For example, in Plutarch's *De Genio Socratis*, one gives oneself over to very hard sporting activities. Or one tempts oneself by placing oneself in front of many tantalizing dishes and then renouncing these appetizing dishes. Then you call your slaves and give them the dishes, and you take the meal prepared for the slaves. Another example is Seneca's eighteenth letter to Lucilius. He prepares for a great feast day by acts of mortification of the flesh in order to convince himself that poverty is not an evil and that he can endure it.

Between these poles of training in thought and training in reality, *meletē* and *gymnasia*, there are a whole series of intermediate possibilities. Epictetus provides the best example of the middle ground between these poles. He wants to watch perpetually over representations, a technique which culminates in Freud. There are two metaphors important from his point of view: the night watchman, who doesn't admit anyone into town if that person can't prove who he is (we must be "watchman" over the flux of thought), and the money changer, who verifies the authenticity of currency, looks at it,

weighs and verifies it. We have to be money changers of our own representations of our thoughts, vigilantly testing them, verifying them, their metal,
weight, effigy.

The same metaphor of the money changer is found in the Stoics and in
early Christian literature but with different meanings. When Epictetus says
you have to be a money changer, he means as soon as an idea comes to mind
you have to think of the rules you must apply to evaluate it. For John
Cassian, being a money changer and looking at your thoughts means
something very different: It means you must try to decipher if, at the root of
the movement which brings you the representations, there is or is not concupiscence or desire—if your innocent thought has evil origins; if you have
something underlying which is the great seducer, which is perhaps hidden,
the money of your thought.

In Epictetus there are two exercises: sophistic and ethical. The first are
exercises borrowed from school: question-and-answer games. This must be
an ethical game; that is, it must teach a moral lesson. The second are ambula-
tory exercises. In the morning you go for a walk, and you test your reactions
to that walk. The purpose of both exercises is control of representations, not
the deciphering of truth. They are reminders about conforming to the rules
in the face of adversity. A pre-Freudian machine of censorship is described
word for word in the tests of Epictetus and Cassian. For Epictetus, the control of representations means not deciphering but recalling principles of acting and thus seeing, through self-examination, if they govern your life. It is a
kind of permanent self-examination. You have to be your own censor. The
meditation on death is the culmination of all these exercises.

In addition to letters, examination, and *askēsis*, we must now evoke a
fourth technique in the examination of the self, the interpretation of dreams.
It was to have an important destiny in the nineteenth century, but it occupied
a relatively marginal position in the ancient world. Philosophers had an
ambivalent attitude toward the interpretation of dreams. Most Stoics are
critical and skeptical about such interpretation. But there is still the popular
and general practice of it. There were experts who were able to interpret
dreams, including Pythagoras and some of the Stoics, and some experts who
wrote books to teach people to interpret their own dreams. There were huge
amounts of literature on how to do it, but the only surviving dream manual
is *The Interpretation of Dreams* by Artemidorus (second century A.D.).
Dream interpretation was important because in antiquity the meaning of a
dream was an announcement of a future event.

I should mention two other documents dealing with the importance of
dream interpretation for everyday life. The first is by Synesius of Cyrene in
the fourth century A.D. He was well known and cultivated. Even though he
was not a Christian, he asked to be a bishop. His remarks on dreams are
interesting, for public divination was forbidden in order to spare the emperor
bad news. Therefore, one had to interpret one's own dreams; one had to be a

self-interpreter. To do it, one had to remember not only one's own dreams but the events before and after. One had to record what happened every day, both the life of the day and the life of the night.

Aelius Aristides' *Sacred Discourses*, written in the second century, records his dreams and explains how to interpret them. He believed that in the interpretation of dreams we receive advice from the gods about remedies for illness. With this work, we are at the crossing point of two kinds of discourses. It isn't the writing of self's daily activities that is the matrix of the *Sacred Discourses* but the ritual inscription of praises to the gods that have healed one.

V

I wish to examine the scheme of one of the main techniques of the self in early Christianity and what it was as a truth game. To do so, I must look at the transition from pagan to Christian culture in which it is possible to see clear-cut continuities and discontinuities.

Christianity belongs to the salvation religions. It's one of those religions which is supposed to lead the individual from one reality to another, from death to life, from time to eternity. In order to achieve that, Christianity imposed a set of conditions and rules of behavior for a certain transformation of the self.

Christianity is not only a salvation religion, it's a confessional religion. It imposes very strict obligations of truth, dogma, and canon, more so than do the pagan religions. Truth obligations to believe this or that were and are still very numerous. The duty to accept a set of obligations, to hold certain books as permanent truth, to accept authoritarian decisions in matters of truth, not only to believe certain things but to show that one believes, and to accept institutional authority are all characteristic of Christianity.

Christianity requires another form of truth obligation different from faith. Each person has the duty to know who he is, that is, to try to know what is happening inside him, to acknowledge faults, to recognize temptations, to locate desires, and everyone is obliged to disclose these things either to God or to others in the community and hence to bear public or private witness against oneself. The truth obligations of faith and the self are linked together. This link permits a purification of the soul impossible without self-knowledge.

It's not the same in the Catholic as in the Reform tradition. But the main features of both are an ensemble of truth obligations dealing with faith, books, dogma, and one dealing with truth, heart, and soul. Access to truth cannot be conceived of without purity of the soul. Purity of the soul is the consequence of self-knowledge and a condition for understanding the text; in Augustine: *Quis facit veritatem* (to make truth in oneself, to get access to the light).

I'd like to analyze the ways by which, in order to get access to the light, the church conceived of illumination: the disclosure of the self. The sacrament of penance and the confession of sins are rather late innovations. Christians of the first centuries had different forms for discovering and deciphering truth about themselves. One of the two main forms of those disclosures can be characterized by the word *exomologēsis*, or "recognition of fact." Even the Latin fathers used this Greek term with no exact translation. For Christians it meant to recognize publicly the truth of their faith or to recognize publicly that they were Christians.

The word also had a penitential meaning. When a sinner seeks penance, he must visit the bishop and ask for it. In early Christianity, penitence was not an act or a ritual but a status imposed on somebody who had committed very serious sins.

Exomologēsis was a ritual of recognizing oneself as a sinner and penitent. It had several characteristics. First, you were a penitent for four to ten years, and this status affected your life. There was fasting, and there were rules about clothing and prohibitions about sex. The individual was marked so he couldn't live the same life as others. Even after his reconciliation, he suffered from a number of prohibitions; for example, he could not marry or become a priest.

Within this status you find the obligation of *exomologēsis*. The sinner seeks his penance. He visits the bishop and asks the bishop to impose on him the status of a penitent. He must explain why he wants the status, and he has to explain his faults. This was not a confession; it was a condition of the status. Later, in the medieval period, *exomologēsis* became a ritual which took place at the end of the period of penance just before reconciliation. This ceremony placed him among the other Christians. Of this recognition ceremony, Tertullian says that wearing a hair shirt and ashes, wretchedly dressed, the sinner stands humbled before the church. Then he prostrates himself and kisses the brethren's knees (*On Repentance* 9–12). *Exomologēsis* is not a verbal behavior but the dramatic recognition of one's status as a penitent. Much later, in the *Epistles* of Jerome, there is a description of the penitence of Fabiola, a Roman lady. During these days, Fabiola was in the ranks of penitents. People wept with her, lending drama to her public chastisement.

Recognition also designates the entire process that the penitent experiences in this status over the years. He is the aggregate of manifested penitential behavior, of self-punishment as well as of self-revelation. The acts by which he punishes himself are indistinguishable from the acts by which he reveals himself. Self-punishment and the voluntary expression of the self are bound together. This link is evident in many writings. Cyprian, for example, talks of exhibitions of shame and modesty. Penance is not nominal but dramatic.

To prove suffering, to show shame, to make visible humility and exhibit modesty—these are the main features of punishment. Penitence in early

Christianity is a way of life acted out at all times by accepting the obligation to disclose oneself. It must be visibly represented and accompanied by others who recognize the ritual. This approach endured until the fifteenth and sixteenth centuries.

Tertullian uses the term *publicatio sui* to characterize *exomologēsis*. *Publicatio sui* is related to Seneca's daily self-examination, which was, however, completely private. For Seneca, *exomologēsis* or *publicatio sui* doesn't imply verbal analysis of deeds or thoughts; it is only a somatic and symbolic expression. What was private for the Stoics was public for the Christians.

What were its functions? First, this publication was a way to rub out sin and to restore the purity acquired by baptism. Second, it was also to show a sinner as he is. That's the paradox at the heart of *exomologēsis*; it rubs out the sin and yet reveals the sinner. The greater part of the act of penitence was not telling the truth of sin but showing the true sinful being of the sinner. It was not a way for the sinner to explain his sins but a way to present himself as a sinner.

Why should showing forth efface the sins? Exposé is the heart of *exomologēsis*. In the Christianity of the first centuries, Christian authors had recourse to three models to explain the relation between the paradox of rubbing out sins and disclosing oneself.

The first is the medical model: One must show one's wounds in order to be cured. Another model, which was less frequent, was the tribunal model of judgment. One always appeases one's judge by confessing faults. The sinner plays devil's advocate, as will the devil on the Day of Judgment.

The most important model used to explain *exomologēsis* was the model of death, of torture, or of martyrdom. The theories and practices of penance were elaborated around the problem of the man who prefers to die rather than to compromise or abandon the faith. The way the martyr faces death is the model for the penitent. For the relapsed to be reintegrated into the church, he must expose himself voluntarily to ritual martyrdom. Penance is the affect of change, of rupture with self, past, and world. It's a way to show that you are able to renounce life and self, to show that you can face and accept death. Penitence of sin doesn't have as its target the establishing of an identity but serves instead to mark the refusal of the self, the breaking away from self: *Ego non sum, ego*. This formula is at the heart of *publicatio sui*. It represents a break with one's past identity. These ostentatious gestures have the function of showing the truth of the state of being of the sinner. Self-revelation is at the same time self-destruction.

The difference between the Stoic and Christian traditions is that in the Stoic tradition examination of self, judgment, and discipline show the way to self-knowledge by superimposing truth about self through memory, that is, by memorizing the rules. In *exomologēsis*, the penitent superimposes truth about self by violent rupture and dissociation. It is important to emphasize that this *exomologēsis* is not verbal. It is symbolic, ritual, and theatrical.

VI

During the fourth century we find a very different technology for the disclosure of the self, *exagoreusis*, much less famous than *exomologēsis* but more important. This one is reminiscent of the verbalizing exercises in relation to a teacher/master of the pagan philosophical schools. We can see the transfer of several Stoic technologies of the self to Christian spiritual techniques.

At least one example of self-examination, proposed by John Chrysostom, was exactly the same form and the same administrative character as that described by Seneca in *De Ira*. In the morning we must take account of our expenses, and in the evening we must ask ourselves to render account of our conduct of ourselves, to examine what is to our advantage and what is prejudicial against us, with prayers instead of indiscreet words. That is exactly the Senecan style of self-examination. It's also important to note that this self-examination is rare in Christian literature.

The well-developed and elaborated practice of the self-examination in monastic Christianity is different from the Senecan self-examination and very different from Chrysostom and from *exomologēsis*. This new kind of practice must be understood from the point of view of two principles of Christian spirituality: obedience and contemplation.

In Seneca, the relationship of the disciple with the master was important, but it was instrumental and professional. It was founded on the capacity of the master to lead the disciple to a happy and autonomous life through good advice. The relationship would end when the disciple got access to that life.

For a long series of reasons, obedience has a very different character in monastic life. It differs from the Greco-Roman type of relation to the master in the sense that obedience isn't based just upon a need for self-improvement but must bear on all aspects of a monk's life. There is no element in the life of the monk which may escape from this fundamental and permanent relation of total obedience to the master. John Cassian repeats an old principle from the oriental tradition: "Everything the monk does without permission of his master constitutes a theft." Here obedience is complete control of behavior by the master, not a final autonomous state. It is a sacrifice of the self, of the subject's own will. This is the new technology of the self.

The monk must have the permission of his director to do anything, even die. Everything he does without permission is stealing. There is not a single moment when the monk can be autonomous. Even when he becomes a director himself, he must retain the spirit of obedience. He must keep the spirit of obedience as a permanent sacrifice of the complete control of behavior by the master. The self must constitute self through obedience.

The second feature of monastic life is that contemplation is considered the supreme good. It is the obligation of the monk to turn his thoughts continuously to that point which is God and to make sure that his heart is pure enough to see God. The goal is permanent contemplation of God.

The technology of the self, which developed from obedience and contemplation in the monastery, presents some peculiar characteristics. Cassian gives a rather clear exposition of this technology of the self, a principle of self-examination which he borrowed from the Syrian and Egyptian monastic traditions.

This technology of self-examination of Oriental origins, dominated by obedience and contemplation, is much more concerned with thought than with action. Seneca had placed his stress on action. With Cassian the object is not past actions of the day; it's the present thoughts. Since the monk must continuously turn his thoughts toward God, he must scrutinize the actual course of this thought. This scrutiny thus has as its object the permanent discrimination between thoughts which lead toward God and those which don't. This continual concern with the present is different from the Senecan memorization of deeds and their correspondence with rules. It is what the Greeks referred to with a pejorative word: *logismoi* ("cogitations, reasoning, calculating thought").

There is an etymology of *logismoi* in Cassian, but I don't know if it's sound: *co-agitationes*. The spirit is *polukinetos*, "perpetually moving" (*First Conference of Abbot Serenus* 4). In Cassian, perpetual mobility of spirit is the spirit's weakness. It distracts one from contemplation of God (*First Conference of Abbot Nesterus* 13).

The scrutiny of conscience consists of trying to immobilize consciousness, to eliminate movements of the spirit that divert one from God. That means we have to examine any thought which presents itself to consciousness to see the relation between act and thought, truth and reality, to see if there is anything in this thought which will move our spirit, provoke our desire, turn our spirit away from God. The scrutiny is based on the idea of a secret concupiscence.

There are three major types of self-examination: first, self-examination with respect to thoughts in correspondence to reality (Cartesian); second, self-examination with respect to the way our thoughts relate to rules (Senecan), third, the examination of self with respect to the relation between the hidden thought and an inner impurity. At this moment begins the Christian hermeneutics of the self with its deciphering of inner thoughts. It implies that there is something hidden in ourselves and that we are always in a self-illusion which hides the secret.

In order to make this kind of scrutiny, Cassian says we have to care for ourselves, to attest to our thoughts directly. He gives three analogies. First is the analogy of the mill (*First Conference of Abbot Moses* 18). Thoughts are like grains, and consciousness is the mill store. It is our role as the miller to sort out amongst the grains those which are bad and those which can be admitted to the mill store to give the good flour and good bread of our salvation.

Second, Cassian makes military analogies (*First Conference of Abbot Serenus* 5). He uses an analogy of the officer who orders the good soldiers to march to the right, the bad to the left. We must act like officers who divide soldiers into two files, the good and the bad.

Third, he uses the analogy of a money changer (*First Conference of Abbot Moses* 20–22). Conscience is the money changer of the self. It must examine coins, their effigy, their metal, where they came from. It must weigh them to see if they have been ill used. As there is the image of the emperor on money, so must the image of God be on our thoughts. We must verify the quality of the thought: This effigy of God, is it real? What is its degree of purity? Is it mixed with desire or concupiscence? Thus, we find the same image as in Seneca, but with a different meaning.

Since we have as our role to be a permanent money changer of ourselves, how is it possible to make this discrimination and recognize if a thought is of good quality? How can this "discrimination" actively be done? There is only one way: to tell all thoughts to our director, to be obedient to our master in all things, to engage in the permanent verbalization of all our thoughts. In Cassian, self-examination is subordinated to obedience and the permanent verbalization of thoughts. Neither is true of Stoicism. By telling himself not only his thoughts but also the smallest movements of consciousness, his intentions, the monk stands in a hermeneutic relation not only to the master but to himself. This verbalization is the touchstone or the money of thought.

Why is confession able to assume this hermeneutical role? How can we be the hermeneuts of ourselves in speaking and transcribing all of our thoughts? Confession permits the master to know because of his greater experience and wisdom and therefore to give better advice. Even if the master, in his role as a discriminating power, doesn't say anything, the fact that the thought has been expressed will have an effect of discrimination.

Cassian gives an example of the monk who stole bread. At first he can't tell. The difference between good and evil thoughts is that evil thoughts can't be expressed without difficulty, for evil is hidden and unstated. Because evil thoughts cannot be expressed without difficulty and shame, the cosmological difference between light and dark, between verbalization and sin, secrecy and silence, between God and the devil, may not emerge. Then the monk prostrates himself and confesses. Only when he confesses verbally does the devil go out of him. The verbal expression is the crucial moment (*Second Conference of Abbot Moses* II). Confession is a mark of truth. This idea of the permanent verbal is only an ideal. It is never completely possible. But the price of the permanent verbal was to make everything that couldn't be expressed into a sin.

In conclusion, in the Christianity of the first centuries, there are two main forms of disclosing self, of showing the truth about oneself. The first is *exomologēsis*, or a dramatic expression of the situation of the penitent as sinner which makes manifest his status as sinner. The second is what was called in the spiritual literature *exagoreusis*. This is an analytical and continual verbalization of thoughts carried on in the relation of complete obedience to someone else. This relation is modeled on the renunciation of one's own will and of one's own self.

There is a great difference between *exomologēsis* and *exagoreusis*; yet we have to underscore the fact that there is one important element in common: You cannot disclose without renouncing. *Exomologēsis* had as its model martyrdom. In *exomologeusis*, the sinner had to "kill" himself through ascetic macerations. Whether through martyrdom or through obedience to a master, disclosure of self is the renunciation of one's own self. In *exagorēsis*, on the other hand, you show that, in permanently verbalizing your thoughts and permanently obeying the master, you are renouncing your will and yourself. This practice continues from the beginning of Christianity to the seventeenth century. The inauguration of penance in the thirteenth century is an important step in its rise.

This theme of self-renunciation is very important. Throughout Christianity there is a correlation between disclosure of the self, dramatic or verbalized, and the renunciation of self. My hypothesis from looking at these two techniques is that it's the second one, verbalization, which becomes the more important. From the eighteenth century to the present, the techniques of verbalization have been reinserted in a different context by the so-called human sciences in order to use them without renunciation of the self but to constitute, positively, a new self. To use these techniques without renouncing oneself constitutes a decisive break.

8

THIS SEX WHICH IS NOT ONE

Luce Irigaray

Source: L. Irigaray, *This Sex Which is Not One*, Ithaca, NY: Cornell University Press, 1988, pp. 23–33.

Female sexuality has always been conceptualized on the basis of masculine parameters. Thus the opposition between "masculine" clitoral activity and "feminine" vaginal passivity, an opposition which Freud—and many others— saw as stages, or alternatives, in the development of a sexually "normal" woman, seems rather too clearly required by the practice of male sexuality. For the clitoris is conceived as a little penis pleasant to masturbate so long as castration anxiety does not exist (for the boy child), and the vagina is valued for the "lodging" it offers the male organ when the forbidden hand has to find a replacement for pleasure-giving.

In these terms, woman's erogenous zones never amount to anything but a clitoris-sex that is not comparable to the noble phallic organ, or a hole-envelope that serves to sheathe and massage the penis in intercourse: a non-sex, or a masculine organ turned back upon itself, self-embracing.

About woman and her pleasure, this view of the sexual relation has nothing to say. Her lot is that of "lack," "atrophy" (of the sexual organ), and "penis envy," the penis being the only sexual organ of recognized value. Thus she attempts by every means available to appropriate that organ for herself: through her somewhat servile love of the father-husband capable of giving her one, through her desire for a child-penis, preferably a boy, through access to the cultural values still reserved by right to males alone and therefore always masculine, and so on. Woman lives her own desire only as the expectation that she may at last come to possess an equivalent of the male organ.

Yet all this appears quite foreign to her own pleasure, unless it remains within the dominant phallic economy. Thus, for example, woman's autoeroticism is very different from man's. In order to touch himself, man needs an instrument: his hand, a woman's body, language ... And this self-caressing requires at least a minimum of activity. As for woman, she touches herself in and of herself without any need for mediation, and before there is any way to distinguish activity from passivity. Woman "touches herself" all the time, and moreover no one can forbid her to do so, for her genitals are formed of two lips in continuous contact. Thus, within herself, she is already two—but not divisible into one(s)—that caress each other.

This autoeroticism is disrupted by a violent break-in: the brutal separation of the two lips by a violating penis, an intrusion that distracts and deflects the woman from this "self-caressing" she needs if she is not to incur the disappearance of her own pleasure in sexual relations. If the vagina is to serve *also*, but *not only*, to take over for the little boy's hand in order to assure an articulation between autoeroticism and heteroeroticism in intercourse (the encounter with the totally other always signifying death), how, in the classic representation of sexuality, can the perpetuation of autoeroticism for woman be managed? Will woman not be left with the impossible alternative between a defensive virginity, fiercely turned in upon itself, and a body open to penetration that no longer knows, in this "hole" that constitutes its sex, the pleasure of its own touch? The more or less exclusive—and highly anxious—attention paid to erection in Western sexuality proves to what extent the imaginary that governs it is foreign to the feminine. For the most part, this sexuality offers nothing but imperatives dictated by male rivalry: the "strongest" being the one who has the best "hard-on," the longest, the biggest, the stiffest penis, or even the one who "pees the farthest" (as in little boys' contests). Or else one finds imperatives dictated by the enactment of sadomasochistic fantasies, these in turn governed by man's relation to his mother: the desire to force entry, to penetrate, to appropriate for himself the mystery of this womb where he has been conceived, the secret of his begetting, of his "origin." Desire/need, also to make blood flow again in order to revive a very old relationship—intrauterine, to be sure, but also prehistoric—to the maternal.

Woman, in this sexual imaginary, is only a more or less obliging prop for the enactment of man's fantasies. That she may find pleasure there in that role, by proxy, is possible, even certain. But such pleasure is above all a masochistic prostitution of her body to a desire that is not her own, and it leaves her in a familiar state of dependency upon man. Not knowing what she wants, ready for anything, even asking for more, so long as he will "take" her as his "object" when he seeks his own pleasure. Thus she will not say what she herself wants; moreover, she does not know, or no longer knows, what she wants. As Freud admits, the beginnings of the sexual life of a girl child are so "obscure," so "faded with time," that one would have to dig down very deep indeed to discover beneath the traces of this civilization, of this history, the vestiges of a more archaic civilization that might give some clue to woman's sexuality. That extremely ancient civilization would undoubtedly have a different alphabet, a different language ... Woman's desire would not be expected to speak the same language as man's; woman's desire has doubtless been submerged by the logic that has dominated the West since the time of the Greeks.

Within this logic, the predominance of the visual, and of the discrimination and individualization of form, is particularly foreign to female eroticism. Woman takes pleasure more from touching than from looking, and her entry into a dominant scopic economy signifies, again, her consignment to passivity: she is to be the beautiful object of contemplation. While her body finds itself thus eroticized, and called to a double movement of exhibition and of chaste retreat in order to stimulate the drives of the "subject," her sexual organ represents *the horror of nothing to see*. A defect in this systematics of representation and desire. A "hole" in its scoptophilic lens. It is already evident in Greek statuary that this nothing-to-see has to be excluded, rejected, from such a scene of representation. Woman's genitals are simply absent, masked, sewn back up inside their "crack."

This organ which has nothing to show for itself also lacks a form of its own. And if woman takes pleasure precisely from this incompleteness of form which allows her organ to touch itself over and over again, indefinitely, by itself, that pleasure is denied by a civilization that privileges phallomorphism. The value granted to the only definable form excludes the one that is in play in female autoeroticism. The *one* of form, of the individual, of the (male) sexual organ, of the proper name, of the proper meaning . . . supplants, while separating and dividing, that contact of *at least two* (lips) which keeps woman in touch with herself, but without any possibility of distinguishing what is touching from what is touched.

Whence the mystery that woman represents in a culture claiming to count everything, to number everything by units, to inventory everything as individualities. *She is neither one nor two.* Rigorously speaking, she cannot be identified either as one person, or as two. She resists all adequate definition. Further, she has no "proper" name. And her sexual organ, which is not *one* organ, is counted as *none*. The negative, the underside, the reverse of the only visible and morphologically designatable organ (even if the passage from erection to detumescence does pose some problems): the penis.

But the "thickness" of that "form," the layering of its volume, its expansions and contractions and even the spacing of the moments in which it produces itself as form—all this the feminine keeps secret. Without knowing it. And if woman is asked to sustain, to revive, man's desire, the request neglects to spell out what it implies as to the value of her own desire. A desire of which she is not aware, moreover, at least not explicitly. But one whose force and continuity are capable of nurturing repeatedly and at length all the masquerades of "feminity" that are expected of her.

It is true that she still has the child, in relation to whom her appetite for touch, for contact, has free rein, unless it is already lost, alienated by the taboo against touching of a highly obsessive civilization. Otherwise her pleasure will find, in the child, compensations for and diversions from the frustrations that she too often encounters in sexual relations per se. Thus maternity fills the gaps in a repressed female sexuality. Perhaps man and woman no longer caress each other except through that mediation between them that the child—preferably a boy—represents? Man, identified with his son, rediscovers the pleasure of maternal fondling; woman touches herself again by caressing that part of her body: her baby-penis-clitoris.

What this entails for the amorous trio is well known. But the Oedipal interdiction seems to be a somewhat categorical and factitious law—although it does provide the means for perpetuating the authoritarian discourse of fathers—when it is promulgated in a culture in which sexual relations are impracticable because man's desire and woman's are strangers to each other. And in which the two desires have to try to meet through indirect means, whether the archaic one of a sense-relation to the mother's body, or the present one of active or passive extension of the law of the father. These are regressive emotional behaviors, exchanges of words too detached from the sexual arena not to constitute an exile with respect to it: "mother" and "father" dominate the interactions of the couple, but as social roles. The division of labor prevents them from making love. They produce or reproduce. Without quite knowing how to use their leisure. Such little as they have, such little indeed as they wish to have. For what are they to do with leisure? What substitute for amorous resource are they to invent? Still . . .

Perhaps it is time to return to that repressed entity, the female imaginary. So woman does not have a sex organ? She has at least two of them, but they are not identifiable as ones. Indeed, she has many more. Her sexuality, always at least double, goes even further: it is *plural*. Is this the way culture is seeking to characterize itself now? Is this the way texts write themselves/are written now? Without quite knowing what censorship they are evading? Indeed, woman's pleasure does not have to choose between clitoral activity and vaginal passivity, for example. The pleasure of the vaginal caress does not have to be substituted for that of the clitoral caress. They each contribute, irreplaceably, to woman's pleasure. Among other caresses . . . Fondling the breasts, touching the vulva, spreading the lips, stroking the posterior wall of the vagina, brushing against the mouth of the uterus, and so on. To evoke only a few of the most specifically female pleasures. Pleasures which are somewhat misunderstood in sexual difference as it is imagined—or not imagined, the other sex being only the indispensable complement to the only sex.

But *woman has sex organs more or less everywhere*. She finds pleasure almost anywhere. Even if we refrain from invoking the hystericization of her entire body, the geography of her pleasure is far more diversified, more multiple in its differences, more complex, more subtle, than is commonly imagined—in an imaginary rather too narrowly focused on sameness.

"She" is indefinitely other in herself. This is doubtless why she is said to be whimsical, incomprehensible, agitated, capricious . . . not to mention her language, in which "she" sets off in all directions leaving "him" unable to discern the coherence of any meaning. Hers are contradictory words, somewhat mad from the standpoint of reason, inaudible for whoever listens to them with ready-made grids, with a fully elaborated code in hand. For in what she says, too, at least when she dares, woman is constantly touching herself. She steps ever so slightly aside from herself with a murmur, an exclamation, a whisper, a sentence left unfinished . . . When she returns, it is to set off again from elsewhere. From another point of pleasure, or of pain. One would have to listen with another ear, as if hearing *an "other meaning" always in the process of weaving itself, of embracing itself with words, but also of getting rid of words in order not to become fixed, congealed in them.* For if "she" says something, it is not, it is already no longer, identical with what she means. What she says is never identical with anything, moreover; rather, it is contiguous. *It touches (upon)*. And when it strays too far from that proximity, she breaks off and starts over at "zero": her body-sex.

It is useless, then, to trap women in the exact definition of what they mean, to make them repeat (themselves) so that it will be clear; they are already elsewhere in that discursive machinery where you expected to surprise them. They have returned within themselves. Which must not be understood in the same way as within yourself. They do not have the interiority that you have, the one you perhaps suppose they have. Within themselves means *within the intimacy of that silent, multiple, diffuse touch*. And if you ask them insistently what they are thinking about, they can only reply: Nothing. Everything.

Thus what they desire is precisely nothing, and at the same time everything. Always something more and something else besides that *one*—sexual organ, for example—that you give them, attribute to them. Their desire is often interpreted, and feared, as a sort of insatiable hunger, a voracity that will swallow you whole. Whereas it really involves a different economy more than anything else, one that upsets the linearity of a project, undermines the goal-object of a desire, diffuses the polarization toward a single pleasure, disconcerts fidelity to a single discourse . . .

Must this multiplicity of female desire and female language be understood as shards, scattered remnants of a violated sexuality? A sexuality denied? The question has no simple answer. The rejection, the exclusion of a female imaginary certainly puts woman in the position of experiencing herself only fragmentarily, in the little-structured margins of a dominant ideology, as waste, or excess, what is left of a mirror invested by the (masculine) "subject" to reflect himself, to copy himself. Moreover, the role of "femininity" is prescribed by this masculine specula(riza)tion and corresponds scarcely at all to woman's desire, which may be recovered only in secret, in hiding, with anxiety and guilt.

But if the female imaginary were to deploy itself, if it could bring itself into play otherwise than as scraps, uncollected debris, would it represent itself, even so, in the form of *one* universe? Would it even be volume instead of surface? No. Not unless it were understood, yet again, as a privileging of the maternal over the feminine. Of a phallic maternal, at that. Closed in upon the jealous possession of its valued product. Rivaling man in his esteem for productive excess. In such a race for power, woman loses the uniqueness of her pleasure. By closing herself off as volume, she renounces the pleasure that she gets from the *nonsuture of her lips:* she is undoubtedly a mother, but a virgin mother; the role was assigned to her by mythologies long ago. Granting her a certain social power to the extent that she is reduced, with her own complicity, to sexual impotence.

(Re-)discovering herself, for a woman, thus could only signify the possibility of sacrificing no one of her pleasures to another, of identifying herself with none of them in particular, *of never being simply one.* A sort of expanding universe to which no limits could be fixed and which would not be incoherence nonetheless—nor that polymorphous perversion of the child in which the erogenous zones would lie waiting to be regrouped under the primacy of the phallus.

Woman always remains several, but she is kept from dispersion because the other is already within her and is autoerotically familiar to her. Which is not to say that she appropriates the other for herself, that she reduces it to her own property. Ownership and property are doubtless quite foreign to the feminine. At least sexually. But not *nearness.* Nearness so pronounced that it makes all discrimination of identity, and thus all forms of property, impossible. Woman derives pleasure from what is *so near that she cannot have it, nor have herself.* She herself enters into a ceaseless exchange of herself with the other without any possibility of identifying either. This puts into question all prevailing economies: their calculations are irremediably stymied by woman's pleasure, as it increases indefinitely from its passage in and through the other.

However, in order for woman to reach the place where she takes pleasure as woman, a long detour by way of the analysis of the various systems of oppression brought to bear upon her is assuredly necessary. And claiming to fall back on the single solution of pleasure risks making her miss the process of going back through a social practice that *her* enjoyment requires.

For woman is traditionally a use-value for man, an exchange value among men; in other words, a commodity. As such, she remains the guardian of material substance, whose price will be established, in terms of the standard of their work and of their need/desire, by "subjects": workers, merchants, consumers. Women are marked phallically by their fathers, husbands, procurers. And this branding determines their value in sexual commerce. Woman is never anything but the locus of a more or less competitive exchange between two men, including the competition for the possession of mother earth.

How can this object of transaction claim a right to pleasure without removing her/itself from established commerce? With respect to other merchandise in the marketplace, how could this commodity maintain a relationship other than one of aggressive jealousy? How could material substance enjoy her/itself without provoking the consumer's anxiety over the disappearance of his nurturing ground? How could that exchange—which can in no way be defined in terms "proper" to woman's desire—appear as anything but a pure mirage, mere foolishness, all too readily obscured by a more sensible discourse and by a system of apparently more tangible values?

A woman's development, however radical it may seek to be, would thus not suffice to liberate woman's desire. And to date no political theory or political practice has resolved, or sufficiently taken into consideration, this historical problem, even though Marxism has proclaimed its importance. But women do not constitute, strictly speaking, a class, and their dispersion among several classes makes their political struggle complex, their demands sometimes contradictory.

There remains, however, the condition of underdevelopment arising from women's submission by and to a culture that oppresses them, uses them, makes of them a medium of exchange, with very little profit to them. Except in the quasi monopolies of masochistic pleasure, the domestic labor force, and reproduction. The powers of slaves? Which are not negligible powers, moreover. For where pleasure is concerned, the master is not necessarily well served. Thus to reverse the relation, especially in the economy of sexuality, does not seem a desirable objective.

But if women are to preserve and expand their autoeroticism, their homosexuality, might not the renunciation of heterosexual pleasure correspond once again to that disconnection from power that is traditionally theirs? Would it not involve a new prison, a new cloister, built of their own accord? For women to undertake tactical strikes, to keep themselves apart from men long enough to learn to defend their desire, especially through speech, to discover the love of other women while sheltered from men's imperious choices that put them in the position of rival commodities, to forge for themselves a social status that compels recognition, to earn their living in order to escape from the condition of prostitute . . . these are certainly indispensable stages in the escape from their proletarization on the exchange market. But if their aim were simply to reverse the order of things, even supposing this to be possible, history would repeat itself in the long run, would revert to sameness: to phallocratism. It would leave room neither for women's sexuality, nor for women's imaginary, nor for women's language to take (their) place.

Note

This text was originally published as "Ce sexe qui n'en est pas un," in *Cahiers du Grif*, no. 5.

9

BODIES THAT MATTER

Judith Butler

Source: J. Butler, *Bodies That Matter: on the discursive limits of "sex"*, London and New York: Routledge, 1993, pp. 27–55.

If I understand deconstruction, deconstruction is not an exposure of error, certainly not other people's error. The critique in deconstruction, the most serious critique in deconstruction, is the critique of something that is extremely useful, something without which we cannot do anything.

> —Gayatri Chakravorty Spivak, "In a Word,"
> interview with Ellen Rooney

... the necessity of "reopening" the figures of philosophical discourse ... One way is to interrogate the conditions under which systematicity itself is possible: what the coherence of the discursive utterance conceals of the conditions under which it is produced, whatever it may say about these conditions in discourse. For example the "matter" from which the speaking subject draws nourishment in order to produce itself, to reproduce itself; the *scenography* that makes representation feasible, representation as defined in philosophy, that is, the architectonics of its theatre, its framing in space-time, its geometric organization, its props, its actors, their respective positions, their dialogues, indeed their tragic relations, without overlooking the *mirror*, most often hidden, that allows the logos, the subject, to reduplicate itself, to reflect itself by itself. All these are interventions on the scene; they ensure its coherence so long as they remain uninterpreted. Thus they have to be reenacted, in each figure of discourse away from its mooring in the value of "presence." For each philosopher, beginning with those whose names define some age in the history of philosophy, we have to point out how the break with material contiguity is made (il faut repérer comment s'opère la coupure d'avec la contiguité materielle), how the system is put together, how the specular economy works.

> —Luce Irigaray, "The Power of Discourse"

Within some quarters of feminist theory in recent years, there have been calls to retrieve the body from what is often characterized as the linguistic idealism of poststructuralism. In another quarter, philosopher Gianni Vattimo has argued that poststructuralism, understood as textual play, marks the dissolution of *matter* as a contemporary category. And it is this lost matter, he argues, which must now be reformulated in order for poststructuralism to give way to a project of greater ethical and political value.[1] The terms of these debates are difficult and unstable ones, for it is difficult to know in either case who or what is designated by the term "poststructuralism," and perhaps even more difficult to know what to retrieve under the sign of "the body." And yet these two signifiers have for some feminists and critical theorists seemed fundamentally antagonistic. One hears warnings like the following: If everything is discourse, what happens to the body? If everything is a text, what about violence and bodily injury? Does anything *matter* in or for poststructuralism?

It has seemed to many, I think, that in order for feminism to proceed as a critical practice, it must ground itself in the sexed specificity of the female body. Even as the category of sex is always reinscribed as gender, that sex must still be presumed as the irreducible point of departure for the various cultural constructions it has come to bear. And this presumption of the material irreducibility of sex has seemed to ground and to authorize feminist epistemologies and ethics, as well as gendered analyses of various kinds. In an effort to displace the terms of this debate, I want to ask how and why "materiality" has become a sign of irreducibility, that is, how is it that the materiality of sex is understood as that which only bears cultural constructions and, therefore, cannot be a construction? What is the status of this exclusion? Is materiality a site or surface that is excluded from the process of construction, as that through which and on which construction works? Is this perhaps an enabling or constitutive exclusion, one without which construction cannot operate? What occupies this site of unconstructed materiality? And what kinds of constructions are foreclosed through the figuring of this site as outside or beneath construction itself?

In what follows, what is at stake is less a theory of cultural construction than a consideration of the scenography and topography of construction. This scenography is orchestrated by and as a matrix of power that remains disarticulated if we presume constructedness and materiality as necessarily oppositional notions.

In the place of materiality, one might inquire into other foundationalist premises that operate as political "irreducibles." Instead of rehearsing the theoretical difficulties that emerge by presuming the notion of the subject as a foundational premise or by trying to maintain a stable distinction between sex and gender, I would like to raise the question of whether recourse to matter and to the materiality of sex is necessary in order to establish that irreducible specificity that is said to ground feminist practice. And here the question is not whether or not there ought to be reference to matter, just as the question never has been whether or not there ought to be speaking about women. This speaking will occur, and for feminist reasons, it must; the category of women does not become useless through deconstruction, but becomes one whose uses are no longer reified as "referents," and which stand a chance of being opened up, indeed, of coming to signify in ways that none of us can predict in advance. Surely, it must be possible both to use the term, to use it tactically even as one is, as it were, used and positioned by it, and also to subject the term to a critique which interrogates the exclusionary operations and differential power-relations that construct and delimit feminist invocations of "women." This is, to paraphrase the citation from Spivak above, the critique of something useful, the critique of something we cannot do without. Indeed, I would argue that it is a critique without which feminism loses its democratizing potential through refusing to engage—take stock of, and become transformed by—the exclusions which put it into play.

Something similar is at work with the concept of materiality, which may well be "something without which we cannot do anything." What does it mean to have recourse to materiality, since it is clear from the start that matter has a history (indeed, more than one) and that the history of matter is in part determined by the negotiation of sexual difference. We may seek to return to matter as prior to discourse to ground our claims about sexual difference only to discover that matter is fully sedimented with discourses on sex and sexuality that prefigure and constrain the uses to which that term can be put. Moreover, we may seek recourse to matter in order to ground or to verify a set of injuries or violations only to find that *matter itself is founded through a set of violations*, ones which are unwittingly repeated in the contemporary invocation.

Indeed, if it can be shown that in its constitutive history this "irreducible" materiality is constructed through a problematic gendered matrix, then the discursive practice by which matter is rendered irreducible simultaneously ontologizes and fixes that gendered matrix in its place. And if the constituted effect of that matrix is taken to be the indisputable ground of bodily life, then it seems that a genealogy of that matrix is foreclosed from critical inquiry. Against the claim that poststructuralism reduces all materiality to linguistic stuff, an argument is needed to show that to deconstruct matter is not to negate or do away with the usefulness of the term. And against those who would claim that the body's irreducible materiality is a necessary precondition for feminist practice, I suggest that that prized materiality may well be constituted through an exclusion and degradation of the feminine that is profoundly problematic for feminism.

Here it is of course necessary to state quite plainly that the options for theory are not exhausted by *presuming* materiality, on the one hand, and *negating* materiality, on the other. It is my purpose to do precisely neither of these. To call a presupposition into question is not the same as doing away with it; rather, it is to free it from its metaphysical lodgings in order to understand what political interests were secured in and by that metaphysical placing, and thereby to permit the term to occupy and to serve very different political aims. To problematize the matter of bodies may entail an initial loss of epistemological certainty, but a loss of certainty is not the same as political nihilism. On the contrary, such a loss may well indicate a significant and promising shift in political thinking. This unsettling of "matter" can be understood as initiating new possibilities, new ways for bodies to matter.

The body posited as prior to the sign, is always *posited* or *signified* as *prior*. This signification produces as an *effect* of its own procedure the very body that it nevertheless and simultaneously claims to discover as that which *precedes* its own action. If the body signified as prior to signification is an effect of signification, then the mimetic or representational status of language, which claims that signs follow bodies as their necessary mirrors, is not mimetic at all. On the contrary, it is productive, constitutive, one might even argue *performative*, inasmuch as this signifying act delimits and contours the body that it then claims to find prior to any and all signification.[2]

This is not to say that the materiality of bodies is simply and only a linguistic effect which is reducible to a set of signifiers. Such a distinction overlooks the materiality of the signifier itself. Such an account also fails to understand materiality as that which is bound up with signification from the start; to think through the indissolubility of materiality and signification is no easy matter. To posit by way of language a materiality outside of language is still to posit that materiality, and the materiality so posited will retain that positing as its constitutive condition. Derrida negotiates the question of matter's radical alterity with the following remark: "I am not even sure that there can be a 'concept' of an absolute exterior."[3] To have the concept of matter is to lose the exteriority that the concept is supposed to secure. Can language simply refer to materiality, or is language also the very condition under which materiality may be said to appear?

If matter ceases to be matter once it becomes a concept, and if a concept of matter's exteriority to language is always something less than absolute, what is the status of this "outside"? Is it produced by philosophical discourse in order to effect the appearance of its own exhaustive and coherent systematicity? What is cast out from philosophical propriety in order to sustain and secure that borders of philosophy? And how might this repudiation return?

Matters of femininity

The classical association of femininity with materiality can be traced to a set of etymologies which link matter with *mater* and *matrix* (or the womb) and, hence, with a problematic of reproduction. The classical configuration of matter as a site of *generation* or *origination* becomes especially significant when the account of what an object is and means requires recourse to its originating principle. When not explicitly associated with reproduction, matter is generalized as a principle of origination and causality. In Greek, *hyle* is the wood or timber out of which various cultural constructions are made, but also a principle of origin, development, and teleology which is at once causal and explanatory. This link between matter, origin, and significance suggests the indissolubility of classical Greek notions of materiality and signification. That which matters about an object is its matter.[4]

In both the Latin and the Greek, matter (*materia* and *hyle*) is neither a simple, brute positivity or referent nor a blank surface or slate awaiting an external signification, but is always in some sense temporalized. This is true for Marx as well, when "matter" is understood as a principle of *transformation*, presuming and inducing a future.[5] The matrix is an originating and formative principle which inaugurates and informs a development of some organism or object. Hence, for Aristotle, "matter is potentiality [*dynameos*], form actuality."[6] In reproduction, women are said to contribute the matter; men, the form.[7] The Greek *hyle* is wood that already has been cut from trees, instrumentalized and instrumentalizable, artifactual, on the way to being put to use. *Materia* in Latin denotes the stuff out of which things are made, not only the timber for houses and ships but whatever serves as nourishment for infants: nutrients that act as extensions of the mother's body. Insofar as matter appears in these cases to be invested with a certain capacity to originate and to compose that for which it also supplies the principle of intelligibility, then matter is clearly defined by a certain power of creation and rationality that is for the most part divested from the more modern empirical deployments of the term. To speak within these classical contexts of *bodies that matter* is not an idle pun, for to be material means to materialize, where the principle of that materialization is precisely what "matters" about that body, its very intelligibility. In this sense, to know the significance of something is to know how and why it matters, where "to matter" means at once "to materialize" and "to mean."

Obviously, no feminist would encourage a simple return to Aristotle's natural teleologies in order to rethink the "materiality" of bodies. I want to consider, however, Aristotle's distinction between body and soul to effect a brief comparison between Aristotle and Foucault in order to suggest a possible contemporary redeployment of Aristotelian terminology. At the end of this brief comparison, I will offer a limited criticism of Foucault, which will then lead to a longer discussion of Irigaray's deconstruction of materiality in Plato's *Timaeus*. It is in the context of this second analysis that I hope to make clear how a gendered matrix is at work in the constitution of materiality (although it is obviously present in Aristotle as well), and why feminists ought to be interested, not in taking materiality as an irreducible, but in conducting a critical genealogy of its formulation.

143

Aristotle/Foucault

For Aristotle the soul designates the actualization of matter, where matter is understood as fully potential and unactualized. As a result, he maintains in *de Anima* that the soul is "the first grade of actuality of a naturally organized body." He continues, "That is why we can wholly dismiss as unnecessary the question whether the soul and the body are one: it is as meaningless to ask whether the wax and the shape given to it by the stamp are one, or generally the matter [*hyle*] of a thing and that of which it is the matter [*hyle*]."[8] In the Greek, there is no reference to "stamps," but the phrase, "the shape given by the stamp" is contained in the single term, "*schema.*" *Schema* means form, shape, figure, appearance, dress, gesture, figure of a syllogism, and grammatical form. If matter never appears without its *schema*, that means that it only appears under a certain grammatical form and that the principle of its recognizability, its characteristic gesture or usual dress, is indissoluble from what constitutes its matter.

In Aristotle, we find no clear phenomenal distinction between materiality and intelligibility, and yet for other reasons Aristotle does not supply us with the kind of "body" that feminism seeks to retrieve. To install the principle of intelligibility in the very development of a body is precisely the strategy of a natural teleology that accounts for female development through the rationale of biology. On this basis, it has been argued that women ought to perform certain social functions and not others, indeed, that women ought to be fully restricted to the reproductive domain.

We might historicize the Aristotelian notion of the *schema* in terms of culturally variable principles of formativity and intelligibility. To understand the *schema* of bodies as a historically contingent nexus of power/discourse is to arrive at something similar to what Foucault describes in *Discipline and Punish* as the "materialization" of the prisoner's body. This process of materialization is at stake as well in the final chapter of the first volume of *The History of Sexuality* when Foucault calls for a "history of bodies" that would inquire into "the manner in which what is most material and vital in them has been invested."[9]

At times it appears that for Foucault the body has a materiality that is ontologically distinct from the power relations that take that body as a site of investments. And yet, in *Discipline and Punish*, we have a different configuration of the relation between materiality and investment. There the soul is taken as an instrument of power through which the body is cultivated and formed. In a sense, it acts as a power-laden schema that produces and actualizes the body itself.

We can understand Foucault's references to the "soul" as an implicit reworking of the Aristotelian formulation. Foucault argues in *Discipline and Punish* that the "soul" becomes a normative and normalizing ideal according to which the body is trained, shaped, cultivated, and invested; it is an historically specific imaginary ideal (*idéal speculatif*) under which the body is effectively materialized. Considering the science of prison reform, Foucault writes, "The man described for us, whom we are invited to free, is already in himself the effect of a subjection [*assujettissement*] much more profound than himself. A 'soul' inhabits him and brings him to existence, which is itself a factor in the mastery that power exercises over the body. The soul is the effect and instrument of a political anatomy; the soul is the prison of the body."[10]

This "subjection," or *assujettissement*, is not only a subordination but a securing and maintaining, a putting into place of a subject, a subjectivation. The "soul brings [the prisoner] to existence"; and not fully unlike Aristotle, the soul described by Foucault as an instrument of power, forms and frames the body, stamps it, and in stamping it, brings it into being. Here "being" belongs in quotation marks, for ontological weight is not presumed, but always conferred. For Foucault, this conferral can take place only within and by an operation of power. This operation produces the subjects that it subjects; that is, it subjects them in and through the compulsory power relations effective as their formative principle. But power is that which forms, maintains, sustains, and regulates bodies at once, so that, strictly speaking, power is not a subject who acts on bodies as its distinct objects. The grammar which compels us to speak that way enforces a metaphysics of external relations, whereby power acts on bodies but is not understood to form them. This is a view of power as an external relation that Foucault himself calls into question.

Power operates for Foucault in the *constitution* of the very materiality of the subject, in the principle which simultaneously forms and regulates the "subject" of subjectivation. Foucault refers not only to the materiality of the body of the prisoner but to the materiality of the body of the prison. The materiality of the prison, he writes, is established to the extent that [*dans la mesure où*] it is a vector and instrument of power.[11] Hence, the prison is *materialized* to the extent that it is *invested with power*; or, to be grammatically accurate, there is no prison prior to its materialization. Its materialization is coextensive with its investiture with power relations, and materiality is the effect and gauge of this investment. The prison comes to be only within the field of power relations, but more specifically, only to the extent that it is invested or saturated with such relations, that such a saturation is itself formative of its very being. Here the body is not an independent materiality that is invested by power relations external to it, but it is that for which materialization and investiture are coextensive.

"Materiality" designates a certain effect of power or, rather, *is* power in its formative or constituting effects. Insofar as power operates successfully by constituting an object domain, a field of intelligibility, as a taken-for-granted ontology, its material effects are taken as material data or primary givens. These material positivities appear *outside* discourse and power, as its incontestable referents, its transcendental signifieds. But this appearance is precisely the moment in which the power/discourse regime is most fully dissimulated and most insidiously effective. When this material effect is taken as an epistemological point of departure, a *sine qua non* of some political argumentation, this is a move of empiricist foundationalism that, in accepting this constituted effect as a primary given, successfully buries and masks the genealogy of power relations by which it is constituted.[12]

Insofar as Foucault traces the process of materialization as an investiture of discourse and power, he focuses on that dimension of power that is productive and formative. But we need to ask what constrains the domain of what is materializable, and whether there are *modalities* of materialization—as Aristotle suggests, and Althusser is quick to cite.[13] To what extent is materialization governed by principles of intelligibility that require and institute a domain of radical *unintelligibility* that resists materialization altogether or that remains radically dematerialized? Does Foucault's effort to work the notions of discourse and materiality through one another fail to account for not only what is *excluded* from the economies of discursive intelligibility that he describes, but what *has to be excluded* for those economies to function as self-sustaining systems?

This is the question implicitly raised by Luce Irigaray's analysis of the form/matter distinction in Plato. This argument is perhaps best known from the essay "Plato's Hystera," in *Speculum of the Other Woman*, but is trenchantly articulated as well in the less well-known essay, "Une Mère de Glace," also in *Speculum*.

Irigaray's task is to reconcile neither the form/matter distinction nor the distinctions between bodies and souls or matter and meaning. Rather, her effort is to show that those binary oppositions are formulated through the exclusion of a field of disruptive possibilities. Her speculative thesis is that those binaries, even in their reconciled mode, are part of a phallogocentric economy that produces the "feminine" as its constitutive outside. Irigaray's intervention in the history of the form/matter distinction underscores "matter" as the site at which the feminine is excluded from philosophical binaries. Inasmuch as certain phantasmatic notions of the feminine are traditionally associated with materiality, these are specular effects which confirm a phallogocentric project of autogenesis. And when those specular (and spectral) feminine figures are taken to be the feminine, the feminine is, she argues, fully erased by its very representation. The economy that claims to include the feminine as the subordinate term in a binary opposition of masculine/feminine excludes the feminine, produces the feminine as that which must be excluded for that economy to operate. In what follows, I will consider first Irigaray's speculative mode of engaging with philosophical texts and then turn to her rude and provocative reading of Plato's discussion of the receptacle in the *Timaeus*. In the final section of this essay, I will offer my own rude and provocative reading of the same passage.

Irigaray/Plato

The largeness and speculative character of Irigaray's claims have always put me a bit on edge, and I confess in advance that although I can think of no feminist who has read and reread the history of philosophy with the kind of detailed and critical attention that she has,[14] her terms tend to mime the grandiosity of the philosophical errors that she underscores. This miming is, of course, tactical, and her reenactment of philosophical error requires that we learn how to read her for the difference that her reading performs. Does the voice of the philosophical father echo in her, or has she occupied that voice, insinuated herself into the voice of the father? If she is "in" that voice for either reason, is she also at the same time "outside" it? How do we understand the being "between," the two possibilities as something other than a spatialized *entre* that leaves the phallogocentric binary opposition intact?[15] How does the difference from the philosophical father resound in the mime which appears to replicate his strategy so faithfully? This is, clearly, no place between "his" language and "hers," but only a disruptive *movement* which unsettles the topographical claim.[16] This is a taking of his place, not to assume it, but to show that it is *occupiable*, to raise the question of the cost and movement of that assumption.[17] Where and how is the critical departure from that patrilineage performed in the course of the recitation of his terms? If the task is not a loyal or proper "reading" of Plato, then perhaps it is a kind of overreading which mimes and exposes the speculative excess in Plato. To the extent that I replicate that speculative excess here, I apologize, but only half-heartedly, for sometimes a hyperbolic rejoinder is necessary when a given injury has remained unspoken for too long.

When Irigaray sets out to reread the history of philosophy, she asks how its borders are secured: what must be excluded from the domain of philosophy for philosophy itself to proceed, and how is it that the excluded comes to constitute negatively a philosophical enterprise that takes itself to be self-grounding and self-constituting? Irigaray then isolates the feminine as precisely this constitutive exclusion, whereupon she is compelled to find a way of reading a philosophical text for what it refuses to include. This is no easy matter. For how can one read a text for what does *not* appear within its own terms, but which nevertheless constitutes the illegible conditions of its own legibility? Indeed, how can one read a text for the movement of that disappearing by which the textual "inside" and "outside" are constituted?

Although feminist philosophers have traditionally sought to show how the body is figured as feminine, or how women have been associated with materiality (whether inert—always already dead—or fecund—ever-living and procreative) where men have been associated with the principle of rational mastery,[18] Irigaray wants to argue that in fact the feminine is precisely what is excluded in and by such a binary opposition. In this sense, when and where women are represented within this economy is precisely the site of their erasure. Moreover, when matter is described within philosophical descriptions, she argues, it is at once a substitution for and displacement of the feminine. One cannot interpret the philosophical relation to the feminine through the figures that philosophy provides, but, rather, she argues, through siting the feminine as the unspeakable condition of figuration, as that which, in fact, can *never be* figured within the terms of philosophy proper, but whose exclusion from that propriety is its enabling condition.

No wonder then that the feminine appears for Irigaray only in *catachresis*, that is, in those figures that function improperly, as an improper transfer of sense, the use of a proper name to describe that which does not properly belong to it, and that return to haunt and coopt the very language from which the feminine is excluded. This explains in part the radical citational practice of Irigaray, the catachrestic usurpation of the "proper" for fully improper purposes.[19] For she mimes philosophy—as well as psychoanalysis—and, in the mime, takes on a language that effectively cannot belong to her, only to call into question the exclusionary rules of proprietariness that govern the use of that discourse. This contestation of propriety and property is precisely the option open to the feminine when it has been constituted as an excluded impropriety, as the improper, the propertyless. Indeed, as Irigaray argues in *Marine Lover* [*Amante marine*], her work on Nietzsche, "woman neither is nor has an essence," and this is the case for her precisely because "woman" is what is excluded from the discourse of metaphysics.[20] If she takes on a proper name, even the proper name of "woman" in the singular, that can only be a kind of radical mime that seeks to jar the term from its ontological presuppositions. Jane Gallop makes this brilliantly clear in her reading of the two lips as both synecdoche and catachresis, a reading which offers an interpretation of Irigaray's language of biological essentialism as rhetorical strategy. Gallop shows that Irigaray's figural language constitutes the feminine in language as a persistent linguistic impropriety.[21]

This exclusion of the feminine from the proprietary discourse of metaphysics takes place, Irigaray argues, in and through the formulation of "matter." Inasmuch as a distinction between form and matter is offered within phallogocentrism, it is articulated through a further materiality. In other words, every explicit distinction takes place in an inscriptional space that the distinction itself cannot accommodate. Matter as a *site* of inscription cannot be explicitly thematized. And this inscriptional site or space is, for Irigaray, a *materiality* that is not the same as the category of "matter" whose articulation it conditions and enables. It is this unthematizable materiality that Irigaray claims becomes the site, the repository, indeed, the receptacle of and for the feminine *within* a phallogocentric economy. In an important sense, this second inarticulate "matter" designates the constitutive outside of the Platonic economy; it is what must be excluded for that economy to posture as internally coherent.[22]

This excessive matter that cannot be contained within the form/matter distinction operates like the supplement in Derrida's analysis of philosophical oppositions. In Derrida's consideration of the form/matter distinction in *Positions*, he suggests as well that matter must be redoubled, at once as a pole within a binary opposition, and as that which exceeds that binary coupling, as a figure for its nonsystematizability.

Consider Derrida's remark in response to the critic who wants to claim that matter denotes the radical outside to language: "It follows that if, and in the extent to which, *matter* in this general economy designates, as you said, radical alterity (I will specify: in relation to philosophical oppositions), then what I write can be considered 'materialist.'"[23] For both Derrida and Irigaray, it seems, what is excluded from this binary is also *produced* by it in the mode of exclusion and has no separable or fully independent existence as an absolute outside. A constitutive or relative outside is, of course, composed of a set of exclusions that are nevertheless *internal* to that system as its own nonthematizable necessity. It emerges within the system as incoherence, disruption, a threat to its own systematicity.

Irigaray insists that this exclusion that mobilizes the form/matter binary is the differentiating relation between masculine and feminine, where the masculine occupies both terms of binary opposition, and the feminine cannot be said to be an intelligible term at all. We might understand the feminine figured within the binary as the *specular* feminine and the feminine which is erased and excluded from that binary as the *excessive* feminine. And yet, such nominations cannot work, for in the latter mode, the feminine, strictly speaking, cannot be named at all and, indeed, is not a mode.

For Irigaray, the "feminine" which cannot be said to *be* anything, to participate in ontology at all, is—and here grammar fails us—set under erasure as the impossible necessity that enables any ontology. The feminine, to use a catachresis, is domesticated and rendered unintelligible within a phallogocentrism that claims to be self-constituting. Disavowed, the remnant of the feminine survives as the *inscriptional space* of that phallogocentrism, the specular surface which receives the marks of a masculine signifying act only to give back a (false) reflection and guarantee of phallogocentric self-sufficiency, without making any contribution of its own. As a topos of the metaphysical tradition, this inscriptional space makes its appearance in Plato's *Timaeus* as the receptacle (*hypodoche*), which is also described as the *chora*. Although extensive readings of the *chora* have been offered by Derrida and Irigaray, I want to refer here to only one passage which is about the very problem of passage: namely, that passage by which a form can be said to generate its own sensible representation. We know that for Plato any material object comes into being only through participating in a Form which is its necessary precondition. As a result, material objects are copies of Forms and exist only to the extent that they instantiate Forms. And yet, where does this instantiation take place? Is there a place, a site, where this reproduction occurs, a medium through which the transformation from form to sensible object occurs?

In the cosmogony offered in the *Timaeus*, Plato refers to three natures that must be taken into account: the first, which is the process of generation; the second, that in which the generation takes place; and the third, that of which the thing generated is a resemblance naturally produced. Then, in what appears to be an aside, we may "liken the receiving principle to a mother, and the source or spring to a father, and the intermediate nature to a child" (50d).[24] Prior to this passage, Plato refers to this receiving principle as a "nurse" (40b) and then as "the universal nature which receives all bodies," according to the Hamilton/Cairns translation. But this latter phrase might be better translated as "the dynamic nature (*physis*) that receives (*dechesthai*) all the bodies that there are (*ta panta somata*)" (50b).[25] Of this all-receiving function, Plato argues, she "must always be called the same, for inasmuch as she always receives all things, she never departs at all from her own nature (*dynamis*) and never, in any way or at any time, assumes a form (*eilephen*) like that of any of the things which enter into her . . . the forms that enter into and go out of her are the likenesses of eternal realities modeled after their own patterns (*diaschematizomenon*) . . ." (50c).[26] Here her proper function is to receive, *dechesthai*, to take, accept, welcome, include, and even comprehend. What enters into this *hypodoche* is a set of forms or, better, shapes (*morphe*), and yet this receiving principle, this *physis*, has no proper shape and is not a body. Like Aristotle's *hyle*, *physis* cannot be defined.[27] In effect, the receiving principle potentially includes all bodies, and so applies universally, but its universal applicability must not resemble at all, ever, those eternal realities (*eidos*) which in the *Timaeus* prefigure universal forms, and which pass into the receptacle. There is here a prohibition on resemblance (*mimeta*), which is to say that this nature cannot be said to be like either the eternal Forms or their material, sensible, or imaginary copies. But in particular, this *physis* is only to be entered, but never to enter. Here the term *eisienai* denotes a going toward or into, an approach and penetration; it also denotes going into a *place*, so that the *chora*, as an enclosure, cannot be that which enters into another enclosure; metaphorically, and perhaps coincidentally, this prohibited form of entry also means "being brought into court", i.e., subject to public norms, and "coming into mind" or "beginning to think."

Here there is also the stipulation not "to assume a form like those that enter her." Can this receptacle, then, be likened to any body, to that of the mother, or to the nurse? According to Plato's own stipulation, we cannot define this "nature," and to know it by analogy is to know it only by "bastard thinking." In this sense the human who would know this nature is dispossessed of/by the paternal principle, a son out of wedlock, a deviation from patrilineality and the analogical relation by which patronymic lineage proceeds. Hence, to offer a metaphor or analogy presupposes a likeness between that nature and a human form. It is this last point that Derrida,

150

accepting Plato's dictum, takes as salient to the understanding of the *chora*, arguing that it can never be collapsed into any of the figures that it itself occasions. As a result, Derrida argues, it would be wrong to take the association of the chora with femininity as a decisive collapse.[28]

In a sense, Irigaray agrees with this contention: the figures of the nurse, the mother, the womb cannot be fully identified with the receptacle, for those are specular figures which displace the feminine at the moment they purport to represent the feminine. The receptacle cannot be exhaustively thematized or figured in Plato's text, precisely because it is that which conditions and escapes every figuration and thematization. *This receptacle/nurse is not a metaphor based on likeness to a human form, but a disfiguration that emerges at the boundaries of the human both as its very condition and as the insistent threat of its deformation; it cannot take a form, a morphe, and in that sense, cannot be a body.*

Insofar as Derrida argues that the receptacle cannot be identified with the figure of the feminine, Irigaray would seem to be in agreement. But she takes the analysis a step further, arguing that the feminine exceeds its figuration, just as the receptacle does, and that this unthematizability constitutes the feminine as the impossible yet necessary foundation of what can be thematized and figured. Significantly, Julia Kristeva *accepts* this collapse of the *chora* and the maternal/nurse figure, arguing in *Revolution in Poetic Language* that "Plato leads us" to this "process . . . [of] rhythmic space."[29] In contrast with Irigaray's refusal of this conflation of the *chora* and the feminine/maternal, Kristeva affirms this association and further asserts her notion of the semiotic as that which "precedes" (26) the symbolic law: "The mother's body is therefore what mediates the symbolic law organizing social relations and becomes the ordering principle of the semiotic *chora*"(27).

Whereas Kristeva insists upon this identification of the *chora* with the maternal body, Irigaray asks how the discourse which performs that conflation invariably produces an "outside" where the feminine which is *not* captured by the figure of the *chora* persists. Here we need to ask, How is this assignation of a feminine "outside" possible within language? And is it not the case that there is within any discourse and thus within Irigaray's as well, a set of constitutive exclusions that are inevitably produced by the circumscription of the feminine as that which monopolizes the sphere of exclusion?

In this sense, the receptacle is not simply a figure *for* the excluded, but, taken as a figure, stands for the excluded and thus performs or enacts yet another set of exclusions of all that remains unfigurable under the sign of the feminine—that in the feminine which resists the figure of the nurse-receptacle. In other words, taken as a figure, the nurse-receptacle freezes the feminine as that which is necessary for the reproduction of the human, but which itself is not human, and which is in no way to be construed as the formative principle of the human form that is, as it were, produced through it.[30]

The problem is not that the feminine is made to stand for matter or for universality; rather, the feminine is cast outside the form/matter and universal/ particular binarisms. She will be neither the one nor the other, but the permanent and unchangeable condition of both—what can be construed as a nonthematizable materiality.[31] She will be entered, and will give forth a further instance of what enters her, but she will never resemble either the formative principle or that which it creates. Irigaray insists that here it is the female power of reproduction that is taken over by the phallogocentric economy and remade into its own exclusive and essential action. When *physis* is articulated as *chora*, as it is in Plato, some of the dynamism and potency included in the meaning of *physis* is suppressed. In the place of a femininity that makes a contribution to reproduction; we have a phallic Form that reproduces only and always further versions of itself, and does this through the feminine, but with no assistance from her. Significantly, this transfer of the reproductive function from the feminine to the masculine entails the topographical suppression of *physis*, the dissimulation of *physis* as *chora*, as place.

The word matter does not occur in Plato to describe this *chora* or *hypodoche*, and yet Aristotle remarks in *The Metaphysics* that this section of the *Timaeus* articulates most closely his own notion of *hyle*. Taking up this suggestion, Plotinus wrote the Sixth Tractate of the *Enneads*, "The Impassivity of the Unembodied," an effort to account for Plato's notion of the *hypodoche* as *hyle* or matter.[32] In a twist that the history of philosophy has perhaps rarely undergone, Irigaray accepts and recites Plotinus's effort to read Plato through Aristotelian "matter" in "Une Mère de Glace."

In that essay, she writes that for Plato matter is "sterile," "female in receptivity only, not in pregnancy . . . castrated of that impregnating power which belongs only to the unchangeably masculine."[33] Her reading establishes the cosmogony of the Forms in the *Timaeus* as a phallic phantasy of a fully self-constituted patrilineality, and this fantasy of autogenesis or self-constitution is effected through a denial and cooptation of the female capacity for reproduction. Of course, the "she" who is the "receptacle" is neither a universal nor a particular, and because for Plato anything that can be named is either a universal or a particular, the receptacle cannot be named. Taking speculative license, and wandering into what he himself calls "a strange and unwonted inquiry" (48d), Plato nevertheless proceeds to name what cannot be properly named, invoking a catachresis in order to describe the receptacle as a universal receiver of bodies even as it cannot be a universal, for, if it were, it would participate in those eternal realities from which it is excluded.

In the cosmogony prior to the one which introduces the receptacle, Plato suggests that if the appetites, those tokens of the soul's materiality, are not successfully mastered, a soul, understood as a man's soul, risks coming back as a woman, and then as a beast. In a sense woman and beast are the very figures for unmasterable passion. And if a soul participates in such passions, it will be effectively and ontologically transformed by them and into the very

152

signs, woman and beast, by which they are figured. In this prior cosmogony, woman represents a descent into materiality.

But this prior cosmogony calls to be rewritten, for if man is at the top of an ontological hierarchy, and woman is a poor or debased copy of man, and beast is a poor or debased copy of both woman and of man, then there is still a *resemblance* between these three beings, even as that resemblance is hierarchically distributed. In the following cosmogony, the one that introduces the receptacle, Plato clearly wants to disallow the possibility of a resemblance between the masculine and the feminine, and he does this through introducing a feminized receptacle that is prohibited from resembling any form. Of course, strictly speaking, the receptacle can have no ontological status, for ontology is constituted by forms, and the receptacle cannot be one. And we cannot speak about that for which there is no ontological determination, or if we do, we use language improperly, imputing being to that which can have no being. So, the receptacle seems from the start to be an impossible word, a designation that cannot be designated. Paradoxically, Plato proceeds to tell us that this very receptacle must always be called the same.[34] Precisely because this receptacle can only occasion a radically improper speech, that is, a speech in which all ontological claims are suspended, the terms by which it is named must be consistently applied, not in order to make the name fit the thing named but precisely because that which is to be named can have no proper name, bounds and threatens the sphere of linguistic propriety, and, therefore, must be controlled by a forcibly imposed set of nominative rules.

How is it that Plato can concede the undesignatable status of this receptacle and prescribe for it a consistent name? Is it that the receptacle, designated as the undesignatable, *cannot* be designated, or is it rather that this "cannot" functions as an "ought not to be"? Should this limit to what is representable be read as a prohibition against a certain kind of representation? And since Plato does offer us a representation of the receptacle, one that he claims ought to remain a singularly authoritative representation (and makes this offer in the very same passage in which he claims its radical unrepresentability), ought we not to conclude that Plato, in authorizing a single representation of the feminine, means to prohibit the very proliferation of nominative possibilities that the undesignatable might produce? Perhaps this is a representation within discourse that functions to prohibit from discourse any further representation, one which represents the feminine as unrepresentable and unintelligible, but which in the rhetoric of the constative claim defeats itself. After all, Plato *posits* that which he claims cannot be *posited*. And he further contradicts himself when he claims that that which cannot be posited ought to be posited in only one way. In a sense, this authoritative naming of the receptacle as the unnameable constitutes a primary or founding inscription that secures this place as an inscriptional space. This naming of what cannot be named is itself a penetration into this receptacle which is at once a violent erasure, one which establishes it as an impossible yet necessary site for all further inscriptions.[35] In this sense, the very *telling* of the story about the phallomorphic genesis of objects *enacts* that phallomorphosis and becomes an allegory of its own procedure.

Irigaray's response to this exclusion of the feminine from the economy of representation is effectively to say, Fine, I don't want to be in your economy anyway, and I'll show you what this unintelligible receptacle can do to your system; I will not be a poor copy in your system, but I will resemble you nevertheless by *miming* the textual passages through which you construct your system and showing that what cannot enter it is already inside it (as its necessary outside), and I will mime and repeat the gestures of your operation until this emergence of the outside within the system calls into question its systematic closure and its pretension to be self-grounding.

This is part of what Naomi Schor means when she claims that Irigaray mimes mimesis itself.[36] Through miming, Irigaray transgresses the prohibition against resemblance at the same time that she refuses the notion of resemblance as copy. She cites Plato again and again, but the citations expose precisely what is excluded from them, and seek to show and to reintroduce the excluded into the system itself. In this sense, she performs a repetition and displacement of the phallic economy. *This is citation, not as enslavement or simple reiteration of the original, but as an insubordination that appears to take place within the very terms of the original, and which calls into question the power of origination that Plato appears to claim for himself.* Her miming has the effect of repeating the origin only to displace that origin *as* an origin.

And insofar as the Platonic account of the origin is itself a *displacement* of a maternal origin, Irigaray merely mimes that very act of displacement, displacing the displacement, showing that origin to be an "effect" of a certain ruse of phallogocentric power. In line with this reading of Irigaray, then, the feminine as maternal does not offer itself as an alternative origin. For if the feminine is said to be anywhere or anything, it is that which is produced through displacement and which returns as the possibility of a reverse-displacement. Indeed, one might reconsider the conventional characterization of Irigaray as an uncritical maternalist, for here it appears that the reinscription of the maternal takes place by writing with and through the language of phallic philosophemes. This textual practice is not grounded in a rival ontology, but inhabits—indeed, penetrates, occupies, and redeploys—the paternal language itself.

One might well ask whether this kind of penetrative textual strategy does not suggest a different textualization of eroticism than the rigorously anti-penetrative eros of surfaces that appears in Irigaray's "When Our Lips Speak Together": "You are not *in me*. I do not contain you or retain you in my stomach, my arms, my head. Nor in my memory, my mind, my language. You are there, like my skin."[37] The refusal of an eroticism of entry and containment seems linked for Irigaray with an opposition to appropriation and possession as forms of erotic exchange. And yet the kind of reading that Irigaray performs requires not only that she enter the text she reads, but that she work the inadvertent uses of that containment, especially when the feminine is sustained as an internal gap or fissure in the philosophical system itself. In such appropriative readings, Irigaray appears to enact the very spectre of a penetration in reverse—or a penetration elsewhere—that Plato's economy seeks to foreclose ("the 'elsewhere' of feminine pleasure can be found only at the price of *crossing back* (*retraversée*) through the mirror that subtends all speculation"[38]). At the level of rhetoric this "crossing back" constitutes an eroticism that critically mimes the phallus—an eroticism structured by repetition and displacement, penetration and exposure—that counters the eros of surfaces that Irigaray explicitly affirms.

The opening quotation of Irigaray's essay claims that philosophical systems are built on "a break with material contiguity," and that the concept of matter constitutes and conceals that rupture or cut (*la coupure*). This argument appears to presume some order of contiguity that is prior to the concept, prior to matter, and which matter works to conceal. In Irigaray's most systematic reading of the history of ethical philosophy, *Éthique de la différence sexuelle*, she argues that ethical relations ought to be based on relations of closeness, proximity, and intimacy that reconfigure conventional notions of reciprocity and respect. Traditional conceptions of reciprocity exchange such relations of intimacy for those characterized by violent erasure, substitutability, and appropriation.[39] Psychoanalytically, that material closeness is understood as the uncertain separation of boundaries between maternal body and infant, relations that reemerge in language as the metonymic proximity of signs. Insofar as concepts, like matter and form, repudiate and conceal the metonymic signifying chains from which they are composed, they serve the phallogocentric purpose of breaking with that maternal/material contiguity. On the other hand, that contiguity confounds the phallogocentric effort to set up a series of substitutions through metaphorical equivalences or conceptual unities.[40]

This contiguity that exceeds the concept of matter is, according to Margaret Whitford, not itself a natural relation, but a *symbolic* articulation proper to women. Whitford takes "the two lips" as a figure for metonymy,[41] "a figure for the vertical and horizontal relationships between women . . . women's sociality".[42] But Whitford also points out that feminine and masculine economies are never fully separable; as a result, it seems, relations of contiguity subsist *between* those economies and, hence, do not belong exclusively to the sphere of the feminine.

How, then, do we understand Irigaray's textual practice of lining up alongside Plato? To what extent does she repeat his text, not to augment its specular production, but to cross back over and through that specular mirror to a feminine "elsewhere" that must remain problematically within citation marks?

There is for Irigaray, always, a matter that exceeds matter, where the latter is disavowed for the autogenetic form/matter coupling to thrive. Matter occurs in two modalities: first, as a metaphysical concept that serves a phallogocentrism; second, as an ungrounded figure, worrisomely speculative and catachrestic, that marks for her the possible linguistic site of a critical mime.

> To play with mimesis is thus, for a woman, to try to recover the place of her exploitation by discourse, without allowing herself to be simply reduced to it. It means to resubmit herself—inasmuch as she is on the side of the "perceptible," of "matter"—to "ideas," in particular to ideas about herself, that are elaborated in/by a masculine logic, but so as to make "visible," by an effect of playful repetition, what was supposed to remain invisible: the cover up of a possible operation of the feminine in language.[43]

So perhaps here is the return of essentialism, in the notion of a "feminine in language"? And yet, she continues by suggesting that *miming* is that very operation of the feminine in language. To mime means to participate in precisely that which is mimed, and if the language mime is the language of phallogocentrism, then this is only a specifically feminine language to the extent that the feminine is radically implicated in the very terms of a phallogocentrism it seeks to rework. The quotation continues, "[to play with mimesis means] 'to unveil' the fact that, if women are such good mimics, it is because they are not simply resorbed in this function. *They also remain elsewhere*: another case of the persistence of 'matter' . . ." They mime phallogocentrism, but they also expose what is covered over by the mimetic self-replication of that discourse. For Irigaray, what is broken with and covered over is the linguistic operation of metonymy, a closeness and proximity which appears to be the linguistic residue of the initial proximity of mother and infant. It is this metonymic excess in every mime, indeed, in every metaphorical substitution, that is understood to disrupt the seamless repetition of the phallogocentric norm.

To claim, though, as Irigaray does, that the logic of identity is potentially disruptible by the insurgence of metonymy, and then to identify this metonymy with the repressed and insurgent feminine is to consolidate the place of the feminine in and as the irruptive chora, that which cannot be figured, but which is necessary for any figuration. That is, of course, to figure that chora nevertheless, and in such a way that the feminine is "always" the outside, and the outside is "always" the feminine. This is a move that at once positions the feminine as the unthematizable, the non-figurable, but which, in identifying the feminine with that position, thematizes and figures, and so makes use of the phallogocentric exercise to produce this identity which "is" the non-identical.

There are good reasons, however, to reject the notion that the feminine monopolizes the sphere of the excluded here. Indeed, to enforce such a monopoly redoubles the effect of foreclosure performed by the phallogocentric discourse itself, one which "mimes" its founding violence in a way that works against the explicit claim to have found a linguistic site in metonymy that works as disruption. After all, Plato's scenography of intelligibility depends on the exclusion of women, slaves, children, and animals, where slaves are characterized as those who do not speak his language, and who, in not speaking his language, are considered diminished in their capacity for reason. This xenophobic exclusion operates through the production of racialized Others, and those whose "natures" are considered less rational by virtue of their appointed task in the process of laboring to reproduce the conditions of private life. This domain of the less than rational human bounds the figure of human reason, producing that "man" as one who is without a childhood; is not a primate and so is relieved of the necessity of eating, defecating, living and dying; one who is not a slave, but always a property holder; one whose language remains originary and untranslatable. This is a figure of disembodiment, but one which is nevertheless a figure of a body, a bodying forth of a masculinized rationality, the figure of a male body which is not a body, a figure in crisis, a figure that enacts a crisis it cannot fully control. This figuration of masculine reason as disembodied body is one whose imaginary morphology is crafted through the exclusion of other possible bodies. This is a materialization of reason which operates through the dematerialization of other bodies, for the feminine, strictly speaking, has no morphe, no morphology, no contour, for it is that which contributes to the contouring of things, but is itself undifferentiated, without boundary. The body that is reason dematerializes the bodies that may not properly stand for reason or its replicas, and yet this is a figure in crisis, for this body of reason is itself the phantasmatic dematerialization of masculinity, one which requires that women and slaves, children and animals be the body, perform the bodily functions, that it will not perform.[44]

Irigaray does not always help matters here, for she fails to follow through the metonymic link between women and these other Others, idealizing and appropriating the "elsewhere" as the feminine. But what is the "elsewhere" of Irigaray's "elsewhere"? If the feminine is not the only or primary kind of being that is excluded from the economy of masculinist reason, what and who is excluded in the course of Irigaray's analysis?

Improper entry: protocols of sexual difference

The above analysis has considered not the materiality of sex, but the sex of materiality. In other words, it has traced materiality as the site at which a certain drama of sexual difference plays itself out. The point of such an exposition is not only to warn against an easy return to the *materiality* of the body or the materiality of sex, but to show that to invoke matter is to invoke a sedimented history of sexual hierarchy and sexual erasures which should surely be an *object* of feminist inquiry, but which would be quite problematic as a *ground* of feminist theory. To return to matter requires that we return to matter as a *sign* which in its redoublings and contradictions enacts an inchoate drama of sexual difference.

Let us then return to the passage in the *Timaeus* in which matter redoubles itself as a proper and improper term, differentially sexed, thereby conceding itself as a site of ambivalence, as a body which is no body, in its masculine form, as a matter which is no body, in its feminine.

The receptacle, she, "always receives all things, she never departs at all from her own nature and, never, in any way or any time, assumes a form like that of any of the things that enter into her" (50b). What appears to be prohibited here is partially contained by the verb *eliephen*—to assume, as in to assume a form—which is at once a continuous action, but also a kind of receptivity. The term means, among other possibilities, to gain or procure, to take, to receive hospitality, but also *to have a wife*, and *of a woman to conceive*.[45] The term suggests a procurement, but also both a capacity to conceive and to take a wife. These activities or endowments are prohibited in the passage above, thus setting limits on the kinds of "receptivity" that this receiving principle can undertake. The term for what she is never to do (i.e., "depart from her own nature") is *existhathai dynameos*. This implies that she ought never to arise out of, become separated from, or be *displaced from* her own nature; as that which is contained in itself, she is that which, quite literally, ought not to be *disordered in displacement*. The *siempre*, the "never," and the "in no way" are insistent repetitions that give this "natural impossibility" the form of an imperative, a prohibition, a legislation and allocation of proper place. What would happen if she began to resemble that which is said only and always to enter into her? Clearly, a set of positions is being secured here through the exclusive allocation of penetration to the form, and penetrability to a feminized materiality, and a full dissociation of this figure of penetrable femininity from the being resulting from reproduction.[46]

Irigaray clearly reads the "assume a form/shape" in this passage as "to conceive," and understands Plato to be prohibiting the feminine from contributing to the process of reproduction in order to credit the masculine with giving birth. But it seems that we might consider another sense of "to assume" in Greek, namely, "to have or take a wife."[47] For she will never resemble—and so never enter into—another materiality. This means that he—remember the Forms are likened to the father in this triad—will never be entered by her or, in fact, by anything. For he is the impenetrable penetrator, and she, the invariably penetrated. And "he" would not be differentiated from her were it not for this prohibition on resemblance which establishes their positions as mutually exclusive and yet complementary. In fact, if she were to penetrate in return, or penetrate elsewhere, it is unclear whether she could remain a "she" and whether "he" could preserve his own differentially established identity. For the logic of non-contradiction that conditions this distribution of pronouns is one which establishes the "he" through this exclusive position as penetrator and the "she" through this exclusive position as penetrated. As a consequence, then, without this heterosexual *matrix*, as it were, it appears that the stability of these gendered positions would be called into question.

One might read this prohibition that secures the impenetrability of the masculine as a kind of panic, a panic over becoming "like" her, effeminized, or a panic over what might happen if a masculine penetration of the masculine were authorized, or a feminine penetration of the feminine, or a feminine penetration of the masculine or a reversibility of those positions—not to mention a full-scale confusion over what qualifies as "penetration" anyway. Would the terms "masculine" and "feminine" still signify in stable ways, or would the relaxing of the taboos against stray penetration destabilize these gendered positions in serious ways? If it were possible to have a relation of penetration between two ostensibly feminine gendered positions, would this be the kind of resemblance that must be prohibited in order for Western metaphysics to get going? And would that be considered something like a cooptation and displacement of phallic autonomy that would undermine the phallic assurance over its own exclusive rights?

Is this a reverse mime that Irigaray does not consider, but which is nevertheless compatible with her strategy of a critical mime? Can we read this taboo that mobilizes the speculative and phantasmatic beginnings of Western metaphysics in terms of the spectre of sexual exchange that it produces through its own prohibition, as a panic over the lesbian or, perhaps more specifically, over the phallicization of the lesbian? Or would this kind of resemblance so disturb the compulsory gendered matrix that supports the order of things that one could not claim that these sexual exchanges that occur outside or in the interstices of the phallic economy are simply "copies" of the heterosexual origin? For clearly, this legislation of a particular version of heterosexuality attests full well to its non-originary status. Otherwise there would be no necessity to install a prohibition at the outset against rival possibilities for the organization of sexuality. In this sense, those improper resemblances or imitations that Plato rules out of the domain of intelligibility do not resemble the masculine, for that would be to privilege the masculine as origin. If a resemblance is possible, it is because the "originality" of the masculine is contestable; in other words, the miming of the masculine, which is never resorbed into it, can expose the masculine's claim to originality as suspect. Insofar as the masculine is founded here through a prohibition which outlaws the spectre of a lesbian resemblance, that masculinist institution—and the phallogocentric homophobia it encodes—is *not* an origin, but only the *effect* of that very prohibition, fundamentally dependent on that which it must exclude.[48]

Significantly, this prohibition emerges at the site where materiality is being installed as a double instance, as the copy of the Form, and as the non-contributing materiality in which and through which that self-copying mechanism works. In this sense, matter is either part of the specular scenography of phallic inscription or that which cannot be rendered intelligible within its terms. The very formulation of matter takes place in the service of an organization and denial of sexual difference, so that we are confronted with an economy of sexual difference as that which defines, instrumentalizes, and allocates matter in its own service.

The regulation of sexuality at work in the articulation of the Forms suggests that sexual difference operates in the very formulation of matter. But this is a matter that is defined not only against reason, where reason is understood as that which acts on and through a countervailing materiality, and masculine and feminine occupy these oppositional positions. Sexual difference also operates in the formulation, the staging, of what will occupy the site of inscriptional space, that is, as what must remain outside these oppositional positions as their supporting condition. There is no singular outside, for the Forms require a number of exclusions; they are and replicate themselves through what they exclude, through not being the animal, not being the woman, not being the slave, whose propriety is purchased through property, national and racial boundary, masculinism, and compulsory heterosexuality.

To the extent that a set of reverse-mimes emerge from those quarters, they will not be the same as each other; if there is an occupation and reversal of the master's discourse, it will come from many quarters, and those resignifying practices will converge in ways that scramble the self-replicating presumptions of reason's mastery. For if the copies speak, or if what is merely material begins to signify, the scenography of reason is rocked by the crisis on which it was always built. And there will be no way finally to delimit the elsewhere of Irigaray's elsewhere, for every oppositional discourse will produce its outside, an outside that risks becoming installed as its non-signifying inscriptional space.

And whereas this can appear as the necessary and founding violence of any truth-regime, it is important to resist that theoretical gesture of pathos in which exclusions are simply affirmed as sad necessities of signification. The task is to refigure this necessary "outside" as a future horizon, one in which the violence of exclusion is perpetually in the process of being overcome. But of equal importance is the preservation of the outside, the site where discourse meets its limits, where the opacity of what is not included in a given regime of truth acts as a disruptive site of linguistic impropriety and unrepresentability, illuminating the violent and contingent boundaries of that normative regime precisely through the inability of that regime to represent that which might pose a fundamental threat to its continuity. In this sense, radical and inclusive representability is not precisely the goal: to include, to speak as, to bring in every marginal and excluded position within a given discourse is to claim that a singular discourse meets its limits nowhere, that it can and will domesticate all signs of difference. If there is a violence necessary to the language of politics, then the risk of that violation might well be followed by another in which we begin, without ending, without mastering, to own—and yet never fully to own—the exclusions by which we proceed.

Formless femininity

Awkwardly, it seems, Plato's phantasmatic economy virtually deprives the feminine of a *morphe*, a shape, for as the receptacle, the feminine is a permanent and, hence, non-living, shapeless non-thing which cannot be named. And as nurse, mother, womb, the feminine is synecdochally collapsed into a set of figural functions. In this sense, Plato's discourse on materiality (if we can take the discourse on the *hypodoche* to be that), is one which does not permit the notion of the female body as a human form.

How can we legitimate claims of bodily injury if we put into question the materiality of the body? What is here enacted through the Platonic text is a violation that founds the very concept of matter, a violation that mobilizes the concept and which the concept sustains. Moreover, within Plato, there is a disjunction between a materiality which is feminine and formless and, hence, without a body, and bodies which are formed through—but not of— that feminine materiality. To what extent in invoking received notions of materiality, indeed, in insisting that those notions function as "irreducibles," do we secure and perpetuate a constitutive violation of the feminine? When we consider that the very concept of matter preserves and recirculates a violation, and then invoke that very concept in the service of a compensation for violation, we run the risk of reproducing the very injury for which we seek redress.

The *Timaeus* does not give us bodies, but only a collapse and displacement of those figures of bodily position that secure a given fantasy of heterosexual intercourse and male autogenesis. For the receptacle is not a woman, but it is the figure that women become within the dream-world of this metaphysical cosmogony, one which remains largely inchoate in the constitution of matter. It may be, as Irigaray appears to suggest, that the entire history of matter is bound up with the problematic of receptivity. Is there a way to dissociate these implicit and disfiguring figures from the "matter" that they help to compose? And insofar as we have barely begun to discern the history of sexual difference encoded in the history of matter, it seems radically unclear whether a notion of matter or the materiality of bodies can serve as the uncontested ground of feminist practice. In this sense, the Aristotelian pun still works as a reminder of the doubleness of the matter of matter, which means that there may not be a materiality of sex that is not already burdened by the sex of materiality.

Some open-ended questions remain: How is it that the presumption of a given version of matter in the effort to describe the materiality of bodies prefigures in advance what will and will not appear as an intelligible body? How do tacit normative criteria form the matter of bodies? And can we understand such criteria not simply as epistemological impositions on bodies, but as the specific social regulatory ideals by which bodies are trained, shaped, and formed? If a bodily schema is not simply an imposition on already formed bodies, but part of the formation of bodies, how might we be able to think the production or formative power of prohibition in the process of morphogenesis?

Here the question is not simply what Plato thought bodies might be, and what of the body remained for him radically unthinkable; rather, the question is whether the forms which are said to produce bodily life operate through the production of an excluded domain that comes to bound and to haunt the field of intelligible bodily life. The logic of this operation is to a certain extent psychoanalytic inasmuch as the force of prohibition produces the spectre of a terrifying return. Can we, then, turn to psychoanalysis itself to ask how the boundaries of the body are crafted through sexual taboo?[49] To what extent does the Platonic account of the phallogenesis of bodies prefigure the Freudian and Lacanian accounts which presume the phallus as the synecdochal token of sexed positionality?

If the bounding, forming, and deforming of sexed bodies is animated by a set of founding prohibitions, a set of enforced criteria of intelligibility, then we are not merely considering how bodies appear from the vantage point of a theoretical position or epistemic location at a distance from bodies themselves. On the contrary, we are asking how the criteria of intelligible sex operates to constitute a field of bodies, and how precisely we might understand specific criteria to produce the bodies that they regulate. In what precisely does the crafting power of prohibition consist? Does it determine a psychic experience of the body which is radically separable from something that one might want to call the body itself? Or is it the case that the productive power of prohibition in morphogenesis renders the very distinction between *morphe* and *psyche* unsustainable?

Notes

1 Gianni Vattimo, "Au dela du matière et du text," in *Matière et Philosophie* (Paris: Centre Georges Pompidou, 1989), p. 5.
2 For a further discussion on how to make use of poststructuralism to think about the material injuries suffered by women's bodies, see the final section of my "Contingent Foundations: Feminism and the Question of Postmodernism," in Judith Butler and Joan Scott, eds., *Feminists Theorize the Political* (New York: Routledge), 1992, pp. 17–19; see also in that same volume, Sharon Marcus, "Fighting Bodies, Fighting Words: A Theory and Politics of Rape Prevention," pp. 385–403.

3 Jacques Derrida, *Positions*, Alan Bass, ed. (Chicago: University of Chicago, 1978), p. 64. On the following page, he writes: "I will not say whether the concept of matter is metaphysical or nonmetaphysical. This depends upon the work to which it yields, and you know that I have unceasingly insisted, as concerns the nonideal exteriority of the writing, the gram, the trace, the text, etc. upon the necessity of never separating them from *work*, a value itself to be thought outside its Hegelian affiliations" (p.65).

4 For a compelling analysis of how the form/matter distinction becomes essential to the articulation of a masculinist politics, see Wendy Brown's discussion of Machiavelli in *Manhood and Politics* (Totowa, N.J.: Rowman & Littlefield, 1988), pp. 87–91.

5 See Marx's first thesis on Feuerbach, in which he calls for a materialism which can affirm the practical activity that structures and inheres in the object as part of that object's objectivity and materiality: "The chief defect of all previous materialism (including Feuerbach's) is that the object, actuality, sensuousness is conceived only in the form of the *object or perception* (*Anschauung*), but not as *sensuous human activity, practice* (*Praxis*), not subjectively" (Karl Marx, *Writings of the Young Marx on Philosophy and Society*, tr. Lloyd D. Easton and Kurt H. Guddat [New York: Doubleday, 1967], p. 400). If materialism were to take account of praxis as that which constitutes the very matter of objects, and praxis is understood as socially transformative activity, then such activity is understood as constitutive of materiality itself. The activity proper to *praxis*, however, requires the transformation of some object from a former state to a latter state, usually understood as its transformation from a natural to a social state, but also understood as a transformation of an alienated social state to a non-alienated social state. In either case, according to this new kind of materialism that Marx proposes, the object is not only transformed, but in some significant sense, the object *is* transformative activity itself and, further, its materiality is established through this temporal movement from a prior to a latter state. In other words, the object *materializes* to the extent that it is a site of *temporal transformation*. The materiality of objects, then, is in no sense static, spatial, or given, but is constituted in and as transformative activity. For a fuller elaboration of the temporality of matter, see also Ernst Bloch, *The Principle of Hope*, tr. Neville Plaice, Stephen Plaice, and Paul Knight (Cambridge, Mass.: MIT Press, 1986); Jean-François Lyotard, *The Inhuman: Reflections on Time*, pp. 8–23.

6 Aristotle, "De Anima," *The Basic Works of Aristotle*, tr. Richard McKeon (New York: Random House, 1941), bk.2, ch.1, 412a10, p. 555. Subsequent citations from Aristotle will be from this edition and to standard paragraph numbering only.

7 See Thomas Laqueur, *Making Sex: Body and Gender from the Greeks to Freud* (Cambridge, Mass.: Harvard University Press, 1990), p. 28; G.E.R. Lloyd, *Science, Folklore, Ideology* (Cambridge: Cambridge University Press, 1983). See also Evelyn Fox Keller, *Reflections on Gender and Science* (New Haven: Yale University Press, 1985); Mary O'Brien, *The Politics of Reproduction* (London: Routledge, 1981).

8 Aristotle, "De Anima," bk.2, ch.1, 412b7–8.

9 Foucault, *The History of Sexuality, Volume One*, p. 152. Original: "Non pas donc 'histoire des mentalités' qui ne tiendrait compte des corps que par la manière dont on les aperçues ou dont on leur a donné sens et valeur; mais 'histoire des corps' et de la manière dont on a *investi* ce qu'il y a de plus *matérial*, de plus vivant en eux," *Histoire de la sexualité 1: La volonté de savoir* (Paris: Gallimard, 1978), p. 200.

10 Michel Foucault, *Discipline and Punish: The Birth of the Prison* (New York: Pantheon, 1977), p. 30. Original: "L'homme dont on nous parle et qu'on invite à

libérer est déjà en lui-même l'effet d'un assujettissement bien plus profond que lui. Une 'âme' l'habite et le porte à l'existence, qui est ellemême une pièce dans la maîtrise que le pouvoir exerce sur le corps. L'âme, effet et instrument d'une anatomie politique; l'âme, prison du corps," Michel Foucault, *Surveillance et punir* (Paris: Gallimard, 1975), p. 34.

11 "What was at issue was not whether the prison environment was too harsh or too aseptic, too primitive or too efficient, but its very materiality as an instrument and vector of power [c'était sa matérialité dans la mesure où elle est instrument et vecteur de pouvoir]," *Discipline and Punish*, p. 30 (*Surveillance et punir*, p. 35).

12 This is not to make "materiality" into the effect of a "discourse" which is its cause; rather, it is to displace the causal relation through a reworking of the notion of "effect." Power is established in and through its effects, where these effects are the dissimulated workings of power itself. There is no "power," taken as a substantive, that has dissimulation as one of its attributes or modes. This dissimulation operates through the constitution and formation of an epistemic field and set of "knowers"; when this field and these subjects are taken for granted as prediscursive givens, the dissimulating effect of power has succeeded. Discourse designates the site at which power is installed as the historically contingent formative power of things within a given epistemic field. The production of material effects is the formative or constitutive workings of power, a production that cannot be construed as a unilateral movement from cause to effect. "Materiality" appears only when its status as contingently constituted through discourse is erased, concealed, covered over. Materiality is the dissimulated effect of power.

Foucault's claim that power is materializing, that it is the production of material effects, is specified in *Discipline and Punish* in the materiality of the body. If "materiality" is an effect of power, a site of transfer between power relations, then insofar as this transfer is the subjection/subjectivation of the body, the principle of this *assujettissement* is "the soul." Taken as a normative/normalizing ideal, the "soul" functions as the formative and regulatory principle of this material body, the proximate instrumentality of its subordination. The soul renders the body uniform; disciplinary regimes train the body through a sustained repetition of rituals of cruelty that produce over the time the gestural stylistics of the imprisoned body. In the *History of Sexuality, Volume One*, "sex" operates to produce a uniform body along different axes of power, but "sex" as well as "the soul" are understood to subjugate and subjectivate the body, produce an enslavement, as it were, as the very principle of the body's cultural formation. It is in this sense that materialization can be described as the sedimenting effect of a regulated iterability.

13

> ... an ideology always exists in an apparatus, and its practice, or practices. This existence is material.
>
> Of course, the material existence of the ideology in an apparatus and its practices does not have the same modality as the material existence of a paving-stone or a rifle. But, at the risk of being taken for a Neo-Aristotelian (NB Marx had a very high regard for Aristotle), I shall say that 'matter is discussed in many senses', or rather that it exists in different modalities, all rooted in the last instance in 'physical' matter

Louis Althusser, "Ideology and Ideological State Apparatuses (Notes towards an Investigation)" in *Lenin and Philosophy and Other Essays* (New York: Monthly Review Press, 1971), p. 166; first published in *La Pensée*, 1970.

14 See *An Ethics of Sexual Difference*, tr. Carolyn Burke (Ithaca: Cornell University Press, 1993); *Éthique de la différence sexuelle* (Paris: Éditions de Minuit, 1984).

15 Bridget McDonald argues that for Irigaray, "the *entre* is the site of difference where uniformity becomes divided . . . every *entre* is a shared space where differentiated poles are not only differentiated, but are also subject to meeting one another in order to exist as differentiated . . .," "Between Envelopes," unpublished ms.

16 For a discussion of a notion of an "interval" which is neither exclusively space nor time, see Irigaray's reading of Aristotle's *Physics*, "Le Lieu, l'intervalle," *Éthique de la Différence*, pp. 41–62.

17 This will be related to the occupation of the paternal name in Willa Cather's fiction. See in particular Tommy's occupation of her father's place in Willa Cather's "Tommy the Unsentimental," considered in chapter five of this text.

18 See Elizabeth Spelman, "Woman as Body: Ancient and Contemporary Views," *Feminist Studies* 8:1 (1982): pp. 109–131.

19 See Elizabeth Weed's "The Question of Style," in Carolyn Burke, Naomi Schor, and Margaret Whitford, eds., *Engaging with Irigaray* (New York: Columbia University Press, forthcoming); and Elizabeth Grosz, *Sexual Subversions* (London: Routledge, 1991).

20 This is my translation even though it is clear that Irigaray in the following uses the term for "being" [être] and not for "essence" [*essence*] based on the sense of the subsequent sentence in which the notion of an "essence" remains foreign to the feminine and the final sentence in which the truth of that being is wrought through an oppositional logic: "Elle ne se constitue pas pour autant en *une*. Elle ne se referme pas sur ou dans une vérité ou une essence. L'essence d'une vérité lui reste étrangère. Elle n'a ni n'est un être. Et elle n'oppose pas, à la vérité masculine, une vérité féminine," Luce Irigaray, "Lèvres voilées," *Amante Marine de Friedrich Nietzsche* (Paris: Éditions de Minuit, 1980), p. 92; "She does not set herself up as the *one*, as a (single) female unit. She is not closed up or around one single truth or essence. The essence of a truth remains foreign to her. She neither has nor is a being. And she does not oppose a feminine truth to a masculine truth," *Marine Lover*, tr. Gillian Gill (New York: Columbia University Press, 1991), p. 86.

Given Naomi Schor's reading of "essence" as itself a catachresis, one might ask whether the discourse of essence cannot be redoubled outside of traditional metaphysical proprieties. Then the feminine could well enjoy an essence, but that enjoyment would be at the expense of metaphysics. Naomi Schor, "This Essentialism Which Is Not One: Coming to Grips with Irigaray," *Differences: A Journal of Feminist Cultural Studies* 2:1 (1989): pp. 38–58.

21 Jane Gallop, *Thinking through the Body* (New York: Columbia University Press, 1990).

22 Strictly speaking, matter as *hyle* does not figure centrally in the Platonic corpus. The term *hyle* is for the most part Aristotelian. In the *Metaphysics* (1036a), Aristotle claims that *hyle* can only be known through analogy. It is defined as potency (*dynamis*), and is isolated as one of the four causes; it is also described as the principle of individuation. In Aristotle, it is sometimes identified with the *hypokeimenon* (*Physics*, 1, 192a), but it is not considered a thing. Although Aristotle faults Plato for failing to differentiate between *hyle* and *steresis* (privation), he nevertheless identifies the Platonic notion of the receptacle (*hypodoche*) with *hyle* (*Physics*, 4, 209b). Like Aristotelian *hyle*, the *hypodoche* is indestructible, can only be known by means of "bastard reasoning" (*Timaeus*, 52a–b), and is that for which no definition can be given ["there is no definition of matter, only of *eidos*" *Metaphysics*, 1035b]. In Plato, *hypodoche* takes on the meaning of place or *chora*. It is only once Aristotle supplies an explicit philosophical discourse on matter that Plotinus writes a reconstruction of the Platonic doctrine of matter. This then becomes the occasion for Irigaray's critical citation of Plato/Plotinus in "Une

Mère de Glace" in *Speculum of the Other Woman*, tr. Gillian Gill (Ithaca: Cornell University Press, 1985), pp. 168–179.

23 Derrida, *Positions*, p. 64.

24 All citations will be to the standard paragraph number and to *Plato: The Collected Dialogues*, Edith Hamilton and Huntington Cairns, eds., Bollingen Series 71. (Princeton: Princeton University Press, 1961).

25 In the *Theatetus* "dechomenon" is described as a "bundle of wax," so Aristotle's choice of the "wax" image in *de Anima* to describe matter might be read as an explicit reworking of the Platonic *dechomenon*.

26 Here *diaschematizomenon* brings together the senses of "to be modelled after a pattern" and "formation," suggesting the strong sense in which schemas are formative. Plato's language prefigures Aristotle's formulation in this specific respect.

27 For a discussion on how *physis* or *phusis* meant genitals, see John J. Winkler's discussion, "*Phusis* and *Natura* Meaning 'Genitals,'" in *The Constraints of Desire: The Anthropology of Sex and Gender in Ancient Greece* (New York: Routledge, 1990), pp. 217–220.

28 This very opposition insists upon the *materiality* of language, what some will call the materiality of the signifier, and is what Derrida proposes to elaborate in "Chora," *Poikilia. Études offertes à Jean-Pierre Vernant* (Paris, EHESS, 1987). To call attention, however, to that word's materiality would not be sufficient, for the point is to gesture toward that which is neither material nor ideal, but which, as the inscriptional space in which that distinction occurs, is neither/nor. It is the neither/nor which enables the logic of either/or, which takes idealism and materialism as its two poles.

Derrida refers to this inscriptional space as a third gender or genre, which he associates on page 280 of the above text with a "neutral space"; neutral because participating in neither pole of sexual difference, masculine or feminine. Here the receptacle is precisely what destabilizes the distinction between masculine and feminine. Consider the way that this inscriptional space is described, especially how the act of inscription works on it: "in a third genre/gender and in the neuter space of a place without place, a place where everything marks it, but which in itself is not marked." Later, on p. 281, Socrates will be said to resemble Chora inasmuch as he is someone or something. "In every case, he takes his place, which is not a place among others, but perhaps *place itself*, the irreplaceable. Irreplaceable, and implacable place . . ." (my translation).

The polarity of idealism/materialism has come under question. But that is not to claim that there are no future question. For what do we make of Irigaray's claim that for Plato, the inscriptional space is a way of figuring and disfiguring femininity, a way of muting the feminine, and recasting it as mute, passive surface. Recall that for Plato the receptacle receives all things, is that through which a certain penetrative generativity works, but which itself can neither penetrate nor generate. In this sense, the receptacle can be read as a guarantee that there will be no destabilizing mimesis of the masculine, and the feminine will be permanently secured as the infinitely penetrable. This move is repeated in Derrida in his references to "the place without place where everything marks it, but which in itself is not marked." Have we discovered here the unmarked condition of all inscription, that which can have no mark of its own, no proper mark, precisely because it is that which, excluded from the proper, makes the proper possible? Or is this unmarked inscriptional space one whose mark has been erased, and is under compulsion to remain under permanent erasure?

"She (is) nothing other than the sum or the process of that which inscribes itself *'on'* her, 'à son sujet, à meme son sujet,'" but she is not the *subject* or the *present support* of all these interpretations, and she does not reduce to these interpretations. That which exceeds any interpretation, but which is itself not any interpretation. This description does not explain, however, why there is this prohibition against interpretation here. Is this not perhaps a virgin spot in or outside of the territory of metaphysics?

Although here Derrida wants to claim that the receptacle cannot be matter, in *Positions* he confirms that matter can be used "twice," and that in its redoubled effect, it can be precisely that which *exceeds* the form/matter distinction. But here, where matter and mater are linked, where there is a question of a materiality invested with femininity, and then subjected to an erasure, the receptacle cannot be matter, for that would be to reinstall it in the binarism from which it is excluded.

29 See Julia Kristeva, "The Semiotic *Chora* Ordering the Drives," in *Revolution in Poetic Language* (New York: Columbia University Press, 1984); abridged and translated version of *La révolution du langage poétique* (Paris: Éditions du Seuil, 1974).

30 For a very interesting discussion of the topography of reproduction in Plato and for a good example of psychoanalytic and classical thinking, see Page DuBois' *Sowing the Body* (Chicago: University of Chicago Press, 1988).

31 Irigaray makes a similar argument in *La Croyance même* (Paris: Éditions Galilée, 1983) in the course of rereading the *fort-da scene* in Freud's *Beyond the Pleasure Principle*. In that text she offers a brilliant rereading of the action of imaginary mastery effected by the little boy in repeatedly throwing his spool out of the crib and retrieving the spool as a way of rehearsing the departures and returns of his mother. Irigaray charts the scenography of this masterful play and locates the substitute for the maternal in the curtains, the folds of the bed linen that receive, hide, and return the spool. Like the *chora*, "she"—the dissimulated maternal support for the scene—is the absent but necessary condition for the play of presence and absence: "Elle y était et n'y était pas, elle donnait lieu mais n'avait pas lieu, sauf son ventre et encore . . . Elle n'y était pas d'ailleurs, sauf dans cette incessante transfusion de vie entre elle et lui, par un fil creux. Elle donne la possibilité de l'entrée en présence mais n'y a pas lieu" (p. 31).

32 *Plotinus' Enneads*, tr. Stephen MacKenna, 2nd ed. (London: Faber & Faber, 1956).

33 Irigaray, "Une Mère de Glace," in *Speculum*, p. 179; original, p. 224.

34 Irigaray makes a similar argument about the *cave* as inscriptional space in *Speculum*. She writes, "The cave is the representation of something always already there, of the original matrix/womb which these men cannot represent . . .," p. 244; original, p. 302.

35 My thanks to Jen Thomas for helping me to think this through.

36 Naomi Schor, "This Essentialism Which Is Not One: Coming to Grips with Irigaray," p. 48.

37 Luce Irigaray, "When Our Lips Speak Together," *This Sex Which Is Not One*, tr. Catherine Porter with Carolyn Burke (Ithaca: New York, 1985), p. 216; *Ce sexe qui n'en est pas un*, (Paris: Editions de Minuit, 1977), p. 215.

38 *This Sex*, p. 77; *Ce sexe*, p. 75.

39 For readings in feminist ethical philosophy which reformulate Irigaray's position in very interesting ways, see Drucilla Cornell, *Beyond Accommodation: Ethical Feminism, Deconstruction, and the Law* (New York: Routledge, 1991); Gayatri Chakravorty Spivak, "French Feminism Revisited: Ethics and Politics," in *Feminists Theorize the Political*, pp. 54–85.

40 Contiguous relations disrupt the possibility of the enumeration of the sexes, i.e., the first and second sex. Figuring the feminine as/through the contiguous thus

implicitly contests the hierarchical binarism of masculine/feminine. This opposition to the quantification of the feminine is an implicit argument with Lacan's *Encore: Le séminaire Livre XX* (Paris: Éditions du Seuil, 1975). It constitutes one sense in which the feminine "is not one." See *Amante marine*, pp. 92–93.

41 Margaret Whitford, *Luce Irigaray: Philosophy in the Feminine* (London: Routledge, 1991), p. 177.

42 Ibid, pp. 180–81.

43 Irigaray, "The Power of Discourse," in *This Sex Which Is Not One*, p. 76.

44 Donna Haraway, responding to an earlier draft of this paper in a hot tub in Santa Cruz, suggested that it is crucial to read Irigaray as reinforcing Plato as the origin of Western representation. Referring to the work of Martin Bernal, Haraway argues that the "West" and its "origins" are constructed through a suppression of cultural heterogeneity, in particular, the suppression of African cultural exchange and influence. Haraway may be right, but Irigaray's point is to expose the violent production of the European "origins" in Greece and so is not incompatible with the view Haraway outlines. My suggestion is that this violence is remaindered within the Platonic doctrine as the "site" of representational inscription and that one way to read Plato and Irigaray for their founding exclusions is by asking, What becomes stored in that receptacle?

45 H. G. Liddell and Robert Scott, *Greek-English Lexicon*, (Oxford: Oxford University Press, 1957).

46 It is important to raise a cautionary note against too quickly reducing sexual positions of active penetration and passive receptivity with masculine and feminine positions within the ancient Greek context. For an important argument against such a conflation, see David Halperin, *One Hundred Years of Homosexuality* (New York: Routledge, 1990), p. 30.

47 What follows may be an overreading, as some of my classicist readers have suggested.

48 Diotima attempts to explain to an apparently witless Socrates that heterosexual procreation not only contains but produces the effects of immortality, thus linking heterosexual procreation with the production of timeless truths. See *The Symposium* 206b–208b. Of course, this speech needs also to be read in the rhetorical context of the dialogue which might be said to assert this heterosexual norm, only later to produce its male homosexual contestation.

49 See Mary Douglas, *Purity and Danger* (London: Routledge & Kegan Paul, 1978); Peter Stallybrass and Allon White, *The Politics and Poetics of Transgression* (Ithaca: Cornell University Press, 1986).

10

TOWARDS A FEMINIST
PHILOSOPHY OF THE BODY

Moira Gatens

Source: B. Caine, E.A. Grosz and M. de Lepervanche (eds), *Crossing Boundaries: feminisms and the critique of knowledge,* Sydney: Allen & Unwin, 1988, pp. 59–70.

Feminists have made women's bodies a focal point around which many campaigns have been fought. The right to the autonomy of the female body has been argued in relation to abortion, contraception and birthing methods. The right to knowledge about the female body, the right to the health of the female body and the insistence on the autonomous pleasure of the female body have all been stressed by feminists in various contexts. Attempts to claim or assert these 'rights' have often involved direct defiance of both church and state. The meaning of the early women's liberation slogan, 'The personal is political', took on an added, and unwelcome, dimension when acts that women saw as *personal* choices were forbidden or penalised by the state. This raises the question of the relation between woman's body and the state. In spite of this social and political concentration on the female body, I would still argue that feminists have offered little by way of a coherent theory of the body. In particular, there has been little critical work done on the *conceptual* dimension of the relations between women's bodies and the state: between the body of woman and the body politic. In the absence of such theory, it is culturally dominant conceptions of the body that, unconsciously, many feminists work with.

What I propose to do in this paper is, first, critically examine some of the features of these dominant conceptions. Second, I will argue that traditional philosophical conceptions of corporeality are counterproductive to the aim of constructing an autonomous conception of women's bodies along with the possibility of women's active participation in the politico-ethical realm. Finally, I will suggest that the onto-ethical writings of Spinoza can provide a rich resource in working towards a feminist theorisation of corporeality.

Whatever else we say about conceptions of the body, it is clear that *how* we conceptualise the body forms and limits the meaning of the body in culture in various ways. The historical and philosophical associations between women and corporeality are multiple and complex (see Spelman, 1982). Significantly, cultural attitudes to both women and corporeality are often negative and function conceptually as the underside to culturally valued terms, such as reason, civilisation and progress. Many philosophers have tended to treat the soul or mind as, in essence, sexually neutral. Apparent differences between minds are generally seen to be due to the influence of the passions of the body. This element of sensuous and passionate corporeality allows philosophers to maintain the essential neutrality of the mind while allowing for individual and sexual differences. The most superior minds suffer least from the intrusions of the body. Women are most often understood to be less able to control the passions of the body and this failure is often located in the a priori disorder or anarchy of the female body itself. Some feminists have argued that this dualist notion of the body involves an implicit alignment between women and irrationality. The ideal conception of the rational is, in other words, articulated in direct opposition to qualities typical of the feminine (Lloyd, 1984; Le Doeuff, 1980).

This notion of the female body as intrinsically anarchic or disordered has repercussions for women's suitability to political participation. Some feminists—especially the egalitarians of the eighteenth and nineteenth centuries—argued that women are not essentially irrational but are *trained* to be so (e.g. Wollstonecraft, Taylor, J.S. Mill). Given proper training, they argued, women would be capable of rational political participation. This does not seem, in our present time, the most productive way of approaching the relation between woman and her access to the political realm. As Lloyd has shown in another context, it is not so much that women are explicitly conceptualised as irrational but rather that rationality itself is defined against the 'womanly'. In this context it may be profitable to explore the idea that it is not so much that women are biologically unsuited to political participation, as political participation has been structured and defined in such a way that it excludes women's bodies. If this is so then fighting to have women included in the present body politic will be counterproductive unless it is accompanied by some analysis of the exclusions of women's corporeality that still define that body politic and a working framework from which to think and live other ways of being, of being political and of being ethical.

Motherless births: the miracle of masculine auto-reproduction

The seventeenth century was witness to at least two births of interest to us here. First, the birth of the human *subject*: who is both the subject *of* governance—of an internal relation of domination, where mind or reason should dominate the body and passion—and one subject *to* governance. Second, the birth of the modern body politic which is represented as a product of reason, designed to govern, manage and administer the needs and desires of its subjects. A twin birth? Clearly, each being presupposes the other. This embryonic contiguity, between the modern body politic and the modern subject, suggests that in order to understand modern conceptions of the human subject, including its corporeality, one needs to understand its reflexive relation to the modern body politic.

Modern political theory typically conceives of political life as a state created by a contract, entered into by rational decision, and designed to ensure the protection and safety of the body and its needs. As it is a contract entered into by men only, one must surmise that it is a contract designed to secure the needs of male bodies and desires. This contract is also thought to create an *artificial* body: Hobbes' leviathan, for example, is an 'artificial man'. What a feminist theorist must consider is woman's relation to this 'artificial man'. Here, I will simply signal the importance of traditional conceptions of the female body and the way these conceptions function in political discourses to justify women's historical (and present) social role.

Woman in fact never makes the transition from the mythical 'state of nature' to the body politic. She *becomes* nature. She is necessary to the functioning of cultural life, she is the very ground which makes cultural life possible, yet she is not part of it. This division between nature and culture, the division between the reproduction of mere biological life as against the production and regulation of social life, is a division reflected in the distinction between the private and the public spheres, the family and the state. These divisions are conceptually and historically sexualised, with woman remaining mere nature, mere body, reproducing in the private familial sphere. These associations are viewed as having their ground in woman's ontology. The distinction between the sexes is taken to be a fundamental feature of nature that could only be represented in culture in this dichotomous way. The notion that culture constructs nature or that cultural practices construct bodies as dichotomously sexed is theoretically *inadmissible* in the modern account.

In the modern view the body is understood as part of 'raw' nature, which is progressively integrated or surpassed by the development of culture. Here I will merely signpost the resonances of this view in feminist theory. Both Firestone and de Beauvoir, for example, have a clear nature/culture, body/social split, where both nature and the body are conceived as outside culture and outside history. Yet the effects or the power of both nature and the body are able to be progressively eroded in history by the advances of culture. The sex/gender distinction, so crucial to early 1970s feminist theory, also displays this acceptance of the division between bodies on one hand and culture on the other (see Gatens, 1983). Sex is understood to be a fact of bodies, gender a socialised addition to sex. It is important to note the extent to which these early feminist critiques share the modern conception of the body as a non-cultural, ahistorical phenomenon. All history and culture can do, on this model, is intervene as a mechanic intervenes into the functioning of an already constituted machine.

The anti-humanist stance marks a definitive break with this tradition. This stance seriously questions the idea that the body has a priori needs, desires or functions which determine the form of culture and politics. Foucault, for example, thoroughly rejects the idea that the body has a fixed character which sets the limits to possible socio-political structures in which that body could 'live'. He inverts the modern problematic and suggests the exploration of how socio-political structures construct particular kinds of bodies with particular kinds of needs and desires. One could argue, for example, that the sexed body is not a product of nature but rather is constituted as dichoto-mously sexed by elaborate and pervasive practices that act on and through the body (see Foucault, 1978; 1980). Rather than viewing the forms and functions of bodies as determinant in the organisation of culture, we can view them as products of the way that culture organises, regulates and remakes itself. This approach allows us to shift the conceptual ground from the question "How is the body taken up in culture?" to the more profitable question 'How does culture construct the body so that it is understood as a biological given?'

The most conspicuous contribution of feminists to the anti-humanist critique involves exposing the masculine bias of the supposed 'neutral' humanist subject. Recent feminist research has shown how paying attention to the specificity of female embodiment disrupts and belies the supposed liberal principles of equal treatment and the right to bodily integrity. However, this critique has paid insufficient attention to the congruence between the (implicitly masculine) subject of these rights and principles on the one hand and representations of the body politic on the other. Many theorists seem to assume that this relation of congruence merely reflects an historical fact about the privilege accorded to masculine experi-ence in the construction of both political life and representations of political life. I think it necessary to go beyond this 'man-as-author' understanding of political life. In particular, I think it is necessary to consider the isomorphism between philosophical representations of the 'neutral' human body and the body politic.

The work of Luce Irigaray is an excellent example of recent feminist criticism which seeks to reveal the masculine bias of western culture. She has argued that an examination of philosophy reveals a certain isomorphism or mirroring of form, between philosophy and the male body, a mirroring which implicitly privileges the masculine form in western constructions of logic, language and metaphysics (Irigaray, 1977). Her main target is metaphysics, which she seeks to undermine by an internal disruption which creates a space to re-present femininity (Irigaray, 1985a). Using aspects of her approach, we can present a challenge to the masculine nature of representations of the human body, the body politic and the links between these two. This may open a space where different political and ethical relations can begin to be thought, a 'space' that will be opened by questioning what is repressed in current representations of politico-ethical life.

In this context Freud offers an interesting observation on the mother–son relation, which is for him the primal 'hinge-relation' between the pre-social and the social. It is this relation, after all, that for Freud lies at the heart of the riddle of culture; it is the riddle the Theban Sphinx poses to Oedipus. Freud writes: 'All his [the son's] instincts, those of tenderness, gratitude, lustfulness, defiance and independence, find satisfaction in the single wish *to be his own father*' (1978: 173). This primal wish, to take the place of the father, is expressed in political terms by the fantasy of the generation of a man-made social body: a body that is motherless and so immortal. Our cultural unconscious is littered with examples that suggest that those *not* born of woman have awesome powers. Macbeth, who smiles with scorn at '. . . swords brandish'd by man that's of woman born', can only be slain by the unbirthed Macduff. The motherless Athena can fearlessly confront the Furies, rebuking them for their vengeful pursuit of the matricide, Orestes. Asserting her authority by sending them (literally) underground she establishes the priority of (male) citizenship over blood ties and thus institutes the classic patriarchal state, which even bears her name: Athens. Unmothered, such beings are autonomous, immortal and quintessentially masculine. The motherless body politic, product of the fecundity of man's reason, is also a body untouched by death. This fantasy of masculine auto-reproduction is not uncommon in western political theory. It appears in Greek, medieval and modern writings and it is a fantasy that feminists need to address.

Discourses on the body and discourses on the body politic each borrow terms from the other. This mutual cross-referencing appears in their shared vocabularies, for example, 'constitution', 'regime' and 'diet'. A philosophically common metaphor for the appropriate relation between the mind and the body is to posit it as a *political* relation, where one (the mind) should dominate, subjugate or govern the other (the body) (see Spelman, 1983). These conceptual interconnections are historically unstable. They take their present form, in whatever definitive sense can be given them, largely in response to a series of dichotomies that came to exist around the seventeenth century.

Descartes, Hobbes, (and later, La Mettrie) are names commonly associated with the mechanisation of the body. This involved positing a faculty of reason able to dominate a body-machine. Seventeenth-century discourses are obsessed with the question of the legitimate exercise of power in at least two contexts: first, how to enforce the legitimate power of reason over the unruly body (see, for example, Descartes' *The Passions of the Soul*); second, how to establish (or discredit) the legitimacy of the power of the King (the head) over the social (body). These debates concerning the legitimacy of social and political authority had considerable effects not only on conceptions of the appropriate governing relation between minds and bodies, kings and subjects, but also on the relations between men and women.

Pateman (1984) has argued against understanding the patriarchal body politic as the 'rule of the father'. She argues that the sons (cf. Locke) may well have defeated the fathers (cf. Filmer and Hobbes) but what they introduced was not a democracy but a fraternity. It is also crucial to stress, in this context, that the triumph of the sons required a strict separation between natural and conventional authority. Although the authority of father over son was questioned, the authority of man over woman was not. In order for men to 'legitimately' dominate women it was necessary to exclude women from the political sphere, i.e. from the 'artificial body'. This involved reducing women to roles that have meaning only in relation to men: wife/mother/daughter. It is worth mentioning that considerable physical coercion was employed in late-seventeenth- and eighteenth-century politics to ensure that women were confined to the private/familial sphere. Any attempt by women to take advantage of the considerable social unrest was often severely quashed. The justification for the often harsh measures used to keep women out of the body politic were commonly put in terms of protecting the health of the social body from invasion, corruption or infection (see Abray, 1975).

One of the many petitions put before the revolutionary government in Paris between 1792 and 1794 demanded that women be given 'a voice' in the newly formed body politic. The terms in which this petition was rejected confirms many of the points I have made here:

> If we take into account the fact that the political education of men is still at its very beginnings, that all the principles are not yet developed, and that we still stammer over the word 'liberty', then how much less enlightened are women, whose moral education has been practically non-existent. Their presence in the *sociétés populaires*, then, would give an active part in government to persons exposed to error and seduction even more than are men. And, let us add that women by their constitution, are open to an exaltation which could be ominous in public life. The interests of the state would soon be sacrificed to all the kinds of disruption and disorder that hysteria can produce. (Abray, 1975:56)

If women are admitted to the social body and given a 'voice', the feminine disease of hysteria may be transposed to the social body which would result in *political* hysteria. We can see in the above passage, the shift that Foucault notes from concern over the wellbeing of the king's body to concern for the health and asepsis of the social body (see 1977; 1978). Amar, the speaker quoted above, was representing the newly formed 'Committee for General Security', a committee whose task it was to police the health and safety of the nascent social body. That part of this task involved the quarantine of women is instructive. As Cixous (1980; 1981), Lyotard (1978), and others have commented, in so far as woman is socially 'initiated', she is initiated by decapitation, either metaphorically (mutism) or literally (recall the guillotining of Mme Roland and Olympe de Gouges). She has nothing to forfeit but her 'voice', her head, her reason. Her relation to the body politic will be limited to the corporeal and to her use as a natural resource. She will continue to function as the repressed term 'body', thus allowing the fantasy of the masculine body politic to 'live'.

Recent feminist writing has responded to the self-representation of philosophers by pointing out that the body politic that men give birth to assumes both the appropriation and the disavowal of woman's ability to reproduce life (Pateman, 1984; Irigaray, 1985a; 1985b). This response allows us to read the modern political writers in a new light. Clearly, many of the writers of this period have in common the fantasy of political man's autonomy from both women and the corporeal, specifically, autonomy from the maternal body. It is tempting to argue that the modern body politic has yet to be *embodied*. Any attempt to begin conceptualising the embodiment of the body politic runs up against immediate problems: the 'neutrality' of the modern subject; women's exclusion from the rational and hence from the political and the ethical also. This situation, then, requires a radical rethinking of the connections between reason, the body and politico-ethical relations. What is required is a theoretical space that is not dominated by the isomorphism between male bodies and political bodies. Part of what I attempted to show in this section is that feminist reflections on modern accounts of embodiment and politics reveal that the philosophers' 'slip' is showing, or perhaps more appropriately, his mother's petticoats.

The lever that this feminist critique provides can be a starting point for exploring other ways of being. Woman's historical exclusion from these discourses and relations can thus be seen as a strength. The construction of alternative perspectives presents us with both practical and theoretical difficulties. The conceptual difficulty of trying to construct other ways to live human corporeality using dominant categories of thought is partly because these categories are tied in complex ways to present forms of social, political and ethical life. Descartes' dualist conception of subjectivity, for example, can be viewed as an essential development in western ontology that has functioned to validate a body politic that is characterised by the notion that the mind, by an act of will, can alienate the labouring capacities of its body-machine in return for a wage. Offering a coherent account of woman's relation to wage-labour has long been problematic for political theorists. It seems fair to suggest that there are conceptual exclusions operating against developing such an account. Of course, theories of being or politics cannot be created *ex nihilo*. We are constrained by our theoretical as well as our practical histories. However, the history of philosophy has a much richer store of conceptions of the body than appears in dominant accounts. For the remainder of this chapter I propose the use of a tradition of conceptualising the body that 'begins' with Spinoza and has been largely neglected in Anglo-American philosophy. This tradition offers a multivalent ontology that may provide a basis from which to develop a multiple and *embodied* politico-ethics.

Spinozistic bodies

It may seem a little odd to return to a seventeenth-century conception of the body given the advances in biology and physiology since then. I think, however, that there are several good reasons to prefer such a remote account as Spinoza's. His theory may offer another perspective from which to assess the claims and findings of a science and a biology that have been articulated in the shadow of dualism. I also think that there is some reason to scrutinise the seventeenth century as it was a crucial transition period in our culture. If women are going to play an active part in contemporary politics then it is important to begin the task of thinking through how one participates in a context where female embodiment is denied any autonomous political or ethical representation. It is important to begin the exploration of other ontologies which would be developed hand in hand with a politico-ethical stance that accommodates *multiple*, not simply dichotomously *sexed* bodies.

It seems important, in this context, to argue that feminists who are in a position of (relative) social power do not use this power to further entrench polarities that function negatively in relation to other social groups as well. Given the history, and the discourses surrounding the history, of the modern body politic it is necessary for feminists to exert a strong counterforce to the explicit and implicit masculinity of that body. This counterforce will necessarily involve the assertion of a certain homogeneity in the specific situations of women. This seems to be a necessary initial response to a substantive historical fact about political society. But this response must be viewed as based in tactical *nous* rather than in an ontological truth about women that is closed to history. It is necessary for feminist theory to develop an open-ended ontology capable of resisting entrenchment in a romanticism which so often accompanies the 'underdog' position.

The kind of political practice that I am suggesting could be developed from Spinozist metaphysics would require the reconsideration of several dominant feminist principles. The polarisation between men and women is a part of our socio-political histories which cannot be ignored. But to accept this dualism uncritically is merely to perpetuate relations whose construction is not fully understood. The kind of political practice envisaged here is one where difference could not be decided a priori but rather recognised in the unfolding of shared (or conflicting) aims and objectives of groups of bodies. To seek to create a politico-ethical organisation where all, in their own manner, seek to maximise the possibilities of their activity must take into account different beings and their desires, and their understandings of their being and their desires. It is an unavoidable (and welcome) consequence of constructing an *embodied* ethics that ethics would no longer pretend to be universal.

Spinozist philosophy is capable of suggesting an account of the body and its relation to social life, politics and ethics that does not depend on the dualisms that dominate traditional modern philosophy. Yet neither is it a philosophy which neutralises difference. Rather it allows a conceptualisation of difference which is neither dichotomised nor polarised. Spinoza's writings offer the possibility of resolving some of the current difficulties in the much-debated relation between feminist theory and dominant theory (see Gatens, 1986). This 'resolution' is not so much concerned with 'answers' to these difficulties as with providing a framework in which it is possible to pose problems in quite 'different' theoretical terms.

The division between the (bodily, natural, feminine) private sphere and the (rational, cultural, masculine) public sphere is a division that has proved particularly resilient to feminist intervention. To address the tension between the political and the familial sphere is to address the tension between the conceptions 'men' and 'women', and so ultimately to address the tension *within* the present politico-ethical structuring of the 'universal' human subject. The Spinozist conceptions of reason, power, activity and conatus (the tendency of all things to persist in their own being) offer a provisional terminology in which to begin working towards dissolving these tensions. By abandoning the dualist ontology of mind versus body, nature versus culture, we can circumvent the either/or impasse of contemporary feminist theory between affirming an essential mental equality, which the progress of civilisation can be entrusted to expose, or affirming an essential bodily difference. The Spinozist view does not lend itself to an understanding of sexual difference in terms of a consciousness/body or sex/gender distinction. For Spinoza the body is not part of passive nature ruled over by an active mind but rather the body is the ground of human action. The mind is constituted by the affirmation of the actual existence of the body, and reason is active and embodied precisely because it is the affirmation of a *particular* bodily existence. Activity itself cannot be related especially to body, mind, nature or culture, but rather to understanding the possibilities of one's participation in one's situation as opposed to the passive 'living' of one's social, political or even brute existence. This active understanding does not, and could not, amount to the mental domination of a body-machine, since thought is dependent for its activity on the character of the body and the manner in which, and the context in which, it recreates itself.

The Spinozist account of the body is of a productive and creative body which cannot be definitively 'known' since it is not identical with itself across time. The body does not have a 'truth' or a 'true' nature since it is a process and its meaning and capacities will vary according to its context. We do not know the limits of this body or the powers that it is capable of attaining. These limits and capacities can only be revealed by the ongoing interactions of the body and its environment.

Traditional political theory takes the body, its passions, its form and function as virtually given. This form is then understood to be taken up in culture in the way that it is because of this a priori or biological nature. Entertaining a non-mechanical view of nature and a non-dichotomised view of nature and culture would involve acknowledging the cultural and historical specificity of bodies. The particular form, structure, character and capabilities of a body confined to the domestic sphere and to the role of wife/mother may then be seen as an historically specific body whose capacities are reduced by its sphere of activity and the conditions under which it recreates itself. This perspective makes essentialist accounts of the female form and its capacities problematic. It allows one to question the traditional alignments between the female body and the private sphere and the male body and the public sphere without disavowing the *historical* facts that support these alignments. One could rather note the ways in which the respective activities of these distinct spheres construct and recreate particular kinds of bodies to perform particular kinds of tasks.

For feminists working in philosophy—or any academic discipline—the most pressing difficulty in relation to affirming the presence of woman is the theoretical exclusions implicit in the discourses we have to deal with. Creating other modes of conceptualising human culture that do not involve the passivity or invisibility of women is obviously of the greatest importance. A philosophy of the body that addresses the connections between representations of sexed bodies on one hand and representations of the politico-ethical on the other is an essential component of any alternative view. Recent work on the body by French feminists (see Marks and Courtivron, 1980; Eisenstein and Jardine, 1980; Irigaray, 1977; 1985a; 1985b) which stress *morphology* over biology, cultural constructions of embodiment over the 'natural' body, break with traditional boundaries between desire and instinct, between consciousness and bodies. Morphological descriptions of the body construct the body as an active, desiring body since the form of the body *is* its being, its form *is* its desiring. I take this conception of morphology to be a useful bridging device—a device that is necessary to get beyond the dilemmas of dualism. Many feminists are working on the creation of an alternative topos from which to reject or work through these dominant dualisms of the mind and the body, nature and culture, biology and psychology, and sex and gender. What I have tried to show in this chapter is that the theorisation or clarification of this topos could benefit from the Spinozist framework. I have suggested that his work offers exciting possibilities in terms of conceptualising the body as productive and dynamic: a conception which defies traditional divisions between knowing and being, between ontology and epistemology, and between politics and ethics.

No doubt there are other non-dualist conceptions of subjectivity that should be explored. I am not presenting Spinoza as a unique exception in the history of philosophy. Some aspects of the work of Nietzsche, or more recently the work of Foucault and Deleuze, may also prove useful to feminists. My personal preference for the remote figure of Spinoza stems from a worry that more contemporary figures may entrap feminism in the transferential position, to which it is so very vulnerable (see Le Doeuff, 1977). Establishing an autonomous relation to one's discipline, and to its history, is a step towards at least *theoretical* independence.

References

Abray, J. (1975) 'Feminism in the French Revolution' in *American Historical Review* 80

Cixous, H. (1980) 'The Laugh of the Medusa' in E. Marks and I. Courtivron (eds) *New French Feminisms* Sussex: Harvester Press Ltd

—— (1981) 'Castration or Decapitation?' in *Signs* 7:1

Eisenstein, H. and A. Jardine (eds) (1980) *The Future of Difference* Boston: G.K. Hall

Foucault, Michel (1977) *Discipline and Punish* London: Allen Lane

—— (1978) *The History of Sexuality* New York: Pantheon

—— (1980) *Herculine Barbin* New York: Random House

Freud, S. (1978) 'A Special Type of Object-Choice Made by Men' in *Standard Edition of Complete Psychological Works of Freud* (ed. J. Strachey) vol. XI

Gatens, M. (1983) 'A Critique of the Sex/Gender Distinction' in J. Allen and P. Patton (eds) *Beyond Marxism? Interventions After Marx* Sydney: Intervention Publications

—— (1986) 'Feminism, Philosophy and Riddles Without Answers' in C. Pateman and E. Gross (eds) *Feminist Challenges: Social and Political Theory* Sydney: Allen & Unwin

Irigaray, L. (1977) 'Women's Exile' *Ideology and Consciousness* 1

—— (1985a) *Speculum of the Other Woman* Cornell University Press

—— (1985b) *This Sex Which is Not One* Cornell University Press

Le Doeuff, M. (1977) 'Women and Philosophy' *Radical Philosophy* 17, Summer, pp.2–11.

—— (1980) *Recherches sur L'imaginaire philosophique* Paris: Payot

Lloyd, G. (1984) *The Man of Reason* London: Methuen

Lyotard, J.F. (1978) 'One of the Things at Stake in Women's Struggles' *Substance* 20

Marks, E. and I. Courtivron (eds) (1980) *New French Feminisms* Sussex: The Harvester Press Ltd

Pateman, C. (1982), What's Wrong with Prostitution?, typescript, University of Sydney

—— (1983) 'Defending Prostitution: Charges against Ericsson' *Ethics* 93, pp. 561–65

—— The Fraternal Social Contract, paper to the Annual American Political Science Assoc., Washington, D.C.

Spelman, E. (1982) 'Woman as Body: Ancient and Contemporary Views' *Feminist Studies* 8, 1

—— (1983) 'The Politicisation of the Soul' in Harding and Hintikka (eds) *Discovering Reality*

11

NOTES TOWARDS A CORPOREAL FEMINISM

Elizabeth Grosz

Source: *Australian Feminist Studies* 5 (1987): 1–16.

> The word 'body', its danger, how easily it gives one the illusory impression of being outside of meaning already, free from the contamination of consciousness-unconsciousness. Insidious return of the natural, of Nature. The body does not belong: it is mortal-immortal; it is unreal, imaginary, fragmentary. Patient. In its patientness the body is thought already—still just thought.
>
> Maurice Blanchot[1]

After a considerable period of distrust regarding the body, feminists today have become increasingly interested in the role the body plays in the social constitution (and problematisation) of sexual identity. Feminist research has effected major changes in the ways bodies are represented and theorised. No longer reduced to naturalistic or essentialist explanations, the body can be seen as *the* primary object of social production and inscription, and can thus be located within a network of socio-historical relations instead of being tied to a fixed essence.

This resurgence of feminist interest is both negatively and positively motivated, an effect, on the one hand, of growing dissatisfaction with humanist notions of subjectivity or identity; and on the other, by a post-humanist recognition that if there is no female essence or *a priori* femininity, then it is only through an understanding of their corporeality that women's identities can be conceived. Humanisms (of all kinds) rely on an (implicit) essentialism; or else on a process of homogenising and recuperating women's specificities, attributes and characteristics, reducing them to a formal equality with men, thus submerging their *positive* particularities.[2] Women are represented as human only through an implicitly male-defined notion of 'humanity'.

If feminists are to avoid a reverse essentialism, in which a determinate form of femininity is universalised, providing a female 'version of humanity', then concepts, which explain both the commonness women share cross-culturally, and their cultural and individual specificities, are necessary for women's positive self-definition. A 'geniune' female universal, if not located in a fixed identity or psyche (as implied by humanism), can be corporeally located. Women's carnal existence, their corporeal commonness, may provide a universal 'raw material', which is nevertheless pliable enough to account for cultural, historical, class and racial specificities distinguishing concrete women from each other. Only a notion like the body — which is both universal in its generality, yet 'open' to any culture's particular significations and requirements — satisfies these two conditions of feminist researches into women's identities.

The female (or male) body can no longer be regarded as a fixed, concrete substance, a pre-cultural given. It has a determinate form only by being socially inscribed. Each sex is not differentiated on the basis of some unique substance or the possession of distinguishing organs alone. Rather, sexual differences are purely *relational*, each sex being defined only by its negative or differential relations to the other sex(es). Out of a spectrum of sexually differential bodies, the continuum is polarised around two sexes, one conceived in terms of the absence, lack or deprivation of the other. The relations between the socially distinguished forms of body, and the positions occupied by each, may help to provide the bases for a non-essentialist, non-humanist conception of sexual/personal identity.

In contesting the prevailing theoretical paradigms through which the body has been theorised (including biology and physiology, at the expense of alternatives which may be based more on social, political, representational and psychological concepts) feminists have articulated a conception of the *constitutive* embodiment of sexed subjects. As a socio-historical 'object', the body can no longer be confined to biological determinants, to an *immanent*, 'factitious', or unchanging social status. It is a political object *par excellence*: its form, capacities, behaviour, gestures, movements, potential are primary objects of political contestation.[3] As a *political* object, the body is not inert or fixed. It is pliable and plastic material, which is capable of being formed and organised in other, quite different ways or according to different classificatory schema than our binarised models. If it is a social object, the body can be redefined, its forms and functions can be contested and its place in culture reevaluated or transformed.

Feminists have attempted to rethink many of their long-term programmes (e.g. abortion, contraception, health, sexuality, violence, harassment etc.) that have centered on the body, but have not been adequately theorised or conceived in corporeal terms. The body need no longer be an object of theoretical aversion and ideological suspicion, for feminists need not commit themselves to essentialism or biologism if the body is conceived in avowedly social terms. Conceptions of the body compatible with transformations or upheavals in social relations, non-biologistic, non-reductionist and anti-essentialist notions of the body, may thus provide some of the critical

181

tools by which the masculinity of prevailing knowledges can be recognised, and women's specific experiences articulated.

I hope to provide some rough notes towards establishing a 'corporeal feminism', that is, an understanding of corporeality that is compatible with feminist struggles to undermine patriarchal structures and to form self-defined terms and representations. First, I examine why the body has occupied a negative place within feminism until relatively recently; second, I examine some of the challenges feminists have posed to prevailing conceptions of the body; and third, I explore some of the implications of theorising the body as a psycho-social object. These are merely preliminary gestures towards the larger project — left untouched here — of formulating a theory of *embodiment* or *corporeal incarnation* compatible with autonomous conceptions of the sexes.

It is apparent from everyday experience that the body plays a crucial role in subjectivity. There are few philosophers willing to deny this claim. However, the problem, articulated throughout the history of philosophy, has been to provide terms and a conceptual space in which their interaction, their togetherness, can be theorised. In starting their researches from the evidence of experience, many feminists begin their researches from a less abstract and self-distanced conception than is generally available in philosophical speculation. Nevertheless, many feminists remain wary of concepts of the body and have considered them a theoretical and political danger. Why has this occurred? In sketching an answer, I will draw on the ways in which the body has been traditionally theorised in the biological or natural sciences, and also on common presumptions governing its position and status in the social sciences and humanities. Given the kinds of theories and conceptions of the body privileged in the social and natural sciences, it is not entirely surprising that feminists tend to remain wary of the idea of the body in their researches, particularly when the notion of the female body has been used to justify women's physical and social subordination.

With rare exceptions in the history of philosophy, the mind and body have been conceived in isolation from each other, functioning as binary or mutually exclusive terms. The attributes of one are incompatible with those of the other. In, for example, Descartes' influential writings[5], the body is defined by its extension, that is, its capacity to be located in, to occupy, space. By contrast, the mind is considered as conceptual, based on Reason. It is non-spatial and the body is non-conceptual. The binary formulation of mind-body relation — that is, *dualism*[5] — identifies subjectivity and personhood with the conceptual side of the opposition while relegating the body to the status of an object, outside of and distinct from consciousness.

This binary opposition is commonly associated with a number of other binary pairs: nature and culture, private and public, self and other, subject and object. These help to provide the mind-body dualism with positive contents. The mind becomes associated with culture, reason, subject and self; while the body is correlated with nature, the passions, object and other. Not unexpectedly, the positive side of the opposition, mind/culture etc. is also associated with masculinity, and their opposites, with femininity.

Significantly, the natural sciences are divided from the social sciences and humanities according to a mind-body dualism. The conceptual side of this opposition becomes the object of the humanities, (their object is consciousness, mind or ideas); the body is given the status of physical object, and becomes the object of a natural scientific investigation. Thus excluded from notions of subjectivity, personhood or identity, the body becomes an 'objective', observable entity, a thing. The human being is distinguished from animals only by mind or reason. As an organism, the human body is merely a more complex version of other organic ensembles. It is not qualitatively distinguished from other types of existence: it poses similar general questions to those raised by animal physiology. The body's sensations, activities, and processes become 'lower order', natural or animalistic factors of the human subject, tying it to nature. It becomes one part of an interconnected chain of organic forms, whether construed in cosmological or ecological terms.

The body has been identified with brute matter in our recent intellectual history. For Descartes, for example, it differs from other material objects only in its degree of complexity. He considers it contiguous with the organic, and part of the physical order. He construes the materiality of the body as fundamentally similar to the materiality of a rock or tree. The natural and life sciences, while distinguishing the organic from the inorganic, nevertheless place them in a(n evolutionary) continuum in which inorganic gives rise, through its increasing complexity, to the organic. The animation and *interiority* of the body, the fact that it is the point of origin of a *perspective* and that it occupies a conceptual, social and cultural point of view, cannot be explained on such a model. The corporeality of a subject *must* differ from the corporeality of a stone or of an animal insofar as the human body is capable of thinking and talking, is subjected to meanings, values, and decisions arising from *within*, while the latter are animated or subjected to meanings only externally. In other words, the *humanness* of the body, its *psychical* status, has been ignored.

Patriarchal oppression justifies itself through the presumption that women, more than men, are tied to their fixed corporeality. They are thus considered *more* natural and biologically governed, and *less* cultural, to be more object, and less subject than men. Women's circumscribed social existence is explained — or rather, rationalised — in biological terms and is thus rendered unchangeable. Relying on essentialism, naturalism and biologism, misogynistic thought confines women by tying them to a biologically and logically necessary dependence on men, ensuring its own continuity through the ascription of a biologically determined female 'nature'.

Women's bodies are not only used as fixed elements to dictate 'efficient' or adaptive roles for women in culture, they are also used to reduce women to a pseudo-evolutionary function in the reproduction of the species, which supposedly acts as a compensation for women's social powerlessness. It supposedly assures women of a socially recognised and validated function — maternity. Women's biologies, it seems, are distinguished from men's insofar as *only* women's reproductive organs and activities characterise them (doctors dealing with so-called 'women's problems', for example, are gynecologists or obstetricians). The allocation of only a reproductive specificity, at the expense of other functions and capacities, once again confirms the presumption that somehow (because of particular biological, physiological and endocrinological transformations that they involuntarily undergo), women are closer to biology, corporeality and nature than men.

Where patriarchs used a fixed, given concept of the body to contain women, it becomes understandable that feminists would resist such conceptions and their implied limits on the possibilities of social change. The hostility directed towards women and femininity is commonly rationalised, explained away, with reference to the functions and capacities of the female body. Yet, although prevalent and socialy legitimised, these biologistic reductions of women's social capacities are not the only possible accounts of female corporeality and sexuality available.

Feminists working in the sciences and humanities increasingly resist these reductions of the body, and have explored alternative concepts of corporeality which, on the one hand avoid biological reductionism, and, on the other, present more appropriate conceptual models to specify women's bodies and experiences than those given in prevailing, male-defined paradigms. In other words, many feminists today seem to agree that the body can be extricated from biologistic and socio-biologistic accounts to provide the basis of a positive identity and representation for women.

There are at least two possible directions in which the body may be rethought in terms outside the limits of biological models, which tend to reduce it to genetic or hereditary factors. Bodies are the result of *more* than biology. Social, economic, psychical and moral relations are not just *experienced* by subjects, but are, in order to be experienced, integrally *recorded* or corporeally *inscribed*. The project known as 'the construction of the subject', which has been focussed on the acquisition of appropriate ideological values can be explained as well on a model of corporeal inscription. Yet claiming that the body is an extra-biological phenomenon does not mean that biology is irrelevant in understanding it. Yet it may imply that biological theories and scientific paradigms, as we know them, now need to be reformulated. Their basic presuppositions and methods can, like other knowledges, be seen as a reflection of the male dominance of culture as a whole. A biological theory, which, for example, takes as its starting point the autonomous definition of two sexes, may provide the conceptual and experimental space in which the female is not seen as an aberration or variant of the male, may develop an altogether different understanding of women's (and men's) corporeality. Theories of the body, those compatible with feminism, should account for both the biological (universal, transhistorical) elements of the body as well as for the body's capacity to be 'molded', 'constructed' or socially in-formed, or culturally specified.

If biology is reconsidered starting from its most fundamental assumptions, it could be regarded in continuity with social, cultural and psychological relations rather than in opposition to them. It would have to refuse the pervasive dichotomisation of mind and body, and nature and culture. *Biology must itself be amenable to psychical and cultural transformation*, to processes of re-tracing or inscription. Moreover, while clearly sharing many features in common with animal bodies, human bodies should also be seen in fundamentally or qualitatively different terms. Among the most relevant differences here is the fact that only human bodies create culture, and, in the process, transform themselves *corporeally* (as well as conceptually). Human biology must be *always already cultural*, in order for culture to have any effect on it. It is thus a threshold term between nature and culture, being both natural and cultural. Or, formulated more paradoxically, it is *naturally social*. That culture, history and language exist at all must, in some broad sense, be in the 'nature' of human biology, if the term 'biology' refers to the complexity of products and the capacities of the organism. This may be the consequence of the fact that 'instincts' have little or no place in sustaining human life in the earliest years; the child *must* (biologically) depend on others for its survival for a far longer period than other animals (indeed, precisely the length of time it takes for the child to acquire language). In human bodies, instinctually governed survival skills are replaced with, or displaced by, emersion in linguistic and learned, culturally meaningful behaviour.

In short, human subjects *give meaning* to their biologies, to their bodies and their existence. They take up attitudes to their bodies that do not correspond to the behaviour of animals. Humans love or hate, have narcissistic or paranoid investments in, their bodies. Their bodies always *mean something*, to themselves and to others. The subject's relation to its body is always *libidinal*: this is a necessary condition of its ability to identify the body as *its own*. The body, when experienced-as-a-whole as well as the preceding phase of motor fragmentation that Lacan has described as 'the body-in-bits-and-pieces' — that is, the body and its various organs and orifices — are always psychically or libidinally mapped, psychically *represented*, as a condition of the subject's ability to use them and to include them in his or her self-image. These libidinal or eroticised investments are not simply or clearly psychological rather than physiological; they blur the boundaries between the psychic and the somatic, bridging their division and making their (conceptual) separation possible. As Freud claims, the *affect* or energy of libido is neither conscious nor unconscious, for it is not psychical but rather the coupling of the psychical or libido and the (erotogenicity of) an organ. This implies that the body itself, which is continually traversed by organic-psychical drives, is *both* biological and psychical. This understanding of the body as a *hinge* or *threshold* between nature and culture makes the limitations of a genetic, or purely anatomical or physiological account of bodies explicit. If the body is purely natural, an object or form, of otherness, that has value and status relative to subjectivity or consciousness, this means that the body's *biological capacity* for consciousness and subjectivity remains uninvestigated.

Feminists have found unexpected allies in the writings of a number of wayward male philosophers (e.g. Spinoza, Leibniz, Nietzsche, Foucault) who have proposed a unified or *monist* rather than a dichotomised or *dualist* understanding of corporeality and subjectivity, and have located the body as a social, historical and political object. However, in their explorations and questioning of the specific ways in which the *female body* can be reconceived, feminists are unlikely to find much support in the writings of, say, a Nietzsche, a Foucault or a Deleuze. With very rare exceptions, these male theorists are blind to or silent about the implications of acknowledging the sexual specificity of different bodies. Each in his own way cannot acknowledge the masculinity, the phallocentrism, of his own position.

Reconceptualising the body in feminist terms entails recognising the existence of *two* kinds of body, two sexes — or rather, of *at least* two. Binary divisions are, of course arbitrary; they divide what may be considered a sexual continuum (a realm of 'pure sexual difference') into mutually exclusive categories. If these divisions are arbitrary, the continuum could be divided in quite different, non-binary, ways. The differences between the sexes do not have universal 'content', meaning or value. Although in our culture, we discern two types of (sexed) bodies, we could also categorise this continuum in ternary or other terms, depending on social needs.

Feminists have increasingly recognised that there is no monolithic category, 'the body'. There are only *particular kinds of bodies*. Where one (the youthful, white, middle-class male body) functions as a representative of *all* bodies, its domination must be overcome through a defiant affirmation of the autonomy of other kinds of bodies/subjectivities. It may turn out that a subversion is accomplished by the proliferation of a number of different types of ideals or representatives for the range and type of bodies.

There are at least two possible lines of research feminists may undertake in reevaluating women's (and men's) corporeal subjectivities. In one case, the body can be approached, not simply as an external object, but from the point of view of its being lived or experienced by the subject. Rather than defining the subject in terms of a mind, as traditional philosophies have done, the subject's corporeal existence can be explored from the 'inside' as it were. Here, psychoanalysis and phenomenology — however incompatible they are — may provide some basis for analysis of the corporeal framework within which all experience is made possible. While neither phenomenology nor psychoanalysis can be considered discourses of 'corporeality', in Freud's and Lacan's understanding of narcissism and the circulation of libido throughout the body, and in Merleau-Ponty's understanding of the body as the threshold of identity and of the subject's being-in-the-world[6] there are at least the rudiments of an account of an embodied subjectivity. In the second case, the corporeal may be approached, as it were, from the outside: it can be seen as a surface, an externality that presents itself to others and to culture as a *writing* or inscriptive surface. (Here, the writings of Nietzsche, Foucault and Lingis may prove fruitful in highlighting the socio-political production of determinate historical bodies.)

Psycho-social explanations of an always embodied and always acculturated subject are crucial to feminist accounts of women's oppression. The techniques through which the body is unified, coordinated, structured and experienced are productive (diet, exercise, movements, pleasures) and constitute, maintain or modify it (shrinking or expanding it, removing some things, adding others by surgical means, requiring a certain type and level of performance from it) are necessary for seeing it as an *interface* between 'privatised' experience and signifying culture. Yet, as a cultural product, the body must not be seen as a mere shell or 'black box' whose interiority has no relevance. Rather, the inscription of its 'external' surface is directed towards the acquisition of appropriate cultural attitudes, beliefs and values. In other words, the metaphor of the body as a writing surface explains the ways in which the body's interiority is produced through its exterior inscription. Theories of subjectivity or experience, which approach the body from the direction of its internal, psychical operations similarly do not merely focus on the subject's wishes, phantasies and attitudes; they are concerned with the ways in which subjects are able to act, to move, to locate themselves within the boundaries of their corporeality. They too can be seen as approaches to the body's externality, its material existence as an object in-the-world and for-others. The exteriority of the body and the confinement of the subject to its interior are effects of the ways in which the subject makes his or her own body meaningful, the way each eroticises the body and lives (in) it as its own.

In refusing self-evident concepts and 'natural' presumptions about the body, feminists may be able to develop new images and representations by which the lived experiences of bodies can be more adequately inscribed. There are a number of different directions in which this research could go, schematically, if somewhat arbitrarily, outlined below. To formulate different conceptions of corporeality, it may be necessary to:

1. Explore non-Euclidean and non-Kantian notions of space. If Euclidean, three dimensional space organises hierarchicised perspectives according to the laws of point-for-point projection, then different 'pre-oedipal' or infantile non-perspectival spaces, for example, may provide the basis for alternatives to those developed in dominant representations of corporeality.[7] This may entail research in post-Einsteinian concepts of space-time; or, in an

altogether different vein, psychological or fantasmatic concepts of space, for example, the kind experienced by the infant before vision has been hierarchically privileged and coordinated the information provided by the other senses into an homogeneous totality.[8] This is necessary if the representational grid which produces conventional patriarchal representations of the body is to be superseded. Exploring other conceptual schemas which rely on different initial premises and different forms of argument prove useful in showing, at the least, that Euclidean/Cartesian conceptions are not the only possibilities;

2. Explore other conceptions of temporality more adequate to the representation of the *two* sexes than patriarchal conceptions. For example, instead of a temporality fundamentally modelled on spatiality — that is, a temporality understood by discrete digital units of regular sequence,[9] a notion modelled on rhythms, cycles and repetitions may provide some clues in this direction. The digital rendering of units of time — a key presumption in notions of chronological progress, lineage, descent — is uniquely unsuitable to represent the bodily cycles and processes located in women's bodies, even if it may describe men's. Solar time is based on the *mathematisation of time*; lunar temporality, by contrast, is based on repetition. A cyclical and non-progressivist time, one beyond the teleological constraints of Hegelian models or Vico's reworkings, however, is not necessarily alien to notions of history, nor even progress, although it does problematise progress conceived as directional or goal-seeking. Repetition and cyclical time, as Nietzsche so astutely understood, is not the repetition of the same, or the (self)-identical, but that by which difference is generated.

Taken together, 1. and 2. question the Cartesian coordinates by which we conventionally represent the space-time grid in which bodies are positioned and conceptualised. At best, it is *one* means of representing space-time, but not the necessary one. The Cartesian grid renders the space-time continuum *quantifiable*; it becomes incapable of representing the experiences of *both* sexes.

3. Redefining the notion of the body also entails reconceiving notions of power: if the body is one of the major objects contested in power relations, then power can no longer be equated with either ideology (in which it is ideas and conceptual systems that are at stake) nor with physical coercion (in which constraint and threat operate directly on the body with brute, repressive force). Rather than see the body as an intervening *medium* between ideological/social systems and individual belief systems, the body can be regarded as the object of dual power relations which inscribe it both socially and idiosyncratically, both 'externally' and 'internally'. The body is both the means by which power is disseminated and a potential object of resistance to power.

Bodies, then, are not outside of power, for power relations constitute them as such. Power generates ideological effects and systems of coercion only through the production of a socially specific body. Individuals' beliefs and value systems, their practices and expectations are propagated through the codification and control of bodies. Prevailing accounts of socialisation or enculturation, that is, theories of imprinting, internalisation or stereotyping (learning theory) presume a passive, pliable subject, indeed a subject incapable of resisting (whatever resistances or imperfections occur, they are effects of inconsistent expectations and cultural demands, not the products of a subject who rebels). Power relations do not simply impose a set of values and preferred practices on individuals; rather, the subject is 'branded' or inscribed, a subject who, while relatively passive during inscription procedures, must nevertheless actively assume the social tattoo as his or her own in order to have a place in culture. In short, power actively produces rather than inhibits the subject's activities.

4. Other systems of signification and representation, which can describe women in their own terms are also necessary. This means not only the creation of new words, syntactical and grammatical rules and formal structures, but the creation of different representational structures, different ways of using language, different contexts in which discourses can function. It implies re-appropriating language by speakers who have been disqualified as such from enunciation. It is thus not a *new* language that is required, but, more feasibly, the construction of new knowledges. This seems necessary insofar as bodies themselves are never brute objects external to discourses and representations; it is relevant then, that the activity of making meaning be reordered so that the bodies it conditions and the social subjectivities it makes possible can be changed.

Biology, for example, could be reformulated, starting from premises that do not automatically regard women as the passive counterparts of men. The humanities and social sciences could become more open to women's interests and perspectives. Indeed, instead of the disinterested objective status of knowledges, they could now be recognised as products of sexually particular perspectives. This recognition would not mean that feminist texts are biased relative to mainstream knowledges, but rather, that *all knowledges*, all discourses, are produced by interests, values and political perspectives. Acknowledging its representational limits may entail the formation of entirely different kinds of knowledge than those which aspire to an eternal, truthful status, a universal validity, or an unambiguous, transparent meaning.

5. Accounts of the sexually differentiated, socially produced body need to transform, integrate, and re-categorise hitherto diverse methodologies and knowledges. This is correlative to the transformations and upheavals in textual norms already suggested. If the boundaries between prevailing knowledges and disciplines remain intact, the body will not be amenable to a psycho-social and biological analysis. Feminist accounts of the body require experiential or phenomenological concepts of the body as the site for an interior or psychical map (of the world, of its own corporeal outlines, of

others) — as well as accounts of the ways in which bodies are manipulated, produced and controlled in order to develop different conceptions of the *lived body*. The 'lived body', the body-and-consciousness has been spuriously defined as 'gender' in most feminist literature on sexual identity.[10] Yet, to avoid the bifurcation between a purely biological 'sex' and a purely social 'gender', which reinforces a mind/body opposition, feminists must take seriously the 'internal' or psychical evidence of the body's externality, and concepts of the body as an external surface which, when appropriately inscribed, engenders psychical or internal attributes. The body's reconceptualisation implies seeing it as a surface for social inscription, a material, external and social writing surface, on which social law is etched; and psychical systems, which are always anchored in the body's perceptual, sensory, and libidinal sensitivity. The introceptive or experiential notion of the body must not be opposed to or seen in distinction from an extroceptive, social concept. These are two sides of a single coin. The social inscription of bodies, particularly in the socialising processes of the kinship structure, produce meanings and structures necessary to live the body as one's own.[11] And the psychical investments in the body's zones and organs, correlatively, is the condition of the body's use for and integration with subjectivity. They mutually condition each other.

The construction of alternative models of corporeal or carnal existence, if they are to represent both sexes adequately and without reductionism, should place special emphasis on women's particular corporeal experiences. Specifically female biological processes like ovulation, menstruation, childbirth, lactation or other processes — have always been inscribed in patriarchal terms and analysed only according to men's interests. Women's bodies are reduced to biology, which in turn presumes them to be passive relative to the (implicitly male) norm of 'humanity'. When women's *psychical experiences of their bodies* are coupled with revised biological models more appropriate to women, can women provide a new starting point for reconceiving their corporeality? For example, women's experiences of menstruation — the archetypal 'symptom' of women's unique biologies — are not simply responses to hormonal and biological imperatives, but are effects, in the first instance, of the ways in which menstruation is represented in culture, and as the way it is lived or experienced by women — its meaning *for them*. In a culture where it is regarded as a wound, a sign of castration, lack or imperfection (as is common in patriarchy), it is likely to be experienced as a dreaded burden or debilitation, unpleasant or painful.

This does not, however, mean that the body's responses to biological processes can be explained by the opposite extreme — psycho-somatic causes, produced by the mind. Rather, it means that lived experiences are made possible and structured as such only through the social construction and inscription of biologies, physiologies or anatomies. Women's specificities, their corporeality and subjectivities, are not inherently resistant to representation

190

or depiction. They may be unrepresentable in a culture in which the masculine can represent others only as versions of itself, where the masculine relies on the subordination of the feminine. But this is not logically or biologically fixed. It can be contested and changed; it can be redefined, reconceived, reinscribed in ways entirely different from those that mark it today.

* I wish to acknowledge the invaluable support for research on this paper provided by the Humanities Research Centre, The Australian National University in 1986.

Notes

1 M. Blanchot *The Writing of Disaster* (University of Nebraska Press), Lincoln, 1986, p. 45.
2 For a feminist critique of egalitarianism, see M. Thornton, 'Sex Equality is Not Enough for Feminism', in C. Pateman and E. Gross *Feminist Challenges. Social and Political Theory* (Allen and Unwin), Sydney, 1986.
3 This seems to be one of the major implications of Foucault's 'genealogical' analyses, in for example, *Discipline and Punish* (Pantheon) New York, 1976; and *The History of Sexuality. Vol. 1 An Introduction* (Pantheon) New York, 1977.
4 For example, in R. Descartes 'The Meditations' in E. Anscombe and P. T. Geach (eds.) *Descartes: Philosophical Writings* (Nelson) Edinburgh, 1954.
5 20th century positions tend to be reductionist rather than monist. Most commonly, modern proponents of mind/body split advocate reducing one to the terms of the other. Where the body is explained in terms of mind, idealism results; and where the mind is explained in terms of the body, materialism is the consequence. Reductionism in both forms simply explains away the 'other' term instead of integrating them or explaining their connections. Today, the materialist reduction of mind to body — particularly the reduction of the mind to the brain — is the most typical 'answer' to the problem of dualism.
6 The psychoanalytic material is located in the various papers centred on the pre-oedipal period — including 'On Narcissism. An Introduction' (S.E. Vol. 14) 'The Three Essays on the Theory of Sexuality' (S.E. Vol. 7) and 'The Ego and The Id' (S.E. Vol. 19) in Freud's work; and the conception of the 'imaginary anatomy' in Lacan's work on the mirror-stage, especially 'The Mirror Stage As Formative of the Function of the I' in *Ecrits. A Selection* (Tavistock), London, 1977, and 'Some Reflections on the Ego', *International Journal of Psychoanalysis*, No. 34, 1953. In the case of Merleau-Ponty and phenomenology, the concept of embodiment is forcefully outlined in *The Primacy of Perception* (Northwestern University Press), Evanston, 1964.
7 The infant's perception of space is not yet structured in terms of adult notions. It has not yet learned to distinguish virtual/specular from real space (Spitz, Merleau-Ponty). It does not understand perspectives or the relations between figure and ground, which require oppositions that the child has not yet acquired. For the infant, space is not yet conceived as a regular grid into which objects are placed or from which they can be removed. Space, in other words, is never 'empty', simply subsisting without objects. This requires an abstraction from its experiences and an ability to position *itself* as an object available for inspection by others. Instead, the child perceives within a pre-oedipal space which is largely orally or kinaesthetically, not visually, structured. The child perceives a 'space of adherence' (Merleau-Ponty), a space that clings to objects and images without distinguishing them.

8 Rather surprisingly this pre-oedipal space — which is occasionally invoked in dreams — is close to mathematical and physicist views which develop non-Euclidian notions of space — Reimannian space, the curved space-time of Einsteinian physics, the 'impossible' space of the Mobius strip and the Klein bottle, Finsler's space are all 'impossible' notions on a Euclidean model.

9 See, for example, Irigaray's comments on the spatialisation of time and the temporalisation of space in her analysis of Kant's *Critique of Pure Reason*, in her text, *L'Ethique de la difference sexuelle* (Edition de Minuit) Paris, 1984.

10 cf. M. Gatens' 'A Critique of the Sex Gender Distinction', in J. Allen and P. Patton (eds.) *Beyond Marxism? Interventions After Marx* (Intervention Publications) Sydney, 1983, pp. 143–162.

11 For a discussion of the conditions under which the body is claimed as one's own, see E. A. Grosz 'Language and the Limits of the Body: Kristeva and Abjection' in *Futur*Fall. Excursions into Post-Modernity*. (Power Foundation), Sydney, 1987.

12

FEMINISM AND THE MATTER OF BODIES

From de Beauvoir to Butler

Alex Hughes and Anne Witz

Source: *Body and Society* 3(1) (1997): 47–60.

Introduction

In this article, we examine the ways in which Simone de Beauvoir and Judith Butler have negotiated, implicitly and explicitly, the complex, unstable distinction between 'sex' and 'gender'. We explore some of the problems intrinsic in this distinction – which de Beauvoir sets up as central to feminist analysis but which Butler subsequently reworks – and, in particular, we scrutinize the complicated connection to it of a third and crucial term: the body. The sex/ gender relation has already been the focus of considerable debate within feminism. Our intention here is to dissect two key propositions which emerge out of our readings of that relation, as it is theorized by de Beauvoir and Butler. The first is that a problematic element of de Beauvoir's legacy to feminism in *The Second Sex* (1949, trans. 1972), is, as Toril Moi puts it, a vision of a female 'body in trouble' (Moi, 1994: 148–78). The second is that Butler's efforts, in the 1980s and 1990s, to retrieve the body for/within gender theory and to allow it to represent more than mere residual facticity eventually attenuate the power of *gender* as a category of analysis.[1] The guiding thread of our discussion, in other words, will be the notion that whereas de Beauvoir privileges gender and elides the body, Butler, ultimately, does the reverse.

In the first part of our paper, we revisit de Beauvoir's *The Second Sex*. This work, as Mary Dietz states, in its 'celebrated declaration of gender' as a socially invested situation, 'frame[d] the field of feminist scholarly enquiry' in the early decades of second-wave feminism (Dietz, 1992: 74). Our aim here is to demonstrate that de Beauvoir's bid, in *The Second Sex*, to escape biologically reductionist explanations of women's situation functions

193

powerfully to diagnose and destabilize patriarchal epistemologies of woman-hood which construct woman within and according to the data of biology. However, there is also an underlying, residual 'ghost in the machine' within de Beauvoir's radical attempt to restore female subjectivity/sociality, which is a female body in trouble. This body, moreover, never fully emerges in *The Second Sex* into a situation where it is not in trouble. Our contention is, then, that if de Beauvoir foregrounds and works productively with the category of gender, she seems unable to do so in a way which avoids sidelining, occulting and 'pathologizing' the female body.

In the second section of our discussion, we turn to an exploration of the powerfully influential work of Judith Butler (as exemplified by *Gender Trouble* [1990] and *Bodies that Matter* [1993]). If we have opted to focus on Butler, it is because she herself focuses explicitly on de Beauvoir's analysis of the sex/gender distinction, precisely because she is keen to escape that 'radical discontinuity between sexed bodies and culturally constructed genders' which is the (problematic) heritage of de Beauvoirian feminism (Butler, 1990: 6; further discussion of de Beauvoir see also Butler, 1990: 10–12, Butler, 1986). In *Gender Trouble*, Butler's escape route proceeds by way of an attempt to wrench 'the body' away from a discrete ontology of substance – designated by the marker of sex – and to instate it *within* the category of gender. In her later book, *Bodies that Matter*, Butler shifts her attention to questions concerning the materialization of the body, specifically its sex. In section two of our discussion, we seek to show how the treatment of the body which Butler offers acts in the end to *obscure* gender, which 'disappears' behind the (discursively regulated) matter of bodies. Our point, then, in this part of our analysis is that in Butler's work, 'gender troubles' are occulted, finally, by 'bodily matters', and occulted in a way that appears highly problematic for feminism.

De Beauvoir on the body

> One is not born but rather becomes a woman. No biological, psychological or economic fate determines the figure that the human being presents in society: it is civilization as a whole that produces this creature indeterminate between male and eunuch which is described as feminine. (de Beauvoir, 1972: 295)

In this much quoted extract from *The Second Sex*, de Beauvoir is doing two things. First, she is articulating the notion that gendering, or becoming a woman or a man, is a productive *social* process. This point came to be absolutely crucial to feminist thinking. Second, she is asserting that biology is not an all-embracing destiny for women. As Moi points out, 'Beauvoir herself insists that hers is a theory of the *social* construction of femininity and masculinity, and, moreover, categorically refuses the idea of a biological or anatomical "destiny" of any kind' (Moi, 1994: 162).

In arguing that anatomy is not destiny, de Beauvoir moves the body off-centre and onto the periphery. She privileges, in other words, the social over the anatomical, and does so precisely in order to explain that which she claims biology cannot explain, i.e. women's *total* situation. This is defined by de Beauvoir as a state of subordination, deriving from a hierarchy of the sexes thanks to which woman 'finds herself living in a world where men compel her to assume the status of the Other' (de Beauvoir, 1972: 29). The bulk of the *The Second Sex* consists of an analysis of women's oppression/ alterity. This analysis establishes how women have been subjected to men economically, socially and politically, in different ways and at different points of history. In writing it, de Beauvoir argues that women exist – and are only conscious of themselves – in ways that men have shaped. She claims that women behave, think and perceive themselves in 'manmade' modes. Woman, she concludes, 'is determined not by her hormones or by mysterious instincts, but by the manner in which her body and her relation to the world are modified through the action of others than herself' (de Beauvoir, 1972: 734).

If biology is not the destiny of woman, then what is the status of 'her body' in de Beauvoir's analysis? On one level, clearly, as the above excerpt from *The Second Sex* suggests, de Beauvoir views the female body as a *socially inflected* body. This is in fact an optimistic position, implying as it does that while woman's body may constitute a problem – because it is socially inflected under patriarchy in an *oppressive* fashion – the problem it represents is not immutable, or wholly devoid of the possibility of change. If 'others' can modify 'her body', and what it 'means', then so too, surely, can woman herself. This account of de Beauvoir's (optimistic) stance vis-à-vis the (mutable) female body does not, however, tell the whole story. As Moi convincingly argues, above and beyond the positive envisioning of a female body open to 'reconstruction' which de Beauvoir occasionally offers us within *The Second Sex*, her essay contains an insistent, haunting vision of the female body as viscerally disgusting: a vision which suggests that de Beauvoir really feels that the female body *is* essentially a 'body in trouble' (see Moi, 1994: 164–74). Moi's point, in other words, is that de Beauvoir's admirable effort to theorize the (oppressive) construction of female embodied subjectivity by/within patriarchy is flawed, and flawed by a failure to escape that revulsion vis-à-vis the female body which inheres in patriarchal culture itself.[2] It seems, then, that de Beauvoir's *The Second Sex* offers a kind of dual perspective on the female body. This perspective incorporates, first, a (positive) vision of a constructed body that is mutable and, second, a more pessimistic vision of a residual, unconstructed, troubled female body – that visceral, menstruating, reproducing, lactating body which is a seemingly intractable part of woman's situation. Catriona MacKenzie (1986) has also argued that de Beauvoir's text creates two oppositional discourses of the female body. One – a constructivist discourse – appears to insist upon the female body as socially constructed, so describes how oppressed women experience their bodies under patriarchy. This is our mutable female body. The other – an oppressive discourse – describes what it is like to experience the world as a body which is fundamentally and inescapably oppressive. This is our female body in trouble.

As Moi rightly contends, discussions of the unconstructed, visceral female body in *The Second Sex* relate to de Beauvoir's theorization of woman's alienation. In the existentialist conceptual framework exploited by de Beauvoir, the tendency of both men and women to alienation is a central feature. However, de Beauvoir believes that while women and men alike *are* their bodies, a *woman's* body (more particularly her reproductive body), unlike a man's, is also something other than herself, and constitutes therefore a profound source of her species alienation. As Moi explains, de Beauvoir's argument seems to be that 'the fact of having a female body is what makes [woman] a woman, yet this very fact also alienates and separates her from herself' (Moi, 1994: 164). In other words, in de Beauvoir's analysis, the body of a woman – that body dogged by 'crises of puberty and the menopause, monthly "curse", long and often difficult pregnancy, painful and sometimes dangerous childbirth, illnesses, unexpected symptoms and complications' (de Beauvoir, 1972: 64) – poses a threat to her personhood, and constantly puts her individuality at risk. This fate is not shared by the male subject, whose sexual life, de Beauvoir (sweepingly) declares, 'is not in opposition to his existence as a person, and biologically . . . runs an even course, without crises and generally without mishap' (de Beauvoir, 1972: 64).

What de Beauvoir seeks to address in statements such as this is the gendered relationship between the body and subjectivity. Her position regarding this relationship can be summarized as follows. Under patriarchy, woman has been reduced to her body; man, however, has not been 'fixed' within/by his. Man does not begin and end with his body, but possesses a consciousness that moves beyond it. Man makes himself what he is, and manhood is a project of becoming. In *The Second Sex*, de Beauvoir seeks to accomplish/ imagine the same situation for woman. Her aim is to recover woman from her imprisonment within the female body, and to understand/envision the female subject in her becoming. Thus, the definition of the possibilities of womanhood above and beyond the female body is the core of the de Beauvoirian project in *The Second Sex*. Her attention focuses primarily upon the constraints and the potentialities of women's becoming. Consequently, 'gender' – the key locus of woman's constraint/becoming – becomes primordial, acquiring the status of both a construct and a project. As Judith Butler puts it, gender not only emerges in *The Second Sex* as 'a cultural construction imposed upon [woman's] identity, but in some sense gender is a process of constructing ourselves' (Butler, 1986: 36). De Beauvoir's dissection of the potential 'reconstructability' of women's gender status constitutes an enabling legacy for feminism. Less enabling, however, is de Beauvoir's (negative) vision of the female body-as-trap, and the doubts which this vision casts upon the degree of its mutability.

For Judith Butler, de Beauvoir's argument in *The Second Sex* is that 'the female body *ought to be* the situation and instrumentality of women's freedom, not a defining and limiting essence' (Butler, 1990: 12). However, Butler also points out that 'the theory of embodiment informing Beauvoir's analysis is clearly limited by the uncritical reproduction of the Cartesian distinction between freedom and the body' (Butler, 1990: 12). This diagnosis is extremely pertinent. In it, Butler is (reluctantly) recognizing that de Beauvoir never fully succeeds in retrieving the female body from its troubled, limiting state, with the result that it remains on the periphery, assuming a residual facticity that is profoundly harmful/antithetical to woman's autonomy.

Two key manifestations of the factitious female 'body in trouble' emerge from the pages of *The Second Sex*. That this is so reflects the particular emphasis which de Beauvoir's essay places upon, first, the *reproductive* body and, second, the *desiring* body. The first of these bodies appears never to assume the status of anything other than a trap and a source of alienation. De Beauvoir's descriptions of pregnancy and childbirth make this apparent:

> The conflict between species and individual, which sometimes assumes dramatic force at childbirth, endows the feminine body with a disturbing frailty. It has been well said that women 'have infirmity in the abdomen'; and it is true that they have within them a hostile element – it is the species gnawing at their vitals. (de Beauvoir, 1972: 63)

De Beauvoir seems however to represent the desiring body as more mutable than its 'sister' and as potentially more free. Our sense of this is confirmed by the fact that, as Moi remarks, de Beauvoir does imagine ways in which heterosexual intercourse, occurring under non-oppressive conditions, might engender 'a profound experience of reciprocity' (Moi, 1994: 172); an experience wherein the female body might function not as a body in trouble, the source/site of alienation and crisis, but rather as a fulfilled, enabling body.[3] However, as Moi also indicates, de Beauvoir's vision of fulfilled, 'healthy' female embodiment is undermined by the indubitable, visceral disgust which the female sexual organs regularly inspire in her, and by the way in which *The Second Sex* insistently implies that anatomical differences mean 'it will *always* be harder for women than for men to experience themselves as sexual beings and free subjects at one and the same time; in some way or other, women will always be up against their anatomy' (Moi, 1994: 172). For de Beauvoir, it seems, even the *desiring* body of a woman is never out of 'trouble' for long.[4]

It appears, in summary, to be the case that de Beauvoir *is* trapped within that Cartesian mind/body dualism which underpins the existentialist conceptualization of freedom as a project of the mind, and as a state of consciousness which transcends the immanence of embodiment, of facticity, of death.[5] Unlike latter-day feminists – Luce Irigaray, for instance – de Beauvoir seems unable/unwilling to recognize that woman might 'think through her body' in order to work towards a non-alienated consciousness and an understanding of what it is to be 'free'. Wedded as she apparently is to the perception that the female body can only in the end be non-transcendent, it seems that de Beauvoir cannot entirely think *beyond* the body of woman, precisely because she cannot think *through* it.[6]

Regardless of de Beauvoir's difficult relationship with the embodied residue of woman, she undoubtedly succeeded in theorizing the previously *un*theorized: that is, the notion of 'gender'. She established that masculinities and femininities are infinitely *more* than their biological facticities, thus providing one of the most powerful political and conceptual tools of second-wave feminism. She may have sidelined the bodily – a fact which recalls Butler's point that 'those trained in philosophy [are] always at some distance from corporeal matters, [and] try in that disembodied way to demarcate bodily terrains: they invariably miss the body or, worse, write against it' (Butler, 1993: ix) – but, as Dorothy Kaufmann asserts, the analysis offered in her essay *is*, indubitably, 'where contemporary feminism begins' (Kaufmann, 1986: 128).

Butler and the matter of bodies

> Gender is the repeated stylization of the body, a set of repeated acts within a highly rigid, regulatory frame that congeal over time to produce the appearance of substance, of a natural sort of being. (Butler, 1990: 33)

> Consider gender, for instance, as a *corporeal style*, an 'act', as it were, which is both intentional and performative, where '*performative*' suggests a dramatic and contingent construction of meaning. (Butler, 1990: 139)

In these extracts from *Gender Trouble*, Butler repositions the body as central to an understanding of gender. Gender is framed here as an enactment, and as involving imitative, *bodily* signification. Gender performances are, moreover, theorized by Butler as regulated by and within 'the obligatory frame of reproductive heterosexuality' (Butler, 1990: 136). They rest upon a kind of reiterated corporeal 'doing', albeit not one that individuals can *choose* to do/decide upon (a point Butler clarifies in her preface to *Bodies that Matter*). Born out of a disciplinary regulation of the flesh – Butler regularly borrows her terminology from Foucault – they are '*fabrications*, manufactured and sustained through corporeal signs and other discursive means' (Butler, 1990: 136). This, in truth, means that the (gendered) body, for Butler, 'has no ontological status apart from the various acts which constitute its reality' – even though 'bodily gestures, movements and styles of various kinds constitute the *illusion* of an abiding gendered self' (Butler, 1990: 136, 140, our emphasis).

The above outline of Butler's complex treatment in *Gender Trouble* of the gender/body relation suggests that Butler's project, up until 1990 at least, was prompted by a desire to reassociate the categories of gender and sex, via the third notion of bodily performativity, or corporeal enactment/stylization.[7] That this was the case is symptomatic of her dissatisfaction with the 'de Beauvoirian' optic wherein 'gender' can only pertain to what culture and society *make* of the residual (female) body and is thus *dissociated* from the sexed body itself. In other words, in *Gender Trouble*, Butler is bent upon 'troubling' the sex/gender distinction. Gender remains her key category of analysis. However, Butler radically *expands* that category, by recuperating sex from the realm of embodiment/immutability and by suggesting that 'this construct called "sex" is as culturally constructed as gender; indeed, it was always already gender, with the consequence that the distinction between sex and gender turns out to be no distinction at all' (Butler, 1990: 7). In *Gender Trouble*, then, she is seeking to correct the assumption that 'sex' is more ontologically 'fixed' than gender; more invariable, more material, more substantive. She is refusing the idea that gender can be made and remade in ways that 'natural' *sex* cannot. She is moving beyond a notion of the sexed body as a substance upon which gender can work, towards a position where the body represents that which gender works through and indeed constitutes. In this she clearly *differs* from de Beauvoir, for whom – as we indicated above – the (female) body never fully moves beyond the status of a limiting materiality out of which gender is culturally interpreted, upon which it is superimposed, and within which the gendered self abides.

In *Bodies that Matter*, Butler's position evolves. She herself confirms this, both in the preface to her text, which sets *Bodies that Matter* up as offering 'a rethinking of some parts of *Gender Trouble*' (Butler, 1993: xii), and in an interview in *Radical Philosophy*, where she states: 'I have shifted, I think I overrode the category of Sex too quickly in *Gender Trouble*. I tried to reconsider it in *Bodies that Matter*, and to emphasize the place of constraint in the very production of sex' (Butler, 1994: 32–3). In opting to move away from a focus on gender as a fabricated bodily performance, she moves towards a preoccupation with the discursively constituted *materiality* of the sexed body. As her Introduction indicates,[8] she reformulates her problematic in order to address those ways in which 'the regulatory norms of "sex" work in a performative fashion to constitute the materiality of bodies, and, more specifically, to materialize the body's sex' (Butler, 1993: 2). She strives to dissect the key question: 'What are the constraints by which bodies are materialized as "sexed", and how are we to understand the "matter" of sex, and of bodies more generally?' (Butler, 1993: xi–xii). Thus, her area of enquiry shifts from a concern with corporeal *styles* to a focus on fleshly *matters*.

What Butler is doing, in *Bodies that Matter*, is tackling head on the matter of bodies, without resorting to a reinstatement of that ontology of substance which *Gender Trouble* swept aside. She avoids such a reinstatement by casting 'the matter of bodies as the effect of a dynamic of power, such that the matter of bodies will be indissociable from the regulatory norms that govern their materialization' (Butler, 1993: 2), i.e. by pursuing a resolutely Foucauldian stance. This stance permits her to 'return to the notion of matter, not as a site or a surface, but as *a process of materialization that stabilizes over time to produce the effect of boundary, fixity, and surface we call matter*' (Butler, 1993: 9). Her adoption of it suggests that her project, in *Bodies that Matter*, is to pose materialist questions without having to revert to a materialist ontological framework.

If Butler decides – as she evidently does – to think through the 'matter' of the body/sex as *materialized*, through regulatory discourses and matrices of power, then it is clear that she has come to recognize that it is unjustifiable to leave the matter of the body untheorized. Implicit in this recognition is an admission that she herself, in *Gender Trouble*, for all her efforts to bring the body into her account of gender performativity, in fact occluded the *matter* of bodies. *Bodies that Matter* represents her attempt to redress that occlusion.

Butler's attempt incorporates a construal of the materiality of the sexed body not as an irreducible given, but as a construction whose contouring and formation issue from 'actions' which, mobilized by the law of 'sex',[9] entail a *citation* of that law which produces *material effects* (see Butler, 1993: 12).[10] Her mode of reasoning rests on the notion that the citational materialization of the sexed body involves the constrained assumption of a bodily norm (Butler, 1993: 3), which is linked to the emergence of subjectivity.[11] This assumption cannot be divorced from the question of identification with the normative dictates of the 'heterosexual imperative'. It is this manifestation of power more than any other, Butler implies, which establishes 'boundaries of bodily life where abjected or delegitimated bodies fail to count as "bodies"' (Butler, 1993: 15), which enables 'certain sexed identifications and forecloses and/or disavows other[s]' (Butler, 1993: 3), and which produces ' "unlivable" and "uninhabitable" zones of social life which are none the less densely populated by those [abjected bodily beings] who do not enjoy the status of the subject' (Butler, 1993: 3).[12] The heterosexual regime, in other words, is centrally implicated in that division of the field of bodies – into 'bodies that matter' and bodies that do not – which Butler takes as a key focus of her analysis.

What troubles us, in Butler's increasingly self-referential and at times dense problematic, are the *erasures* it effects. Before discussing some of these, however, we wish to acknowledge the productive dimensions of the Butlerian project. Butler's conceptualization of the materialization of the sexed body opens up a mode of radical 'bodily thinking' which is absent not only in de Beauvoir's *The Second Sex* but also in Butler's own *Gender Trouble*. Further, her linking of the regulated assumption of bodily norms to issues of subjectivity and abjection introduces new possibilities for reflection and critique. Butler's arguments encourage us to think productively about the workings of those mechanisms through which some modalities of bodily being are banished 'from the proper domain of "sex" ' (Butler, 1993: 23), and from subjectivity, while others are legitimated. More importantly, her accounts of the contestatory possibilities intrinsic in the domain of objected bodies emphasize what she terms the 'political promise' of citationality (Butler, 1993: 21), and contribute powerfully to contemporary queer (re)formulations of bodily 'abjection', which read the 'abject' defiantly, in order to generate an 'enabling disruption, the occasion for a radical rearticulation of the symbolic horizon in which bodies come to matter at all' (Butler, 1993: 23).[13]

What, then, of the erasures that operate in *Bodies that Matter*? In the preface to her text, Butler alludes to that body which lives and dies, eats and sleeps, feels pain and pleasure, endures illness, violence and so forth, in order to pinpoint the way in which its dogged materiality seems to defy containment within post-structuralist theories of constructivism which 'reduce all materiality to linguistic stuff' (Butler, 1993: xi, 29–30).[14] She herself, she insists, wants to find 'new ways for bodies to matter' (Butler, 1993: 30). She seeks to discover new modes of thinking which neither presume nor negate materiality, and endeavours in so doing to move beyond the legacies of post-structuralist *and* de Beauvoirian feminism. However, Butler's own constructionist framework does not, in our view, succeed in recuperating those 'substantive' aspects of bodies – that 'lost matter of bodies' – evoked in her prefatory remarks and in her first chapter. More particularly, her speculations lose sight of certain 'matters' characterizing the living *female* body, notably those pertaining to the (de Beauvoirian) reproductive 'body in trouble' on which earlier sections of our article focused. This omission points up the fact that Butler is actively striving, in *Bodies that Matter*, to refute the classical philosophical association of femininity and materiality (see Butler, 1993: 31–2). It is symptomatic, further, of her desire to prevent us from thinking about bodies naively, as 'matters' which we 'experience'. However, in encouraging us to abandon this type of thinking, she leaves little space for a consideration of the ways in which women may actually 'live' their bodies *precisely as such*. She offers, moreover, scant scope for a recognition of the fact that there may be, for women, *gendered* modes of bodily materiality – modes relating for instance to issues of menstruation, conception, contraception, and the colonization/control of the female body by new reproductive technologies – which cannot be understood *simply* as constructions contoured by the (hegemonic, heterosexual) law of *Sex*. Butler, in other words – because she concentrates so intensely upon the ways in which the body comes to be materialized *within the regulatory framework of normative heterosexuality* – allows whole areas of (female) bodily being to elude the bounds of her analysis and thus to disappear from her problematic. If, then, her work offers us tools through which to theorize the constrained materialization of the sexed body, it nonetheless obscures key matters of gender-inflected embodiment which are central to an understanding of women's experience/oppression, and which feminism can ill afford to ignore. Early on in *Bodies that Matter*, Butler exhorts us to remember that 'the "body" comes in genders' (Butler, 1993: ix). This fact, however, is something that she herself seems in the end never fully to address.

It is not only those doggedly fleshy, troubling matters of female embodiment which are obscured by Butler. Butler also occults the analytic *category* of gender, by causing it intermittently to 'disappear' mysteriously behind 'sex' (where 'sex' represents a cultural norm governing the materialization of bodies). It is not as if Butler *never* speaks of gender in *Bodies that Matter*. Her final chapter, 'Critically Queer' is for instance devoted in large part to a discussion of 'resignificatory' modes of gender performativity and their relation to queer politics. However, in those sections of her text where the regulatory, normative power of 'sex' comes to prominence, gender magically collapses, ceasing to figure in any meaningful way. Consequently, in our opinion at least, Butler's working through of the sex/gender/body triad – that triad which led her down her analytical path from the troubles of gender to the matter of bodies – ultimately foregrounds and elides two of its terms (sexed bodies) at the expense of the third (gender). Butler herself, particularly in the Introduction to *Bodies that Matter*, seems keen to imply that in her most recent theoretical schema, gender, sex and the body remain in 'touch' with each other. How, though, can this actually be the case, within a framework which addresses the 'matter of bodies' in such a way as to occlude the 'matter of gender' behind the overarching regulatory citationality of the heterosexual law?

Conclusion

De Beauvoir's problematic legacy to modern feminism – the female body in trouble – was one of the disabling consequences of her use of Sartreian existentialism. Sartre's horror of 'the slimy', or the in-itself that threatens to overwhelm the project of individual being for-itself, was incarnated in the female body – which, for Sartre, represented an enveloping matter 'comparable to the flattening out of the overripe breasts of a woman lying on her back' (Sartre, quoted in Le Doeuff, cited in Grosz, 1989: 214). We have argued that de Beauvoir was ultimately unable to retrieve the female body from the fleshly, troubling state that it occupies in existentialist philosophy. It is worth noting, however, that while we have stressed the disabling influence of existentialism upon de Beauvoir and upon the modern feminist project that she inspired, Le Doeuff suggests that it is precisely because de Beauvoir did *not* identify with the notion of a shared female embodiment that she was able to step back from women's bodily being and produce the analysis for which she is feted: an analysis that turns on the contention that women's situation is more than bodily. Arguably, then, the curbing of de Beauvoir's capacity to conceive of the fleshiness of woman as anything other than a troubling state which existentialism effected was counterbalanced by the way in which de Beauvoir's existentialist stance enabled her to think beyond woman's corporeality and to envisage feminine agency in a new and radical way.

For all Le Doeuff's exculpation of de Beauvoir, we must not forget that de Beauvoir's feminist imaginary enabled women to think beyond, but not *through*, their bodies. Still working with the Hegelian-inflected framework of existentialist phenomenology (which linked women to the sphere of natural, immanent reproduction whilst working with an idealized notion of the male body as a rational body, under the control of the intellect and capable of transcending its own embodied limitations), de Beauvoir is left grappling with the issue of how woman can achieve subjectivity *despite* her reproductive capacity (Mackenzie, 1986). Nonetheless, de Beauvoir's feminist imaginary influenced modern feminism by opening up the possibility of conceptualizing the sociality of woman although at the same time foreclosing the possibility of conceptualizing women's corporeality. It is therefore unsurprising that the sex/gender distinction that conceptually drove much modern feminist thought was toppled, in the 1980s, from its position of conceptual dominance. Feminists' reluctance to conceptualize the female body was corrected in the 1980s by the enthusiastic insertion of 'the body' into the very centre of poststructuralist feminism. However, as Grosz (1995) argues, this insertion has taken the form of a radical discursivization of bodies, at the heart of which lies a denial of bodily corporeality. As Grosz points out, 'analyses of the representation of bodies abound, but bodies in their material variety still wait to be thought' (Grosz, 1995: 31). We see Judith Butler's work as working both within and against the trajectory of feminist poststructuralism which Grosz evokes. On the one hand, Butler attempts to correct the radical discursivization of the corporeal to which Grosz refers, and to return to the 'matter' of bodies. Butler's notion of the 'materialization' of bodies (articulated most forcefully in *Bodies that Matter*) represents her attempt to effect just such a return. Ultimately though, as we suggested earlier, Butler's heavy reliance on the notion of 'citationality' and its relation to the overarching influence of the heterosexual law works to occlude gendered corporeality behind the materialization of sexed bodies, i.e. loses its hold on the lived, fleshly, experienced matter of (womanly) bodies.

In the post-de Beauvoirian feminist climate, then, has gender really gone away? If, as much of our argument has suggested, gender is a disappearing category, then does this actually matter at all? Some critics – Grosz (1996) for example – appear to applaud the demise of the category 'gender' on the grounds that, in a post-Foucauldian age, it constitutes a wholly redundant category of feminist analysis; others – Gatens (1996) included – are renegotiating their analyses of corporeality in such a way as to retrieve a gendered perspective. Our conceptual and political loyalties lie with the latter group. We want to suggest that gender constitutes a vital category within the analysis of the matter of bodies, and to argue in favour of a feminist pragmatics that does not throw the baby (gender) out with the bathwater (the lost or untheorized matter of bodies). We think that the matter of bodies provides a vitally important third term within feminist analysis. However, we are also convinced that bodies of analysis in which the body and sexuality/sexual difference play a central role must also incorporate – or at least not preclude – a phenomenologically inflected understanding of embodiment as a lived, gendered materiality. Embodiment, in other words, can and must be conceptualized as a lived matter of gender.

Notes

1 The notion of facticity will recur in our discussion. It signifies all of those things which form part of the situation of a human being but which he/she has not chosen, and which seem to constitute a limitation.

2 Moi argues further that if de Beauvoir cannot manage to avoid being horrified by the female body, this is for two reasons. The first is that she exploits Sartrean categories and a disgust for the female body inheres in Sartrean thinking (see Moi, 1994: 168). The second is that de Beauvoir herself is driven by unconscious fears relating to the *mother's* body (Moi, 1994: 173). Other commentators who address de Beauvoir's fear of (female) biology are Elaine Marks (1986) and Mary Evans (1984: 61–6, 128).

3 Moi locates traces of this body not only in *The Second Sex* but also in de Beauvoir's novel *The Blood of Others* (1945), in which a female character, Hélène, appears to enjoy, with her lover, Jean Blomart, an experience of freedom-in-desire (see Moi, 1994: 172–3). It is worth noting that the credible status of that experience and its 'emancipatory' effect is attenuated by the fact that we are never given access to *Hélène's* own view of the sexual encounter in question; this being 'focalized' through *Jean's* narrative perspective/consciousness.

4 Elaine Marks remarks upon the way in which de Beauvoir's autobiographical texts 'pathologize' woman's sexual body, noting that in them 'urination, abundant, excessive urination by women becomes the metaphor for everything that is embarrassing in sexuality. . . . And the metaphor always involves the feminine' (Marks, 1986: 192).

5 Both Moi (in 'Ambiguous Women') and Butler (in *Gender Trouble*) acknowledge this fact. In *Gender Trouble*, Butler reverses therefore her earlier contention, contained in 'Sex and Gender in Simone de Beauvoir's *Second Sex*', that 'not only is it questionable whether [de Beauvoir] accepts [in *The Second Sex*] a view of consciousness of freedom which is in any sense beyond the body . . . but her discussion of the Other permits a reading which is highly critical of the masculine project of disembodiment' (Butler, 1986: 43). She herself recognizes this volte-face (Butler, 1990: 12).

6 In this context, Tina Chanter's observations regarding de Beauvoir's vision of sexual difference are illuminating:

> Beauvoir [argues] that while men risk their lives, create values, and introduce novelty into the world, women do not. While men take initiatives, women stick to biological rhythms. Having set up the problem in this way, the only solution she can find is for women to become more creative, more like the subjects they fundamentally are – less feminine, more masculine. To put this in terms of the sex/gender distinction, Beauvoir's answer to women's situation is to ignore the fact that the female sex is different from the male sex. . . . (Chanter, 1995: 75)

7 Butler's 'reconnection' of gender, the body and sex does not mean that she is not alive to the subversive possibilities inherent in gender performances which disorganize that 'coherence' of anatomy, sexuality and gender identity which is the heterosexual ideal. For an account of the way such performances – drag, for instance – reveal the false, cultural naturalization of what Butler frames as *contingently* related dimensions of corporeality, see *Gender Trouble* (137–9), and *Bodies that Matter* (Chapter 4).

8 Our discussion of *Bodies that Matter* will focus primarily on its Introduction, partly for reasons of space and, more importantly, because this is where Butler sets up the key parameters/issues of her debate.

9 'Sex' is defined as 'a cultural norm which governs the materialization of bodies' (Butler, 1993: 3).

10 As Butler reveals in Chapter 3 of *Bodies that Matter*, 'Phantasmatic Identification and the Assumption of Sex', her view is that the 'law' of sex is not so much that which precedes/produces materializing bodily citations as that which is constituted through them: 'the embodying of sex would be a kind of "citing" of the law, but neither sex nor the law can be said to preexist their various citings' (1993: 108). Thus, she argues, the authority of the law – which she labels here, in Lacanian terms, as the 'symbolic' – comes into being through a kind of 'recursive turn'. Another way of putting this point is that the 'power of the symbolic is itself *produced* by the citational instance by which the law is embodied' (Butler, 1993: 108).

11 Butler suggests that we need to rethink 'the process by which a bodily norm is assumed, appropriated, taken on as not, strictly speaking, undergone *by a subject*', because, she suggests, 'the subject, the speaking "I", is formed by virtue of having undergone such a process of assuming a sex' (Butler, 1993:3). She considers, further, that those 'abject' individuals who assume bodily norms in a way which fails to meet the heterosexual ideal find themselves not in the domain of the subject but in its 'constitutive outside' (Butler, 1993; 3) so that 'proper' subjectivity is denied them.

12 Butler does acknowledge that 'normative heterosexuality is clearly not the only regulative regime operative in the production of bodily contours or setting the limits to bodily intelligibility' (Butler, 1993: 17), and goes on to address questions of race, both in her Introduction and in Chapters 4 and 6.

13 In various essays in *Bodies that Matter*, Butler addresses the ways in which abject bodies can function as a critical resource in the struggle to redefine symbolic legitimacy, *and* discusses the complex relationship between abjection, subversion and agency. These discussions focus on practices such as drag. Fascinating as they are, there is sadly no space to gloss them here.

14 In this context, she quotes Gianni Vattimo's concern that poststructuralism 'marks the dissolution of matter as a contemporary category' (Butler, 1993: 27–8) and indicates that she is sympathetic to his search for 'this lost matter'.

References

de Beauvoir, Simone (1972) *The Second Sex*. Harmondsworth: Penguin Books. (Orig. pub. 1949.)

Butler, Judith (1986) 'Sex and Gender in Simone de Beauvoir's *Second Sex*', *Yale French Studies* 72: 35–49.

Butler, Judith (1990) *Gender Trouble*. London and New York: Routledge.

Butler, Judith (1993) *Bodies that Matter: On the Discursive Limits of Sex*. London and New York: Routledge.

Butler, Judith (1994) 'Gender as Performance: an Interview', *Radical Philosophy* 67: 32–5.

Chanter, Tina (1995) *Ethics of Eros: Irigaray's Rewriting of the Philosophers*. London and New York: Routledge.

Dietz, Mary (1992) 'Introduction: Debating Simone de Beauvoir', *Signs* 18: 74–88.

Evans, Mary (1984) *Simone de Beauvoir: A Feminist Mandarin*. London and New York: Tavistock.

Gatens, Moira (1996) *Imaginary Bodies: Ethics, Power and Corporeality*. London and New York: Routledge.

Grosz, Elizabeth (1989) *Sexual Subversions*. Sydney: Allen and Unwin.

Grosz, Elizabeth (1995) *Space, Time and Perversion*. London and New York: Routledge.

Kaufmann, Dorothy (1986) 'Simone de Beauvoir: Questions of Difference and Generation', *Yale French Studies* 72: 121–31.

Mackenzie, Catriona (1986) 'Simone de Beauvoir: Philosophy and/or the Female Body', in C. Pateman and E. Grosz (eds) *Feminist Challenges: Social and Political Theory*. Sydney and London: Allen and Unwin.

Marks, Elaine (1986) 'Transgressing the (In)cont(in)ent Boundaries: The Body in Decline', *Yale French Studies* 72: 181–200.

Moi, Toril (1994) *Simone de Beauvoir: The Making of an Intellectual Women*. Oxford: Blackwell.

13

BODY IMAGE

Seymour Fisher

Source: D. Sills (ed.), *International Encyclopaedia of the Social Sciences*, New York: Macmillan & Glencoe: Freepress, 1968, pp. 113–116.

"Body image" can be considered synonymous with such terms as "body concept" and "body scheme." Broadly speaking, the term pertains to how the individual perceives his own body. It does not imply that the individual's concept of his body is represented by a conscious image; rather, it embraces his collective attitudes, feelings, and fantasies about his body without regard to level of awareness.

Basic to most definitions of body image is the view that it represents the manner in which a person has learned to organize and integrate his body experiences. Body image concepts are important for an understanding of such diverse phenomena as adjustment to body disablement, maintenance of posture and spatial orientation, personality development, and cultural differences.

At a common-sense level, the pervasive significance of the body image is evident in widespread preoccupation with myths and stories that concern body transformation (such as the change from human to werewolf form). It is evident, too, in the vast expenditure of time and energy that goes into clothing and reshaping the body (for example, plastic surgery) for the purpose of conforming to idealized standards of appearance.

Historical background

Interest in the body image appeared first in the work of neurologists who observed that brain damage could produce bizarre alterations in a person's perception of his body. Patients suffering from brain damage manifested such extreme symptoms as the inability to recognize parts of their own bodies and the assignment of entirely different identities to the right and left sides of their bodies. Interest in body image phenomena was further reinforced by observations that neurotic and schizophrenic patients frequently had unusual body feelings. Paul Schilder (1935), neurologist, psychiatrist, and early influential theorist, reported the following kinds of distortions in the schizophrenic patient: a sense of alienation from his own body (depersonalization), inability to distinguish the boundaries of his body, and feelings of transformation in the sex of his body. Surgeons recorded unusual body experiences in patients with amputations and noted that amputees typically hallucinated the absent member as if it were still present. The hallucinated body member was designated a "phantom limb."

The neurologist Henry Head, another early influential theorist, took the view that a body schema was essential to the functioning of the individual (Head et al. 1920). He theorized that each person constructs a picture or model of his body that constitutes a standard against which all body movements and postures are judged. He applied the term "schema" to this standard. His description of the body schema underscored its influence upon body orientation, but he noted also that it served to integrate other kinds of experiences.

Equally prominent in early body image formulations was the psychoanalytic work of Sigmund Freud. Freud considered the body concept basic to the development of identity and ego structure. He conceived of the child's earliest sense of identity as first taking the form of learning to discriminate between his own body and the outer world. Thus, when the child is able to perceive his own body as something apart from its environs, he presumably acquires a basis for distinguishing self from nonself.

Freud's theory of libidinal development was saturated with key references to body attitudes. He conceptualized the individual's psychosexual development in terms of the successive localization of energy and sensitivity at oral, anal, and genital body sites. It was assumed that as each of these sites successively acquired increased prominence and sensitivity, corresponding needs were aroused to seek out agents capable of providing stimulation. Presumably, too, when a person failed to mature and was fixated at one of the earlier erogenous zones (oral or anal), he was left to deal with adult experiences in terms of a body context more appropriate to the way of life of a child.

Many of Freud's concepts of personality development assign importance to changes in the perceptual and erogenous dominance of body sectors. Psychoanalytic theorists continue to focus upon body attitudes as significant in understanding many forms of behavior deviance (for example, schizophrenia and fetishism). Indeed, psychoanalytical concepts have had a major influence upon body image theory and research.

Schilder drew attention to other body image phenomena in his book *The Image and Appearance of the Human Body* (1935), where he formulated a variety of theoretical concepts that were phrased largely in psychoanalytic terms. He suggested that the body image is molded by one's interactions with others, and to the extent that these interactions are faulty, the body image will be inadequately developed. Schilder's book contained rich descriptions of how the individual perceives his own body in diverse situations. He ana-lyzed body experiences that characterize awakening, falling asleep, assuming unusual body positions, ingesting certain drugs, and undergoing schizo-phrenic disorganization. One idea he particularly emphasized was that sensa-tions of body disintegration are likely to typify those who masochistically direct anger against themselves.

Schilder concerned himself with determining whether specific brain areas are linked with the body image. He was one of a group of neurologists who made persistent attempts to relate body image distortions observed in brain-damaged patients to the sites of the brain lesions. Considerable evidence has accumulated that damage to the parietal lobes selectively disrupts the individual's ability to perceive his body realistically.

Phantom limb

Historically, the phantom limb phenomenon has played a significant role in calling attention to the problems of organizing body perceptions. Such observers as Head and his colleagues (1920), Lhermitte (1939), and Schilder (1935) were puzzled by the fact that normal persons typically hallucinated the presence of body members lost through injury or amputation. Such hal-lucinations implied that the individual had a "picture" of his body which persisted even when it was no longer realistically accurate. Controversy still exists about whether the phantom experience is primarily a result of a com-pensatory process occurring in the central nervous system or of persisting peripheral sensations evoked by injured tissue in the stump. Evidence indi-cates that while stump sensations play a part in the phantom experience, central factors are of greater importance. Interesting questions have been stimulated by observations of the phantom limb: for example, why does the duration of phantom experiences vary markedly between individuals? And why does the phantom not appear when body parts are gradually absorbed (as in leprosy) rather than suddenly removed?

Research

Well-controlled experiments in the area of body image are relatively new, most scientific studies having been carried out since 1945.

Human figure drawing

One of the oldest and most frequently used techniques for the study of the body image makes use of human figure drawing. It has been suggested that when an individual is asked to draw a picture of a person, he projects into his drawing indications of how he experiences his body. Some investigators have proposed that such indicators as the size of the figure drawn and difficulty in depicting specific body areas provide information about the individual's body concept. There have been claims that the figure drawing can be used to measure such variables as feelings of body inferiority and anxiety about sexual adequacy. However, despite a profusion of studies, there is no evidence that figure drawing is an effective method of tapping body image attitudes. It is true that in some instances it has proved sensitive to the existence of actual body defects. For example, individuals with crippling defects have been shown to introduce analogous defects in their figure drawings. Moreover, there have been some demonstrations that figure-drawing indicators of body disturbance are higher in schizophrenic than in normal subjects. However, no consistently successful indices of body attitudes have been derived. Indeed, the problem of using the figure drawing to evaluate body image has been enormously complicated by evidence that artistic skill may so strongly influence the characteristics of drawings as to minimize the importance of most other factors.

Attitudes toward the body

Another approach to evaluating the body image has revolved about measuring the subject's dissatisfaction with regions of his body. Procedures have been devised that pose for him the task of indicating how positively or negatively he views his body. These procedures vary from direct ratings of dissatisfaction with parts of one's body to judgments regarding the comparability of one's body to pictured bodies. It has been found that men are most likely to be dissatisfied with areas of their bodies that seem "too small"; whereas women focus their self-criticism upon body sectors that appear to be "too large." Also, evidence has emerged that dissatisfaction with one's body is accompanied by generalized feelings of insecurity and diminished self-confidence.

Perceived body size

One of the most promising lines of body image research has dealt with perceived body size. This work concerns the significance to be attached to the size an individual ascribes to parts of his body. The individual's concept of his body size is often inaccurate and exaggerated in the direction of largeness or smallness as a function of either situational influences or specific body attitudes. It has been demonstrated that estimates of body size vary in relation to the total spatial context of the individual, the degree of sensory input to his skin, the nature of his ongoing activities, and many other variables (Wapner et al. 1958). For example, subjects judge their heads to be smaller when heat or touch emphasizes the skin boundary than when such stimulation is absent. It has further been shown that subjects perceive their arms as longer when pointed at an open, unobstructed vista than when pointed at a limiting wall. The subject's mood, his attitudes toward himself, his degree of psychiatric disturbance, and a number of other psychological factors have been found to play a part in his evaluation of his own body size. For example, persons exposed to an experience of failure see themselves as shorter than they do under conditions of nonfailure. Schizophrenic, as compared to normal, subjects unrealistically exaggerate the size of their bodies. Normal subjects who ingest psychotomimetic drugs, which produce psychoticlike disturbance, likewise overestimate the sizes of their body parts. At another level, it has been noted that the relative sizes an individual ascribes to regions of his body (for example, right side versus left side, back versus front) may reflect aspects of his personality organization.

Aside from the formal research efforts that have highlighted the importance of perceived body size as a body image variable, there is a long history of anecdotal and clinical observation supporting a similar view. Vivid experiences of change in body size have been described in schizophrenic and brain-damaged patients, in patients with migraine attacks, and in various other persons exposed to severe stress demands. Clearly, there is a tendency for experiences to be translated into changes in perceived body size.

Projective techniques

Responses to ambiguous stimuli, such as ink blots, briefly exposed pictures, and incomplete representations of the human form, have been widely utilized to measure body attitudes. It is assumed that when a person is asked to interpret or give meaning to something as vague as an ink blot, he projects self feelings and self representations into his interpretations. In this vein, it has been found that persons with localized body defects focus their attention upon corresponding body areas when studying pictures containing vague representations of the human figure. The frequency of references to body sensations (such as pain, hunger, fatigue) in stories composed in response to pictures has been shown by D. J. van Lennep (1957) to vary developmentally and to differ between the sexes. Females were found to show a moderate increase in body references beyond the age of 15, whereas males were typified by a pattern of decline in such references. It has been suggested by van Lennep that in Western culture men are supposed to transcend their bodies and to turn their energies toward the world. Women, on the other hand, are given approval for continuing and even increasing their investments in their bodies.

Fisher and Cleveland (1958) have developed a method for scoring responses to ink blots which measures how clearly the individual is able to experience his body as possessing boundaries that differentiate it from its environs. This boundary measure has been able to predict several noteworthy aspects of behavior, including the desire for high achievement, behavior in small groups, the locus of psychosomatic symptomatology, and adequacy of adjustment to body disablement.

Perspectives and problems

The investigation of body image phenomena has become a vigorous enterprise. One dominant fact that has emerged is that the individual's body is a unique perceptual object. The individual responds to his own body with an intensity of ego involvement that can rarely be evoked by other objects. The body is, after all, in a unique position as the only object that is simultaneously perceived and a part of the perceiver. In studying an individual's manner of experiencing and conceptualizing his body, one obtains rich data about him that is not readily available from other sources.

It is difficult to know what priorities to assign to the body image issues that still need to be clarified. Speaking broadly, one may say there is an emphatic need to ascertain the principal axes underlying the organization of the body image. It remains to be established whether the body image is built around the spatial dimensions of the body, the specialized functions of different body regions, or perhaps the private and symbolic meanings assigned to body areas by the culture. There is also a need to examine the relationships between body attitudes and socialization modes in different cultures. There is evidence in the anthropological literature that body attitudes may differ radically in relation to cultural context. Another important problem for research is the assessment of the role that body image plays in the development and definition of the individual's sense of identity.

Bibliography

CRITCHLEY, MACDONALD 1953 *The Parietal Lobes*. London: Arnold.

FISHER, SEYMOUR; and CLEVELAND, SIDNEY E. 1958 *Body Image and Personality*. Princeton, N.J.: Van Nostrand.

FREUD, SIGMUND (1888–1938) 1959 *Collected Papers* 5 vols. Authorized translation under the supervision of Joan Riviere. Volume 5 edited by James Strachey. International Psycho-analytic Library, No. 7–10, 34. New York: Basic Books; London: Hogarth. → Translation of *Sammlung kleiner Schriften zur Neurosenlehre* and additional papers. A ten-volume paperback edition was published in 1963 by Collier Books.

HEAD, HENRY et al. 1920 *Studies in Neurology*. 2 vols. London: Hodder & Stoughton. → These papers consist mainly of a republication of papers published in *Brain* between 1905 and 1918.

LENNEP, D. J., VAN 1957 Projection and Personality. Pages 259–277 in Henry P. David and Helmut von Bracken (editors), *Perspectives in Personality Theory*. New York: Basic Books.

LHERMITTE, JACQUES J. 1939 *L'image de notre corps*. Paris: Éditions de la Nouvelle Revue Critique.

SCHILDER, PAUL (1935) 1950 *The Image and Appearance of the Human Body: Studies of the Constructive Energies in the Psyche*. New York: International Universities Press.

WAPNER, SEYMOUR; WERNER, H.; and COMALLI, P. E. 1958 Effect of Enhancement of Head Boundary on Head Size and Shape. *Perceptual and Motor Skills* 8:319–325.

WAPNER, SEYMOUR; and WERNER, HEINZ (editors) 1965 *The Body Percept*. New York: Random House.

14

BODY RITUAL AMONG THE NACIREMA

Horace Miner

Source: *American Anthropologist* 6(8) (1956): 503–507.

The anthropologist has become so familiar with the diversity of ways in which different peoples behave in similar situations that he is not apt to be surprised by even the most exotic customs. In fact, if all of the logically possible combinations of behavior have not been found somewhere in the world, he is apt to suspect that they must be present in some yet undescribed tribe. This point has, in fact, been expressed with respect to clan organization by Murdock (1949:71). In this light, the magical beliefs and practices of the Nacirema present such unusual aspects that it seems desirable to describe them as an example of the extremes to which human behavior can go.

Professor Linton first brought the ritual of the Nacirema to the attention of anthropologists twenty years ago (1936:326), but the culture of this people is still very poorly understood. They are a North American group living in the territory between the Canadian Cree, the Yaqui and Tarahumare of Mexico, and the Carib and Arawak of the Antilles. Little is known of their origin, although tradition states that they came from the east. According to Nacirema mythology, their nation was originated by a culture hero, Notgnih-saw, who is otherwise known for two great feats of strength—the throwing of a piece of wampum across the river Pa-To-Mac and the chopping down of a cherry tree in which the Spirit of Truth resided.

Nacirema culture is characterized by a highly developed market economy which has evolved in a rich natural habitat. While much of the people's time is devoted to economic pursuits, a large part of the fruits of these labors and a considerable portion of the day are spent in ritual activity. The focus of this activity is the human body, the appearance and health of which loom as a dominant concern in the ethos of the people. While such a concern is certainly not unusual, its ceremonial aspects and associated philosophy are unique.

The fundamental belief underlying the whole system appears to be that the human body is ugly and that its natural tendency is to debility and disease. Incarcerated in such a body, man's only hope is to avert these characteristics through the use of the powerful influences of ritual and ceremony. Every household has one or more shrines devoted to this purpose. The more powerful individuals in the society have several shrines in their houses and, in fact, the opulence of a house is often referred to in terms of the number of such ritual centers it possesses. Most houses are of wattle and daub construction, but the shrine rooms of the more wealthy are walled with stone. Poorer families imitate the rich by applying pottery plaques to their shrine walls.

While each family has at least one such shrine, the rituals associated with it are not family ceremonies but are private and secret. The rites are normally only discussed with children, and then only during the period when they are being initiated into these mysteries. I was able, however, to establish sufficient rapport with the natives to examine these shrines and to have the rituals described to me.

The focal point of the shrine is a box or chest which is built into the wall. In this chest are kept the many charms and magical potions without which no native believes he could live. These preparations are secured from a variety of specialized practitioners. The most powerful of these are the medicine men, whose assistance must be rewarded with substantial gifts. However, the medicine men do not provide the curative potions for their clients, but decide what the ingredients should be and then write them down in an ancient and secret language. This writing is understood only by the medicine men and by the herbalists who, for another gift, provide the required charm.

The charm is not disposed of after it has served its purpose, but is placed in the charm-box of the household shrine. As these magical materials are specific for certain ills, and the real or imagined maladies of the people are many, the charm-box is usually full to overflowing. The magical packets are so numerous that people forget what their purposes were and fear to use them again. While the natives are very vague on this point, we can only assume that the idea in retaining all the old magical materials is that their presence in the charm-box, before which the body rituals are conducted, will in some way protect the worshipper.

Beneath the charm-box is a small font. Each day every member of the family, in succession, enters the shrine room, bows his head before the charm-box, mingles different sorts of holy water in the font, and proceeds with a brief rite of ablution. The holy waters are secured from the Water Temple of the community, where the priests conduct elaborate ceremonies to make the liquid ritually pure.

In the hierarchy of magical practitioners, and below the medicine men in prestige, are specialists whose designation is best translated "holy-mouth-men." The Nacirema have an almost pathological horror of and fascination with the mouth, the condition of which is believed to have a supernatural influence on all social relationships. Were it not for the rituals of the mouth, they believe that their teeth would fall out, their gums bleed, their jaws shrink, their friends desert them, and their lovers reject them. They also believe that a strong relationship exists between oral and moral characteristics. For example, there is a ritual ablution of the mouth for children which is supposed to improve their moral fiber.

The daily body ritual performed by everyone includes a mouth-rite. Despite the fact that these people are so punctilious about care of the mouth, this rite involves a practice which strikes the uninitiated stranger as revolting. It was reported to me that the ritual consists of inserting a small bundle of hog hairs into the mouth, along with certain magical powders, and then moving the bundle in a highly formalized series of gestures.

In addition to the private mouth-rite, the people seek out a holy-mouth-man once or twice a year. These practitioners have an impressive set of paraphernalia, consisting of a variety of augers, awls, probes, and prods. The use of these objects in the exorcism of the evils of the mouth involves almost unbelievable ritual torture of the client. The holy-mouth-man opens the client's mouth and, using the above mentioned tools, enlarges any holes which decay may have created in the teeth. Magical materials are put into these holes. If there are no naturally occurring holes in the teeth, large sections of one or more teeth are gouged out so that the supernatural substance can be applied. In the client's view, the purpose of these ministrations is to arrest decay and to draw friends. The extremely sacred and traditional character of the rite is evident in the fact that the natives return to the holy-mouth-men year after year, despite the fact that their teeth continue to decay.

It is to be hoped that, when a thorough study of the Nacirema is made, there will be careful inquiry into the personality structure of these people. One has but to watch the gleam in the eye of a holy-mouth-man, as he jabs an awl into an exposed nerve, to suspect that a certain amount of sadism is involved. If this can be established, a very interesting pattern emerges, for most of the population shows definite masochistic tendencies. It was to these that Professor Linton referred in discussing a distinctive part of the daily body ritual which is performed only by men. This part of the rite involves scraping and lacerating the surface of the face with a sharp instrument. Special women's rites are performed only four times during each lunar month, but what they lack in frequency is made up in barbarity. As part of this ceremony, women bake their heads in small ovens for about an hour. The theoretically interesting point is that what seems to be a preponderantly masochistic people have developed sadistic specialists.

The medicine men have an imposing temple, or *latipso*, in every community of any size. The more elaborate ceremonies required to treat very sick patients can only be performed at this temple. These ceremonies involve not only the thaumaturge but a permanent group of vestal maidens who move sedately about the temple chambers in distinctive costume and headdress.

The *latipso* ceremonies are so harsh that it is phenomenal that a fair proportion of the really sick natives who enter the temple ever recover. Small children whose indoctrination is still incomplete have been known to resist attempts to take them to the temple because "that is where you go to die." Despite this fact, sick adults are not only willing but eager to undergo the protracted ritual purification, if they can afford to do so. No matter how ill the supplicant or how grave the emergency, the guardians of many temples will not admit a client if he cannot give a rich gift to the custodian. Even after one has gained admission and survived the ceremonies, the guardians will not permit the neophyte to leave until he makes still another gift.

The supplicant entering the temple is first stripped of all his or her clothes. In every-day life the Nacirema avoids exposure of his body and its natural functions. Bathing and excretory acts are performed only in the secrecy of the household shrine, where they are ritualized as part of the body-rites. Psychological shock results from the fact that body secrecy is suddenly lost upon entry into the *latipso*. A man, whose own wife has never seen him in an excretory act, suddenly finds himself naked and assisted by a vestal maiden while he performs his natural functions into a sacred vessel. This sort of ceremonial treatment is necessitated by the fact that the excreta are used by a diviner to ascertain the course and nature of the client's sickness. Female clients, on the other hand, find their naked bodies are subjected to the scrutiny, manipulation and prodding of the medicine men.

Few supplicants in the temple are well enough to do anything but lie on their hard beds. The daily ceremonies, like the rites of the holy-mouth-men, involve discomfort and torture. With ritual precision, the vestals awaken their miserable charges each dawn and roll them about on their beds of pain while performing ablutions, in the formal movements of which the maidens are highly trained. At other times they insert magic wands in the supplicant's mouth or force him to eat substances which are supposed to be healing. From time to time the medicine men come to their clients and jab magically treated needles into their flesh. The fact that these temple ceremonies may not cure, and may even kill the neophyte, in no way decreases the people's faith in the medicine men.

There remains one other kind of practitioner, known as a "listener." This witch-doctor has the power to exorcise the devils that lodge in the heads of people who have been bewitched. The Nacirema believe that parents bewitch their own children. Mothers are particularly suspected of putting a curse on children while teaching them the secret body rituals. The counter-magic of the witch-doctor is unusual in its lack of ritual. The patient simply tells the "listener" all his troubles and fears, beginning with the earliest difficulties he can remember. The memory displayed by the Nacirema in these exorcism sessions is truly remarkable. It is not uncommon for the patient to bemoan the rejection he felt upon being weaned as a babe, and a few individuals even see their troubles going back to the traumatic effects of their own birth.

217

In conclusion, mention must be made of certain practices which have their base in native esthetics but which depend upon the pervasive aversion to the natural body and its functions. There are ritual fasts to make fat people thin and ceremonial feasts to make thin people fat. Still other rites are used to make women's breasts larger if they are small, and smaller if they are large. General dissatisfaction with breast shape is symbolized in the fact that the ideal form is virtually outside the range of human variation. A few women afflicted with almost inhuman hypermammary development are so idolized that they make a handsome living by simply going from village to village and permitting the natives to stare at them for a fee.

Reference has already been made to the fact that excretory functions are ritualized, routinized, and relegated to secrecy. Natural reproductive functions are similarly distorted. Intercourse is taboo as a topic and scheduled as an act. Efforts are made to avoid pregnancy by the use of magical materials or by limiting intercourse to certain phases of the moon. Conception is actually very infrequent. When pregnant, women dress so as to hide their condition. Parturition takes place in secret, without friends or relatives to assist, and the majority of women do not nurse their infants.

Our review of the ritual life of the Nacirema has certainly shown them to be a magic-ridden people. It is hard to understand how they have managed to exist so long under the burdens which they have imposed upon themselves. But even such exotic customs as these take on real meaning when they are viewed with the insight provided by Malinowski when he wrote (1948:70):

Looking from far and above, from our high places of safety in the developed civilization, it is easy to see all the crudity and irrelevance of magic. But without its power and guidance early man could not have mastered his practical difficulties as he has done, nor could man have advanced to the higher stages of civilization.

References cited

LINTON, RALPH 1936 The Study of Man. New York, D. Appleton-Century Co.
MALINOWSKI, BRONISLAW 1948 Magic, Science, and Religion. Glencoe, The Free Press.
MURDOCK, GEORGE P. 1949 Social Structure. New York, The Macmillan Co.

15

BODY-SUBJECT/BODY-POWER

Agency, inscription and control in Foucault and Merleau-Ponty

Nick Crossley

Source: *Body and Society* 2(2) (1996): 99–116.

A division is forming in the social theory of the body. We are being asked to choose. Should we study 'the body' as 'lived' and active or as acted upon, as historically 'inscribed' from without. Elizabeth Grosz (1993), in her paper, 'Bodies and Knowledges', recognizes the value of both approaches but she doubts whether they are reconcilable or even commensurable. And she is not alone in her doubt. Similar views are expressed by both David Levin (1989) and by Bryan Turner (1984).

In this article I argue, contra Grosz, that we do not need to choose between the lived body and the inscribed body. These conceptions, I maintain, are not only commensurable and compatible, they are mutually informing and complementary. They are two sides of the same coin and there are considerable gains to be achieved by recognizing this.

My argument focuses on two writers who, in the view of Grosz, Turner and Levin, clearly exemplify the supposed competing accounts of 'the body'. Maurice Merleau-Ponty (1908–61) is taken as a representative of the 'lived' approach and Michel Foucault (1926–84) is taken as a representative of the inscription approach. My contention is, as it has been elsewhere (Crossley, 1993a, 1994), that there is a common ground between these two writers which allows their work – and particularly their work on embodiment, power and subjectivity – to be brought into a mutually informing and enriching dialogue. A discussion of their work effectively shows that the distinction between the lived body and the inscribed body cannot be maintained.

The article begins with a discussion of the socio-historical conception of the body which, I argue, is shared by both Merleau-Ponty and Foucault.

Next I consider the relation of human agency to power (body-subject to body-power) in the work of each writer. This involves a discussion of body-space relations, of forms of body mastery and of forms of body awareness. Following this I consider the work of two feminist authors, Iris Young (1980) and Sandra Lee Bartky (1988), who have used the work of Merleau-Ponty and Foucault, respectively, to constitute a feminist politics of comportment and motility. Their work, I argue, shows clearly how the approaches of Merleau-Ponty and Foucault can be brought into dialogue in relation to a specific and important concrete issue. This section is followed by a discussion section which concludes the article.

A socio-historical conception of the body

Before considering the differences between Foucault's and Merleau-Ponty's conceptions of the body, it is important to identify and explicate the common ground which underpins (without undermining) these differences. In the first instance, both writers identify a neglect of the question of the body in traditional philosophy and both advocate opposition to this neglect. Moreover, each claims to combat the neglect by focusing upon the body in his philosophical work. Second, each opposes the dominant, Western (academic) conception of the body as a closed, object-like, physiological system, or rather, each opposes the notion that the body is only an object-like system. The challenge of the philosophy of the body, for each of them, is to offer an alternative to this conception. Finally, and most importantly, in their respective alternative conceptions, they each focus upon socio-historical conducts or behaviour. The body, each maintains, should be conceived as a bearer of such conducts. It should be understood in terms of its habit-based actions and those actions, in turn, should be understood as derivatives or expressions of a common cultural stock. The difference between their two positions, in the final instance, lies in the manner in which each develops these presuppositions.

Merleau-Ponty argues his case, at considerable length and in considerable depth, in his first two major works: i.e. *The Structure of Behaviour* (1965) and *The Phenomenology of Perception* (1962). In the former, he considers the distinctiveness of human behaviour (in relation to animal behaviour) and, partly on this basis, he launches a two-pronged attack on behaviourist and mentalist (or intellectualist) conceptions of human being. Human behaviour, qua embodied action, is intelligent, purposive and skilful, he argues, but its purpose and intelligence, etc. are not derived from a specific (mental) act of intellection, etc. which is prior to or separate from it. In a fashion similar to Gilbert Ryle (1949), he maintains that intelligence, purpose and the like are features of embodied actions themselves and he rejects the notion of an inner 'mental' realm which is separate from such actions. Unlike Ryle, however, Merleau-Ponty identifies the historical and social bases of such actions.

Embodied action, he argues, is based in 'habit' (i.e. acquired skills, schemas and techniques) and these habits are drawn, in part at least, from a social stock or habitus.

This notion of the social-historical base of habituated, embodied action is developed in *The Phenomenology of Perception* (1962). In this text, Merleau-Ponty discusses the social (habitual) bases of our perceptual, linguistic, affective and practical forms of behaviour. Embodied activity, which is our very way of being-in-the-world, he argues, takes up these habitual schemas and deploys them, in situ, with competence and skill. It applies them and modifies them as and when appropriate.

The term 'body-subject' was later applied to this conception by Merleau-Ponty and, as the term suggests, this understanding of the active body was used to displace the traditional philosophical subject in his work. Human beings do not stand in relation to their world as a subject to an object, at least not in the first instance, he maintains. Their primordial relation to their world consists in their embodied (practical) action within it. They belong to their world, as an active part of it. Moreover, Merleau-Ponty identifies social, embodied action with the production of meaning. Meaning is not produced by a transcendental or constituting consciousness but by an engaged body-subject.

The key concern of Merleau-Ponty's account, at least for our purposes, is the manner in which acquired corporeal habits form the basis of our being-in-the-world. We are our (habit-based) actions, in this conception, and it is by virtue of those carnal actions that we take up a position in (and thus also sustain) the social world.

In contrast to this, Foucault's philosophical engagement with embodiment is rather vague and underdeveloped. He is less concerned to establish his ideas in the usual academic ways (i.e. argument and evidence) and his views are nowhere coherently laid out. Nevertheless, in the essay 'Nietzsche, Genealogy and History', he outlines a position which is relatively consist-ently maintained throughout his later work:

> We believe, in any event, that the body obeys the exclusive laws of physiology and that it escapes the influence of history, but this too is false. The body is broken down by a great many distinct regimes; it is broken down by rhythms of work, rest and holidays; it is poisoned by food or values, through eating habits or moral laws; it constructs resistances. (Foucault, 1977:153)

'Effective history', Foucault (1977:153) continues, recognizes no constants. It reveals and analyses a body which is 'totally imprinted by history . . .'. The examples which are given of this are sentiments or feelings, ways of seeing ('the eye was not always intended for contemplation . . . the eye ini-tially responded to the requirements of hunting and warfare' [Foucault

1977:148]), love and instinct. Furthermore, like Merleau-Ponty, Foucault stresses that this historical body is not subordinated to or controlled by a substantial soul or self which is somehow external to it. He eschews mentalism, and transcendentalism. Insofar as it is legitimate to refer to a soul or a self which subordinates the body, in Foucault's schema, this too must be understood as a result of historical inscriptions upon the body (Merleau-Ponty has a similar notion to this).[1] There is no pre-given, spiritual or psychological faculty – distinct from the engaged body – which corresponds to this function.

What Foucault is effectively arguing then, like Merleau-Ponty, is that 'the body' must, in addition to being considered as a physiological system, be considered in terms of its conduct or behaviour (its ways of seeing, loving and its emotional conduct, etc.) And he is arguing that the latter consideration should not be reduced in terms of the former. Embodied behaviour, for Foucault as for Merleau-Ponty, cannot be reduced to the body qua pre-given physiological system. It is irreducibly historical. It is structured through human values and the exigencies of the historical world. Furthermore, Foucault is refusing to refer this behaviour back to a substantial inner mental realm. Like Merleau-Ponty, he is arguing that the surfaces of behaviour are the extent of the depth of human being. In contrast to Merleau-Ponty, however, he is identifying and stressing the historical variability of forms of conduct and he is identifying a politics with the acquisition of such conducts. Furthermore, he is suggesting that, within the context of this politics of acquisition at least, the behaving-body is not the subject of historical forms of conduct but is rather subject to such forms of conduct. *Discipline and Punish* (1979) best illustrates and supports this point. In this text, Foucault details the historical emergence of complex social practices which work on human conduct, moulding it and forcing the bearer of such conducts to take responsibility for them. It is an account, in other words, of systems of historical inscription.

This very sketchy account of the differences in the way in which Foucault and Merleau-Ponty respectively develop their socio-historical conception of the body can be sharpened up into an account of three clear differences. Each of these differences must be identified and discussed if we are to challenge the pseudo-distinction between 'lived' and 'inscribed' conceptions of the body.

The first key difference between the two writers is that while Merleau-Ponty understands historical behaviours or habits in terms of their existential functions, as ways of being-in-the-world, Foucault understands them in terms of their political history and functions. Both, for example, would accept Merleau-Ponty's claim that, 'Feelings and passional conduct are invented like words' (1962:189), but where Merleau-Ponty would call for an analysis of feelings as ongoing, situated forms of conduct which constitute a person's mode of being with others or with certain objects, Foucault would call for a historical (genealogical) analysis of such feelings and their (in all probability) ignoble, petty and malicious roots. Moreover, he would seek out their role in contemporary political life.

This difference, given its basis in a common conception of 'feeling' (i.e. as a historical form of conduct rather than a biological or 'mental' given), does not amount to an incommensurability or conflict. Indeed, it suggests that a genealogical and a phenomenological analysis, of the same 'feeling', would be potentially mutually informing. Each approach, because they both constitute their object in the same fashion, is able to contribute to the account provided by the other, in a coherent way. The value of such a dialogue will be made apparent later in the article.

The second difference concerns the issue of change and stability. Merleau-Ponty tends to suggest that the body-subject derives stability (in its relation to itself and its world) from its habits. The habitual body, for him, provides a stable bedrock upon which (relatively)[2] free agency is based. Foucault, by contrast, stresses instability and change in his account. Nothing in 'man' (sic) is stable, he argues, 'not even his body' (1977:153). The contrast between the two writers is considerable in this respect but, as with the first difference, it does not amount to an incommensurability or conflict between the two positions. The reason for this is that Merleau-Ponty and Foucault work within different temporal frames. Merleau-Ponty is concerned (in his work on the body-subject) with stability on an hour-by-hour, day-to-day basis, while Foucault is concerned with change and instability in a long-term historical perspective. There is no reason to assume that Merleau-Ponty would be opposed to the notion of corporeal change and instability in the (historical) long term or that Foucault would oppose the notion of a day-to-day stability. Indeed, given Merleau-Ponty's concern for the historical contingency of the present and given Foucault's concern that conduct is historically regulated (i.e. made regular) by systems of power and 'moulded by a great many regimes' (i.e. cast into a specific mould), I suggest that their views converge on the question of stability, when we hold time-scale constant.

Having made this point, one qualification is necessary. Merleau-Ponty's 'body' is clearly potentially equally as historical as Foucault's (i.e. totally). Everything about the body (as actor) is historical for Merleau-Ponty; except, that is, for its historicity. The habits and forms of conduct of the body and thus our very ways of being-in-the-world are always open to historical change, for Merleau-Ponty, but the fact that we are able to acquire habits and forms of conduct, and that we are able to deploy them, is not. And neither is the competent, flexible and creative way in which those habits are used. These dimensions of the body (unless one adopts a longer-term, evolutionary perspective – which Merleau-Ponty is by no means opposed to and which Foucault's metaphors are sometimes suggestive of) are historically stable. In other words, while our habits may change, the fact that we are creatures of habit (as opposed to having fixed instincts) does not.

Foucault makes no comparable qualification to this. Nevertheless, the point applies equally to him. If he wants to maintain that human bodies are moulded historically and that they are historically variable, then he must maintain that they are consistently open to such historical moulding processes.

The third point of difference between Foucault and Merleau-Ponty concerns the issues of agency and power, and activity and passivity. This difference is the focus of the next section of this article.

Agency and power

In the view of David Levin (1989), Merleau-Ponty's and Foucault's conceptions of the body are radically opposed with respect to the issue of passivity/activity. Foucault, on Levin's account, views the body as a passive receptacle of historical and political forces. Levin points to the overwhelming technologies of power discussed in *Discipline and Punish* and to passages in other texts, such as that cited above, where Foucault explicitly describes the body in terms of passivity: e.g. 'The body is moulded by a great many distinct regimes' (Foucault, 1977:153). Furthermore, he argues, Foucault adopts a functionalist position on this passivity; he reduces the body's (behavioural) functioning to the requirements of the social system writ large. The evidence for this is to be found in Foucault's 'Body-Power' interview: 'One needs to study what kind of body that the current society needs . . .' (Foucault, 1980: 58). Merleau-Ponty, in Levin's view, adopts a very different stance to this. While he stresses the cultural basis of action, Merleau-Ponty emphasizes the extent to which the body actively takes up and uses conventionalized (rule-bound) forms of conduct. The body is dependent upon cultural repertoires and skills, in Merleau-Ponty's account, but is equally responsible for the reproduction of those repertoires and skills. Moreover, in this sense, it is the habituated or instituted actions of bodies which are responsible for the reproduction of the social formation and of historical time. Merleau-Ponty's 'body' acts, according to Levin, where Foucault's 'body' is acted upon.

This account has a certain validity – which I will return to. As it stands it is incorrect however. A thorough reading of the work of Foucault and Merleau-Ponty reveals that, for both, the body is both active and acted upon: a locus of action and a target of power. Moreover, both contend, in opposition to traditional (consciousness-centred) approaches to political philosophy, that political control and stability are achieved at this corporeal or intercorporeal level:[3]

> . . . consciousness can do nothing without its body and can only act upon others by acting upon their bodies. It can only reduce them to slavery by making nature an appendix of its body, by appropriating nature to itself and establishing in nature its instruments of power. (Merleau-Ponty, 1969:102)

> I believe the great fantasy is the idea of a social body constituted by
> the universality of wills. Now the phenomenon of the social body is
> an effect not of a consensus but of the materiality of power operat-
> ing on the very bodies of individuals. (Foucault, 1980:55)

Social and political order, such as it is, they both maintain, is achieved, in the
first instance, neither by ideological manipulation (at least not in the narrow–
ideational–sense) nor by free consensus and contract. It is achieved by direct
and active attempts to control, direct, delimit and co-opt the actions of the
body: body-power.

In the case of Merleau-Ponty, the relation of body-power to embodied
agency is never discussed as such. His discussion of agency in *The Phenomenology of Perception* (1962) does include consideration of the political
situation of agents in relations of oppression and control. Moreover, the
discussion of oppression and control in *Humanism and Terror* (1969) does
include a detailed discussion of agency. Nevertheless, the relationship of
power to agency is not explored at length in either text. In Foucault's work,
however, and particularly his later work, power and agency are quite clearly
viewed in relational terms. In the essay, 'The Subject and Power', for
example, Foucault moves towards a sophisticated view of the necessary
interrelation of agency and power. Power, he maintains in this essay, is
constituted by 'A set of actions upon other actions' (1982:220). It is a
relationship between active persons and is only sustained insofar as each is
'thoroughly recognised and maintained to the very end as a person who
acts' (1982:220). It consists in an attempt, by one agent, to conduct the
conduct – Foucault likes the word play – of the other. If either (or any)
person in the relationship ceases to act then we must cease to refer to that
relationship in terms of power and must redefine it in terms of physical
determination, sheer physical restraint or death, depending, of course, upon
the reason for the person having ceased to act. In this sense then, power is
only possible for Foucault by virtue of agency. It requires a person who acts
and a person who acts upon those actions.

The active/passive distinction cannot be sustained with respect to the work
of Merleau-Ponty and Foucault then. Not only do both writers affirm that
bodies are active and acted upon, but Foucault provides a model within
which both aspects are shown to interrelate. Active bodies are acted upon.

Bodies, spaces and power

The model that Foucault posits provides a possible mechanism through
which his position and that of Merleau-Ponty can be brought into a more
sustained dialogue. This is particularly so given the (above mentioned) con-
vergence of the two writers, regarding the political significance which they
both attribute to – what Foucault calls – 'body-power': i.e. as the key to

political control and stability. Before such a dialogue can be effected however, there are further obstacles to be removed.

One such obstacle stems from the fact that Merleau-Ponty and Foucault,
while they both accept a definition of the body as active and acted upon,
tend to emphasize a different pole within this duality. Merleau-Ponty tends
to concentrate upon the active pole, while Foucault tends to stress the acted-
upon pole. This difference, at one level, further confirms the need for dialogue. Each can complement and supplement the other. At another level,
however, it creates complications because it leads to apparently quite
opposed conceptions of other corporeal relations. A key example of this
concerns their respective conception of the body's relation to space. Both
writers view the body as inseparably joined to space but their conception of
this join differs considerably.

For Merleau-Ponty, the body's active relation to its environment creates a
functional space around it. Using its acquired schemas and habits, he maintains, the active body positions its world around itself and constitutes that
world as 'ready-to-hand', to use Heidegger's (1962) expression. For Foucault,
by contrast, bodies are organized and controlled through the organization
and control of space. He describes the historical emergence of an 'art of
distributions' (1979: 141) by which attempts have been made to maximize the
efficiency and usefulness of bodies. In Foucault's schema, contra Merleau-
Ponty, the body does not position space around itself. It is positioned in space.
Furthermore, it does not render its space functional; rather, it is made functional by means of space. Thus Foucault (1979: 141) describes the practices of
enclosure, partitioning, functional codification and differentiation of spaces,
which have been deployed in factories, workshops, schools, prisons, etc., as a
means of securing some control over the bodies who populate them.

The one-sidedness of each of these perspectives – and it is legitimate to
speak of one-sidedness because each nominally accepts that the body is both
active and acted upon – amounts to a major weakness in both. It does not
amount to an incommensurability, however, and it does not prevent dialogue
between the two perspectives. To say, as Foucault does, that the body is made
useful, efficient and functional through the organization of space, is also to
say that the body can make space useful, functional and efficient. It is to say
that the body is conducted to perform such an operation. To designate a
space, within a workshop or on a production line, for sawing and cutting, for
example, is to presuppose a body which is able to transform space and the
equipment in it by sawing and cutting and, moreover, to ensure that bodies
actually perform this function; likewise, a rest room can only ever be a rest
room by virtue of the thought that persons will rest in it (and nowhere else)
and by virtue of the success of those who designate it as such to enforce their
designation by ensuring that people do rest in it (and nowhere else). It
depends upon the use of space. In this sense, the body can only be acted upon
and co-opted, by means of space, to the extent that it acts and that it uses and

co-opts space through its action. The proof of this pudding lies with the fact that an inert body, such as a dead body, or an unmastered body, such as a very young child's body, could not be controlled in this way. It would make no sense to attempt to control a young child through a functional differentiation of spaces (e.g. into a washroom, laundry, workshop, etc.) because such functions are beyond a young child's corporeal capabilities. The child cannot be controlled by means of these spatial tactics because she is unable to animate and transform space in the manner required by these tactics.

Clearly a space can be designed, equipped and organized to enable effective control over bodies, quite independently of those (particular) bodies, but such spaces can only serve their political function to the extent that they are populated by bodies who will animate and execute that function. Space is not an (external) object-like force which imposes itself on the body from without. It is a lived and shared dwelling whose 'effects' cannot be understood or accounted for independently of the human action which animates them. It is the use of space, as an ongoing, situated activity, that constitutes body-power. And this demands that the body is both active and acted upon, and, indeed, that these two modes of corporeal involvement are understood as twin aspects of a single situation.

The issue of resistance – which was central to Foucault's (1981a, 1982) later understanding of power – should also be discussed here. Clearly it is the active role of the subject, in her own subjection, and the skills and competence that are presupposed on her behalf, which provides the space for effective resistance. It is because body-power (as a spatial phenomenon) harnesses the action of those whom it subjects, that those subjects are in a position to resist. And they do resist. The functionality of space is under constant threat from resistances, as the teacher, who tells her pupils that they are 'not in the playground now' and the athlete, who is told to 'save it for the dressing room' both bear witness to.

The definition of body-space (which includes both 'bodies' and 'spaces') that we are moving to here is that it is both overdetermined and contestable. Body-spaces are constituted through their architectural design, their actual construction, their organization and their equipment, their enforcement agents (supervisors, managers, etc.) and their subject population. Each of these levels (which are in fact levels of human action) acts upon the others in a transformative manner. And power, space and agency thereby overlap and intertwine. A chiasm is formed, in which the functionality of space, the functionality of embodied human action and the directionality and effectivity of power are constituted in one and the same moment.

Investing the body

There is a possible objection to my argument that requires some consideration: namely, that it overlooks the extent to which bodies are actually ('internally') invested by power, according to Foucault's analysis. At one level this is an argument about the historical construction of self-policing and conscience. I have discussed this with respect to Foucault and Merleau-Ponty elsewhere (Crossley, 1993a, 1994) and will not repeat myself here. At another level, however, the objection concerns Foucault's claim that the human musculature itself is invested and controlled by the effects of power:

> Mastery and awareness of one's own body can be acquired only through the effect of an investment of power in the body: gymnastics, exercises, muscle building, nudism, glorification of the body beautiful. All of this belongs to the pathway leading to the desire of one's own body, by way of the insistent, persistent, meticulous work of power on the bodies of children or soldiers, the healthy bodies. But once power produces this effect, there inevitably emerge the responding claims and affirmations, those of one's own body against power, of health against the economic system, of pleasure against the moral norms of sexuality, marriage, decency. Suddenly, what had made power strong becomes used to attack it. Power, after investing itself in the body, finds itself exposed to a counter-attack in the same body. (Foucault, 1980:56)

In this passage Foucault adds a further dimension to the relation between power and agency or embodied subjectivity. He identifies 'Mastery and awareness of one's body', that is, embodied subjective agency, as an effect of the investment of power in the body. Surely, it will be argued, this notion contradicts Merleau-Ponty's understanding of the lived body.

In order to consider this idea and its implications it is necessary to unpick the rather enigmatic gloss, 'investment of power in the body'. To this end I will examine 'mastery' and 'awareness' of the body separately.

In relation to the question of mastery, the investment gloss translates as training. In the passage above, for example, Foucault refers to 'gymnastics, exercises [and] muscle building' as forms of power. Moreover, in *Discipline and Punish*, which is the key text in terms of a description of body-power, there is no form of power described that could not be redescribed as a training technique. Foucault refers to exercises and to economies of reward and punishment as forms of power for example. In effect then, the investment of power in the body consists in its being trained in specific modes of comportment, motility, etc., under specific conditions, by virtue of specific techniques, to a more or less stipulated and specific end.

By redescribing 'investment' in this way we can identify four important points of possible interchange between Foucault and Merleau-Ponty. In the first instance, we can eliminate the possibility that the work of Foucault and Merleau-Ponty is incommensurable with respect to the issue of the 'investment' of the body. Merleau-Ponty too posits that the body is trained and if this is what is meant by investment then he is in (basic) agreement with Foucault.

It is interesting in this respect, furthermore, to note that Foucault describes the effect of investment as 'Mastery' and that he allows for the possibility that the body will take up the skills and dispositions that are imposed upon it, and use them against those who impose them. He does not adopt the behaviourist option of viewing the result of training as a simple propensity to repeat certain actions. In this respect, he agrees with Merleau-Ponty (1962, 1965), who was very critical of behaviourism, on this issue. Training, Merleau-Ponty argued, gives rise to competence, to a flexible power of action and reaction; it is empowering. This is the second point.

Third, it is clear that Foucault's gloss facilitates a criticism of Merleau-Ponty. It points to Merleau-Ponty's failure to consider the political function and the political conditions of training – these functions and conditions being what enables us to equate training with 'power'. Merleau-Ponty, in other words, only identifies the empowering aspect of training. He does not recognize the control function that is, in some instances at least, embodied in the training process. Moreover, in this respect, Foucault's work allows us to fill a hiatus in Merleau-Ponty's work, with respect to the question of body-power. For Merleau-Ponty, as I noted above, the co-option and control of the body-subject is the key means by which social and political order is achieved; and yet he never outlines how this is possible or even what form it takes. With the help of Foucault we can see that the answer to Merleau-Ponty's problem lies disguised in his own writings: that is, in the concept of training that he (Merleau-Ponty) is so keen to elucidate.

Fourth, Merleau-Ponty's own position on training allows us to develop a criticism of Foucault. For Merleau-Ponty, training is only possible by virtue of an element of mastery that is always already there in the active body-subject. Training is an active process, in Merleau-Ponty's approach, and as such it presupposes certain capabilities on the behalf of the (active) training body. For example, it presupposes a degree of hand to eye co-ordination and more general co-ordination, which allows an agent to observe and then copy. Moreover, as Merleau-Ponty observes, the trained often have to copy the results of their trainers' actions, without being able to see how those actions are performed – the acquisition of language is a key example of this – or again, when they see those actions from the 'wrong way round', because the trainer is facing them. In addition to this, training presupposes the power of conservation, which allows set exercises to be repeated at intervals, with a gradual improvement, until a skill or technique is naturalized. In this sense then, Merleau-Ponty would call for a reformulation of Foucault's point. Power, he would argue, does increase mastery in both a qualitative and quantitative sense but it does not effect mastery per se. A germ of mastery, however small, is always presupposed in the training process.

There is no recognition of this notion in Foucault's work but it is clear that he has no reply to it. He does, albeit unwittingly, presuppose some degree of carnal mastery in his account of the power mechanisms by means of which such mastery is inscribed in the body. To say that 'exercise' and 'gymnastics' are forms of power which invest the body and afford body mastery, for example, is clearly to presuppose a body which is capable of the level of co-ordination and control necessary to take on an exercise or gymnastics routine. This is not to say that corporeal routines and skills cannot be immensely transformed but it is to say that they can only be transformed because there is some effective basis to work with. It is to affirm, effectively, what Foucault affirms elsewhere: viz. that power is constituted by means of a set of actions upon other actions. And it is to take this further by noting that 'action' must therefore always be presupposed on the behalf of the subjected, in any account of power, and that so too, therefore, must the effective conditions of action (i.e. a degree of body mastery). By taking this route, we can maintain that Foucault's account must presuppose some notion of a body-subject. Without such a notion, his account of investment and mastery would not work.

It is not only a body-subject which is presupposed here moreover. It is communicative intersubjectivity. Space will not permit a detailed discussion of this issue here. Suffice it to say, however, that the 'transmission' of body routines and habits, is more often than not facilitated by communicative interactions and symbolic processes. The investment of the body by power requires a fabric of intersubjectivity. This 'phenomenology of power' has been discussed in more detail elsewhere (Crossley, 1993a, 1994) and is to be the subject of a further paper.

Embodied awareness of embodiment

In addition to 'Mastery', the above passage suggests that 'awareness of one's own body' is the outcome of a positive investment of power in the body. This point is vaguely elaborated by reference to 'nudism and glorification of the body beautiful' as cultural practices but it is not expanded upon. Moreover, it is nowhere properly expanded upon in Foucault's work. *Birth of the Clinic* (1976) and the studies of sexuality (1981a, 1986, 1987) and discipline (1979), refer to the emergence of particular discursive constitutions of the body, and these can be described as forms of awareness – in the sense that they represent the manner in which the body is given to discursive reflection in specific instances – but, even so, Foucault never discusses the question of awareness in any detail.

Notwithstanding this, however, what he seems to be suggesting, contra some versions of humanism, is that one's experience of one's body is not immediate (i.e. without medium) but is mediated by power. Power in this sense refers to particular discursive and perceptual schemas which are linked to given instituted forms of social practice. It could be said, for example, that we only have a 'medical awareness' of our bodies and thus that we only experience our various ticks and flushes as signs of disease, by virtue of a historically contingent web of discourses and practices to which we subscribe (however unwittingly) and which, at least in part, are tied to the practices of sanitation, surveillance and control which regulate our everyday being. Moreover, it could be added, we subject ourselves to this regulation by virtue of our identification of ourselves or our experiences through the medical model.

In dealing with this claim it is important to flesh out some of the presuppositions that it involves. There are three in particular that I will deal with. In the first instance, awareness is presupposed. Unless power is granted the occult status of being able to make an unaware being aware, that is, to create one form of being out of another, then we must grant that power works upon already existing forms of awareness. These forms of awareness need not amount to 'self-awareness'. Indeed, if Foucault's account is to have any meaning and substance then self-awareness cannot be presupposed; awareness, however, must be present. This brings us to the second presupposition; viz. that Foucault presupposes a critique of the notion of privileged access to self and a notion of a being who can only achieve self-awareness and knowledge by means of a cultural medium. Third, Foucault presupposes that the being who conforms to these various requirements is also capable of taking up the cultural devices that his account refers to; that is, of acquiring language, entering a particular language game and applying the rules of that game appropriately, so as to be correctly aware of their body. None of these presuppositions are or can be accounted for in Foucault's work (precisely because they are presuppositions).

Again this opens the door for dialogue with Merleau-Ponty. Throughout his major writings, Merleau-Ponty (1962, 1965, 1968) maintains the notion that the body-subject is, in the first instance, aware but not self-aware. Although it develops an awareness and understanding of its environment, it is not an object of its own awareness in any straightforward sense.[4] This does not mean that the body-subject is perpetually unaware of itself however. Rather, Merleau-Ponty maintains that it acquires such awareness by means of its engagement in a cultural world. He discusses the role of Lacan's (1988) 'mirror stage' in the development of specular self-awareness (Merleau-Ponty, 1964), for example, and he discusses the role which language acquisition and 'taking the point of view of the other' play in the formation of an objectification of one's own carnal-being (and thus an awareness of self) (Merleau-Ponty, 1962, 1973). This account (which I cannot outline in detail here) provides for Foucault's presuppositions. The body-subject is precisely the being who takes up the mechanisms of culture and achieves a (culturally bound) awareness of itself (qua body) in the process.

The converse side of this is that Merleau-Ponty would gain an account of the politics of identity and self-awareness. As with the account of 'Mastery', he would be able to see how the child development processes (of gaining self-awareness) that he seeks to understand (philosophically), are bound to relations of power and control; that is, he would see that the perspective of otherness, which makes the perspective of self (and self-awareness) possible, has a political aspect; that it intertwines with relations of power. It would be wrong to say that Merleau-Ponty's work does not contain some recognition of this already but it is clearly via Foucault that such recognition can be developed into a proper framework of analysis.

With respect to the question of carnal awareness then, as with those issues discussed previously, Merleau-Ponty's 'body-subject', complements and enriches Foucault's 'body-power' (and vice versa).

The gender politics of comportment

Hitherto the dialogue between the work of Merleau-Ponty and Foucault has been conducted at an abstract level. The value of the dialogue is not restricted to this level however. It clearly has a more concrete application and use. This can be best illustrated by reference to the gender politics of comportment.

The gender division in (human) bodily comportment, motility, etc. is a much remarked upon phenomenon. One of the most detailed empirical studies of this phenomenon, from a feminist perspective, is Mariane Wex's (1979) photographic study, *Let's Take Back Our Space*. This study clearly illustrates 'typical' differences in the manner in which women and men perform basic and mundane human actions (e.g. sitting and standing). It is an account of gender differences in what Marcel Mauss (1979) referred to as 'body techniques' (see Crossley, 1993b, 1995b).

These differences are not registered by either Merleau-Ponty or Foucault. Both talk of bodies in general, making little to no reference to gender differences. Notwithstanding this however, it is an issue which has been taken up by feminist readers of both. Iris Young's (1980) paper, 'Throwing Like a Girl', takes up the case from a Merleau-Pontyian stance. And Sandra Lee Bartky's (1988) paper, 'Foucault, Femininity and the Modernisation of Patriarchal Power', takes up the issue from a Foucauldian perspective. In both cases, in Bartky in particular, some attention to empirical detail is lacking. Nevertheless it is clear to see, from these papers, how the two perspectives can be fruitfully engaged in an understanding of the gender politics of comportment.

Bartky's Foucauldian contribution involves a consideration of the technologies by which comportment styles are invested in the body. She criticizes

Foucault for failing to see the gender divisions which are perpetuated by the disciplinary mechanisms that he studied in *Discipline and Punish*. And she thereby identifies the sites in which those mechanisms manifest as sites of gender reproduction. Moreover (in accord with Foucault's later political writings), she argues that some of the techniques which control comportment are self-administered. Women and men, she notes, may actively fashion themselves as subjects of a particular gait, etc.

From this position we are able to identify and critically analyse and discuss the sources of gender differences that studies such as those of Wex (1979) outline. It is difficult to ascertain or discuss the significance (political or otherwise) of this however, particularly as some of those mechanisms are apparently voluntarily taken up by the subject. There are of course extreme cases where the harms of specific body techniques are obvious, but what of different ways of walking or throwing? What does it matter if there is a specifically feminine way (or ways) of walking or throwing? It is in relation to this question that Iris Young's (1980) contribution can best be appreciated. Young, as a Merleau-Pontyian, is concerned with the (habit-based) body as a means of being-in-the-world and, from this position, she is precisely able to consider the consequences of throwing, running and lifting (etc.) 'like a girl'.

The manner in which women move and engage with their environment, Young observes, is inhibited in relation to that of men. She explores this inhibition in some depth but for our purposes it will suffice to say that it consists, first, in a hesitancy and cautiousness which precedes action; second, in a reactive rather than a proactive engagement with objects, e.g.:

> Men more often move out toward a ball in flight and confront it with their own countermotion. Women tend to wait for and then react to its approach rather than going forth to meet it. We frequently respond to the motion of a ball coming towards us as though it were coming at us, and our immediate bodily impulse is to flee, duck, or otherwise protect ourselves from its flight. (Young, 1980:143)

Third, there is a tendency for women to use only 'parts' of the body, rather than putting the whole body behind an action (e.g. lifting with the arms rather than the back, shoulders and arms). This inhibition, Young maintains, leads to a relative lack in female agency capacity. Women are less able to command a control over their immediate environment. An obvious example of this would be that, irrespective of muscular power, an agent who lifts with her arms only will not be able to lift such heavy things as one who lifts with her back, shoulders and arms. The female manner of (bodily) being-in-the-world in other words, works to the relative disadvantage of women, considered as practical agents.

233

Young considers two possible explanations of women's inhibited comportment. She cites differences in training and she cites the manner in which women are made aware of themselves as objects (i.e. by the objectifying gaze of men). Their training makes women less equipped to act in space, she argues, while objectification constitutes an inhibition in female embodiment, a self-consciousness which obviates 'trust' in the pre-reflective capabilities of the body: women feel unable to 'let go' and let their body guide them to the same extent as their male counterparts. These are important points but Young does not pursue them and her Merleau-Pontyian framework would not help her to do so. What is required is precisely a consideration of the means by which 'Mastery and awareness of one's body' is achieved; i.e. a Foucauldian perspective, such as that pursued by Bartky.

The dialogue between Young's and Bartky's account illustrates the interpenetration between the concept of the body as a surface of inscription and as a (lived) way of being-in-the-world at the political level. Not only can we maintain, as we did earlier, that inscription is only possible by virtue of an active body, we can maintain that it is only of political significance because the body is our (active) way of being-in-the-world. It is because we exist by means of embodied action that it matters how our bodies are treated and how they perform. What would be the meaning of 'body-power' if the body were nothing but flesh and bone?

Body-subject/body-power

I have argued in this article that the concept of the lived body, as posited in the work of Merleau-Ponty, and the concept of the inscribed body, as posited in the work of Foucault, are not incommensurable: that they are compatible and complementary at both the theoretical and the political levels. I have not dissolved or argued for the dissolution of the two concepts into one, however. Rather, I have kept them in tension with each other. I have suggested that the body is both active and acted upon (by other bodies) (see also Crossley, 1994, 1995a). This tension, I contend, is precisely what constitutes the human body qua socio-historical being. The body as a mastered and self-aware being is, as I have argued, formed in this interstice. Likewise, as I have shown with regard to spatiality, the modalities of the body-subject are formed in this tension: it positions and is positioned, functions and makes function.

This tension is not a clash of opposites. Its poles are, as Merleau-Ponty (1968) would say, reversibilities within a single flesh; that is, relational dimensions of a single structure. One side presupposes, rather than negates the other. Moreover, if we follow Foucault, this tension and this structure, are the very stuff of history itself:

> There are revolts and that is fact. It is through revolt that subjectivity
> (not that of great men but that of whomever) introduces itself into

history and gives it the breath of life . . . it is due to such voices [of revolt] that the time of man does not have the form of an evolution, but precisely that of history. (Foucault, 1981b: 8)

History is formed in the tension or agonism between a body which has broken free of evolutionary time, thereby constituting a human world and the multiple, manifold and dispersed forms of control and restraint that have been constituted in that self-same world; a play of unstable dominations.

It remains for future work to trace this relational and reversible tension of body-subject and body-power in the multiple sites which they simultaneously occupy and constitute and to observe and critique their diverse forms and consequences. We must resist the 'either/or' temptation and study body-subject and body-power as twin aspects of a single structure of action-upon-action.

Notes

1   See particularly his discussion of superego development in 'The Child's Relations With Others' (Merleau-Ponty, 1964).
2   Merleau-Ponty posits a notion of situated freedom (which is distinct from Sartre's understanding of absolute freedom) in the final chapter of *The Phenomenology of Perception* (1962).
3   In *Humanism and Terror* (1969), Merleau-Ponty argues this from a Marxist position. He later drops the Marxism but not the critical perspective in *Adventures of the Dialectic* (1973). Foucault argues the point from a Nietzschean (i.e. non-dialectical, fragmented) position. For a closer political comparison of the two writers see Crossley (1994).
4   The body has a tacit or proprioceptive awareness of itself according to Merleau-Ponty (1962); that is, it knows where its various parts are and it knows how to move them, 'without thinking' but it is not aware of itself in an explicit or thematic way. It is not an object for itself (see Crossley, 1995a).

References

Bartky, S. (1988) 'Foucault, Femininity and the Modernisation of Patriarchal Power', pp. 61–86 in I. Diamond and L. Quinby (eds) *Feminism and Foucault: Reflections On Resistance*. Boston: Northeastern University Press.

Crossley, N. (1993a) 'The Politics of the Gaze; Between Foucault and Merleau-Ponty', *Human Studies* 16(4): 399–419.

Crossley, N. (1993b) 'Body Techniques and Human Agency in Mauss, Merleau-Ponty and Foucault', *Working Paper*, Centre for Psychotherapeutic Studies, Department of Psychiatry, University of Sheffield.

Crossley, N. (1994) *The Politics of Subjectivity: Between Foucault and Merleau-Ponty*. Ashgate: Avebury.

Crossley, N. (1995a) 'Merleau-Ponty, the Elusive Body and Carnal Sociology', *Body & Society* 1(1): 43–63.

Crossley, N. (1995b) 'Body Techniques, Agency and Intercorporeality', *Sociology* 29(1): 132–49.

Foucault, M. (1976) *The Birth of the Clinic*. London: Tavistock.

Foucault, M. (1977) 'Nietzsche, Genealogy and History', pp. 139–64 in D. Bouchard (ed.) *Language, Counter-Memory, Practice*. Ithaca, NY: Cornell University Press.

Foucault, M. (1979) *Discipline and Punish*. Harmondsworth: Penguin.

Foucault, M. (1980) 'Body-Power', pp. 55–63 in C. Gordon (ed.) *Power/Knowledge*. Brighton: Harvester.

Foucault, M. (1981a) *The History of Sexuality, Vol. 1*. Harmondsworth: Penguin.

Foucault, M. (1981b) 'Is It Useless to Revolt?', *Philosophy and Social Criticism* 8(1): 3–9.

Foucault, M. (1982) 'The Subject and Power: An Afterword', pp. 208–26 in H. Dreyfus and P. Rabinow (1982) *Michel Foucault: Beyond Structuralism and Hermeneutics*. Brighton: Harvester.

Foucault, M. (1986) *The Use of Pleasure*. Harmondsworth: Penguin.

Foucault, M. (1987) *The Care of the Self*. London: Allen Lane.

Grosz, E. (1993) 'Bodies and Knowledges: Feminism and the Crisis of Reason', in A. Alcoff and E. Potter (eds) *Feminist Epistemologies*. London: Routledge.

Heidegger, M. (1962) *Being and Time*. Oxford: Blackwell.

Lacan, J. (1988) 'The Mirror Stage as Formative of the Function of the I as Revealed in Psychoanalytic Experience', pp. 1–7 in *Ecrits: A Selection*. London: Tavistock/Routledge.

Levin, D. (1989) 'The Body Politic: The Embodiment of Praxis in Foucault and Habermas', *Praxis International* 9(1/2):112–32.

Mauss, M. (1979) 'Body Techniques', pp. 95–123 in *Sociology and Psychology*. London: Routledge and Kegan Paul.

Merleau-Ponty, M. (1962) *The Phenomenology of Perception*. London: Routledge and Kegan Paul.

Merleau-Ponty, M. (1964) 'The Child's Relations With Others', pp. 96–155 in *The Primacy of Perception and Other Essays*. Evanston, IL: Northwestern University Press.

Merleau-Ponty, M. (1965) *The Structure of Behaviour*. London: Methuen.

Merleau-Ponty, M. (1968) *The Visible and the Invisible*. Evanston, IL: Northwestern University Press.

Merleau-Ponty, M. (1969) *Humanism and Terror*. Boston: Beacon.

Merleau-Ponty, M. (1970) 'The Concept of Nature 1', pp. 130–55 in *In Praise of Philosophy and Other Essays*. Evanston, IL: Northwestern University Press.

Merleau-Ponty, M. (1973) *Adventures of the Dialectic*. Evanston, IL: Northwestern University Press.

Ryle, G. (1949) *The Concept of Mind*. Harmondsworth: Penguin.

Turner, B. (1984) *Body and Society*. Oxford: Blackwell.

Wex, M. (1979) *Let's Take Back Our Space*. Berlin: Frauenliteratervlag Hermine Fees.

Young, I. (1980) 'Throwing Like a Girl: A Phenomenology of Feminine Bodily Comportment', *Human Studies* 3:137–56.

16

THE BODY AND THE REPRODUCTION OF FEMININITY

A feminist appropriation of Foucault

Susan R. Bordo

Source: A. M. Jaggar and S. R. Bordo (eds), *Gender/Body/Knowledge: feminist reconstructions of being and knowing*, New Brunswick: Rutgers University Press, 1989, pp. 13–31.

Reconstructing feminist discourse on the body

The body—what we eat, how we dress, the daily rituals through which we attend to the body—is a medium of culture. The body, as anthropologist Mary Douglas has argued, is a powerful symbolic form, a surface on which the central rules, hierarchies, and even metaphysical commitments of a culture are inscribed and thus reinforced through the concete language of the body. The body may also operate as a metaphor for culture. From quarters as diverse as Plato and Hobbes to French feminist Luce Irigaray, an imagination of body-morphology has provided a blueprint for diagnosis and/or vision of social and political life.

The body is not only a *text* of culture. It is also, as anthropologist Pierre Bourdieu and philosopher Michel Foucault (among others) have argued, a *practical*, direct locus of social control. Banally, through table manners and toilet habits, through seemingly trivial routines, rules, and practices, culture is "*made* body," as Bourdieu puts it—converted into automatic, habitual activity. As such it is put "beyond the grasp of consciousness . . . [untouchable] by voluntary, deliberate transformation" (1977:94). Our conscious politics, social commitments, strivings for change may be undermined and betrayed by the life of our bodies—not the craving, instinctual body imagined by Plato, Augustine, and Freud but the docile, regulated body practiced at and habituated to the rules of cultural life.

Throughout his later "genealogical" works (*Discipline and Punish, History of Sexuality*), Foucault constantly reminds us of the primacy of practice over belief. Not chiefly through "ideology," but through the organization and regulation of the time, space, and movements of our daily lives, our bodies are trained, shaped, and impressed with the stamp of prevailing historical forms of selfhood, desire, masculinity, femininity. Such an emphasis casts a dark and disquieting shadow across the contemporary scene. For women, as study after study shows, are spending more time on the management and discipline of our bodies than we have in a long, long time. In a decade marked by a reopening of the public arena to women, the intensification of such regimens appears diversionary and subverting. Through the pursuit of an ever-changing, homogenizing, elusive ideal of femininity—a pursuit without a terminus, a resting point, requiring that women constantly attend to minute and often whimsical changes in fashion—female bodies become what Foucault calls "docile bodies,"—bodies whose forces and energies are habituated to external regulation, subjection, transformation, "improvement."[1] Through the exacting and normalizing disciplines of diet, make-up, and dress—central organizing principles of time and space in the days of many women—we are rendered less socially oriented and more centripetally focused on self-modification. Through these disciplines, we continue to memorize on our bodies the feel and conviction of lack, insufficiency, of never being good enough. At the farthest extremes, the practices of femininity may lead us to utter demoralization, debilitation, and death.

Viewed historically, the discipline and normalization of the female body— perhaps the only gender oppression that exercises itself, although to different degrees and in different forms, across age, race, class, and sexual orientation —has to be acknowledged as an amazingly durable and flexible strategy of social control. In our own era, it is difficult to avoid the recognition that the contemporary preoccupation with appearance, which still affects women far more powerfully than men, even in our narcissistic and visually oriented culture,[2] may function as a "backlash" phenomenon, reasserting existing gender configurations *against* any attempts to shift or transform power-relations. Surely we are in the throes of this backlash today. In newspapers and magazines daily we encounter stories that promote traditional gender relations and prey on anxieties about change: stories about latch-key children, abuse in day-care centers, the "new woman" 's troubles with men, her lack of marriageability, and so on. A dominant visual theme in teenage magazines involves women hiding in the shadows of men, seeking solace in their arms, willingly contracting the space they occupy. The last, of course, also describes our contemporary aesthetic ideal for women, an ideal whose obsessive pursuit has become the central torment of many women's lives.[3] In such an era we desperately need an effective *political* discourse about the female body, a discourse adequate to an analysis of the insidious, and often paradoxical, pathways of modern social control.

Developing such a discourse requires reconstructing the "old" feminist body-discourse of the late 1960s and early 1970s, with its political categories of oppressors and oppressed, villains and victims. Here, I believe that a feminist appropriation of some of Foucault's later concepts can prove useful. Following Foucault, we must first abandon the idea of power as something possessed by one group and leveled against another, and we must think instead of the network of practices, institutions, and technologies that sustain positions of dominance and subordination within a particular domain. Second, we need an analytics adequate to describe a power whose central mechanisms are not repressive, but *constitutive*: "a power bent on generating forces, making them grow, and ordering them, rather than one dedicated to impeding them, making them submit, or destroying them" (Foucault 1978: 136). Particularly in the realm of femininity, where so much depends upon the seemingly willing acceptance of various norms and practices, we need an analysis of power "from below," as Foucault puts it (1978:94): for example, the mechanisms that shape and proliferate, rather than repress, desire, generate and focus our energies, construct our conceptions of normalcy and deviance. Third, we need a discourse that will enable us to account for the subversion of potential rebellion, a discourse that, while insisting on the necessity of "objective" analysis of power relations, social hierarchy, political backlash, and so forth, will nonetheless allow us to confront the mechanisms by which the subject becomes enmeshed, at times, into collusion with forces that sustain her own oppression.

This essay will not attempt to produce a "theory" along these lines. Rather, my focus will be the analysis of one particular arena where the interplay of these dynamics is striking and perhaps exemplary. It is a limited and unusual arena—a group of gender-related and historically localized disorders: hysteria, agoraphobia, and anorexia nervosa.[4] I recognize, too, that these disorders have been largely class and race specific, occurring overwhelmingly among white middle- and upper middle-class women.[5] Nonetheless, anorexia, hysteria, and agoraphobia may provide a paradigm of one way in which potential resistance is not merely undercut but *utilized* in the maintenance and reproduction of existing power relations.[6]

The central mechanism I will describe involves a transformation (or, if you wish, duality) of meaning, through which conditions that are "objectively" (and on one level, experientially) constraining, enslaving, and even murderous, come to be experienced as liberating, transforming, and life-giving. I offer this analysis, although limited to a specific domain, as an example of how various contemporary critical discourses may be joined to yield an understanding of the subtle and often unwitting role played by our bodies in the symbolization and reproduction of gender.

The body as a text of femininity

The continuum between female disorder and "normal" feminine practice is sharply revealed through a close reading of those disorders to which women

239

have been particularly vulnerable. These, of course, have varied historically: neurasthenia and hysteria in the second half of the nineteenth century; agoraphobia and, most dramatically, anorexia nervosa and bulimia in the second half of the twentieth century. This is not to say that anorexics did not exist in the nineteenth century—many cases were described, usually within the context of diagnoses of hysteria (Showalter 1985:128–129)—or that women no longer suffer from classical hysterical symptoms in the twentieth century. But the taking up of eating disorders on a mass scale is as unique to the culture of the 1980s as the epidemic of hysteria was to the Victorian era.[7]

The symptomatology of these disorders reveals itself as textuality. Loss of mobility, loss of voice, inability to leave the home, feeding others while starving self, taking up space and whittling down the space one's body takes up—all have symbolic meaning, all have *political* meaning within the varying rules governing the historical construction of gender. Working within this framework, we see that whether we look at hysteria, agoraphobia, or anorexia, we find the body of the sufferer deeply inscribed with an ideological construction of femininity emblematic of the periods in question. That construction, of course, is always homogenizing and normalizing, erasing racial, class, and other differences and insisting that all women aspire to a coercive, standardized ideal. Strikingly, in these disorders the construction of femininity is written in disturbingly concrete, hyperbolic terms: exaggerated, extremely literal, at times virtually caricatured presentations of the ruling feminine mystique. The bodies of disordered women in this way offer themselves as an aggressively graphic text for the interpreter—a text that insists, actually demands, it be read as a cultural statement, a statement about gender.

Both nineteenth-century male physicians and twentieth-century feminist critics have seen, in the symptoms of neurasthenia and hysteria (syndromes that became increasingly less differentiated as the century wore on), an exaggeration of stereotypically feminine traits. The nineteenth-century "lady" was idealized in terms of delicacy and dreaminess, sexual passivity, and a charmingly labile and capricious emotionality (Vicinus 1972:x–xi). Such notions were formalized and scientized in the work of male theorists from Acton and Kraft-Ebbing to Freud, who described "normal," mature femininity in such terms.[8] In this context, the dissociations of hysteria, the drifting and fogging of perception, the nervous tremors and faints, the anaesthesias, and the extreme mutability of symptomatology associated with nineteenth-century female disorders can be seen to be concretizations of the feminine mystique of the period, produced according to rules governing the prevailing construction of femininity. Doctors described what came to be known as the "hysterical personality" as "impressionable, suggestible, and narcissistic; highly labile, their moods changing suddenly, dramatically, and for seemingly inconsequential reasons ... egocentric in the extreme ... essentially asexual and not uncommonly frigid" (Smith-Rosenberg 1985:203)—all characteristics normative of femininity in this era.

As Elaine Showalter points out, the term "hysterical" itself became almost interchangeable with the term "feminine" in the literature of the period (1985:129).

The hysteric's embodiment of the feminine mystique of her era, however, seems subtle and ineffable compared to the ingenious literalism of agoraphobia and anorexia. In the context of our culture this literalism makes sense. With the advent of movies and television, the rules for femininity have come to be culturally transmitted more and more through the deployment of standardized visual images. As a result, femininity itself has come to be largely a matter of constructing, in the manner described by Erving Goffman, the appropriate surface presentation of the self. We no longer are told what "a lady" is or of what femininity consists. Rather, we learn the rules directly through bodily discourse: through images which tell us what clothes, body shape, facial expression, movements, and behavior is required.

In agoraphobia and even more dramatically in anorexia, the disorder presents itself as a virtual, though tragic, parody of twentieth-century constructions of femininity. The 1950s and early 1960s, when agoraphobia first began to escalate among women, represented a reassertion of domesticity and dependency as the feminine ideal. "Career woman" became a dirty word, much more so than it had been during the war, when the survival of the economy depended on women's willingness to do "men's work." The reigning ideology of femininity, so well described by Betty Friedan and perfectly captured in the movies and television shows of the era was childlike, nonassertive, helpless without a man, "content in a world of bedroom and kitchen, sex, babies and home" (1962:36). The house-bound agoraphobic lives this construction of femininity literally. "You want dependency? I'll give you dependency!" she proclaims with her body, "You want me in the home? You'll have me in the home—with a vengeance!" The point, which many therapists have commented on, does not need laboring. Agoraphobia, as I. G. Fodor has put it, seems "the logical—albeit extreme—extension of the cultural sex-role stereotype for women" in this era.[9]

The emaciated body of the anorexic, of course, immediately presents itself as a caricature of the contemporary ideal of hyperslenderness for women, an ideal that, despite the game resistance of racial and ethnic difference, has become the norm for women today. But slenderness is only the tip of the iceberg, for slenderness itself requires interpretation. "C'est le sens qui fait vendre," said Barthes, speaking of clothing styles—it's meaning that makes the sale. So, too, it is meaning that makes the body admirable. To the degree that anorexia may be said to be "about" slenderness it is about slenderness as a citadel of contemporary and historical meaning, not as an empty "fashion" ideal. As such, the interpretation of slenderness yields multiple readings, with some related to gender, some not. For the purposes of this essay I will offer an abbreviated, gender-focused reading. But I must stress that this reading illuminates only partially, and that many other currents not discussed here—economic, psychosocial, and historical, as well as ethnic and class dimensions—figure prominently.[10]

We begin with the painfully literal inscription, on the anorexic's body, of the rules governing the construction of contemporary femininity. That construction is a "double-bind" that legislates contradictory ideals and directives. On the one hand, our culture still widely advertises domestic conceptions of femininity, the ideological moorings for a rigorously dualistic sexual division of labor, with woman as chief emotional and physical nurturer. The rules for this construction of femininity (and I speak here in a language both symbolic and literal) require that women learn to feed others, not the self, and to construe any desires for self-nurturance and self-feeding as greedy and excessive. Thus, women are required to develop a totally other-oriented emotional economy.

Young women today are still being taught such a construction of the self. On television, the Betty Crocker commercials symbolically speak to men of the legitimacy of their wildest, most abandoned desires: "I've got a passion for you; I'm wild, crazy, out of control" the hungering man croons to the sensuously presented chocolate cake, offered lovingly by the (always present) female. Female hunger, on the other hand, is depicted as needful of containment and control, and female eating is seen as a furtive, shameful, illicit act, as in the Andes Candies and "Mon Cheri" commercials, where a "tiny bite" of chocolate, privately savored, is supposed to be ample reward for a day of serving others (Bordo 1986). Food is not the real issue here, of course; rather, the control of female appetite for food is merely the most concrete expression of the general rule governing the construction of femininity that female hunger—for public power, for independence, for sexual gratification—be contained, and the public space that women be allowed to take up be circumscribed, limited (Bordo 1989). On the body of the anorexic woman such rules are grimly and deeply etched.

At the same time as young, "upwardly mobile" women today continue to be taught traditionally "feminine" virtues, to the degree that the professional arena has opened up to them, they must also learn to embody the "masculine" language and values of that arena—self-control, determination, cool, emotional discipline, mastery, and so on. Female bodies now speak symbolically of this necessity in their slender spare shape and the currently fashionable menswear look. Our bodies, as we trudge to the gym every day and fiercely resist both our hungers and our desires to soothe and baby ourselves, are also becoming more and more practiced at the "male" virtues of control and self-mastery. The anorexic pursues these virues with single-minded, unswerving dedication. "Energy, discipline, my own power will keep me going," says ex-anorexic Aimée Liu, recreating her anorexic days, "psychic fuel. I need nothing and no one else. . . . I will be master of my own body, if nothing else, I vow" (1979:123).

The ideal of slenderness, then, and the diet and exercise regimens that have become inseparable from it, offer the illusion of meeting, through the body, the contradictory demands of the contemporary ideology of femininity. Popular images reflect this dual demand. In a single issue of *Complete Woman* magazine, two articles appear, one on "Feminine Intuition," the other asking "Are You the New Macho Woman?" In *Vision Quest*, the young male hero falls in love with the heroine, as he says, because "she has all the best things I like in girls and all the best things I like in guys," that is, she's tough and cool, but warm and alluring. In the enormously popular *Aliens*, the heroine's personality has been deliberately constructed, with near comic-book explicitness, to embody traditional nurturant femininity alongside breathtaking macho-prowess and control; Sigourney Weaver, the actress who portrays her, has called the character "Rambolina."

In the pursuit of slenderness and the denial of appetite the traditional construction of femininity *intersects* with the new requirement for women to embody the "masculine" values of the public arena. The anorexic, as I have argued, embodies this intersection, this double-bind, in a particularly painful and graphic way.[11] I mean double-bind quite literally here. "Masculinity" and "femininity," at least since the nineteenth century and arguably before, have been constructed through a process of mutual exclusion. One cannot simply add the historically feminine virtues to the historically masculine ones to yield a "New Woman," a "New Man," a new ethics, or a new culture. Even on the screen or on television, embodied in created characters like the *Aliens* heroine, the result is a parody. Unfortunately, in this image-bedazzled culture, we have increasing difficulty discriminating between parodies and possibilities for the self. Explored as a possibility for the self, the "androgynous" ideal ultimately exposes its internal contradiction and becomes a war that tears the subject in two—a war explicitly thematized, by many anorexics, as a battle between male and female sides of the self (Bordo 1985).

Protest and retreat in the same gesture

In hysteria, agoraphobia, and anorexia, the woman's body may thus be viewed as a surface on which conventional constructions of femininity are exposed starkly to view, through their inscription in extreme or hyperliteral form. They are also written, of course, in languages of horrible suffering. It is as though these bodies are speaking to us of the pathology and violence that lurks just around the edge, waiting at the horizon of "normal" femininity. It is no wonder, then, that a steady motif in the feminist literature on female disorder is that of pathology as embodied *protest*—unconscious, inchoate, and counterproductive protest without an effective language, voice, or politics—but protest nonetheless.

American and French feminists alike have heard the hysteric speaking a language of protest, even or perhaps especially when she was mute. Dianne Hunter interprets Anna O's aphasia, which manifested itself in an inability to speak her native German, as a rebellion against the linguistic and cultural rules of the father and a return to the "mother-tongue": the semiotic babble of infancy, the language of the body. For Hunter, and for a number of other feminists working with Lacanian categories, the return to the semiotic level is both regressive and, as Hunter puts it, an "expressive" communication "addressed to patriarchal thought," "a self-repudiating form of feminine discourse in which the body signifies what social conditions make it impossible to state linguistically" (1985:114). "The hysterics are accusing; they are pointing," writes Catherine Clément in *The Newly Born Woman*; they make a "mockery of culture" (1986:42). In the same volume, Hélène Cixous speaks of "those wonderful hysterics, who subjected Freud to so many voluptuous moments too shameful to mention, bombarding his mosaic statute/law of Moses with their carnal, passionate body-words, haunting him with their inaudible thundering denunciations" (1986:95). For Cixous, Dora, who so frustrated Freud, is "the core example of the protesting force in women."

The literature of protest includes functional as well as symbolic approaches. Robert Seidenberg and Karen DeCrow, for example, describe agoraphobia as a "strike" against "the renunciations usually demanded of women" and the expectations of housewifely functions such as shopping, driving the children to school, accompanying their husbands to social events, and so on (1983:31). Carroll Smith-Rosenberg presents a similar analysis of hysteria, arguing that by preventing the woman from functioning in the wifely role of caretaker of others, of "ministering angel" to husband and children, hysteria "became one way in which conventional women could express—in most cases unconsciously—dissatisfaction with one or several aspects of their lives" (1983:208). A number of feminist writers, among whom Susie Ohrbach is the most articulate and forceful, have interpreted anorexia as a species of unconscious feminist protest. The anorexic is engaged in a "hunger strike," as Ohrbach calls it, stressing this as a political discourse in which the action of food refusal and dramatic transformation of body-size "expresses with [the] body what [the anorectic] is unable to tell us with words"—her indictment of a culture that disdains and suppresses female hunger, makes women ashamed of their appetites and needs, and demands women's constant work on the transformation of their bodies (1985:102).[12]

The anorexic, of course, is unaware that she is making a political statement. She may, indeed, be hostile to feminism and any other critical perspectives that she views as disputing her own autonomy and control or questioning the cultural ideals around which her life is organized. Through embodied rather than discursive demonstration she exposes and indicts those ideals, precisely by pursuing them to the point where their destructive potential is revealed for all to see. The very same gesture that expresses protest, moreover, can also signal retreat; this, indeed, may be part of the symptom's attraction. Kim Chernin argues, for example (1985), that the debilitating anorexic fixation, by halting or mitigating personal development, assuages this generation's guilt and separation anxiety over the prospect of surpassing our mothers, of living less circumscribed, freer lives. Agoraphobia, too, which often develops shortly after marriage, clearly functions in many cases as a way to cement dependency and attachment in the face of unacceptable stirrings of dissatisfaction and restlessness.

Although we may talk meaningfully of protest, then, I would emphasize the counterproductive, tragically self-defeating (indeed self-deconstructing) nature of that protest. Functionally, the symptoms of these disorders isolate, weaken, and undermine the sufferers; at the same time they turn the life of the body into an all-absorbing fetish, beside which all other objects of attention seem pale and unreal. On the symbolic level, too, the protest dimension collapses into its opposite and proclaims the utter defeat and capitulation of the subject to the contracted female world. The muteness of hysterics and their return to the level of pure, primary bodily expressivity have been interpreted, as we have seen, as rejecting the symbolic order of patriarchy and recovering a lost world of semiotic, maternal value. But *at the same time*, of course, muteness is the condition of the silent, uncomplaining woman—an ideal of patriarchal culture. Protesting the stifling of the female voice through one's own voicelessness, that is, employing the language of femininity to protest the conditions of the female world, will always involve ambiguities of this sort. Perhaps this is why symptoms crystallized from the language of femininity are so perfectly suited to express the dilemmas of women living in periods poised on the edge of gender change: the late nineteenth century, the post–World War II period, and the late twentieth century. In these periods gender has become as issue to be discussed, and discourse proliferates about "The Woman Question," "The New Woman," "What Women Want," "What Femininity Is," and so on.

Of course, such dilemmas are differently experienced, depending on class, age, and other aspects of womens' situations. Agoraphobia and anorexia are, after all, chiefly disorders of middle- and upper middle-class women—women for whom the anxieties of *possibility* have arisen, women who have the social and material resources to carry the language of femininity to symbolic excess. Clearly, we need separate analyses of the effects of homogenizing feminine practice on various class and racial groups and the different modes of protest that may be employed.

Collusion, resistance, and the body

The pathologies of female protest function, paradoxically, as if in collusion with the cultural conditions that produce them, reproducing rather than transforming precisely that which is being protested. In this connection, the fact that hysteria and anorexia have peaked during historical periods of cultural backlash against attempts at reorganization and redefinition of male and female roles is significant. Female pathology reveals itself here as an extremely interesting social formation, through which one source of potential for resistance and rebellion is pressed into the service of maintaining the established order.

How is this collusion established? Here, "objective" accounts of power relations fail us. For whatever the objective social conditions are that "produce" a pathology, the symptoms themselves must still be produced (however unconsciously or inadvertently) by the subject. That is, the body must become invested with meanings of various sorts. Only by examining this "productive" process on the part of the subject can we, as Mark Poster has put it, "illuminate the mechanisms of domination in the processes through which meaning is produced in everyday life" (1984:28); that is, only then can we see how the desires and dreams of the subject become implicated in the matrix of power relations.

Here, examining the context in which the anorexic syndrome is produced may be illuminating. Anorexia will erupt, typically, in the course of what begins as a fairly moderate diet regime, undertaken because someone, often the father, has made a casual critical remark. Anorexia *begins*, emerges out of what is, in our time, conventional feminine practice. In the course of that practice, for any variety of individual reasons that I cannot go into here, the practice is pushed a little farther than the parameters of moderate dieting. The young woman discovers what it feels like to crave and want and need and yet, through the exercise of her own will, to triumph over that need. In the process, a new realm of meanings is discovered, a range of values and possibilities that western culture has traditionally coded as "male" and rarely made available to women: an ethic and aesthetic of self-mastery and self-transcendence, expertise, and power over others through the example of superior will and control. The experience is intoxicating, habit-forming. Aimée Liu writes: "The sense of accomplishment exhilarates me, spurs me to continue on and on. . . . I shall become an expert [at losing weight]. . . . The constant downward trend [of the scale] somehow comforts me, gives me visible proof that I can exert control" (1979:36).

At school, she discovers that her steadily shrinking body is admired, not so much as an aesthetic or sexual object but for the strength of will and self-control it projects. At home, she discovers, in the inevitable battles her parents fight to get her to eat, that her actions have enormous power over the lives of those around her. As her body begins to lose its traditional feminine curves, its breasts and hips and rounded stomach, and begins to feel and look more like a spare, lanky male body, she begins to feel untouchable, out of reach of hurt, "invulnerable, clean and hard as the bones etched into my silhouette," as one woman described it. She despises, in particular, all those parts of her body that continue to mark her as female. "If only I could eliminate [my breasts]," says Liu, "cut them off if need be" (1979:99). For her, as for many anorexics, the breasts represent a bovine, unconscious, vulnerable, side of the self (Bordo 1985). Liu's body symbolism is thoroughly continuous with dominant cultural associations. Brett Silverstein's studies on the "Possible Causes of the Thin Standard of Bodily Attractiveness for Women," testify empirically to what is obvious from every comedy routine involving a dramatically shapely woman: namely, our cultural association of curvaceousness and incompetence. The anorexic is also quite aware, of course, of the social and sexual vulnerability involved in having a female body; many, in fact, were sexually abused as children.

Through her anorexia, on the other hand, she has unexpectedly discovered an entry into the privileged male world, a way to become what is valued in our culture, a way to become safe, above it all; for her, they are the same thing. She has discovered this, paradoxically, by pursuing conventional feminine behavior—in this case, the discipline of perfecting the body as an object —to excess, to extreme. At this point of excess, the conventionally feminine "deconstructs," we might say, into its opposite and opens onto those values our culture has coded as male. No wonder the anorexia is experienced as liberating and that she will fight family, friends, and therapists in an effort to hold onto it—fight them to the death, if need be. The anorexic's experience of power is, of course, deeply and dangerously illusory. To reshape one's body into a male body is *not* to put on male power and privilege. To *feel* autonomous and free while harnessing body and soul to an obsessive body-practice is to serve, not transform, a social order that limits female possibilities. And, of course, for the female to become male is only to locate oneself on a different side of a disfiguring opposition. The new "power look" in female body-building, which encourages women to develop the same hulk-like, triangular shape that has been the norm for male body-builders, is no less determined by a hierarchical, dualistic construction of gender than was the conventionally "feminine" norm that tyrannized female body-builders such as Bev Francis for years.

Although the specific cultural practices and meanings are different, similar mechanisms, I suspect, are at work in hysteria and agoraphobia. In these cases too, the language of femininity, when pushed to excess—when shouted and asserted, when disruptive and demanding—deconstructs into its opposite and makes available to the woman an illusory experience of power previously forbidden to her by virtue of her gender. In the case of nineteenth-century femininity, the forbidden experience may have been the breaking out of constraint, of bursting fetters—particularly moral and emotional fetters. John Conolly, the asylum reformer, recommended institutionalization for women who "want that restraint over the passions without which the female character is lost" (Showalter 1985:48). Hysterics often infuriated male doctors for lacking just this quality. S. Weir Mitchell described them as "the despair of physicians" whose "despotic selfishness wrecks the constitution of nurses and devoted relatives, and in unconscious or half-conscious self-indulgence destroys the comfort of everyone around them" (Smith-Rosenberg 1985:207). It must have given the Victorian patient some illicit pleasure to be viewed as capable of such disruption of the staid nineteenth-century household. A similar form of power, I believe, is part of the experience of agoraphobia.

This does not mean that the primary reality of these disorders is not one of pain and entrapment. In anorexia, too, there is clearly a dimension of physical addiction to the biochemical effects of starvation. But whatever the physiology involved, the ways in which the subject understands and thematizes her experience cannot be reduced to mechanical process. The anorexic's ability to live with minimal food intake allows her to feel powerful and worthy of admiration in a "world," as Susie Ohrbach describes it, "from which at the most profound level [she] feels excluded" and unvalued (1985:103). The literature on both anorexia and hysteria is strewn with battles of will between the sufferer and those trying to "cure" her; the latter, as Ohrbach points out, very rarely understand that the psychic values she is fighting for are often more important to the woman than life itself.

Textuality, praxis, and the body

The "solutions" offered by anorexia, hysteria, and agoraphobia, I have suggested, develop out of the practice of femininity itself, the pursuit of which is still presented as the chief route to acceptance and success for women in our culture. Too aggressively pursued, that practice leads to its own undoing, in one sense. For if femininity, as Susan Brownmiller has said, is at its very core a "tradition of imposed limitations" (1984:14), then an unwillingness to limit oneself, even in the pursuit of femininity, breaks the rules. But, of course, in another sense everything remains fully in place. The sufferer becomes wedded to an obsessive practice, unable to make any effective change in her life. She remains, as Toril Moi has put it, "gagged and chained to [the] feminine role" (Bernheimer and Kahane 1985:192), a reproducer of the docile body of femininity.

This tension between the psychological meaning of a disorder, which may enact fantasies of rebellion and embody a language of protest, and the practical life of the disordered body, which may utterly defeat rebellion and subvert protest, may be obscured by too exclusive a focus on the symbolic dimension and insufficient attention to praxis. As we have seen in the case of some Lacanian feminist readings of hysteria, the result of this can be a one-sided interpretation, romanticizing the hysteric's symbolic subversion of the phallocentric order while confined to her bed. This is not to say that confinement in bed has a transparent, univocal meaning—in powerlessness, debilitation, dependency, and so forth. The "practical" body is no brutely biological or material entity. It, too, is a culturally mediated form; its activities are subject to interpretation and description. The shift to the practical dimension is not a turn to biology or nature, but to another "register," as Foucault puts it (1979:136) of the cultural body: the register of the "useful body" rather than the "intelligible body." The distinction can prove useful, I believe, to feminist discourse.

The intelligible body includes our scientific, philosophic, and aesthetic representations of the body—our cultural *conceptions* of the body, norms of beauty, models of health, and so forth. But the same representations may also be seen as forming a set of *practical* rules and regulations through which the living body is "trained, shaped, obeys, responds," becoming, in short, a socially adapted and "useful body" (Foucault 1979:136). Consider this particularly clear and appropriate example: The nineteenth-century "hourglass" figure, emphasizing breasts and hips against a wasp-waist, was an "intelligible" symbolic form, representing a domestic, sexualized ideal of femininity. The sharp cultural contrast between the female and male form, made possible by the use of corsets, bustles, and so forth, reflected, in symbolic terms, the dualistic division of social and economic life into clearly defined male and female spheres. At the same time, to achieve the specified look, a particular feminine *praxis* was required—straitlacing, minimal eating, reduced mobility—rendering the female body unfit to perform activities outside of its designated sphere. This, in Foucauldian terms, would be the "useful body" corresponding to the aesthetic norm.

The intelligible body and the useful body are two arenas of the same discourse; they often mirror and support each other, as in the above illustration. Another example can be seen in the seventeenth-century philosophic conception of the body as a machine, mirroring an increasingly more automated productive machinery of labor. But the two bodies may also contradict and mock each other. A range of contemporary representations and images, for example, have coded the transcendence of female appetite and its public display in the slenderness ideal in terms of power, will, mastery, the possibilities of success in the professional arena, and so forth. These associations are carried visually by the slender superwomen of prime-time television and popular movies and promoted explicitly in advertisements and articles appearing routinely in women's fashion magazines, diet books, and weight-training publications. The equation of slenderness and power emerges most dramatically when contemporary anorexics speak about themselves. "[My disorder] was about power," says Kim Morgan in an interview for the documentary *The Waist Land*, "that was the big thing . . . something I could throw in people's faces, and they would look at me and I'd only weigh this much, but I was strong and in control, and hey, *you're* sloppy."[13]

Yet of course the anorexic is anything *but* "strong" and "in control," and not only full-blown anorexics live such contradictions. Recent statistics—for example, the widely publicized University of California study of fourth-grade girls in San Francisco—suggest that, at least in some American cultures, more and younger girls (perhaps as many as 80 percent of the nine-year-olds surveyed) are making dedicated dieting the central organizing principle of their lives. These fourth-graders live in constant fear, reinforced by the reactions of the boys in their classes, of gaining a pound and thus ceasing to be "sexy," "attractive," or, most tellingly, "regular." They jog daily, count their calories obsessively, and risk serious vitamin deficiencies (not to mention fully developed eating disorders and delayed sexual and reproductive maturation).[14] We may be producing a generation of young women with severely diminished menstrual, nutritional, and intellectual functioning.

Exposure and cultural analysis of such contradictory and mystifying relations between image and practice is only possible if one's analysis includes attention to and interpretation of the "useful" or, as I prefer to call it, practical body. Such attention, although often in inchoate and theoretically unsophisticated form, was central to the beginnings of the contemporary feminist movement. In the late 1960s and early 1970s the objectification of the female body was a serious political issue. All the cultural paraphernalia of femininity, learning to please visually and sexually through the practices of the body—media imagery, beauty pageants, high heels, girdles, make-up, simulated orgasm—were seen as crucial in maintaining gender domination.

Disquietingly, for the feminisms of the present decade, such focus on the politics of feminine praxis, although still maintained in the work of individual feminists,[15] is no longer a centerpiece of feminist cultural critique. On the popular front, we find *Ms.* magazine presenting issues on fitness and "style," the rhetoric reconstructed for the 1980s to pitch "self-expression" and "power." Although feminist theory surely has the tools, it has not provided a critical discourse to dismantle and demystify this rhetoric. The work of French feminists has provided a powerful framework for understanding the inscription of phallocentric, dualistic culture on gendered bodies. But so far, French feminism has offered very little in the way of concrete, material analyses of the female body as a locus of practical cultural control. Among feminist theorists in this country, the study of cultural "representations" of the female body has flourished, and it has often been brilliantly illuminating and instrumental to a feminist rereading of culture.[16] But the study of cultural representations alone, divorced from consideration of their relation to the practical lives of bodies, can obscure and mislead.

Here, Helena Michie's significantly titled *The Flesh Made Word* offers a striking example. Examining nineteenth-century representations of women, appetite, and eating, Michie draws fascinating and astute metaphorical connections between female eating and female sexuality. Female hunger, she argues, and I agree, "figures unspeakable desires for sexuality and power" (1987:13). The Victorian novel's "representational taboo" against depicting women eating (an activity, apparently, that only "happens offstage," as Michie puts it) thus functions as a "code" for the suppression of female sexuality, as does the general cultural requirement, exhibited in etiquette and sex manuals of the day, that the well-bred woman eat little and delicately.

250

The same coding is drawn on, Michie argues, in contemporary feminist "inversions" of Victorian values, inversions that celebrate female sexuality and power through images exulting in female eating and female hunger, depicting it explicitly, lushly, and joyfully.

Despite the fact that Michie's analysis centers on issues concerning women's hunger, food, and eating practices, she makes no mention of the grave eating disorders that surfaced in the late nineteenth century and that are ravaging the lives of young women today. The "practical" arena of women dieting, fasting, straitlacing, and so forth is, to a certain extent, implicit in her examination of Victorian gender ideology. But when Michie turns, at the end of her study, to consider recent feminist literature celebrating female eating and female hunger, the absence of even a passing glance at how women are *actually* managing their hungers today casts her analysis adrift from any concrete social moorings.

Michie's sole focus is on feminist literature's inevitable failure to escape "phallic representational codes" (1987:149). But the feminist celebration of the female body did not merely "deconstruct" on the written page or canvas. Largely located in the feminist counterculture of the 1970s, it has been culturally displaced by a very different contemporary reality; its celebration of female flesh now presents itself in jarring dissonance with the fact that women, feminists included, are starving themselves to death in our culture. The rising incidence of eating disorders, increasing dissatisfaction and anxiety among girls and women concerning how they look, and the compulsive regimens of bodily "improvement" in which so many of us engage suggest that a *political* battle is being waged over the energies and resources of the female body, a battle in which at least *some* feminist agendas for women's empowerment are being defeated.

I do not deny the benefits of diet, exercise, and other forms of body "management." Rather, I view our bodies as a site of struggle, where we must *work* to keep our daily practices in the service of resistance to gender domination, not in the service of "docility" and gender normalization. This requires, I believe, a determinedly skeptical attitude toward the seeming routes of liberation and pleasure offered by our culture. It also demands an awareness of the often contradictory relations between image and practice, between rhetoric and reality. Popular representations, as we have seen, may speak forcefully through the rhetoric and symbolism of empowerment, personal freedom, "having it all." Yet female bodies, pursuing these ideals, may find themselves as distracted, depressed, and physically ill as female bodies in the nineteenth century, pursuing a feminine ideal of dependency, domesticity, and delicacy. The recognition and analysis of such contradictions, and of all the other collusions, subversions, and enticements through which culture enjoins the aid of our bodies in the reproduction of gender, requires that we restore a focus on female praxis to its formerly central place in feminist politics.

Notes

The analysis presented in this essay is part of a larger study, presently in progress (*Food Fashion and Power: The Body and the Reproduction of Gender*; forthcoming, University of California Press). Other pieces of this larger analysis appear in several other papers: "Anorexia Nervosa: Psychopathology as the Crystallization of Culture" (Bordo 1985; reprinted in Diamond and Quinby 1988), "Reading the Slender Body" (in Jacobus, Keller, and Shuttleworth 1989), and "The Contest for the Meanings of Anorexia" (in *The Body in Medical Thought and Practice*, ed. Drew Leder and Mary Rawlinson; Reidel, 1990). See also "How Television Teaches Women To Hate Their Hungers," *Mirror Images* 1986.

I wish to thank Douglass College for the time and resources made available to me as the result of my Visiting Scholarship for the Laurie Chair in Women's Studies, spring 1985. My time there, and my participation in the Women's Studies Seminar, greatly facilitated much of the initial research for this piece. Earlier versions of this paper were delivered at the philosophy department of State University of New York at Stony Brook, the University of Massachussetts conference on "Histories of Sexuality," and at the 21st Annual Conference of the Society for Phenomenology and Existential Philosophy at University of Toronto. To all those who commented on those versions I express my appreciation for stimulating suggestions and helpful criticisms.

1 On "docility," see Foucault 1979, 135–169. For a Foucauldian analysis of feminine practice, see Bartky 1988; see also Brownmiller 1984.
2 Over the last decade, there has been an undeniable increase in male concern over appearance. Study after study confirms, however, that there is still a large "gender gap" in this area. Research conducted at the University of Pennsylvania in 1985 found men to be generally satisfied with their appearance, often, in fact, "distorting their perceptions [of themselves] in a positive, self-aggrandizing way." See "Dislike of Own Bodies Found Common Among Women," *New York Times*, March 19, 1985. Women, however, were found to exhibit extreme negative assessments and distortions of body perception. Other studies have suggested that women are judged more harshly than men when they deviate from dominant social standards of attractiveness. *Psychology Today* (April 1986) reports that while the situation for men has changed recently, the situation for women has more than proportionately worsened, too. Citing results from 30,000 responses to a 1985 survey of perceptions of body image and comparing similar responses to a 1972 questionnaire, the magazine reports that the 1985 respondents were considerably more dissatisfied with their bodies than the 1972 respondents, and it notes a marked intensification of concern among men. Among the 1985 group, the group most dissatisfied of all with their appearance, however, were teen-age women. Women today are by far the largest consumers of diet products, attenders of spas and diet centers, and subjects of intestinal by-pass and other fat reduction operations.
3 On our cultural obsession with slenderness, see Chernin 1981; Ohrbach 1985; Bordo 1985, 1989. For recent research on incidence and increase in anorexia nervosa and bulimia, see Greenfield et al. 1987; Rosenzweig and Spruill 1987.
4 On the "gendered" and historical nature of these disorders: The number of female to male hysterics has been estimated as anywhere from two to one to four to one, while as many as 80 percent of all agoraphobics are female (Brodsky and Hare-Mustin 1980:116, 122). Although more cases of male eating disorders are being reported recently, it is estimated that close to 90 percent of all anorexics are

female (Garfinkel and Garner 1982:112–113). For a sociohistorical account of female psychopathology, with particular attention to nineteenth-century disorders but having, unfortunately, little mention of agoraphobia or eating disorders, see Showalter 1985. For a discussion of social and gender issues in agoraphobia, see Seidenberg and DeCrow 1983. On the clinical history of anorexia nervosa, see Garfinkel and Garner; for cultural, historical, and gender perspectives, see Bordo 1985, 1986; Ohrbach 1985, 1989.

5 There is evidence that in the case of eating disorders this is rapidly changing. Anorexia and bulimia, originally almost exclusively limited to upper- and upper middle-class white families, are now touching ethnic populations (e.g., blacks, East Indians) previously unaffected and all socioeconomic levels (Garfinkel and Garner 1982:102–103). Although there are cultural reasons for such changes, equally interesting and crucial to study are the cultural factors which have "protected" certain ethnic groups from the disorders (see, for example, Hsu's study of eating disorders among blacks).

6 In constructing such a paradigm, I do not pretend to do justice to any of these disorders in its individual complexity as "pathology" or as cultural formation. My aim is to chart some points of intersection, to describe some similar patterns, as they emerge through a particular reading of the phenomena—a "political" reading, if you will.

7 For studies suggestive of a striking increase in the frequency of eating disorders over the last twenty years, see Garfinkel and Garner 1982:100; Greenfeld et al. 1987; and Rosenzweig and Spruill 1987. On the "epidemic" of hysteria and neurasthenia, see Showalter 1985; Smith-Rosenberg 1985.

8 See Nadelson and Notman 1982:5; Vicinus 1972:82. For more general discussions, see Gay 1984, Showalter 1985. The delicate lady, an ideal that had very strong class connotations (as does slenderness today), is not the only conception of femininity to be found in Victorian cultures. But it was arguably the single most powerful ideological representation of femininity in that era, affecting women of all classes, including those without the material means to fully realize the ideal. See Michie 1987 for dicussions of the control of female appetite and Victorian constructions of femininity.

9 See Fodor 1974:119; see also Brehony 1983.

10 For other interpretive perspectives on the slenderness ideal, see Bordo 1985, 1989; Chernin 1981; Ohrbach 1985.

11 Striking, in connection with this, is Catherine Steiner-Adair's 1984 study of high-school women, which reveals a dramatic association between problems with food and body-image and emulation of the cool, professionally "together" *and* gorgeous Superwoman. On the basis of a series of interviews, the high schoolers were classified into two groups—one that expressed scepticism over the Superwoman ideal, the other that thoroughly aspired to it. Later administration of diagnostic tests revealed that 94 percent of the Superwomen group fell into the eating disordered range of the scale. Of the other group, 100 percent fell into the noneating disordered range. Media images notwithstanding, young women today appear to sense, either consciously or through their bodies, the impossibility of simultaneously meeting the demands of two spheres whose values have been historically defined in utter opposition to each other.

12 When one looks into the many autobiographies and case studies of hysterics, anorexics, and agoraphobics, one is struck by the fact that these are, indeed, the sorts of women one might expect to be frustrated by the constraints of a specified female role. Freud and Breuer, in *Studies on Hysteria* (and Freud, in the later *Dora*) constantly remark on the ambitiousness, independence, intellectual ability, and creative strivings of their patients. We know, moreover, that many women who

later became the leading social activisits and feminists of the nineteenth century were among those who fell ill with hysteria or neurasthenia. It has become a virtual cliché that the typical anorexic is a perfectionist, driven to excel in all areas of her life. Though less prominently, a similar theme runs throughout the literature on agoraphobia.

One must keep in mind that in drawing on case studies, one is relying on the perceptions of other, acculturated individuals. One suspects, for example, that the popular portrait of the anorexic as a relentless "overachiever" may be colored by the lingering or perhaps resurgent Victorianism of our culture's attitudes toward ambitious women. One does not escape this hermeneutic problem by turning to autobiography. But in autobiography one is at least dealing with social constructions and attitudes that animate the subject's own psychic reality. In this regard the autobiographical literature on anorexia in particular is strikingly full of anxiety about the domestic world and other themes which suggest deep rebellion against traditional notions of femininity; see Bordo 1985.

13 "The Waist Land: Eating Disorders In America," 1985, Gannett Corporation, MTI Teleprograms.

14 "Fat or Not, 4th-Grade Girls Diet Lest They Be Teased or Unloved," *Wall Street Journal*, February 11, 1986.

15 A focus on the politics of sexualization and objectification remains central to the antipornography movement (e.g., in the work of Andrea Dworkin, Catherine MacKinnon). Feminists exploring the politics of appearance include Sandra Bartky, Susan Brownmiller, Wendy Chapkis, Kim Chernin, and Susie Ohrbach. Recently, too, a developing feminist interest in the work of Michel Foucault has begun to produce a poststructuralist feminism oriented toward practice; see, for example, Diamond and Quinby 1988.

16 See, for example, Jardine 1985; Suleiman 1986; Michie 1987.

References

Bartky, Sandra. 1988. "Foucault, Femininity, and the Modernization of Patriarchal Power." In *Feminism and Foucault: Reflections on Resistance*, ed. Irene Diamond and Lee Quinby. Boston: Northeastern University Press.

Bernheimer, Charles, and Claire Kahane, eds. 1985. *In Dora's Case: Freud—Hysteria—Feminism*. New York: Columbia University Press.

Bordo, Susan. 1985. Anorexia Nervosa: Psychopathology as the Crystallization of Culture." *The Philosophical Forum* 17, no. 2 (Winter):73–103. Reprinted in Diamond and Quinby 1988.

——— .1986. "How Television Teaches Women To Hate Their Hungers." *Mirror Images* [newsletter of Anorexia/Bulimia Support, Syracuse, N.Y.] 4:1, 8–9.

——— . 1989. "Reading the Slender Body." In *Women, Science, and the Body Politic: Discourses and Representations*, ed. Mary Jacobus, Evelyn Fox Keller, and Sally Shuttleworth. New York: Methuen.

Bourdieu, Pierre. 1977. *Outline of a Theory of Practice*. Cambridge: Cambridge University Press.

Brehony, Kathleen. 1983. "Women and Agoraphobia." In *The Stereotyping of Women*, ed. Violet Frank and Esther Rothblum. New York: Springer Press.

Brodsky, Annette, and Rachel Hare-Mustin. 1980. *Women and Psychotherapy*. New York: Guilford Press.

Brownmiller Susan. 1984. *Femininity*. New York: Fawcett Columbine.

Chernin, Kim. 1981. *The Obsession: Reflections on the Tyranny of Slenderness*. New York: Harper & Row.

——. 1985 *The Hungry Self: Women, Eating, and Identity*. New York: Harper & Row.

Clement, Catherine, and Hélène Cixous. 1986. *The Newly Born Woman*. Trans. Betsy Wing. Minneapolis: University of Minnesota Press.

Diamond, Irene, and Lee Quinby, eds. 1988. *Feminism and Foucault: Reflections on Resistance*. Boston: Northeastern University Press.

Fodor, I. G. 1974. "The Phobic Syndrome in Women." In *Women in Therapy*, ed. V. Franks and V. Burtle. New York: Bruner/Mazel.

Foucault, Michel. 1978. *The History of Sexuality*, Vol. I. New York: Pantheon.

——. 1979. *Discipline and Punish*. New York: Vintage.

Friedan, Betty. 1962. *The Feminine Mystique*. New York: Dell.

Garfinkel, Paul, and David Garner. 1982. *Anorexia Nervosa: A Multidimensional Perspective*. New York: Bruner/Mazel.

Gay, Peter. 1984. *The Bourgeois Experience*, Vol. I. New York: Oxford University Press.

Greenfeld, D., et al. 1987. "Eating Behavior in an Adolescent Population." *International Journal of Eating Disorders* 6:1 (January 1987):99–112.

Hunter, Diane. 1985. "Hysteria, Psychoanalysis and Feminism." In *The (M)Other Tongue*, ed. Shirley Garner. Claire Kahane, and Madelon Sprenger. Ithaca, N.Y.: Cornell University Press.

Jardine, Alice. 1985. *Gynesis*. Ithaca, N.Y.: Cornell University Press.

Liu, Aimée. 1979. *Solitaire*. New York: Harper & Row.

Michie, Helena. 1987. *The Flesh Made Word*. New York: Oxford.

Nadelson, Carol, and Malkah Notman. 1982. *The Female Patient*. New York: Plenum.

Ohrbach, Susie. 1985. *Hunger Strike: The Anorectic's Struggle as a Metaphor for Our Age*. New York: Norton.

Poster, Mark. 1984. *Foucault, Marxism and History*. Cambridge: Polity Press.

Rosenzweig, M., and J. Spruill. 1987. "Twenty Years After Twiggy: A Retrospective Investigation of Bulimic-Like Behaviors." *International Journal of Eating Disorders* 6, no. 1 (January):59–66.

Seidenberg, Robert, and Karen DeCrow. 1983. *Women Who Marry Houses*. New York: McGraw-Hill.

Showalter, Elaine, 1985. *The Female Malady*. New York: Pantheon.

Smith-Rosenberg, Carroll. 1985. *Disorderly Conduct*. Oxford: Oxford University Press.

Steiner-Adair, C. 1987. "The Body Politic: Normal Female Adolescent Development and Eating Disorders." Ph.D. diss., Harvard University Graduate School of Education.

Suleiman, Susan, ed. 1986. *The Female Body in Western Culture*. Cambridge, Mass.: Harvard University Press.

Vicinus, Martha. 1972. *Suffer and Be Still*. Bloomington: Indiana University Press.

17

FOUCAULT'S DISAPPEARING BODY

Greg Ostrander

Source: A. Kroker and M. Kroker (eds), *Body Invaders, Sexuality and the Postmodern Condition*, London: Macmillan Educational, 1988, pp.169–182.

In the folds of the reduction to language, Foucault's thought discovers the body although this discovery is not stamped with the problematic of origin:

> The body is the inscribed surface of events (traced by language and dissolved by ideas), the locus of a dissociated Self (adopting the illusion of substantial unity), and a volume in disintegration. Genealogy, as an analysis of descent, is thus situated within the articulation of the body and history. Its task is to expose a body totally imprinted by history and the process of history's destruction of the body.[1]

History has thus destroyed the body. Certainly one day which, with Foucault, has perhaps arrived, in asking about our bodies and how they have been formed, we will discover how very little we know of them. Secular philosophies of the soul, related in this to a "positivism" of the body, have conspired to limit knowledge of the history of the body. If the body was not considered to be the despised prison of the soul, it was considered to be a sort of residual datum in which immediacy was deposited. There can be, within this positivism, a powerful de-mystifying tendency. Feuerbach's critique of Hegel's sense consciousness as originating inevitably in the body or the reduction, by the young Marx of Hegel's theory of sovereignty, to the body of the sovereign are two examples of this. But the history of the body — how it became what it became, not biologically, but politically; how it moves in this way rather than another way; why it enjoys in this way rather than another — this history has only begun to be written and it bears the name of Foucault.

Foucault teaches us that the soul is the prison of the body, an historical reality and the effect of relations of power. The soul is not merely a religious illusion but rather it is a "reality-reference" on which diverse concepts and fields of research have been engraved — the so-called human sciences:

> This is the historical reality of this soul, which, unlike the soul represented by Christian theology, is not born in sin and subject to punishment, but is born rather out of methods of punishment, supervision and constraint. This real, non-corporeal soul is not a substance; it is the element in which are articulated the effects of a certain type of power and the reference of a certain type of know-ledge, the machinery by which the power relations give rise to a possible corpus of knowledge and knowledge extends and reinforces the effects of this power. On this reality-reference, various concepts have been constructed and domains of analysis carved out: psyche, subjectivity, personality, consciousness, etc; on it have been built sci-entific techniques and discourses, and the moral claims of human-ism. But let there be no misunderstanding: it is not that a real man, the object of knowledge, philosophical reflection or technical inter-vention, has been substituted for the soul, the illusion of the theo-logians. The man described for us, whom we are invited to free, is already in himself the effect of a subjection much more profound than himself. A "soul" inhabits him and brings him to existence, which is itself a factor in the mastery that power exercises over the body. The soul is the effect and the instrument of a political anatomy; the soul is the prison of the body.[2]

Foucault discovers in his investigation of disciplinary power, the arcane history of the body, the reasons for why such a history has not previously been possible. The third part of *Discipline and Punish* on "Discipline"[3] from the Man-the-machine of La Mettrie to the Panopticon of Bentham is a powerful essay on the politics of details and bodies. It demonstrates the possible meaning of a microphysics of power and what it might mean to manufacture an individual.[4] Foucault examines here the evolution from the invention of the spy-glass to the development of new techniques of surveil-lance based on the model of the military camp.[5] And, as suggested by the telescope, the trick is to see without being seen:

> The exercise of discipline presupposes a mechanism that coerces by means of observation; an apparatus in which the techniques that make it possible to see induce effects of power, and in which, con-versely, the means of coercion make those on whom they are applied clearly visible. Slowly, in the course of the classical age, we see the construction of those 'observatories' of human multiplicity about which the history of the sciences has so little good to say. Side by side with the major technology of the telescope, the lens and the light

beam, which were an integral part of the new physics and cosmology, there were the minor techniques of multiple and intersecting observations, of eyes that see without being seen; using techniques of subjection and methods of exploitation of an obscure art of light and the visible was secretly preparing a new knowledge of man.[6]

It was probably inevitable that Foucault, after investigating first madness, then that master of life and death, the medical gaze, and finally the prison, would find himself confronted with that astute production of bodies and of codified reciprocity that is discipline. The mad individual, the ill, the prisoner but also the soldier, the student and the worker, are all entangled in a network of diffuse and anonymous micropowers. We must ask ourselves whether, with the discovery of the significance of discipline, we have not found the historical ground of the dialectic of recognition — a ground that is located outside the existentialist mythologies and consisting of the technology of bodies, not the labor of the spirit. We must also ask whether or not Marxism intentionally neglected the importance of these corporeal powers and if this has compromised any liberation struggles. But Marx, as Foucault notes, insisted in several places on the analogy that exists between the problems of the division of labour and those of military tactics.[7] This is the disciplinary red thread that connects the oppression in the factory with that within the army. According to Foucault, Marx was also aware of the importance of surveillance as a power mechanism.[8] With these traditional references and his strong praise for the "great work",[9] *Punishment and Social Structures*, by Frankfurt Marxists Rusche and Kirchheimer, Foucault attempts to defuse anticipated Marxist criticism of his perspective. He fails to note that Marx only examined these techniques (surveillance, discipline, etc.) as they were applied to capital. The problem of the inter-relation of the abstract domination of capital, which is based on the creation of the commodity, labor power, and the fine texture of individuated micropowers remains open. Without referring to these micropowers, it seems we certainly cannot account for the imprisonment of the mad whose chains appear not in the night of the medieval ages but rather at the dawn of an age that supposedly saw the breaking of man's chains. Neither can we account for the passage from the glorious tortures of an earlier age to the planned surveillance of today's prisons. These and other relations of power are not reducible to the capital-labor relationship.

In the process of unearthing these micropowers, Foucault has consciously condemned the traditional theory of power which saw the latter focussed exclusively on the concept of the state. Foucault's new concept means that power can no longer be seen as a property but rather must be now viewed as a stragey. Its model is that of

> a perpetual battle rather than a contract regulating a transaction or the conquest of a territory. In short, this power is exercised rather

than possessed; it is not the "privilege," acquired or preserved, of the dominant class, but the overall effect of its strategic positions – an effect that is manifested and sometimes extended by the position of those who are dominated. Furthermore, this power is not exercised simply as an obligation or a prohibition on those who "do not have it"; it invests them, is transmitted by them and through them; it exerts pressure upon them, just as they themselves, in their struggle against it, resist the grip it has on them.[10]

Foucault's microphysics considers the state to be a point in the strategy of power, certainly an important point, but not the most important. It is not the organ of power *par excellence* precisely because such an organ does not exist. Beneath and surrounding the state operate a thousand techniques for ranking bodies. This type of approach is especially valuable today as a counter to the new forms of statolatry characteristic of much modern political theory. (Witness, for example, neo-Marxism's absorption in new theories of the state.) Politics, the regulating Technique, the supreme Jacobin 'ratio', has its domain continually eroded by the micropowers. Its autonomy is seen to be quite 'relative' with Foucault's theory. Even if the substantiality of the state is radically put into question, it is very difficult to finally eliminate that current of political thought that has always worshipped its power. The state is revived in some radical theories (especially, Leninist theory) as the model of a pure will to power to which even the party itself must adapt. Foucault has furnished tools that allow us to criticize this false autonomy of the state and explore the zone in which the political interweaves with the social to achieve domination. Foucault's approach is a micropolitical one that bases itself upon all of the recent work in the field of anti-psychiatry. However, unlike certain currents of the latter, he avoids any temptation of embarking on a cure of the soul.

The political investment of the body, which characterizes disciplinary society, involves a total inversion of the processes of individuation:

> In certain societies, of which the feudal regime is only one example, it may be said that individualization is greatest where sovereignty is exercised and in the higher echelons of power. The more one possesses power or privilege, the more one is marked as an individual, by rituals, written accounts or visual reproductions. The 'name' and the genealogy that situate one within a kinship group, the performance of deeds that demonstrate superior strength and which are immortalized in literary accounts, the ceremonies, that mark, the power relations in their very ordering, the monuments or donations that bring survival after death, the ostentation and excess of expenditure, the multiple, intersecting links of allegiance and suzerainty, all these are procedures of an 'ascending' individualization. In a

disciplinary regime, on the other hand, individualization is "descending": as power becomes more anonymous and more functional, those on whom it is exercised tend to be more strongly individualized.[11]

This means that, for Foucault, the individual is not simply an ideological production — that atom which is at the base of political theory of the seventeenth and eighteenth centuries. The individual is also a reality fabricated by disciplinary power. This new power uses the ritual of the examination as the means to achieve "the pinning down of each individual in his own particularity."[12] In this new system, "the individual receives as his status his own individuality . . . and is linked by his status to the features, the measurements, the gaps, the 'marks' that characterize him and make him a 'case.'"[13]

The new theory of the individual is an important result of Foucault's investigations. It leads to a different status being conferred on the individual and it throws new light on the anthropological disciplines that make of the individual their proper object of research. Foucault also contributes to the liberation of research from the somewhat ingenuous separation of ideology and science — as if ideology was the chaff and science the wheat — that characterizes the human sciences. Foucault shows that not only the theoretical choices but also the very object of study of these sciences are products of power. In a Nietzschean fashion, power produces truth — power is always power/knowledge and no knowledge can flourish outside of power.

For Adorno, on the contrary, utopia would be precisely an anti-power truth which for this reason abides in a state of ineffectuality.[14] Utopia cannot survive within the relation of power/knowledge. Utopia, for Adorno, remains committed to the idea of objective truth — it flees the vice of instrumental reason and forms the point of escape from power relations. Foucault, however, believes that this escape or utopia does not exist or only existed as the goal of the socialisms of the nineteenth century. The counter-attack against existing institutions must, today, base itself on experience. Perhaps, Foucault argues, a new society is delineated in the experiences of drugs, sexuality and community life. He himself stresses the experiential bases of his own theoretical innovations: his early experiences as a mental health worker in France, his experience of the "non-repressive" welfare-state of Sweden and of the overtly repressive society of Poland. Especially important, he argues was his encounter with the students of Tunisia during the mid-sixties who attempted to formulate a radically new political ethic *despite* their nominal adhesian to Marxism. Thus, much more than May '68 in France, March '68 in Tunisia, marked a decisive turning-point, in his intellectual/practical career. One also, of course, thinks of his work in the prisoners' rights movement in France (his founding of the G.I.P. and its theoretical effects: *Discipline and Punish*).

The source of new experiences, Foucault believes, will never be those who benefit from a given system of governmentality. Rather, new heterogeneous practices are always thrown up from below, from the plebs. In this, he agrees with Bataille against the more romantic notions deriving from Nietzsche, notions Bataille believed infected the surrealist movement of his own time. This romanticism resulted in an idealist longing for a "reconstruction of the foundation of humanity before human nature was enslaved by the necessity for technical work . . . or tied to ends dictated by exclusively material conditions."[15] The surrealists sought an idealistic overcoming of society in the sacred realm of "surreal" art or in a very restricted concept of surreal *activity*. They did not realize that heterogeneity, art or the sacred simply *are* a part of society. Bataille owed his understanding of this to his reading of Durkheim on the elementary forms of religious life. Even the surrealists' self-proclaimed materialism failed to come to grips with the actual links between art and life and, thus, earned Bataille's contempt: "If one determined under the name of *materialism* an offensive emanation of human life poisoned by its own moral system, a recourse, to all that is shocking, impossible to destroy and even abject — all that debases and ridicules the human spirit — it would be possible to determine at the same time *surrealism* as an infantile disease of this base materialism."[16] For Foucault, the linkage between these experiences of resistance and politics must always remain rather mysterious since the truth, for him, is always completely absorbed in power/knowledge and, thus, the movement against present-day power is prevented from generating clear social and political perspectives.

Just as he refutes the notion of utopia, Foucault suspects that of ideology because this always involves the reference to something which poses as the truth as opposed to error. Archaeology, on the other hand, realizes that it is the discursive practices which constitute the channels within which we necessarily speak and think. Genealogy merely claims to bring to light the knowledges deposited in these practices. There are only limited references in Foucault to something that might subterranneously determine the outcome — discourse itself is the first and last level on which the genealogist installs himself. Or as Foucault stated in his inaugural address to the Collège de France in 1970:

> It is as though discourse, far from being a transparent, neutral element, allowing us to disarm sexuality and to pacify politics, were one of those privileged areas in which they exercised some of their more awesome powers. In appearance, discourse may well be of little account, but the prohibitions surrounding it soon reveal its links with desire and power. This should not be very surprising, for psychoanalysis has already shown us that discourse is not merely the medium which manifests — or dissembles — desire; it is also the object of desire. Similarly, historians have constantly impressed upon us that discourse is no mere verbalisation of conflicts and systems of domination, but that it is the very object of man's conflicts.[17]

Foucault knows how to carry out a profound analysis of unconscious ideologies (that is, ideologies that are not ordered around a subject but, rather, are prior to any subject), seizing their quality of being merely circulating discourses.[18] However, in eliminating the concept of ideology, Foucault loses the nexus appearance/reality — a loss which has the ideology of the primacy of discourse as its correlate. Discourses only retain the reality side of this nexus. They are dense realities, charged with power/knowledge — positivities or monuments which can be exhumed from time which has concealed them. How, then, can they be criticized? To this question, Foucault gives no response. The critique of ideology, as developed, for instance, by the Frankfurt School, has always attempted to demonstrate the non-correspondence of reality with its concept and, consequently, revealing the character of socially necessary appearance that the latter assumes is false consciousness. This means that ideology has real social force. This is often forgotten in certain vulgar tendencies within Marxist theory. Foucault has broken with this (not innocent) neglect and has turned his attention on those discourses which, although presenting themselves as sciences, nevertheless engage themselves within a network of powers. This is the case, for example, of discipline; a subtle discourse involving the technology of bodies and the formation of subjects (that is, of the subjugated). Discipline is an unconscious ideology, which despite its lack of recognition remains, nonetheless, terribly efficacious.

An analysis, however, which insistently remains at the level of the positivity of a discourse, risks only attaining its object in part. Discipline is a necessary connection that produces subjects and of which subjects act as supports — it operates a continuous totalization. An ideological analysis would not only reveal the whole that disciplinary power constitutes, it would also indicate the space from which the possibility of breaking through this whole may emerge. The analyses of Foucault, by remaining at the level of the exhumed positivities, are prevented from seeing the internal possibilities of change. This is without a doubt imputable to the panic that Foucault (similar to Deleuze) feels for any theory of liberation — a theory that, for him, must always involve a new counter-productive totalization. Thus, Foucault's microphysics has a kind of fore-shortened perspective and is proud of it. The abandonment of the concept of ideology is, consequently, a sign of his disgust with utopia — the point of escape for radical theories.

The philosophy of desire remains more committed to the survival of the subject despite its efforts to disperse it. Whether desire is pre-formed à la Lacan or not, the subject remains tossed in the current of desire. This philosophy tells us nothing about the subject in its impact with the body. Thus, in both of its extreme forms (Lacan's pre-formed desire or originary desire), desire is hypostatized in the effort to demolish the hypostatization of the subject. A desire liberated from the subject is a "quid pro quo" that can flourish perhaps in a mythological vision of madness. Desire springs up together with the subject of which it constitutes the other face. A dispersion occurs only insofar as a totalization was first posited. Desire is grafted in the political investment of the body. And the body, which is not merely a linguistic element, is irreducible. Its sufferings and enjoyments are not simply a matter of signs but rather of nerves and muscles. Since Foucault draws all of the implicit consequences from the archaeological finding of the body, from the discovery that the body itself is pre-formed, the result is a profound change in the orientation of his thought. The first aspect to be eliminated is the reduction to language. To be precise, Foucault refuses to align himself with the philosophy of desire (despite his admiration for Deleuze) and his barely commenced research on sexuality proves this. His study is focussed on bodies and their pleasures rather than on desire. He seeks to study the "apparatus of sexuality" as a field of micropowers rather than sex as a desirable object:

> It is the agency of sex that we must break away from if we aim — through a tactical reversal of the various mechanisms of sexuality — to counter the grips of power with the claims of bodies, pleasures and knowledges, in their multiplicity and their possibility of resistance. The rallying point for the counterattack against the deployment of sexuality ought not to be sex-desire, but bodies and pleasures.[19]

However, in his 1963 "A Preface to Transgression," we see the reduction to language at work:

> Sexuality is only decisive for our culture as spoken, and to the degree it is spoken: not that it is our language which has been eroticized now for nearly two centuries. Rather, since Sade and the death of God, the universe has absorbed our sexuality, denatured it, placed it in a void where it establishes its sovereignty and where it incessantly sets up as the Law the limits it transgresses. In this sense, the appearance of sexuality as a fundamental problem marks the transformation of a philosophy of man as worker to a philosophy based on a being who speaks.[20]

Six years later, when his historical research dragged behind it only the wreckage of a problematic compromised by ontology, Foucault described the work of the sexual archaeologist in the following terms:

> . . . instead of studying the sexual behaviour of men at a given period (by seeking its law in a social structure, in a collective unconscious, or in a certain moral attitude), instead of describing

what men thought of sexuality (what religious interpretation they gave it, to what extent they approved or disapproved of it, what conflicts of opinion or morality it gave rise to), one would ask oneself whether, in this behaviour, as in these representations, a whole discursive practice is not at work; whether sexuality quite apart from any orientation towards a scientific discourse, is not a group of objects that can be talked about (or that it is forbidden to talk about), a field of possible enunciation (whether in lyrical or legal language), a group of concepts (which can no doubt be presented in the elementary form of notions or themes), a set of choices (which may appear in the coherence of behaviour or in systems of prescription). Such an archaeology would show, if it succeeded in its task, how the prohibitions, exclusions, limitations, values, freedoms and transgressions of sexuality, all its manifestations, verbal or otherwise, are linked to a particular discursive practice. It would reveal, not of course as the ultimate truth of sexuality, but as one of the dimensions in accordance with which one can describe it, a certain "way of speaking"; and one would show how this way of speaking is invested not in scientific discourses, but in a system of prohibitions and values.[21]

As we can observe from the above passage, Foucault in 1969 believes that discourse is one among several possible ways of approaching sexuality. By 1976, however, and the first volume of *The History of Sexuality*, this becomes *the* approach *par excellence* to the study of sexuality. In this study, sexuality appears exclusively insofar as it is put into discourse or spoken by an insatiable will to know. From medieval Christianity, with its technique of meticulous confession, through *Les Bijoux Indiscrets*, to modern psycho-analysis (in which sexuality itself speaks), sexuality constitutes the field of an immense discourse and the object of a continual enjoyment via the discourse which is its basis. The transgression of the system of prohibitions defined by the discourse on sexuality is possible within this same discourse. The prohibition is posited in language as is the transgression — the prohibition incites the transgression and, consequently, the resultant pleasure. Thus, to demonstrate the way in which bodies revolt and engage in a strategic struggle against the moves of the dominant power, Foucault takes the example of auto-eroticism.

The restrictions on masturbation hardly start in Europe until the eighteenth century. Suddenly, a panic theme appears: an appalling sickness develops in the Western world. Children masturbate. Via the medium of families, though not at their initiative, a system of control of sexuality, an objectivisation of sexuality, through thus becoming an object of analysis and concern, surveillance and control, engenders at the same time an intensification of each individual's desire, for, in and over his body. The body thus became the issue of a conflict between parents and children, the child and the instances of control. The revolt of the sexual body is the reverse effect of this encroachment.[22]

Foucault's discourse maintains within itself an interesting duplicity — if sexuality is a discourse, it is a discourse traversed by conflicts. This undoubtedly represents something which was not present in his writings on literature. The will to know, which provides the impulse for discourse, is completely involved in a Nietzschean fashion with power. A power/enjoyment corresponds to the power/knowledge. Power and pleasure do not contradict one another but rather support one another. Where there is desire there is already present a relation of power. Even perversions are continually solicited by discourse which itself induces these transgressions. Unlike Marcuse's concept of the polymorphously perverse, sexuality is not a free zone but, instead, constitutes part of the power/pleasure complex. This is important because it indicates the elimination of the traditional concept of repression in Foucault's perspective. Sexuality consists of a network of micropowers, analogous to the disciplinary powers that, far from repressing the individual, permits and encourages his pleasures. The concept of repression, for Foucault, cannot avoid (as in Reich or Marcuse) making reference to a certain uncontaminated "humanity" to which each individual will some fine day have to return. Foucault, who in *Madness and Civilisation* was very much influenced by this concept, breaks with it in *Discipline and Punish*.

In his research on the history of sexuality, the break with the notion of repression is very marked, especially in his new concept of "power over life."[23] This is a power that channels but also provokes life — a power which compels us to live. This new "bio-power"[24] replaces the earlier right of life and death of the sovereign over the subject (the right to kill or to *allow* to live) and signifies the beginning of a positive political investment of life and the body. Sexuality, as an apparatus, can, thus, only be grasped against the background of this power. Power presents sex as desirable and even more than desirable. Power links sex very intimately with death which remained the 'outside' in Foucault's earlier work. The death instinct that traverses sex is an historically determined fact — it is entangled in the contemporary apparatus of sexuality. Foucault describes this employment of 'sex' as strategic ideal used in the domination of bodies in a concluding passage of *The History of Sexuality*:

> It is through sex — in fact, an imaginary point determined by the deployment of sexuality — that each individual has to pass in order to have access to his own intelligibility (seeing that it is both the hidden aspect and the generative principle of meaning), to the whole of his

body (since it is a real and threatened part of it, while symbolically constituting the whole), to his identity (since it joins the force of a drive to the singularity of a history). Through a reversal that doubtless had its surreptitious beginnings long ago — it was already making itself felt at the time of the Christian pastoral of the flesh — we have arrived at the point where we expect our intelligibility to come from what was for many centuries thought of as madness; the plenitude of our body from what was long considered its stigma and likened to a wound; our identity from what was perceived as an obscure and nameless urge. Hence the importance we ascribe to it, the reverential fear with which we surround it, the care we take to know it. Hence, the fact that over the centuries it has become more important than our soul, more important almost than our life; and so it is that all the world's enigmas appear frivolous to us compared to this secret, miniscule in each of us, but of a density that makes it more serious than any other. The Faustian pact, whose temptation has been instilled in us by the deployment of sexuality, is now as follows: to exchange life in its entirety for sex itself, for the truth and the sovereignty of Sex. Sex is worth dying for. It is in this (strictly historical) sense that sex is indeed imbued with the death instinct. When a long while ago the West discovered love, it bestowed on it a value high enough to make death acceptable; nowadays it is sex that claims this equivalence, the highest of all. And while the deployment of sexuality permits the techniques of power to invest life, the fictitious point of sex, itself marked by that deployment, exerts enough charm on everyone for them to accept hearing the grumble of death within it.[25]

Thus, the circle within Foucault's work is closed. That which was initially the ontological experience of death and origin (and of their collapsing one into the other in an eternal recurrence), is now the experience of a power that seizes us. The Other of desire is now the Same of discourse.

To locate the unthought in a pure outside means to abandon it, finally, to the web of micropowers. For a long time, these micropowers have occupied what seemed to be an outside and have, thus, made nonsense of ontology. Origin, death, desire, transgression — all are not at all outside but rather inside these networks. The theory that wishes to forget this runs headlong into them. This is no cause for despair, however. It simply means that contradiction must be conceived immanently although this, of course, is no panacea. That bodies appear in Foucault only as subjugated is due to the fact that they really are such, rather than due to the reduction to discourse carried out by him. This reduction *illustrates* a reality but, because it prohibits the radical questioning of this reality, it remains to a considerable extent politically impotent. Discourse, thus, becomes the monologue of power or rather, the chorus of the micropowers. The radical challenging of reality would involve the question, in what way is it possible to think, always negatively, the breaking of this network of power that holds bodies? Perhaps it will be necessary to start with the negative experience of the difference that opens in every enjoyment between the enjoyment itself and the totality that surrounds it. Perhaps, we could locate at this point, the possibility of an 'unhappy consciousness' of the body. We do not yet know. All we know — and the later work of Foucault has taught us this — is that the 'liberation' has already taken place. We must now liberate ourselves from liberation.

Notes

1   Michel Foucault, "Nietzsche, Genealogy, History," in *Language, Counter-Memory, Practice: Selected Essays and Interviews*, ed. Donald Bouchard (Ithaca: Cornell University Press, 1977), p. 148.
2   Idem, *Discipline and Punish: The Birth of the Prison*, (New York: Pantheon, 1977), pp. 29–30 (hereafter cited as Foucault, *Discipline*).
3   Ibid., pp. 135–228.
4   One thinks of the case of President Schreber who was the subject of a famous study by Freud which revealed the pathogenic effects of the disciplinary machines invented by Schreber's father.
5   Foucault quotes from "Rules for the Prussian Infantry" (1973) to show how the new power of the gaze reshaped these initial observatories:

> In the parade ground, five lines are drawn up, the first is sixteen feet from the second; the others are eight feet from one another; and the last is eight feet from the arms depots. The arms depots are ten feet from the tents of the junior officers, immediately opposite the first tent-pole. A company street is fifty-one feet wide ... All tents are two feet from one another. The tents of the subalterns are eight feet from the last soldiers' tent and the gate is opposite the captains' tent ... The captains' tents are erected opposite the streets of their companies. The entrance is opposite the companies themselves.

> Foucault then goes on the explain the functioning of this new alert, discrete source of power: The camp is the diagram of a power that acts by means of a general visibility. For a long time, this model of the camp or at least its underlying principle was found in urban development, in the construction of working-class housing estates, hospitals, asylums, prisons, schools: the spatial "nesting" of hierarchized surveillance. The principle was one of "embedding" ("encastrement"). The camp was to the rather shameful art of surveillance what the camera obscura was to the great science of optics." (translation corrected; Foucault, *Discipline*, pp. 172–173.

6   Foucault, *Discipline*, p. 171.
7   In Foucault, *Discipline*, pp. 163–164, Foucault quotes several passages including the following passage from *Capital*, Vol. I:

> Just as the offensive power of a squadron of cavalry, or the defensive power of a regiment of infantry, is essentially different from the sum of the offensive or defensive powers of the individual cavalry or infantry soldiers taken separately, so the sum total of the mechanical forces

exerted by isolated workmen differs from the social force that is developed, when many hands take part simultaneously in one and the same undivided operation.

8 See Foucault, *Discipline*, p. 175 for this passage from *Capital*, Vol. I: "The work of directing, superintending and adjusting becomes one of the functions of capital, from the moment the labor under the control of capital, becomes cooperative. Once a function of capital, it requires special characteristics."

9 Foucault, *Discipline*, p. 24 and p. 54.

10 Ibid., pp. 26–27.

11 Ibid., pp. 192–193.

12 Ibid., p. 192.

13 Ibid.

14 Theodor Adorno, *Negative Dialectics*, trans. E.B. Ashton (New York: Seabury Press, 1973).

15 Georges Bataille, *Complete Works*, Volume VII: *L'Economie à la mesure de l'universe. La Part maudite, la Limite de l'utile (fragments, Théorie de la religion, Conférences, 1947–1948)*, ed. Thadée Klossowski (Paris: Gallimard, 1976), p. 386.

16 Idem, *Complete Works*, Volume II: *Ecrits posthumes, 1922–1940*, ed. Denis Hollier (Paris: Gallimard, 1970), p. 93.

17 Michel Foucault, "Orders of Discourse," *Social Science Information*, 10:2 (April 1971): 2–3 (translation corrected).

18 There is no doubt that Marxism has for too long neglected the critical exploration of unconscious ideologies. It has too long lingered on the analysis of intellectuals as producers of ideology and consensus and, consequently, on the analysis of those ideologies which have attained a certain level of conceptual systematization. These ideologies can be conceived of as being the product of subjects and of being, at least apparently, a matter of free choice. The inverse is the case of unconscious ideologies which circulate without even allowing the questions of 'believing' in them or consensus around them to be posed.

19 Michel Foucault, *The History of Sexuality*, Volume I: *An Introduction*, trans. David Hurley (New York: Pantheon, 1976), p. 157 (hereafter cited as Foucault, *Sexuality*).

20 Idem, "A Preface to Transgression," in *Language, Counter-Memory, Practice: Selected Essays And Interviews*, ed. Donald Bouchard (Ithaca: Cornell University Press, 1977), p. 50.

21 Idem, *The Archaeology of Knowledge*, trans. A.M. Sheridan Smith (New York: Random House, 1970), p. 193.

22 Idem, *Power/Knowledge: Selected Interviews and Other Writings, 1972–1977*, ed. with a preface by Colin Gordon, trans. Colin Gordon, Leo Marshall, John Mepham, and Kate Soper (Brighton, Sussex: The Harvester Press, 1980), pp. 56–57.

23 See Foucault, *Sexuality*, pp. 133–159.

24 Ibid., p. 143.

25 Ibid., pp. 155–156.

18

THE MEANING OF BODY IN CLASSICAL CHINESE PHILOSOPHY

Roger T. Ames

Source: *International Philosophical Quarterly* 24(1) (1984): 157–177.

I

A first step in comparative philosophy must be to identify and excavate those shared yet usually unconscious presuppositions or premises that are implicit in the philosophical reflections of all members of a particular cultural tradition. F. M. Cornford, the British classicist, took this as the one sustained principle of all his work:

> In every age the common interpretation of the world of things is controlled by some scheme of unchallenged and unsuspected presupposition; and the mind of any individual, however little he may think himself to be in sympathy with his contemporaries, is not an insulated compartment, but more like a pool in one continuous medium—the circumambient atmosphere of his place and time. This element of thought is always, of course, most difficult to detect and analyse, just because it is a constant factor which underlies all the differential characters of many minds.[1]

A. N. Whitehead, seeing himself more as moving among philosophical epochs than distinct cultures, reinforced Cornford's very important concern:

> When you are criticizing the philosophy of an epoch, do not chiefly direct your attention to those intellectual positions which its exponents feel it necessary to defend. There will be some fundamental assumptions which adherents of all the variant systems within the epoch unconsciously presuppose.[2]

269

Another observation, frequently made by social scientists, is that a cultural tradition is an organismic growth in which the personality of the tradition is established in its infancy. To a greater or lesser extent, the distinctive traits of any cultural tradition, like those of the human analog, are an elaboration and extension of characteristics imprinted very early in the career of the organism.

The specific project of this chapter is a preliminary investigation of the classical Chinese conception of body in an effort to identify and articulate its peculiar features. Before this can be undertaken, it is necessary to engage in a kind of conceptual "strip mining" to lay bare, assay, and register those relevant assumptions subscribed to by most if not all early thinkers in this particular culture and epoch, which constitute their shared ground and which ramify through their philosophical observations. With these presuppositions in hand, I can then attempt a conceptual reconstruction of "body" through a mutually corroborative philological and philosophical analysis. This will require first an examination of the language in which this notion of "body" is couched, and then a verification of the direction established by this analysis by pursuing its philosophical implications in the broad tradition. I say "direction" here rather than "conclusions" in recognition of the speculative and hence tentative nature of this kind of hermeneutical analysis. It provides us with an explicatory apparatus and with definite clues, perhaps, but not with conclusive proof.

In this paper, I want to attempt to reinstate the notion of body in our understanding of the early Chinese philosophical literature as a corrective against what I perceive to be an inappropriate "psychologization" of the materials. I want to claim that mind and body are polar rather than dualistic concepts, and as such, can only be understood by reference to each other. On this basis, I shall argue that in classical Chinese philosophy, "person" is properly regarded as a "psychosomatic process."

II

It is a widely proclaimed feature of classical Chinese philosophy that, in contrast to the early Greeks, it all but lacks a developed cosmogony.[3] There have been many reasons suggested in explanation of this phenomenon, from sexual inhibitions in the culture to disparate notions of creativity.[4] I would like to borrow and elaborate the distinction between *dualism* and *polarism* that David L. Hall develops in explanation of the non-cosmogonic nature of early Chinese thought. This distinction, I believe, can be an important instrument in disclosing underlying premises as a starting point for our discussion of body.[5]

A *dualism* exists in *ex nihilo* doctrines because a fundamentally indeterminate, unconditioned power is posited as determining the essential meaning and order of the world. It is a "dualism" because of the radical separation between the trancendent and nondependent creative source, and the determinate and dependent object of its creation. The creative source does not require reference to its creature for explanation. This dualism, in many various forms, has been a prevailing force in the development of Western-style cosmogonies, and has been a veritable Pandora's box in the elaborated pattern of dualisms that have framed Western metaphysical speculations: supernatural/natural, reality/appearance, being/becoming, knowledge/opinion, self/other, subject/object, substance/attribute, mind/matter, form/matter, agent/act, animate/inanimate, birth/death, *creatio ex nihilo/destructio in nihilum* and so forth.

Polarism, on the other hand, has been a major principle of explanation in the initial formulation and evolution of classical Chinese metaphysics. By "polarism," I am referring to a symbiosis: the unity of two organismic processes which require each other as a necessary condition for being what they are. In this paradigm, each existent is auto-generative and self-determinate. Each participant in existence is "so-of-itself," and does not derive its meaning and order from some transcendent source. Do we not have some inconsistency, however, in asserting that each particular is self-creative yet can only be accounted for by its symbiotic relationship with every other particular? As Hall observes:

> The great difficulty for the radical view of creativity is to account for the apparent interconnectedness of things given the fact that each process is self-creative. It is the polar character of each process that establishes the ground for such an explanation.[6]

In other words, the notion of "self" in the locution "so-of-itself" has a polar relationship with "other." In the process ontology underlying this system, each particular is a consequence of every other, such that there is no contradiction in saying that each particular is both self-determinate and determined by every other particular. That is, the "other" particulars which make up existence are, in fact, constitutive of "self." The principle distinguishing feature of polarism is that each "pole" can only be explained by reference to the other. "Left" requires "right," "up" requires "down," *yin* requires *yang*, and "self" requires "other."

The separateness implicit in dualistic explanations of relationships conduces to an essentialistic interpretation of the world, a world of "things" characterized by discreteness, finality, closedness, determinateness, independence, a world in which one thing is related to the "other" extrinsically. By contrast, a polar explanation of relationships gives rise to an organismic interpretation of the world, a world of "processes" characterized by interconnectedness, interdependence, openness, mutuality, indeterminateness, complementarity, correlativity, coextensiveness, a world in which continuous processes are related to each other intrinsically.

Not only are the dualistic categories mentioned above inappropriate to the orientation of polar metaphysics, they are a source of serious distortion. Polarism has its own correlative sets of terminologies which are applied in explanation of the dynamic cycles and processes of existence: differentiating/condensing, scattering/amalgamating, dispersing/coagulating, waxing/waning. Further, since all existents fall on a shared continuum differing in degree rather than in kind, the distinctions which obtain among them are only qualitative: clear (*ch'ing*[a])/turbid (*cho*[b]); correct (*cheng*[c])/one-sided (*p'ien*[d]); thick (*hou*[e])/thin (*po*[f]); hard (*kang*[g])/soft (*jou*[h]); genial (*wen*[i])/overbearing (*pao*[j]). And, since these existents constitute one order of being, the changes which they undergo cannot be fairly described as "substantial."

Returning to the contrasting notions of genesis and transformation operative in the early Chinese and Western traditions, the polar character of early Chinese thought discouraged the interpretation of creativity in terms of *creatio ex nihilo* and *destructio in nihilum*. The historian Michael Loewe goes so far as to assert that for the classical Chinese context, "in neither mythology nor philosophy can there be found the idea of *creatio ex nihilo*."[7] The *Chuang Tzu*, as an example of this tradition, challenges the principle of an absolute beginning:

> There is a beginning. There is not yet begun to be a beginning. There is not yet begun to not yet begin to be a beginning. There is something. There is nothing. There is not yet begun to be nothing. There is not yet begun to not yet begin to be nothing. Suddenly there is something and nothing. And yet I don't know what follows from there "being" nothing. Is it something or is it nothing?[8]

The organismic process of existence, generating its own motion by the interaction of psycho-physical forces, is fundamentally cyclical. There is no final beginning or end in this process; rather, there is the identifiable rhythm, order, and cadence of cycle. Relative to this observation, it is perhaps significant that the notion of "birth" and the process of "growth" (or "life") are not clearly differentiated in Chinese, both denoted by the character *sheng*.[k] Given that reality in the early Chinese tradition is conceived of in terms of cyclical process, the absence of cosmogony is compensated for by an elaborate cosmological tradition, to which the *I Ching*, and the Taoist, *Yin-yang* and *Wu-hsing* schools bear witness.

The implications of this dualism/polarism distinction are both many and important in the kinds of philosophical questions that were posed by the Chinese thinkers and the responses that they provoked. For example, Loewe suggests that in this culture, "no linear concept of time develops from the need to identify a single beginning from which all processes followed."[9] Again, the notion of a purposeful, anthropomorphic creator is found in the classical literature—the *tsao wu che*[l] of the Taoists, for example. However, the polar relationship between creator and creature rendered this idea still-born.[10] The classical Chinese alternative to the final, dualistic distinction between creator and creature is a polar continuum: human being in realizing himself *is* deity. In the *Mencius*, we read:

> The admirable person is called "good." The one who has integrity is called "true." To be totally genuine is called "beautiful," and to radiate this total genuineness is called "greatness." Being great, to be trans-formed by it is called "sageliness." And being sagely, to be unfathomable is called "divinity."[11]

Tu Wei-ming develops this theme in his interpretative study of the Confucian *Chung-yung*, frequently translated as *The Doctrine of the Mean*, but perhaps better rendered *Hitting the Mark in the Everyday*:

> The relationship between Heaven and man is not an antinomic bi-unity but an indivisibly single oneness. In this sense, the sage as the most authentic manifestation of humanity does not coexist with Heaven; he forms a coincidence with Heaven. Accordingly, *ch'eng*[m] as the ultimate reality is conceived not as a unity of opposites but as a continuous, lasting and homogeneous whole. Despite the possibility of a conceptual separation between Heaven and man, inwardly, in this deepest reality, they form an unbreakable organismic continuum.[12]

As a corrective against reading passages from these classical texts such as "what Heaven (*t'ien*[n]) mandates is called human nature"[13] and "Heaven gives birth to the integrating potency (*te*[o]) in me"[14] as a doctrine of transcendent deity, we do well to pay careful attention to discussions in the same texts which clearly collapse the human/Heaven distinction. The *Chuang Tzu*, for example, repeatedly describes the realizing human being as "the comple-ment/counterpart (*p'ei*[p]) of Heaven,"[15] and goes even further in describing him as "being one with all things."[16] This is not simply Taoist mysticism. The *Mencius* asserts that "the myriad things are fully here in me"[17] and "one who knows his nature knows Heaven."[18] The *Chung-yung* moves from "the sage is the complement of Heaven"[19] to the more explicit:

> So earnest, he is humanity (*jen*[q]),
> So profound, he is an abyss (*yuan*[r]),
> So pervasive, he is Heaven (*t'ien*[n]).[20]

Tu Wei-ming is cautious about the implications of these *Chung-yung* pas-sages: "Of course, 'counterpart' here does not mean to suggest that Confu-cius is, in a sense, being deified."[21] The fact is, however, that Confucius *does* "deify" himself in the sense that he achieves a quality of integration in the world that dissolves any obstructive distinction between part and whole. Of course, this notion of deification has a profoundly different import from what "becoming one with Other" would entail in a dualistic Western paradigm. In the classical Chinese context, it is not "either/or"; as Tu himself has rightly observed, humanity and divinity are continuous.

Yet another implication of this dualism/polarism distinction is that it highlights the absence of a substance ontology in the early Chinese tradition. A. C. Graham alludes to this important contrast is his analysis of Mohist thought:

> The Western philosophical tradition has conceived qualities as inhering in something underlying them called "substance." But the Mohist seems to conceive the object as the composite "filling" of a space, and to think of its mutually pervasive components (shape and consciousness, hardness and whiteness) only in relation to the space filled.[22]

If this tradition is in fact grounded in a polar metaphysics, a reasonable expectation would be that this metaphysics is manifested in the main concerns of classical Chinese thought: social and political philosophy. Benjamin Schwartz among others has observed that this is indeed the case. Schwartz identifies several "polarities"—these poles being described as "inseparably complementary"—which are grounded in classical Confucianism and which pervade the tradition: "personal cultivation" (*hsiu shen*[s]) and "political administration" (*chih kuo*[t]), "inner" (*nei*[u]) and "outer" (*wai*[v]), and the familiar "knowledge" (*chih*[w]) and "action" (*hsing*[x]).[23]

III

One of the most significant implications of this dualism/polarism distinction lies in the perceived relationship between mind and body. If we can take Plato as a fair representative of the Western tradition, the dualistic relationship between *psyche* and *soma* is plagued with problems of interaction analogous to those inherent in his Form/particular distinction. In the polar metaphysics of the classical Chinese tradition, the correlative relationship between the psychical and the somatic militated against the emergence of a mind/body problem. It was not that the Chinese thinkers were able to "reconcile" this dichotomy; rather, it did not arise.

Since body and mind were not regarded as different "kinds" of existence in any essential way, they did not generate different sets of terminologies necessary to describe them. For this reason, the qualitative modifiers that we usually associate with matter do double duty in Chinese to characterize both the physical and the psychical. *Hou*, for example, can mean either physically thick or generous, *po* can mean either physically thin or frivolous. Roundness (*yuan*[y]) and squareness (*cheng*[c]) can characterize both physical and psychical

dispositions. In fact, the consummate person in this tradition is conventionally distinguished by his "size"; great (ta^z), abysmal ($yuan^r$), and so forth.
Similar yet perhaps less pervasive metaphors in Western languages might
hark back to a pre-dualistic interpretation of person. At the least, they
reflect an interesting inconsistency between theory and metaphor in our
tradition.

When we combine the process ontology of the early Chinese tradition with
its polar conception of the psychical and physical, it would follow that "person" was seen holistically as a psychosomatic process. If this is the case, it
would stand to reason that what we tend to interpret as Chinese "psychology" might in fact be better understood as a uniquely Chinese "psycho-
somatology." In other words, in reducing classical Chinese discussions of
person to assertions about the *psyche* at the expense of the physical, we
might inadvertently be misconstruing or even impoverishing this concept in a
serious way. We can take the prominent Confucian notion *jen* as a case in
point. It is translated variously as "benevolence," "love," "altruism," "kind-
ness," "charity," "compassion," "magnanimity," "perfect virtue," "goodness," "human-heartedness," and "humanity." As these renderings clearly
indicate, there has been a tendency for scholars to "psychologize" *jen* as a
"subjective" feeling made manifest in "objective" social norms or mores
which we submit to or accord with in ritual conduct (li^{aa}).[24] *Jen* is interpreted
as psychological dispositions of which ritual actions are overtly physical
demonstrations. Herbert Fingarette warns us against the dangers of this kind
of reductionistic interpretation:

> *Jen* seems to emphasize the individual, the subjective, the character,
> feelings and attitudes; it seems, in short, a psychological notion. The
> problem of interpreting *jen* thus becomes particularly acute if one
> thinks, as I do, that it is of the essence of the *Analects* that the thought
> expressed in it is not based on psychological notions. And, indeed, one
> of the chief results of the present analysis of *jen* will be to reveal how
> Confucius could handle in a nonpsychological way basic issues which
> we in the West naturally cast in psychological terms . . . The move from
> *jen* as referring us to a person on to *jen* as "therefore" referring us to his
> inner mental or psychic condition or process finds no parallel in the
> *Analects.*[25]

I suggest that both *jen* and ritual conduct (*li*) are psycho-physical disposi-
tionings. The *jen* disposition of mind is inseparable from its physical disclosure in comportment, poise, dignity, and can only be explained by such
reference. Ritual actions, on the other hand, as *formal* demonstrations of
psychosomatic *jen*, are the structured and refined expression of a state of
mind and its correlative physical dispositions. The distinction between *jen*
and ritual action is not that between a subjective, psychological disposition

of mind and an objective physical demonstration, but rather between a non-formalized psychosomatic dispositioning and a formalized and refined psychosomatic dispositioning. *Jen*, as a homophone of "person" (*jen*[ab]) denoting achieved personhood, is the whole human process: body and mind.

IV

A first step in recovering the notion of body in our understanding of classical Chinese philosophy is to analyze the language in which this idea was captured. It is interesting that the term "body" in English has a speculated etymological association with the Old High German, *botahha:* "tub," "vat," "cask"; hence, the expression, a "tubby" person. Consistent with this etymology, as Eliot Deutsch has pointed out, the dominant metaphors in the Western tradition have been "container" images: the prison-house, the temple, the machine.[26] By contrast, the notion of body in the Chinese tradition tends to be couched in "process" rather than substance language. The human body is frequently discussed as the shape or disposition of the human process. An analysis of the three most prominent terms for body— *shen*,[ac] *hsing*,[ad] and *t'i*[ae]—will bear this observation out. In the classical lexicons, we turn circles as these three terms are used in definition of each other.

V

Although *shen* is possibly a profile pictograph of the human physique[af] and can certainly be used to denote one's physical being, it seems to be used frequently to refer to one's entire psychosomatic person.[27] Since the physical body is an important focus of self, it is not unexpected that in those passages where *shen* does denote "body," it is one's "lived body" seen from within rather than "body as corpse" experienced from without. In fact, the phonological association between śien/śien/*shen* and ńien/ńzien/*jen* taken together with their respective semantic functions might suggest that *jen* is "person" with the connotation of "other," while *shen* is "person" with the connotation of "self." It is perhaps because *shen* is not clearly and specifically physical that graphically related characters were necessary to make such a distinction clear: *ch'u*[ag] and *kung*,[ah] for example, are more decidedly anatomical terms.

In the *Shih-ming*,[ai] a lexicon of the latter Han, *shen* is defined with its homophone, *shen*,[aj] meaning "to stretch out" or "to extend." Further, there is the cognate *shen*[ak] meaning "spirit." This is suggestive that person was seen as an "extending" or "presencing," having correlative physical and spiritual (or psychical) aspects denoted by *shen*[ac] and *shen*[ak] respectively.

VI

The second character frequently used to represent the early Chinese notion of body is *hsing*: the form or shape, the three-dimensional disposition or configuration of the human process. *Hsing* is defined in the *Kuang-ya*[al] glosses as *hsien*[am] meaning "to appear" or "to presence," and generally, has a morphological rather than a genetic or schematic nuance.

Given that all of existence is conceived of as a continuum of one order of being differing only as a matter of degree, macrocosm/microcosm analogies abound in the explanation of phenomena, especially of the human being. Two very common analogies are the correlations established between the Heaven-and-earth (*tien-ti*[an]) and the *yin-yang*[ao] vapors on the one hand, and the human intellect (*yi*[ap]) and physical form (*hsing*) on the other. The *Kuan Tzu*, for example, uses the Heaven-and-earth analog to describe the human form as the shape or disposition of the intellect:

> The life of the human being is such
> That Heaven (*t'ien*) unfolds his distilled essence (*ching*[aq])
> And earth (*ti*) unfolds his form (*hsing*).
> The combination of these constitutes the human being.
> Where there is concord, he lives;
> Where there is not, he does not.[28]

This is not to say that Heaven and earth are some transcendent Creator which "authors" humanity. Rather, the human being like all of existence is autogenerative, and arises within Heaven-and-earth. Wang Ch'ung, the Eastern Han sceptic, makes this observation in his definition of "self-so-ing" (*tzu-jan*[ar]):

> Now, Heaven covers above and the earth looks up from below. The *ch'i*[as] below steams upward; the *ch'i* above descends. The myriad things are self-engendered out of their midst . . . When the child is in the mother's womb, the father cannot have any knowledge of it. The child is formed of its own accord. How could Heaven and earth or the parents have any knowledge of it?[29]

He goes on to explain the form and intellect of the human being in terms of the symbiotic relationship between *yin* and *yang*:

> That out of which the human being is born and grows is the *yin* and the *yang ch'i*. The *yin ch'i* constitutes his vital spirit. In the life of the human being, where the *yin* and *yang ch'i* amalgamate, the bones and flesh are firm, and the vital spirit is replete; the vitality constitutes the intellect, the bones and flesh make him strong; the vital spirit is verbal, the physical

form is firm and robust. Where these congeal in mutual support, being always visible, they do not perish.[30]

In explanation of disembodied spirits, he goes on:

When the *yang ch'i* is replete but lacking in *yin*, it can produce a semblance but not the form itself. Being only the vital spirit without bones or flesh, it is vague and hazy, and once appearing, it soon disappears.

The physical form is frequently portrayed as a disclosure of some intellectual condition:[31]

> Where a person is able to be correct and tranquil,
> His skin will be ample,
> His senses will be keen,
> He will have protruding muscles
> And strong bones.
> He will be able to bear up the circular firmament
> And walk on the square earth.

As I have suggested above, in the Western tradition, the most familiar metaphors for body are "container" images. The early Chinese tradition, by contrast, is dominated by organic imagery. The intellect is the "wellspring" or the "fountainhead" which keeps the body nourished and firm. Intellect is the "essence" (*ching*) of body, not in the sense of some underlying permanent and unchanging substratum to be distinguished from its supporting attributes, but rather as the *concentrated* form of a single reality.[32] It is because "essence" or "intellect" is not a different order of being from body that it is the means whereby the human being can pervade the cosmos. The notion of imperceptible influence and efficacy—the intellect stretching across space and the understanding penetrating everywhere—is a familiar theme in the classical tradition, and is grounded in the correlative relationship between the psychical and the physical:

> . . . The internal repository (i.e. the distilled essence) is a
> fountainhead;
> Floodlike, placid, it is a source of *ch'i*.
> Where this source does not dry up.
> The body will be sturdy;
> Where the fountain is not exhausted,
> The nine orifices will have clear passage,
> And one will be able to exhaust the cosmos
> And cover the whole earth.

His integrating potency (*te*) is daily renewed. He knows the world every-where and penetrates exhaustively to the four extremities.[33]

There is no perceived problem of interaction in the non-corporeal, intan-gible, and imperceptible intellect reaching out to move the corporeal, tan-gible, and perceptible world.

As I have suggested above, the classical Chinese tradition is generally committed to a process rather than a substance ontology: the body is a "pro-cess" rather than a "thing," something "done" rather than something one "has." This being the case, there is a symbiotic relationship between intellect and physical form such that the disposition of the intellect is disclosed in the comportment of the person:

> If one harbors no misgivings within, he will encounter no catastrophes without. If the heart-and-mind is wholesome within, the form will be whole without. The person who encounters neither natural calamity nor human disaster is called the sage . . . Where a wholesome heart-and-mind lies within, it cannot go hidden. It is evident in one's form and bearing, and is apparent in his complexion . . . Where the *ch'i* of this kind of heart-and-mind is made manifest in the physical form, a person becomes more illustrious than the sun and moon.[34]

Not only is the disposition of the body determined by and revealing of the conditions of one's intellect, but further, there are situations in which the physical disposition of the body fades into the background and becomes, in a sense, imperceptible. What is "seen" is solely the disposition of the mind:

> There was a crippled, hunchbacked hairlip who counselled Duke Ling of Wei. Duke Ling was so pleased with him that when he looked at normal men their backs were too straight. There was a man with a jug-sized goitre who counselled Duke Huan of Ch'i. Duke Huan was so pleased with him that when he looked at normal men their necks were too thin. Thus it is that to the extent that one achieves integra-tion, the physical form is forgotten. When people forget what is usually remembered, and do not forget what is usually lost, this then is true forgetting.[35]

In these several passages, the notion of body is understood consistently as a disposition which can only be understood by reference to the intellect.

VII

The third character that I want to examine as designating body is *t'i*. The organic connotation of this character is immediately apparent in its longstanding abbreviated forms in which it is represented as "root."[at] The notion of organismic transmission is found in the *Li-chi* (*Record of Rituals*) in which one's person is described as "the inherited body of one's parents."[36] In the *Mo Tzu*, *t'i* is defined as "a share of the whole."[37]

The most revealing aspect of *t'i*, however, is its cognate relationship with ritual actions (*li*): formal behaviors which define interpersonal relationships in community, commonly rendered "rites," "propriety," "decorum," and so forth. As Peter Boodberg observes, these are the only two common Chinese characters which share the *li*[au] phonetic, "ritual vase." Further, he suggests that these two characters are related in their overlapping connotation of "organic form"; " 'Form,' that is, 'organic' rather than geometrical form, then, appears to be the link between the two words, as evidenced by the ancient Chinese scholiasts who repeatedly used *t'i* to define *li* in their glosses."[38] Both body (*t'i*) and ritual action (*li*) are also frequently defined by the character *ti*[av] meaning "order" in the sense of "sequence" or "arrangement."

It is a relatively easy matter to recover the shared ground between *li* and *t'i* from the perspective of *li*, ritual actions. To accomplish this, we need to explore the notion of ritual (*li*) and register those ways in which it evidences connotations of body (*t'i*). If we examine the notion of ritual in the classical literature in a way sensitive to the intimate relationship between this kind of action and the concept of "rightness/significantion" (*yi*),[aw39] we find that these rituals can be more elaborately described as an inherited tradition of formalized human actions that evidence both a cumulative investment of meaning by one's precursors in a cultural tradition, and an openness to reformulation and innovation within the framework of the tradition.

The notion of formal *li* action overlaps with *t'i*, body, in that a *li* action is an em*bodi*ment or *form*alization of meaning and value that accumulates to constitute a cultural tradition. This ritual action, like body, is of variable "shape," appropriating much of its definition from its context. It is morphological rather than schematic in that changing participants and environments result in an altered disposition of the ritual. Ritual action, invested with the accumulated meaning of the tradition, is a formalized structure on which the continuity of the tradition depends and through which a person in the tradition pursues cultural refinement. Like a *body* of literature or a *corpus* of music, these rituals continue through time as a repository of the moral, rational and aesthetic insights of those who have gone before. A person engaged in the performance of a particular formal action, appropriating meaning from it while seeking himself to be appropriate to it, derives meaning and value from this embodiment, and further strengthens it by his contribution of novel meaning and value. He pursues "rightness" and "significance" both in an imitative and a creative sense.

The concept of body (*t'i*) also figures into divination practices as the configuration of the divining apparatus which reveals to the forecaster the most auspicious and appropriate course of action. This association with divination further suggests an important religious significance conjoining physical and ritual form.

Finally, the body of ritual actions and institutions constitutes the root which supports and sponsors the innovation and creativity of a cultural tradition. Like the human body, it is a profoundly organic entity which must be nurtured and cultivated to preserve its integrity, and which must be constantly revitalized and adapted to prevailing circumstances in order to retain its influence. It is at once the fruit of the past and the ground out of which the future will grow.

Significant in the correlation between ritual action and body is the polar rather than dualistic relationship between form and matter, action and body. Any particular ritual action can be understood only by reference to a formalized body of actions, a cultural tradition; meaning and value can be enacted only by embodiment in ritual actions.

VIII

Above, I have tried to extend our understanding of the classical Chinese conception of ritual action by developing its correlative relationship with *t'i*, body. In so doing, it has been necessary to suspend the familiar dualistic categories such as mind/matter, form/matter, actor/action, and so forth. The perhaps more difficult project that remains is to approach this in reverse; to expand and enrich our understanding of the classical Chinese notion of body by amplifying its polar relationship with ritual. This task is complicated by the fact that with our categories of mind and body, we are inclined to regard the former as active and the latter as acted upon. In cashing out the full consequence of classical Chinese body, it will be necessary to highlight its dynamic aspects as compensatory to this passive interpretation.

First, tradition has it that the Sage-rulers of antiquity observed regularity and order implicit in the natural process and sought to devise formal rules of conduct, or *li*, that would enable human beings to make the same cosmological patterns explicit in their own lives. These formal behaviors, serving to structure human life within and integrate it without, are a microcosm of the *li*[ax] (veins, fibers) of the macrocosm. Similarly, throughout the early literature, the human form, with its wind, orifices, lumimaries, circulation, and so forth, is treated as a microcosm which functions in a way analogous to the whole. Further, both ritual action and body as imitations of cosmic functions share a sense of mysterious power, sanctity, and efficacy.

Secondly, *li*, from its earliest meaning of those sacrifices whereby the ruler established a relationship with deity, has always had a strong "relational" import. Ritual action establishes, conditions, and bonds relationships at every level of human experience, from one's own introspective dialog to the broadest social and political matrixes. Similarly, the physical form is profoundly relational as a means of engaging, appropriating form, and contributing to its environs.

Thirdly, ritual actions are not perceived as divinely established and maintained norms informing the cosmos which mankind must obey in service to some higher will. If they have normative force, it is because they have been generated out of the human situation, and hence render informed access to it. They are patterns of behavior initiated and transmitted by man to regulate life in community, and to refine and enhance it. Similarly, the human body is contingent rather than divinely established and maintained: it is neither man fashioned in God's image nor some immutable Aristotelian species. It is a changing configuration of processes that have been embodied as a creative response to circumstances. There is no ideal physical form; rather, the kinds of skills and faculties embodied are generated out of the situations with which they seek to integrate. The body is a variable statement of meaning and value achieved in effort to refine and enhance human life within the changing parameters of context.

Fourthly, the corpus of ritual actions, beginning as a set of practices initiated to give human beings access to other-worldly realms, became an apparatus for personal spiritual integration within the broad cultural continuity of this world. The religious element was sustained in this process of evolution in that ritual actions were consistently interpreted as a formal construct directed at relating part to whole. The quality of the religious component in the ritual-structured experience is a function of the extent to which one is able to overcome a preoccupation with ego-self (i.e., to $k'o\ chi^{ay}$) and to achieve the level of person-in-context. In that ego-self is delimiting, it is seen as an unfortunate inhibition to the fundamentally religious experience of integrating part with whole. Similarly, to the extent that the personal body can be construed as a dimension of ego-self, it too must be overcome. Yet when extended out into the world, body has an analogous religious function in relating part to whole. To appreciate this paradigm, it is crucial to resist equating ego-self with particularity. That is, the process of integration, far from being a surrender of part to whole, is the extension and celebration of the particular in its integral, organismic relationship to the whole. The *Chuang Tzu*, for example, describes the "breaking up of the bones and body" as a necessary condition for finding integration with the whole: "becoming one with all things."[40] Kuo Hsiang,[az] the fourth century A.D. commentator, explains this process by suggesting that: "When a man is unaware of his own person (*shen*) internally and knows nothing of a cosmos outside, he then constitutes one body (*t'i*) with the process of change and pervades everything and everywhere."[41] The *Lao Tzu* makes the same comment in a positive way:

> Why do we say that concern for one's person (*shen*) should be the same as concern over a great disaster?

The reason that we have great disasters is because we have our
persons . . .
Only when one can govern the empire with the same attitude as he
esteems his own person
Can he be trusted with the empire; . . .[42]

One must extend his physicality beyond the personal in order to achieve
integration. Throughout the classical tradition generally, integration represented by physical efficacy is a characteristic of the consummating person,
whether it is Confucius holding up the portcullis to allow his men to escape[43]
or Ting the butcher cutting up an ox.[44]

IX

Ritual actions (*li*) have several specific functions derived from their relationship with *yi*: aesthetic, rational and moral meaning/rightness. And these
functions have their physical counterpart.

Ritual actions have a heuristic or pedagogical function. A person in learning and reflecting upon ritual, the encapsulated insights embedded in and
inherited out of the cultural tradition, seeks in them the *yi*: their aesthetic,
rational, and moral meaning, their value. In so doing, this person stimulates,
develops, and refines his own *yi* intuition. While the *yi* of past generations is
impressed on the inherited cultural tradition and is a rich source for the
cultivating person, it is still incumbent upon this person to engage his own *yi*
judgment in evaluating and appropriating from his inheritance, and to contribute his own meaning and value to the development and refinement of this
tradition.

T'i, "body," like ritual action, has an intimate and important relationship
with *yi* in that it can be interpreted as a physical rendering of meaning and
value. By investigating and evaluating the physical dispositions inherited in the
tradition, a person stimulates and refines his own sense of what is physically
"right," and can appropriate it for himself. At the same time, his own selection
and embellishment of the physical constitutes a *reform*ation and refinement of
the tradition. Thus, body, as a repository of *yi*, has its heuristic function.

A second *yi*-related function of ritual action is that ritual provides a formal apparatus for realizing and displaying one's own aesthetic, moral, and
rational meaning. It is clear in the tradition that ritual actions lack significance when they consist merely of bald imitation. It is ritual vitalized so as to
disclose "meaning" that constitutes truly "meaning-full" action. Body is also
a formal apparatus for actualizing and displaying meaning and value. Physical dispositions communicate moral, rational, and aesthetic sensitivities and
commitments in their engagement with the world.

The third *yi*-related function of ritual action is that it is a currency through
which one's own creativity can be introduced. Formal actions are a means

for reifying one's own novel insights. The ritual structures inherited out of the tradition are only counsel, open to appropriation and creative elaboration. Similarly, the physical disposition as inherited is only a suggestion informed by the insights of those who have gone before. Importantly, it is malleable; wax into which one's novelty can be impressed.

X

Above, I have argued for a polar rather than a dualistic interpretation of the classical Chinese conception of the relationship between mind and body, actor and action. The implications of this interpretation of body, when disengaged from its cultural context and brought to bear on our own physical experience in the world, are significant. It justifies our feelings of varying degrees of intellectuality and physicality. It can accommodate the notion of "multiple bodies" in the Nietzschean sense; my "teacher body," my "father body," my "lover body," my "athletic body."[45] It offers a more suitable framework for understanding psychosomatic disease and physiologically inspired pathological conditions.[46]

Importantly, it can be employed in accounting for what I would call the "psychosomatic merge" phenomenon of the consummate ballet dancer or the karate master. In the dance or in the *kata*[ba] experience, there seems to be a point at which the physical and the conscious become inseparably integrated and in which the experience seems to leave behind the commonly identifiable and conflicting characteristics of either consciousness or physicality. It can be argued that it is the category of experience in which we come to feel most wholly human. If this holistic interpretation of person provides such a rich, multidimensional ground for explaining our cultural sensorium: our religious, moral, aesthetic, and rational experience, we might be well advised to remedy what Nietzsche identifies as one of the "tremendous blunders" of Western philosophical reflection: "They despised the body: they left it out of the account: more, they treated it as an enemy."[47]

Notes

1 See F. M. Cornford, *Thucydides Mythistoricus* (London: Routledge & K. Paul, 1907), ix. That this pursuit of presuppositions was Cornford's guiding principle is underscored in W. K. C. Guthrie's Introduction to Cornford's posthumous collection of essays, *The Unwritten Philosophy* (Cambridge: Cambridge University Press, 1967).

2 See A. N. Whitehead, *Science and the Modern World* (New York: New American Library, 1925), 71.

3 See, for example, M. Loewe, *Life and Death in Han China*, 63; K. Schipper. "The Taoist Body" in *History of Religions* 17:3; 4,371; D. L. Hall, *Eros and Irony* (Albany: State University of New York Press, 1982), 246–49; Tu Wei-ming, *Centrality and Commonality: An Essay on Chung-yung* (Honolulu, University Press of Hawaii, 1976), 118–19.

4 The former belongs to Schipper, *Taoist Body*: "And it is a fact that in China, as in our society, the female sexual and reproductive functions have been much more tabooed than the male ones. I cannot help wondering if this taboo could not also help to explain the almost total denial of this creation myth in Chinese classical literature." The latter is D. Hall's. See his paper, "Process and Anarchy: A Taoist Vision of Creativity" in *Philosophy East and West* 28(3):271–85, and his *Eros and Irony*, 118–19.

5 Hall, *Eros and Irony*, 118–19.

6 Ibid., 248.

7 Loewe, *Life and Death*, 63.

8 *Chuang Tzu*, Harvard-Yenching Index Series 5.2.49ff.

9 Loewe, *Life and Death*, 63.

10 See *Chuang Tzu*, 17.6.48ff; and *Lieh Tzu*, 3.

11 *Mencius*, Harvard-Yenching Index Series 57.7B.25.

12 Tu Wei-ming, *Centrality and Commonality*, 129.

13 *Chung-yung*, 1.

14 *Analects*, Harvard-Yenching Index Series 13.7.23.

15 *Chuang Tzu*, 29.12.21–25.

16 Ibid., 5.2.53; 12.5.7.

17 *Mencius*, 51.7A.4.

18 Ibid., 50.7A.1.

19 *Chung-yung*, 31.

20 Ibid., 32.

21 Tu Wei-ming, *Centrality and Commonality*, 135–36.

22 A. C. Graham, *Later Mohist Logic, Ethics and Science* (Hong Kong: Chinese University Press, 1978), 202.

23 Benjamin Schwartz, "Some Polarities in Confucian Thought," in *Confucianism in Action* (Stanford: Stanford University Press, 1959), 50–62. This characterization was later elaborated by Yu Ying-shih, and most recently by Hoyt Tillman, *Utilitarian Confucianism: Ch'en Liang's Challenge to Chu Hsi* (Cambridge: Harvard University Press, 1982).

24 See, for example, D. Bodde, *Essays on Chinese Civilization*, ed. C. Le Blanc and D. Borei (Princeton: Princeton University Press, 1981), 399–401, in which he discusses the virtues of translating *jen* as "love."

25 H. Fingarette, *Confucius–Secular as Sacred* (New York: Harper & Row, 1972), 37, 43.

26 See Eliot Deutsch, "The Concept of Body," Chapter 1, above.

27 In surveying popular translations of the *Tao Te Ching*, we find that D. C. Lau and W. T. Chan usually translate *shen* as "one's person" with the exception of chapter 13 where they render it "body." In Chang Chung-yuan's Heideggerian translation, he renders it consistently as "one's self," while in my own translation (Ch'en Ku-ying, *Lao Tzu: Text, Notes and Comments* [San Francisco: Chinese Materials Center, 1977]), I translate it throughout as "person."

28 *Kuan Tzu* (Ssu-pu pei-yao, ed.), 16.4a.

29 Lun-heng, 54.

30 Lun-heng, 65.

31 Kuan Tzu, 16.4a.

32 Peter Boodberg, in a review of D. Bodde's translation of Fung Yulan's *History of Chinese Philosophy* (see *Far Eastern Quarterly* 13 (1954):334–37), criticizes Bodde's translation of *t'i* as "substance." Bodde replies to Boodberg in his paper "On Translating Chinese Philosophic Terms," *ibid.*, describing *t'i* as "the inherent, enduring and fundamental (hence 'internal') qualities of a thing." This is, at least

as it applies to the classical Chinese tradition, unsupportable. Boodberg's criticism is a fair one. The number of prominent scholars that Bodde is able to muster to defend his translation only serves to demonstrate the seriousness of this misconception.

33 *Kuan Tzu*, 16.4a–b.

34 Ibid.

35 *Chuang Tzu*, 14.5.49ff.

36 *Li-chi*, Harvard-Yenching Index Series 24.35.

37 *Mo Tzu*, Harvard-Yenching Index Series 65.40.1. Graham, 26, translates this passage as "A *t'i* (unit/individual part) is a portion of a *chien*[bb] (total/collection/whole)."

38 P. Boodberg, "The Semasiology of Some Primary Confucian Concepts," in *Philosophy East and West* 2(4):326–27.

39 See David L. Hall and Roger T. Ames, *Thinking Through Confucius* (Albany, NY: SUNY Press, 1987), 71–110.

40 *Chuang Tzu*, 2.6.

41 See Kuo Ch'ing-fan,[bc] *Chuang Tzu chi-shih*, [bd] vol. 1 (Peking: Chung-hua shu-chii, 1961), 285.

42 *Lao Tzu*, 13.

43 For a discussion of this anecdote and its development, see D. C. Lau (trans.) *The Analects* by Confucius (Middlesex: Penguin, 1979), introduction and appendix 1. By the time of the *Huai Nan Tzu* (c. 140 B.C.), it is Confucius himself who demonstrates this physical prowess.

44 *Chuang Tzu*, 7.3.2ff.

45 See Friedrich Nietzsche, *Thus Spoke Zarathustra*, trans. R. J. Hollingdale (Middlesex: Penguin, 1961), 61: "The body is a great intelligence, a multiplicity with one sense, a war and a peace, a herd and a herdsman." and Friedrich Nietzsche, *The Will to Power*, trans. W. Kaufmann (New York: Random House, 1968), 281: "The evidence of the body reveals a tremendous multiplicity." Nietzsche also seems to treat the physiological and the psychical as one order of being: (Nietzsche, *Zarathustra*, 62) "Behind your thoughts and feelings, my brother, stands a mighty commander, an unknown sage—he is called Self. He lives in your body, he is your body." And *ibid.*, 101. "Our mind flies upward: thus it is an image of our bodies, an image of an advance and elevation . . . Thus the body goes through history, evolving and battling. And the spirit—what is it to the body? The herald, companion and echo of its battles and victories."

46 Cf. Wilhelm Reich, *Character Analysis* (New York: Straus and Giroux, 1949), esp. his notion of "character armor" in which psychological stress is made manifest in physiological strain.

47 Nietzsche, *The Will to Power*, 131.

Glossary of Chinese characters

a	清	t	治國	am	見(現)	
b	濁	u	內	an	天地	
c	正	v	外	ao	陰陽	
d	偏	w	知	ap	意	
e	厚	x	行	aq	精	
f	薄	y	圓	ar	自然	
g	剛	z	大	as	氣	
h	柔	aa	禮	at	体(躰)	
i	溫	ab	人	au	豐	
j	暴	ac	身	av	第	
k	生	ad	形	aw	義	
l	造物者	ae	體	ax	理	
m	誠	af		ay	克己	
n	天	ag	軀	az	郭象	
o	德	ah	躬(躳)	ba	形	
p	配	ai	釋名	bb	兼	
q	仁	aj	伸	bc	郭慶藩	
r	淵	ak	神	bd	莊子集釋	
s	修身	al	廣雅			

287

19

HUMAN EMBODIMENT

Indian perspectives

John M. Koller

Source: T. P. Kasulis, R.T. Ames & Dissanayake, *Self as Body in Asian Theory and Practice*, New York: SUNY Press, 1993, pp. 45–58.

Overview

When we ask, "How does the Indian philosophical tradition view the human body?" we must be prepared for a multitude of answers, for the tradition is made up of many subtraditions, each with its own answer. Furthermore, these traditions are continuously changing, so that the answers vary across time, as well as across traditions. Nonetheless, allowing for necessary qualifications, there are two common features that these different answers have in common, features which constitute a rudimentary shared core of understanding across traditions and time. First of all, the human body is viewed as a living process that integrates a complex variety of mental and physical processes. That is, the human body is really a body-mind, rather than a mere body or a body to which a mind is somehow attached. And this body-mind is not viewed statically, as an ontologically completed being capable of undergoing various accidental changes, but is seen as a karmic process, a continuing process of making and unmaking, a process which has no beginning and which is never completed. Furthermore, it is a process constituted by interaction with other processes in an ever-widening sphere that extends ultimately to the whole world, linking each person to other persons and beings in a web of interconnections that extends to all times and places. Indeed, what we think of as individual persons or beings are viewed within the tradition as junctures within the karmic network, analogous to the knots in a fishnet.[1]

In the *Bhagavad Gītā* this karmic view of the body-mind is presented in the image of a field on which the various physical and mental forces interact with and modify each other:

This body is called the field. . . . Described briefly, this field, with its modifications, is constituted by the great elements (either, air, fire, water, and earth), sense-of-self, intelligence, the unmanifested, the ten senses and the mind, the five sense realms, desire, aversion, happiness and suffering, the embodied whole, consciousness and steadfastness.[2]

This is, of course, a brief description of a person seen not as an individual mental-physical thing but as a field of interacting energies of different kinds and intensities, a field which is simultaneously interacting with innumerable other fields. The body-mind is a juncture or constellation of these interactions, born and reborn out of successively intersecting energy-fields.

Secondly, the Indian tradition, with the exception of Buddhism and Cārvāka, tends to regard the body-mind as the instrument of a Self that is essentially transcendent and independent of its embodied condition. Chapter 13 of the *Gītā*, quoted in the previous paragraph, refers to this Self as "the knower of the field" and declares, "This imperishable supreme Self, beginningless and without qualities, though abiding in the body, Arjuna, neither acts nor is polluted."[3] The view dominating the tradition regards this Self as being held hostage by the body-mind, and emphasizes strategies and techniques for its liberation. This view is captured well by the author of the *Knife Upaniṣad* in the following verses:

> As a migratory bird
> Imprisoned within a net
> Flies upward toward the heavens
> When the captive's cords are cut;
>
> So the Self of the adept
> Set free from passion's bondage
> By the keen knife of yoga
> Escapes *saṁsāra*'s prison.[4]

According to this view, the Self, essentially autonomous and independent of the mind-body complex, is held fast by the karmic bonds of passion and ignorance. This bondage, which constitutes the ground for suffering, can be terminated only by liberating the Self from the body-mind. This means that the Indian tradition draws an ontological line between the body-mind, which has both physical and mental characteristics, and the Self, which transcends both the physical and the mental. Unlike modern Western philosophy, which draws the line between the mind and the body, regarding them as substantially different, and sometimes exclusive, kinds of entities, Indian philosophers have tended to see the mental and physical as aspects of an integrated process, seeing the body as conscious and consciousness as bodily activity. This means that from the Indian perspective, body is never rejected in favor of mind as the authentic self, a rejection characteristic of much Western thought since Descartes. However, it also means that both body and mind (i.e., body-mind) are rejected as the authentic self of a person by most Indian systems. Thus, whereas modern Western philosophy faces a serious philosophical problem in trying to relate body and mind to each other, in the Indian tradition a similar problem appears in the effort to relate Self and body-mind to each other.

Although it is true that for most of the Indian philosophical systems it is the pure Self that is of paramount value, the lived body-mind is of central importance in every system. Buddhism and Cārvāka, despite the profound differences between them, agree in taking this lived body-mind as ultimate, rejecting any Self beyond the lived body-mind. The other systems, precisely because of their emphasis on liberation of the pure Self from the samsaric bonds of embodied existence, attach great importance to the body-mind as the key to liberation. Because the bonds to be loosened are those created by the body-mind, and because the path to liberation is followed by the embodied self, full knowledge of body-mind is seen as a necessary condition for liberation of the pure Self from its bondage.

Although all the systems view the human body as an integrated complex of mental and physical processes, and all but Cārvāka and Buddhism view this body-mind as embodying the transcendent, pure Self, which in its own nature is autonomous and not dependent on the body-mind, the nature of body-mind and its relation to the Self have been understood in a great variety of ways. A sense of this diversity can be provided by briefly characterizing a number of different views of the body and its relation to the Self.

In the Ṛg Veda, where a religious holism that regards body and consciousness as instrumentalities of agency, particularly the instruments of sacrificial agency, is maintained, there is no trace of body-mind/Self dualism. Seeing the Self fundamentally in terms of agency, it appeared obvious to Ṛg Vedic thinkers that the human body is the locus of consciousness since bodily movements directed by volition are impossible without consciousness.

The Upaniṣads contain many interpretations of body-mind and its relation to the ultimate Self (*Ātman/Brahman*). Most of these provide an organic, holistic account of existence. The Muṇḍaka, for example, suggests that even as a spider produces its web, as plants grow from the earth, and hair from a person's body, so does the universe arise from the ultimate (*Ātman/Brahman*).[5] The body-mind also arises from that ultimate Self: "From Him are born life, mind, the sense-organs, and also ether, air, fire, water, and earth, all supported."[6] The Taittirīya says that "From this Self (*Brahman*) arose ether; from ether, air, from air, fire; from fire, water; from water, earth; from earth, herbs, from herbs, food; from food the person."[7] It then goes on to give a picture of a person as an integral, organic layered process, where the physical processes envelop the life processes, which envelop the perceptual processes, which envelop the processes of understanding, which envelop joy, the innermost self, the *Ātman* which is the source and ground of the person.[8] The Kaṭha explains the Self and its relation to the body-mind with the image of a chariot: "Self should be known as lord of the chariot, body as chariot, intelligence as chariot driver, mind as reins, senses as horses, and sense objects the paths; The Self, associated with body, senses and mind, is the enjoyer."[9]

The Cārvākans, of course, are infamous for taking the body-mind complex to be the ultimate self, denying the existence of any Self separate from this complex, and the possibility of liberation. Since mind is inseparable from body, Cārvākans regard the death of the body as also the death of the mind, thus the final termination of a person's life. Although they were regarded as materialists by adherents of the other systems, they were not materialists in the usual Western sense of that term, for they viewed the body of a person as imbued with consciousness.

Buddhists also denied the existence of a Self separate from the lived body-mind complex. Unlike the Cārvākans, however, they recognized the possibility of liberating a person from the karmic bondage resulting from thoughts and actions rooted in ignorance and selfish desires.

Sāṅkhya philosophers were frankly dualistic, claiming two ultimately different kinds of being, *puruṣa* and *prakṛti*, corresponding roughly to pure consciousness which can never be object, and physical-mental existence, which is always object. The body-mind is of the nature of *prakṛti*, and the true Self is *Puruṣa*, which, although it occasions the various movements of *prakṛti*, remains forever distinct and separate from it.

Advaita philosophers, as the name suggests, denied this duality, claiming that reality was not-two, that Self (*Ātman/Brahman*) alone is real, and that the body-mind and all the other processes constituting the world are *māyā*, or only apparent reality.

Jainism divides reality into life-principle (*jīva*) and matter (*pudgala*), with the living person regarded as the embodiment of the life-principle in matter. Corresponding to finer and coarser grades of matter are different bodies in which the *jīva* dwells. Within this large physical body, a material organism made up of earth, water, fire, and air aggregates which constitute the body-mind organs and the vital breath that enlivens it, is a subtle body made up karmic matter (*kārmāṇa-śarīra*), and within the karmic body is a luminous body (*taijasa-śarīra*), in which the *jīva* dwells. Most Jainas insist that embodiment is merely the association of the *jīva* with matter, that there is no actual contact, let alone integration of *jīva* and matter, for the pure bliss, awareness, and energy that constitutes *jīva* is held to be incompatible with matter. At the same time, since bondage is experience of suffering and liberation experience of bliss, and since experience is possible only in the context of some kind of embodiment, Jainas have difficulty making sense out of karmic bondage if the *jīva* is not actually embodied.

In *Nyāya*, the conviction that consciousness is inoperative except through the body-mind organism is so powerful that the pure Self (*Ātman*) in disembodied condition is held to be without consciousness or knowledge. The explanation given is that consciousness is an accidental attribute of the Self, the accident being its relation to the body-mind.[10]

Tantra, of course, is a continuing vital effort to spiritualize the body, an attempt to overcome the dominant tradition's tendency to devalue the body.

Although this suggests the diversity of views found in Indian thought about embodied existence, when we begin a detailed analysis of specific views and arguments it quickly becomes clear that a summary or survey of the whole tradition is too much to attempt here. However, by selecting for examination three quite different perspectives on the nature of embodied existence and its relation to self, it is possible to give a fuller sense of the tradition's understanding of personal existence without ignoring its rich diversity. These three perspectives, dualistic Sāṅkhya-Yoga, the nondualistic Vedānta of Śaṅkara, and the holistic process view of Buddhism, will offer some insights into the role of the body in accounting for experience and for the unity and continuity of personal existence within the Indian philosophical tradition.

Sāṅkhya

The Sāṅkhya account of a person is explicitly dualistic, for it views a person as the conjunction of two fundamentally different and eternally opposed realities, *puruṣa* and *prakṛti*. *Puruṣa* is pure consciousness, eternal, unchanging, and self-shining. It is the true Self, the pure subject which can never become an object. The prakṛtic body-mind, on the other hand is always of the nature of object, in itself unconscious, constantly changing, illuminated only by the light of *puruṣa*. Experience and knowledge are possible only because *prakṛti* is capable of reflecting the consciousness of *puruṣa*. That is, even though the prakṛtic body-mind is itself unconscious, it can become the instrument of a consciousness which shines through it because of its sattvic nature.

But this is problematic, for if *prakṛti* is by nature unconscious, and if consciousness as *puruṣa* is totally different from the prakṛtic objects it is said to illuminate, how can there be any interaction between the two? How can *puruṣa* illumine what is totally unconscious, and how can *prakṛti*, whose nature is to be unconscious, be illumined by consciousness? After all, these two realities are regarded as ontologically exclusive of each other. The traditional answer is that one of the constituent strands of *prakṛti*, *sattva*, is transparent, capable of taking illumination from consciousness. But this is also problematic, for either *sattva* is *prakṛti*, and therefore unconscious, or else the strict dualism is given up. The other alternative, that the sattvic manifestations of *prakṛti* as embodied awareness (*buddhi*) is not absolutely different from the *puruṣa*, also destroys the dualism. Since *puruṣa* is unchanging and *prakṛti* ever-changing, for *puruṣa* to take the form of *buddhi* means that it cannot be *puruṣa*.

Sāṅkhya philosophers have made many attempts to overcome the problems this rigid dualism presents, but they all appear to stumble at the critical juncture, the juncture where supposedly *puruṣa* and *prakṛti* meet. No matter how *buddhi* and *sattva* are construed, as long as they are admitted to be prakṛtic, they must be said to be essentially unconscious. This apparently serves the soteriological-metaphysical interest of Sāṅkhya, for it supports the claim that *puruṣa* is never in fact in bondage to *prakṛti*, that the true Self, the *puruṣa*, is always free and that liberation is simply the realization of this truth.

One of the fundamental reasons for holding to this rigid dualism is to account for the fact that there is never experience unless there is an experiencing subject and an experienced object. That is, to account for the self-reflective character of experience in which a person not only experiences, but is also aware that she is experiencing, it is thought necessary to posit a transcendent Self, a Self that remains always a subject totally different from the object experienced. But as we have seen, the very dualism that helps explain the self-reflective character of experience makes experience itself problematic, for experience requires a genuine meeting of subject and object, a meeting this dualism renders problematic.

What is especially interesting about the Sāṅkhya account of body-mind is that despite the metaphysical problems presented by *puruṣa/prakṛti* dualism, *prakṛti*, including its body-mind manifestation, is seen as the instrument of *puruṣa*, manifesting consciousness. Indeed, the very first manifestation or evolution of *prakṛti*, triggered by the presence of *puruṣa*, is *buddhi* (awareness), out of which self-awareness (*ahaṁkāra*), mind and the various capacities for sensation, perception, and action evolve—and out of which eventually physical matter and bodies evolve. Clearly this *prakṛti*, as the ground for existence, is not merely material, at least not in the sense of inert or unconscious matter, for it is the ground from which embodied consciousness evolves. Accordingly, if *prakṛti* is taken to be a kind of materiality, it will have to be taken as a conscious materiality. We might say it is a consciousness embodied within the very processes constitutive of existence, though from a Sāṅkhya point of view it would be more accurate to say that consciousness embodies materiality, for what are regarded as physical elements or bodies are declared to evolve out of *buddhi*, or reflected consciousness, which is the first manifestation of *prakṛti*. On this view, the body and mind are both seen as conscious, and experience interpreted in terms of the play between the various constituents of *prakṛti*, between the more and less conscious, rather than between the conscious subject and the unconscious object. Here we find no hard line between body and mind or between Self and body-mind. Rather, consciousness is seen as a pervasive and integral constituent of bodily existence.

The metaphysics underwriting this corporeal view of embodied consciousness, though extremely subtle in its details, is simple in its outlines. *Prakṛti*, a unified whole, is seen as constituted by three interpenetrating kinds of energy or force fields, which are revealed in the tendencies to manifestation found in the experienced world. *Rajas* is the vibrant energy that drives the entire manifestation process, which, if the *sattvic* energy level is high, appears as predominantly consciousness-like, and if the *tamasic* energy level predominates, appears as predominantly physical body or object-like. However, these constituent *guṇas*, or force fields, are always present together in some proportion in every manifestation of *prakṛti* so that consciousness and physical existence are mutually dependent, always to be found together.

The Yoga system, which accepts much of Sāṅkhya's metaphysical anthropology and cosmology, focuses on the prakṛtic embodiment of consciousness as it constitutes the experiential life of a person. Drawing out the implications of the Sāṅkhya view of embodied existence as the continuing intersection of the energy-fields constituting all persons and things, Yoga notes that human actions have the effect (*karmāśaya*) of changing both the surrounding world and the actor, disposing him or her in manifold ways. These dispositions (*saṃskāras*) condition subsequent experience and action, investing them with the traces (*vāsanās*) of previous acts. These traces or seeds (*bīja*) perpetuate the experiential stream, producing various afflictions, memories, and expectations. At death all the as yet unrealized karmic effects, collected in the subtle body of consciousness, move out of the physical body and enter an appropriate new body at its moment of conception. Thus, whatever is born is already conditioned and disposed by prior actions, for embodied existence is a continuous creative process in which the effects of prior experience are transformed into present life, which, in turn, conditions future experience.

Advaita vedānta

As we have seen, the Sāṅkhya problem of the apparent irrelevance of theories of prakṛtic existence to a theory of the self is connected to its main problem of explaining how genuine interaction between the dual realities of *puruṣa* and *prakṛti* can occur, a problem Advaita hopes to avoid with its non-dual stance. Śaṅkara's view, as expressed in the *Upadeśasāhasrī*, for example, is that the pure consciousness (*cidātman*) alone is ultimately real; everything else is only appearance. The Self (*ātman*) that I truly am, he says, is "ever free, pure, transcendentally changeless, invariable, immortal, imperishable, and thus always bodiless."[11] Further, being bodiless means that the true self neither experiences nor acts. In Śaṅkara's words, "The false belief that Ātman is doer is due to the belief that the body is Ātman."[12] Thus, the *Upadeśa-sāhasrī* recounts that when a student approached his teacher, a

knower of Brahman, and asked how he could obtain release from the suffering of this transmigratory existence, the teacher advised him that he must
overcome the ignorance through which he mistakenly thinks that he is an
agent, an experiencer and a transmigrator, when in fact he is none of these,
but the highest *Ātman*.[13]

It would seem then that Śaṅkara cannot be expected to have a philosophy
of the body. After all, from his perspective, though I frequently identify with
this body, this identification (*adhyāsa*) is a mistake, the result of ignorance,
for the truth is that I am pure consciousness, *Ātman*, eternal and unchanging,
having nothing to do with body. But how is this mistake to be explained?
What is this ignorance wherein I identify with the body and regard myself as
actor and experiencer? For the sake of showing that this identification is a
mistake, that it results from ignorance, Śaṅkara needs to develop a philosophy of human existence that explains what the body-mind is and how it
comes to be falsely imposed on *Ātman*. Thus, he says that if the student
seeking the sacred knowledge which brings release from *saṁsāra* says, "I am
eternal and different from the body. The bodies come and go like a person's
garment," the teacher should say, "you are right," and then should explain
how the body is different from the Self.[14]

There follows a remarkable passage in which Śaṅkara explains what the
body is and how it comes to be. Positing an unmanifest name-and-form
(*avyākṛte nāmarūpa*), Śaṅkara declares that this unmanifest evolved into the
world of name-and-form as we know it through an evolutionary process
according to which it first became manifest as ether, air, fire, water, and earth,
in that order. As each of these elements became impregnated with the previous elements, finally earth appeared, as a combination of all five elements.
He goes on to say,

> And from earth, rice, barley, and other plants consisting of the five
> elements are produced. From them, when they are eaten, blood and
> sperm are produced, related respectively to the bodies of women and
> men. Both blood and sperm, produced by churning with the churning
> stick of sexual passion driven by ignorance (*avidyā*) and sanctified with
> sacred formulas, are poured into the womb at the proper time. Through
> the penetration of fluid from the womb, they become an embryo and it is
> delivered in the ninth or tenth month.[15]

He then explains how this body is named at birth, how it gets its student
name, its householder name, and also the name of the forest dweller and
sannyāsin. Repeating that "the body is different from you (*Ātman*)," Śaṅkara
says that the teacher should remind the student that the mind and the
sense organs consist only of name-and-form, and quotes passages from the
Chāndogya Upaniṣad (VI. 5, 4; 6, 5; and 7, 6) which declare that the mind
consists of food.[16]

Like the prakṛtic self of Sāṅkhya, this self of name-and-form is said to be unconscious ("like food") but nonetheless constituted by an awareness enabling it to experience, act, and identify itself (mistakenly) as a transmigrating, experiencing, acting self. Thus, according to Advaita, a person consists of a physical body, made up of material substances: the senses (eye, ear, etc.); mind; agencies of speech, movement, sex, excretion, and grasping; sense-of-self (ahaṁkāra); as well as the internal embodied consciousness (antaḥkaraṇa), all of which are disposed and conditioned according to previous experiences.

The distinction between physical and subtle bodies (sthūlaśarīra and sūkṣmaśarīra) is very important, for it recognizes a distinction between mere physicality and humanly embodied physicality. It is a way of insisting on the bodily character of what we think of as mental functions, for the sūkṣmaśarīra, constituted by the five vital airs, the buddhi and manas through which the antaḥkaraṇa functions, as well as the ten organs (five cognitive-sensory; five conative-motor), is not only itself viewed as a body, but is itself further embodied in the sthūlaśarīra. Only for the embodied self are the knowledge and action needed for liberation possible (or necessary). The senses are seen as instruments of the mind, linking mind with the outside world, just as mind links senses with reflective consciousness, and reflective consciousness links up with Self. But senses, vital force, mind, and reflective consciousness can function only when embodied; ultimately the inner organ (antaḥkaraṇa) cannot function except through the bodily self; through its indriya, or senses.

To avoid the problems of dualism, Śaṅkara denies that name-and-form is ultimately real or that it really embodies the Self. For him this account functions to explain only the *appearance* of experience and the world, the reality of which is never admitted. This view is deeply problematic, however, as Śaṅkara himself recognized when he said not only that avyākṛte nāmarūpa evolved from Ātman, but also that it is different in essence from Ātman. How can it be both essentially different from and evolved from Ātman in a philosophy committed to satkāryavāda? Satkāryavāda, as a causal principle, insists that what is produced, the effect, cannot be a different kind of reality than its cause. Thus, Ātman could produce only Ātman, never nāma-rūpa, which is non-Ātman.

The analogy Śaṅkara introduces to explain this evolution of nāmarūpa from Ātman reveals the problem, for he says,

> In this manner this element named "ether" arose from the highest Ātman as dirty foam from clear water. Foam is neither water nor absolutely different from water, since it is not seen without water. But water is clear and different from foam, which is of the nature of dirt. Likewise, the highest Ātman is different from nāmarūpa, which corresponds to foam; Ātman is pure, clear, and different in essence from it.[17]

296

Clearly, this analogy breaks down, for foam combines two different things, clear water and dirt. Since Śaṅkara cannot admit such a duality, he denies the reality of *nāma-rūpa*, relegating it to the level of *māyā* or appearance, as superimposition on *Ātman* through ignorance. Thus, Advaita confronts a dilemna: though body-mind must be assumed to account for experience, action, and transmigration; but to preserve the nondualism that allows nothing other than *Ātman* to be real, its reality must be denied.

Buddhist analysis

For both Sāṅkhya and Śaṅkara, the insistence that the real Self is of the nature of pure consciousness, eternal and unchanging, stands in the way of seeing the Self in bodily terms, as an experiencing, acting, living process. Buddhism does not admit a non-karmic self or realm of existence. It denies the existence of a transcendent self that is pure consciousness, declaring the truth of no-Self (*anātman*), teaching that all existence is devoid or empty (*śūnya*) of Self. This insistence of no-Self is not the nihilistic view that nothing exists, a view to be avoided as carefully as the view that there is an eternal Self to whom mind and body somehow belong. The positive view of no-Self is brought out in the teaching of *madhyamā pratipad*, the middle way that denies both being and non-being in favor of becoming. This middle way means that existence is to be understood in terms of *pratītya samutpāda*, or interdependent arising. Becoming is seen as a creative process, a continuous arising and perishing, in which everything is related to everything else in mutually dependent ways. What *anātman* and *śūnyatā* deny is that selves and things exist separately and in some absolute sense, a denial intended to make room for an affirmation of existence as a dynamic, integrated whole wherein the unity and continuity of experience is not destroyed by bifurcation.

Instead of analyzing personal existence in terms of a self which in some sense "has" a body and mind, Buddhists analyze it in terms of the processes involved in experience. This analysis distinguishes five interrelated groups of processes, which, in their interdependent functioning, give rise to what we call a "person." *Rūpa* constitutes the so-called bodily processes, giving a person his or her corporeal dimensions, while the other four, feeling/sensation (*vedanā*), perceptual processes (*saṁjñā*), impulses to action (*saṁskāras*), and the processes of consciousness (*vijñāna*) constitute the so-called mental processes. These processes, all together in their interdependent functioning, *are* the self. The assumption of a separate self is seen as a mistake.

But it is also a mistake to see the distinctions between these five groups as boundary lines marking totally separate processes, for as the Abhidharma analysis clearly shows, there is no consciousness without impulses, perception, sensation/feeling, or bodily processes. *Dhātus, āyatanas*, and *dharmas* are terms of analysis of experience intended to show not only that these five groups are empty of Self, but that in their interdependent functioning they constitute unified and continuous personal existence. Thus, the twelve *āyatanas*, or bases of perception, reflect the unity of the senses and their objects grounded in lived bodily experience, and the eighteen *dhātus*, or constituents of consciousness, reflect the unity of consciousness and conceptual objects grounded in the bases of perception. Further analysis of experience yields the eighty-nine *dharmas*, or factors constituting the interdependent flow of processes we call a "person."

What needs to be stressed here is that *skandhas, āyatanas, dhātus*, and *dharmas* are terms of *analysis* of experience and not the lived experience itself. The lived experience is a holistic, continuous process. To see it in terms of analysis pointing to a complex built up out of static and separate parts is a mistake. Not only is it a mistake to see experience as constituted by contact between an independently given subject and object, or relationship between a body and mind conceived of as essentially separate from each other, but it is also a mistake to see experience in terms of *skandhas, āyatanas, dhātus* or *dharmas* if these are taken to be self-sufficient units of existence. Thus, the *Heart Sūtra* declares that *skandhas* and *dharmas* are both empty; and, of course, emptiness is also empty.

This insistence on emptiness constitutes a rejection of the position that there is an already constituted existent with which a person can be identified. Practically all Indian philosophers—except Cārvākans—denied that there was an already constituted physical being—a body—with which one's true existence could be identified. But they held that there was an *Ātman*, or *puruṣa*, or *jīva*—some spiritual being—with which a person can be truly identified. And this spiritual being, one's true being, is an eternal being, of the nature of pure, unembodied consciousness; it does not perish and is not subject to change. Buddhists, however, in their insistence on *anātman* and *śūnyatā*, not only deny that there is an already constituted physical being or body which is a person's true identity but also deny that there is an already constituted transcendent being or self which is a person's true identity.

Instead, Buddhists see a person as a continuous creative process, integrally linked to all the other creative processes constituting existence. The *skandhas* and *dharmas* are not seen as constituting the person, but as factors or conditions out of which a person-in-the-making (along with all other beings existing in mutual interdependence) continuously creates herself/himself. In the sense that this creative process is not dependent on a logically separate and prior agent, it is spontaneous. But it is not spontaneous in the sense that it is without conditions. Indeed, it is the conditionedness of this process that allows for intentional direction, that allows a person to be an interdependent set of processes of mutual self-creativity. The *arhant* or *bodhisattva* is a person who is not determined by the facticity of existence but who, rather, is continuously creating himself out of the conditions that the ignorant take to be the given facticity of their existence. The ignorant grasp at the factors of existence as though they were already made elements of their being. The wise know that this is the mistake of substituting the terms of analysis for the living process.

Typical attempts to account for the identity and continuity of the immediate experiential process, of the lived body, seek the underlying causal factors on which the process depends. But causal understanding is inherently atomistic; it cuts up the holistic process, regarding it as constituted by distinct factors that can stand in a causal relation to each other such that A causes B, B causes C, and so on. But A can cause B only if A is other than B. This is the same kind of thinking that leads philosophers to say that experience proves that subjects and objects have independent existence—that there could be no experience unless there were an experiencer and something to be experienced separate from each other, whereas, in truth, it is precisely their mutual interdependence that makes experience possible.

By insisting on the interdependence of the processes of existence and on the unity and continuity of personal experience, Buddhists resist the tendency to see persons as two different kinds of being—either Self and body-mind, or mind and body—in some inexplicable relationship. Instead of being forced to see the body as somehow foreign to oneself, as an object-like being appended to or imprisoning the self, the Buddhist perspective facilitates seeing oneself as a creative, unified, and continuous process of becoming—as a lived-conscious-body capable of actualizing the potential represented by the so-called objective factors of existence.

Notes

1 Yoga *Sūtra Bhāṣya* 2.13.
2 *Bhagavad Gītā* 13.5.
3 Ibid., 13.31.
4 Kṣurika Upaniṣad, 1.25.
5 Muṇḍaka Upaniṣad, 1.1.7.
6 Ibid., 2.1.3.
7 Taittirīya Upaniṣad, 2.1.
8 Ibid., 2.2–5.
9 Kaṭha Upaniṣad, 1.3.3–4.
10 *Nyāya Vārttika*, 2.1.22.
11 *Upadeśasāhasrī*, 1.13.3. As translated by Sengaku Mayeda in *A Thousand Teachings: The Upadeśasāhasrī of Śaṅkara* (Albany, New York: State University Press, 1992).
12 Ibid., 1.12.16.
13 Ibid., 2.2.50.
14 Ibid., 2.1.12,13.
15 Ibid., 2.1.20.
16 Ibid., 2.1.21.
17 Ibid., 2.1.19.